LIFE IN THE AGE OF DRONE WARFARE

LIFE IN THE AGE OF DRONE WARFARE

LISA PARKS AND CAREN KAPLAN, *Editors*

DUKE UNIVERSITY PRESS

DURHAM AND LONDON

2017

CONTENTS

ACKNOWLEDGMENTS

Life in the Age of Drone Warfare emerged through a series of dialogues between media, communication, and cultural studies scholars, artists, sociologists, feminists, geographers, journalists, philosophers, and science and technology studies specialists during the past several years. The collection began to germinate during the Drones at Home conference at the University of California–San Diego in 2012, organized by Jordan Crandall and Ricardo Dominguez, and further evolved during the Sensing the Long War: Sites, Signals and Sounds workshop at the University of California–Davis, the Life in the Age of Drones symposium at the University of California–Santa Barbara in 2013, and the Eyes in the Skies: Drones and the Politics of Distance Warfare conference at UC Davis in 2016. We are grateful to the Militarization Research Group, the Mellon Digital Cultures Initiative, the Department of American Studies, and the Cultural Studies Graduate Group at UC Davis and the Center for Information Technology and Society, Interdisciplinary Humanities Institute, and Department of Film and Media Studies at UC Santa Barbara, whose support enabled us to deepen and expand our discussions and understandings of drone technologies and processes of militarization. We also thank Arthur and Marilouise Kroker for their vital interventions at the UC San Diego and UC Santa Barbara events. Their provocations continue to reverberate and have marked this project in numerous ways. In addition, we are grateful to all the conference, workshop, and symposium participants for their stimulating presentations and artworks, many of which are included in this book. Other scholars and activists who have supported and inspired us include Javier Arbona, M. Ryan Calo, Deborah Cowen, Lindsey Dillon, Kris Fallon, Emily Gilbert, Casey Cooper Johnson, Léopold Lambert, Nancy Mancias (CODE PINK), Minoo Moallem, Trevor Paglen, Marko Peljhan, Kriss Ravetto-Biagioli, Alex Rivera, Rebecca Stein, Jennifer Terry, and Federica Timeto. We also thank Abby Hinsman for editorial assistance as this project was getting off the ground.

As our ideas for the *Life in the Age of Drone Warfare* collection began to cohere, we were very fortunate to connect with editor Courtney Berger, who has been supportive, thoughtful, and enthusiastic throughout the editorial process. We are grateful for her commitment to this project and the manner in which she helped it come to fruition. We also thank Sandra Korn and Susan Albury at Duke University Press for their careful readings and attention to detail and for being extremely helpful editorial associates. We are indebted to this book's contributors for their significant chapters, ongoing commitment to the project and the issues it addresses, and their collegiality. Our deepest gratitude goes to Andrea Miller, who worked tirelessly as an editorial assistant during various stages of the manuscript's preparation. Simply put, the project could not have happened without her myriad efforts. Finally, the project benefited from the insightful reviews of three anonymous readers, whose comments were enormously helpful as we moved the project toward completion.

Beyond those mentioned above, we would like to thank Brandon Bryant for his openness to participate in this project, despite challenges he continues to face as a veteran and whistleblower. Caren Kaplan thanks her faculty and graduate student colleagues in American Studies (especially her department chair, Julie Sze) and Cultural Studies at UC Davis for sharing their work and supporting her research interests with such enthusiasm. She also thanks Eric Smoodin and Sofia Smoodin-Kaplan for all kinds of support on the home front and Marisol de la Cadena, Inderpal Grewal, Meredith Miller, Minoo Moallem, Ella Shohat, and Jennifer Terry for their friendship and interest in this work. She also extends a big thanks to Lisa Parks for conceiving this project and getting it started before inviting her to join as coeditor—working together has been a joyful experience. Lisa Parks thanks the faculty, graduate students, and staff in the Department of Film and Media Studies at UC Santa Barbara for providing a stimulating, supportive, and fun work environment for so many years, and expresses gratitude to her new colleagues in Comparative Media Studies/Writing at MIT for creating new opportunities and a dynamic place to work. She also thanks from the bottom of her heart John Harley, Jennifer Holt, Moya Luckett, Constance Penley, Rita Raley, Cristina Venegas, and Janet Walker for their incredible friendship and support over the years, and conveys her deepest gratitude to Caren Kaplan for being an exceptional coeditor, scholar, and friend.

INTRODUCTION

LISA PARKS AND CAREN KAPLAN

SINCE 2009, U.S. news media have had a virtual love affair with the drone. Celebrating the alleged novelty and flexibility of the technology, reporters have pointed to a proliferating array of quirky or surprising drone uses, ranging from pizza delivery to pornography recording, from the maintenance of energy plants to the protection of wildlife, from graffiti writing to traffic monitoring.[1] Drones, we are told, are used in sectors as diverse as real estate, art photography, natural resource development, insurance, sports, meteorology, and activism.[2] They perform tasks that are too risky, remote, or mundane for humans, whether monitoring lava inside a volcano, measuring winds inside a hurricane, or performing safety inspections on aircraft. Toy Predators are sold out because of their popularity. Fears of proliferating drones in domestic airspace have spurred new regulations and legislation, prompting Chicago to become a no-drone zone.[3] Despite such regulations, drones have even fallen on the White House lawn.[4] It is impossible to keep up with all the drone news. So much reporting on drones has appeared that Caren Kaplan refers to it in her chapter in this book as the "drone-o-rama"—an immersion in the sights and sounds of an expanding "military-industrial-media-entertainment network" that now includes views captured by robotic hummingbirds and remote-controlled quadcopters.[5]

In addition to this flood of news features about the playful and pragmatic potentials of drones, the drone-o-rama has included a steady stream of reporting on the more somber topics of drone warfare and targeted killing. Investigative reporter Jane Mayer first broke the story about the Central Intelligence Agency's (CIA) drone war in Pakistan in 2009.[6] Since then, a whirlwind of public commentary has emerged on drone warfare. The United Nations (UN) has conducted special investigations, activists have protested, policy experts have deliberated, news agencies have queried, and researchers have published lengthy reports.[7] The drone obsession has also struck the

U.S. Congress, which now runs an "unmanned systems caucus" made up of fifty members from twenty-nine states (with the co-chairs from border states California and Texas). Since 2009, the caucus's congressional members have garnered close to two million dollars from drone manufacturers such as Northrup Grumman, General Atomics, and Lockheed Martin.[8] Thus, drones are not only envisioned as a pivotal technology in U.S. counterterrorism efforts, but politicians and manufacturers have colluded to ramp up the expansion of the civilian drone sector. In 2014 digital behemoth Google purchased drone manufacturer Titan Aerospace, promising to use drones to bring Internet access to the planet's most remote and underserved regions.

While some news media have played up the friendlier, neoliberal side of the technology, emphasizing its capacity to handle a multitude of tasks and, in the process, make life easier while expanding the global economy,[9] other reports have raised serious questions about the ethics of drone warfare, covered anti-drone demonstrations, or honed in on instances of technological failure. Some drone coverage has even verged on the uncanny. Pointing simultaneously to the intrusiveness and frailty of the drone, several reports, for instance, have featured eagles attacking drones in midair, whether as part of a natural predator hierarchy or as a result of training by military or police units.[10] To be sure, the drone has become a contested object. While drone strikes are routinely reported in most mainstream news outlets, what is often missing from the reportage is an understanding of the material ecologies through which drones are operationalized. These ecologies have been depicted in fictional television series such as *Homeland* and *24*, films such as *Eye in the Sky*, and computer games like *Drone: Shadow Strike* and the *Call of Duty* series, yet the narrative logic of these media often (though not always) works to legitimate or reinforce militaristic drone use, even if providing windows of opportunity to question it.

Life in the Age of Drone Warfare zeroes in on the militaristic histories, uses, cultures, and affects of drone technology. Heeding Derek Gregory's call to move beyond the "technical (or techno-cultural) object" to the wider "matrix of military violence" that such "remote platforms help to activate," this volume brings together scholars and artists who explore the historical, juridical, geopolitical, and cultural dimensions of drone technology and warfare and sets out to deepen and expand the public discussions initiated by investigative reporters, activists, and nongovernmental organizations (NGOs).[11] While 91 percent of the U.S. public is aware of U.S. military drone operations,[12] oppositional voices are often marginalized and sidelined in public sphere discussions, as evidenced by activists who have infiltrated congressional hearings and protested at manufacturers' gates in efforts to have their voices heard. Sometimes these voices come from within military institutions. Whistleblowers such as Brandon Bryant, who has a chapter in this book, and Michael Haas decided to break the code of silence and speak publicly about their grim experiences as drone sensor operators, and have appeared in news media such as Bryant's 2013 interview with NBC's Richard Engel or in documentaries such as *Drone* (2014), directed by Tonje Hessen Schei. Artivist projects, such as James Bridle's Dronestagram, which links Google imagery to drone target details circulated by the Bureau of Investigative Journalism, or the "Out of Sight, Out of Mind" narrative data visualization project by the Pitch Interactive design studio, offer thought-provoking challenges to U.S. officials and publics who continue to ignore the devastating effects of drone warfare.[13] In an effort to draw further attention to U.S. drone wars, artist Joseph DeLappe's 2014 project, *In Drones We Trust*, asks participants to rubber stamp a tiny image of a Predator drone onto the empty sky on the back of U.S. currency. Describing this crowd-sourced intervention, DeLappe indicates: "It seems appropriate, considering our current use of drones in foreign skies, to symbolically bring them home to fly over our most notable patriotic structures."[14]

Militarized Unmanned Aerial Vehicles

Drones or unmanned aerial vehicles (UAVs) were first developed for military reconnaissance, surveillance, and intelligence during the early twentieth century and were part of a major push toward "airpower" and aerial policing that had colonial roots.[15] By the early twentieth century, aircraft could fly in the sky unmanned and be remotely controlled to gather information about objects or activities on the ground. During World War II, the United States began arming experimental aerial drones with bombs and missiles in efforts to compete with Japanese kamikazes, as discussed in Katherine Chandler's chapter in this book. The use of U.S. drones for surveillance continued during the Vietnam War. In the early 1980s, the Israeli Air Force successfully integrated drones into a full-fledged battle plan, and, as Lisa Hajjar discusses in her chapter, by the 1990s, Israel and the United States were using drones to support military operations and conduct targeted killings in the Occupied Territories and the former Yugoslavia, respectively. These situations proved that drones could be used not only to locate and monitor "suspects" or "enemies" but also to assassinate them from above. After 9/11, the drone warfare practices tested during the 1990s were redirected to fight a global war on terror, and U.S. use of drones for targeted killings dramatically escalated. As Hugh Gusterson has argued, drones "respatialize war, change its pace, and rework conventional military notions of honor and courage."[16] The respatialization of war has produced what Keith Feldman refers to as "racialization from above," recasting "Orientalist imagined geography" through new scales of relation and division along with transformations in the temporality of "pre-emption and endurance."[17]

Since the 9/11 attacks, the United States has increased its use of drones in two parallel programs, one overtly operated by the military and the other a covert program of the CIA. Ostensibly directed against al-Qaeda operatives in Pakistan and Yemen and Al-Shabaab forces in Somalia, and now increasingly deployed in relation to actions taken against the Islamic State in greater Syria, the U.S. drone program has raised many legal, cultural, and political questions, including the following: What and where is the battlefield? Who is a combatant? Which laws apply?[18] Public discomfort and suspicion of targeted assassinations conducted by remote pilots stationed in air-conditioned rooms on bases thousands of miles away from the zone of conflict have not led to any appreciable change in policy. While proponents of autonomous weaponry characterize it as a "humane" form of warfare, highlighting its alleged efficiency, surgical precision, and minimal casualties, critics insist that drone war is far from humane since it has been waged in an undeclared and illegal fashion, killed or injured thousands of civilians, and traumatized people living in places that become geopolitically designated as "trouble spots." Since 2001, U.S. drone operators have killed and/or injured thousands of suspected "terrorists" and innocent civilians in Afghanistan, Iraq, Pakistan, Yemen, and Somalia, many of whom have never been counted or identified.[19] The explosive force of Hellfire missiles dropped by U.S. drones often incinerates bodies, leaving them unrecognizable. These extrajudicial killings by the United States have drawn staunch criticism from the international community and have catalyzed organizations such as CODE PINK, the Bureau of Investigative Journalism, Global Drones Watch, Ban Weaponized Drones, No Drones Network, Reprieve, and the Campaign to Stop Killer Robots to work with activists and NGOs in South Asia and the Middle East to form an anti-drone movement and seek redress for victims. Increasingly, as accounts from former drone operators like Brandon Bryant and others suggest, remote warfare using high-resolution digital imaging can result in adverse effects on those who conduct war remotely.

Just as there has been a surge in news media coverage on drone technology and anti-drone activism, so too has there been a burst of scholarly publishing on the topic. When we started working on this project in 2012, there was only one book focused exclusively on military drone use—*Drone Warfare: Killing by Remote Control* by CODE PINK founder Medea Benjamin—and a handful of other books and articles featured discussions of the technology. More recently, the amount of scholarly work on drones has skyrocketed.[20] That scholars from so many fields have gravitated to the drone in droves motivates us to ask why. Multiple possible explanations exist. First, we are living through an era of dramatic technological transformation, of digitization, automation, and robotics, and the drone is both driving and manifesting these processes and as such fits neatly into research on key technological questions. Second, the unprecedented use of drones by the United States for targeted killings in the context of the war on terror has prompted scholars to consider how these circumstances challenge existing theories of sovereignty, warfare, and ethics and whether they violate national and/or international law. Third, the technical infrastructures that support drone operations facilitate the orchestration of war from a distance—as a system of remote control played out at game-like interfaces—and such conditions have provoked scholarly interest in the labor, psychic, and affective dimensions of drone warfare, particularly among drone operators or "remote pilots." Finally, there has been a plethora of scholarship on the optics or visualities and other sensing practices of drone warfare, which ranges from analyses of military drone screens and visions of the world to considerations of "drone phenomenologies" to tactical drone media created by artists/activists who set out to publicize these optics as a way of contesting this military paradigm.[21] In short, the drone has been such an avid object of scholarly focus precisely because it connects to so many different issues, from digitization to sovereignty, from surveillance to geopolitics, from labor to affect. The question is, how long will scholarly focus on the drone persist? What kinds of questions about violence, politics, and targeting are engendered through these debates and conversations? Most importantly, we have to ask whether critical scholarly responses to the rapid rise of the use of unmanned aerial vehicles in specifically designated theaters of war will have any impact on the policies surrounding drone operations, the next generation of the technology, or those impacted by its use.[22]

Dronology: Recent Works on Drone Warfare

While books and articles about drone technology and warfare abound, there are several works that informed this book project in its early stages. As already mentioned, in addition to Jane Mayer's *New Yorker* article, Medea Benjamin's *Drone Warfare: Killing by Remote Control* was the first book to critique the CIA's drone war in Afghanistan and Pakistan, document the explosive growth of the drone industry, and signal the rise of anti-drone activism. Also in the activist vein was Nick Turse and Tom Englehardt's *Terminator Planet: The First History of Drone Warfare, 2001–2050*. In 2012 Shahzad Bashir and Robert D. Crews published *Under the Drones: Modern Lives in the Afghanistan-Pakistan Borderlands*, a work that, despite its title, addresses a very wide array of social, cultural, and political issues in the region beyond the threats drones pose to civilians. Discussions of the technology have surfaced, as well, in other widely read recent works such as P. W. Singer's *Wired for War: The Robotics Revolution and Conflict in the Twenty-First Century*, M. Shane Riza's *Killing without Heart: Limits on Robotic Warfare in an Age of Persistent Conflict*, and Adam Rothstein's *Drone*. In addition, there has been a recent spate of critical scholarship on the politics of verticality, which we deem to be relevant to drone research: for example, the work of Eyal Weizman, Stephen Graham, and Laura Kurgan.[23] Finally, the explosion of scholarship on algorithmic practices and preemption of risk in security cultures is particularly germane to any examination of the political and technological context of drone warfare; here we are thinking specifically of the work of Louise Amoore and Marieke de Goede as well as Jutta Weber.[24]

Derek Gregory and Grégoire Chamayou have published some of the most influential and widely cited critical scholarship on drone technology and warfare. In a series of key articles, Gregory has addressed a range of issues, from the "new visibilities" and "scopic regime" of drone war to its expanding definition of the "civilian" in a "drone geography," from the lethal logistics of the "kill chain" to the screened intimacies of drone operators.[25] The geographies of drone warfare in Gregory's groundbreaking work move from the ground control stations, where sensor operators practice the doctrine of "projecting power without vulnerability," to the variable scales of intimacy and distance as mediated through material relations and technologies, to the transforming battlefield as targeting shifts from an area or structure, to, in many cases of assassination, an individual.[26] There is probably no other cultural critic at work today who has done more to trace these geographies of military power and the ways in which political violence is enacted, justified, and resisted. Gregory's newest research on drone warfare, which appears in the first chapter of this book, offers a painstaking analysis of the rise of "targeted killing" and its production of "spaces of exception."

With the recent English translation of Grégoire Chamayou's *Théorie du drone*, this French philosopher's work has circulated more widely and generated more comment. Chamayou begins with the assumption that the drone has altered the general conditions of war and undertakes a philosophical, ethical, and genealogical analysis of the technology. His genealogy moves from automatons in the early twentieth century to kamikazes during World War II, from unmanned systems deployed in Israel and Vietnam to the Predators and Reapers currently aloft. For Chamayou, the drone turns humans into prey and war into a "militarized manhunt" that idealizes asymmetry, enabling the hunter-killer to kill without being killed and to see without being seen.[27] Chamayou confronts a range of vital issues—from relations of reciprocity to necro-ethics, from precision to automation—yet, as Ian Shaw has argued, in privileging ethics, the book has other agendas than to engage drone technology as inherent to a "history of U.S. empire and global violence," evacuating key historical instances, such as the Cold War.[28] This kind of metaphysics, Benjamin Noys insists, can ascribe "agency and activity that flatters the drone as object" while eliding "the intricate meshing with human labor that makes drone operations possible."[29] The balance between material analysis and metaphysical theory, between new or misrecognized sources and classic Eurocentric histories, and other antinomies of long standing can be difficult to negotiate. Considered together, recent work on drone warfare advances our understanding of the "full matrix," as Gregory puts it, of the ways in which war is being conducted "everywhere" as well as "somewhere" with significant repercussions for everyday life in an era of shifting battlespaces.[30]

Along these lines, *Life in the Age of Drone Warfare* provides contexts, concepts, and examples that encourage further interrogation and critique of drone warfare and drone-related militarization. What distinguishes this book from other works, however, is a privileging of critical humanities, poststructuralist, and feminist perspectives. *Life in the Age of Drone Warfare* explores how the imagination and usage of military drones has made possible or affected particular kinds of material conditions and embodiments, whether in Israel/Palestine or the Horn of Africa, the Federally Administered Tribal Areas (FATA) region of Pakistan or the U.S.-Mexico border. To think about life in the age of drone warfare is to recognize the stretch between ground and sky as a field of strategic operations, world histories, and biopolitics. It is to recognize the ways military technologies are entangled with modes of perception and practices of knowledge. And it is to acknowledge the need for sustained critical inquiry around foundational categories such as body and machine, distance and proximity, self and Other, life and death. To think about life in the age of drone warfare, in other words, is to situate this flying apparatus within the frictions and factions of power. That the drone has maneuvered into so many sectors is also suggestive of the capacity of its militarizing tendencies to permeate life conditions. Too often the discussion of drones transpires in broad brushstrokes and top-down modes that often have the effect of endorsing current drone policy and practice rather than questioning the technology's public subsidies, uses, and effects. What is missing from existing scholarly work on drones is a critique of the technology that recognizes its imbrication within cultural imaginaries, biopolitics, difference, and perception.

To expand the critical analysis of drone technology, this book engages with perspectives from fields such as media and communications studies, geography, sociology, art, literary studies, journalism, feminist and queer theory, and subaltern studies, fields that approach the drone as a technology of power as well as a part of everyday life. Some of the questions explored in this book are: How does drone use intensify power asymmetries in the world and where? How do uses of this "unmanned" technology relate to issues of embodiment, subjectivity, and subjectivation? How is everyday life in different parts of the world changing in relation to the use of drones? What does it mean to sense the Earth's surface from the perspective of the drone, and how does that information manifest and circulate? What kinds of political practices and imaginaries are produced by the new forms of spatialization in targeting and the reorganization of lived experience produced by drone warfare? *Life in the Age of Drone Warfare* builds upon and extends the work mentioned above by drawing more focused attention to juridical relations, cultural imaginaries, and biopolitical formations.

Despite decades of feminist research on science, technology, and militarization, only a handful of recently published drone-related articles explicitly engage with feminist epistemologies.[31] Crucially, some of this research builds upon Donna Haraway's critique of science and technology to foreground the gendered dynamics of unmanned systems and the agential capacities of drone interfaces.[32] Most drone research averts feminist perspectives either by ignoring them completely or absorbing their basic arguments and precepts without acknowledgment. This book, in embracing an openly feminist approach, takes as axiomatic that gender/sexuality, race/ethnicity, class, and national identities are constituted intersectionally and transnationally; that humans, animals, and technologies are materially integrated and hybridized; that militarization and violence are embodied in multiple ways; that the rule of law is applied differentially and unevenly within territories and upon bodies; and that postcolonial tensions persist, subalterns speak, and hegemonies are scattered.[33] Feminist epistemologies have guided us not only to shape and coedit this collection but also to spend much of our academic careers conceptualizing, researching, and analyzing the relationships between aerial and satellite technologies, militarization, power, and violence.[34] *Life in the Age of Drone Warfare* addresses readers who are interested in learning about, interrogating, and reflecting on the politics of drone technology and its relation to life worlds on Earth.

Drone Formations

Formulating research practices through multidisciplinary engagements, the contributors to this book draw upon a range of fields, including science and technology studies, poststructuralist and transnational feminisms, postcolonial criticism, critical legal studies, media studies, geography, and art, and analyze aspects of drone technology and warfare in relation to five critical themes. First, contributors explore drones as part of *cultural imaginaries*. Rather than treat the drone as a technical system that can be concealed away in secret CIA campaigns or hidden in the proprietary clean rooms of manufacturers, this book approaches the drone as a technology that draws upon and generates particular ways of perceiving and understanding the world. Drones are not idle machines hovering above; they are loaded with certain assumptions and ideologies. They operationalize fantasies and produce psychological states ranging from fear to fury, vulnerability to vengeance, anxiety to security. Drones should not only be thought of as the high-tech machines of militaries or states; they are also ideas, designs, visions, plans, and strategies that affect civilians on the ground, pilots in the remote cockpit, and consumers in the marketplace. The contributors to *Life in the Age of Drone Warfare* critically engage a wide spectrum of imaginaries that are deployed through and with unmanned aerial vehicles.

Second, this book approaches drones as technologies of *power* or as *biopolitical* machines that have the potential to alter life in a most material way. Far from being wholly "autonomous" or "unmanned," drones are fusions or hybrids of human labor and technical objects and processes. Their network connections and vertical maneuvers enable the application of power from sky to ground, across patches of earth, within life worlds, and upon bodies. As they carry out or execute particular kinds of tasks for their human operators, they at times go rogue, malfunction, or crash. As such, drones are vital sites for studying how power works through human-technical assemblages. Just as drones have been used to patrol, target, and kill from above, some have been designed from the bottom up, as it were, for grassroots or "artivist" projects. By deploying conceptual art, reverse engineering, and do-it-yourself (DIY) engagements, activists have contested militarized drones through alternative design and visioneering. Art is a crucial technique for demonstrating and analyzing the logics and logistics of militarization, probing the politics of forensic evidence, and exploring the parameters of aesthetics in the age of airpower.

Third, as our contributors consider the cultural imaginaries and biopolitics of drones, they also explore the critical issues of *difference* and *affect*. As drones are used throughout the world for an array of purposes, it is vital to consider whose lives are most shaped by these technologies and how. Chapters throughout the book describe specific drone uses across different (trans)national, regional, or local contexts and analyze the effects of drone operations from diverse social perspectives, from those who build, design, and pilot drones to civilians who live daily beneath their unwavering eye. One of the intentions of the book is to foreground the affective experiences of subaltern and minority subjects whose lives are too often eclipsed in scholarly discussions of drone technology and warfare. These discussions tend to favor the technical, juridical, and geopolitical over the biopolitical and the affective, sidestepping the everyday social realities of ordinary people who live in the vicinity of drone operations. To engage with diverse social experiences, contributors use multiple approaches—from interviews to site visits, from discourse analysis to performance art—and they consider multiple sites, from Israel/Palestine to the U.S.-Mexico border and from Pakistan to Somalia and Yemen.

Fourth, contributors to *Life in the Age of Drone Warfare* approach drones through the registers of the *sensory* and the *perceptual*. In this way, the book builds on prior work on the histories of aerial observation and remote sensing by considering how the drone promises to refine and intensify aerial practices that have evolved over centuries. Contributors consider how this airborne machine generates images of the Earth, what those images are made of, and how they are mobilized to intervene in life on Earth. Engaging critically with the drone's sensing devices, contributors explore how the technology participates in the radiographic episteme, detecting and digitizing phenomena beyond the visible light portion of the electromagnetic spectrum so that it can become part of the knowledge economy. In addition to analyzing the epistemological dimensions of drone imagery, contributors explore how the drone itself has become a spectacle, serving, on the one hand, as a flying fetish that symbolizes the quest for planetary management and remote control, and, on the other, as the latest handheld device that enables civilians to sense, perceive, and privatize the Earth's surface. To approach the drone as a technology of sensing and perception involves considering uses that extend from militarized interventions to civilian experimentation.

Finally, chapters in this book explore the juridical dimensions of drone war and its relation to systems of governance, rationalization, and what has been termed *lawfare*. In the context of the war on terror, national and international laws have been mobilized to authorize acts of war without defining them as such and to legitimate targeted killings. One of the effects of exercising juridical power in this way has been to establish a new class of disenfranchisement—people who are targeted as suspects or who live in the vicinity of or have relations with those targeted suspects. Strategic uses of juridical power have undermined the civil rights and liberties of people around the world, particularly Muslims and people of color, forcefully impeding their mobility, infringing upon their privacy, and detaining them without cause. Drone technology and warfare have been used both to extend juridical power and, at the same time, to avoid it. The preemptive killing of suspects and incineration of bodies by drones has a way of neatly eliminating problems of legal breach or overreach. Now, more than ten years into the U.S. global drone war, the repetitive pattern of extrajudicial killings has had the effect of normalizing and sanctioning this method as part of a new world order, even as other heads of state who commit such atrocities are brought before international war crimes tribunals.

Weaving together the voices of scholars, artists, journalists, and activists, the book features multiple kinds of interventions—from research chapters to artistic provocations, from investigative reporting to personal correspondence—and is organized into three sections: Juridical, Genealogical, and Geopolitical Imaginaries; Perception and Perspective; and Biopolitics, Automation, and Robotics. Throughout the book, the critical themes discussed above surface and interlink contributors' chapters in multiple ways. The first section presents chapters that situate drone technology and warfare within different juridical, historical, and territorial constellations to draw attention to the technology's constitutive relation to concepts such as sovereignty, territory, borders, and verticality. It opens with Derek Gregory's chapter, "Dirty Dancing: Drones and Death in the Borderlands," which provides a comprehensive analysis of the rise of "targeted killing." Gregory argues that for the first time in its history, the CIA has combined covert bombing with a sustained and systematic approach to assassination. This shift in the doctrine of airpower, incorporating both "area" and "precision" attacks from above with new forms of surveillance through "persistent presence" and "pattern of life" analysis, leads to the production of "spaces of exception" in the Federally Administered Tribal Areas in northwestern Pakistan. In this incisive work, Gregory shows how the emergence of new battlefield spaces enables the killing of a range of subjects, from Taliban leaders to grandmothers in their gardens, as multiple powers compete, collide, and collaborate to permit states to assert, enact, and enforce a claim over bodies-in-space.

Lisa Hajjar's chapter, "Lawfare and Armed Conflicts: A Comparative Analysis of Israeli and U.S. Targeted Killing Policies and Legal Challenges against Them," explores U.S. and Israeli legal justifications for targeted killing practices. Hajjar distinguishes the concept of lawfare from what she refers to as "state lawfare." While lawfare describes the ways bodies of law are deployed to challenge specific forms of statecraft within international and domestic courts, *state lawfare*, according to Hajjar, refers to "the practices of officials to reinterpret international humanitarian law (IHL) or human rights laws in ways that deviate from prevailing internationally accepted understandings in order to 'legalize' state practices that would otherwise constitute violations." Hajjar constructs a genealogy of state lawfare to explain how the United States and Israel have defined vague categories such as "unlawful combatants," expressed territorial concerns related to exercises of military force, and legally obfuscated or justified accountability in targeted killing practices. Working through particular legal cases, Hajjar points to the tenuousness of state lawfare, noting that attempts toward legitimation have persistently been met by resistance to these legal maneuverings and state violence.

Shifting from the historical conjuncture of the war on terror to World War II, Katherine Chandler's chapter, "American Kamikaze: Television-Guided Assault Drones in World War II," provides a historical analysis of the first television-guided assault drone, discussing key projects from 1939 to 1944. Blending critical science and technology studies and archival research, she excavates the sociopolitical frameworks and players that shaped and tested early assault drones. Drawing upon memoirs, military documents, scientific reports, and a test film, Chandler focuses not on the "invention" of the drone but on the co-constitution of "drone" and "human" during this period. She reveals how the drone was positioned in relation to a series of key issues, including human/nonhuman relations, interpretive flexibility, the politics of failure, and geopolitical relations between the United States and Japan. As the U.S. military combined automated flight, television, and targeting in a single machine, it also sought to remove the human pilot from danger and assert U.S. technical superiority, generating a variety of conflicting viewpoints and feelings among the players involved.

Returning to some of the concerns raised by Lisa Hajjar, Andrea Miller's chapter, "(Im)material Terror: Incitement to Violence Discourse as Racializing Technology in the War on Terror," explores the preemptive logic of drone warfare as symptomatic of a more pervasive phenomenon of preemption as a racializing technology in the war on terror, where action in the present is undertaken to contain and mitigate perceived future threats. Specifically, Miller examines the deployment of "incitement to violence" discourse as a mode of statecraft by exploring the 2011 case of Anwar al-Awlaki, the first U.S. citizen explicitly targeted and killed by a drone strike in Yemen, and the 2012 case of Tarek Mehanna, a twenty-nine-year-old Boston pharmacist sentenced to seventeen and a half years in prison for providing material support for terrorism and conspiring to kill in a foreign country. In both cases, disciplinary and lethal force were enacted against al-Awlaki and Mehanna not for actions they actually committed but for actions they were imagined to inspire others to commit in a conditional and indeterminate future. Within preemptive governance, then, incitement to violence discourse functions as a particularly insidious mode of racialization that seeks to criminalize and render actionable the realms of desire, imagination, and inspiration for Muslim and Arab bodies in the war on terror.

Also addressing the current historical conjuncture, Lisa Parks's chapter, "Vertical Mediation and the U.S. Drone War in the Horn of Africa," provides a critical analysis of the material restructuring and effects of U.S. drone operations in this region. Since 2002, the U.S. Joint Special Operations Command (JSOC) and the CIA have orchestrated a covert drone war from Camp Lemonnier in the African country of Djibouti, monitoring and striking alleged al-Qaeda and Al-Shabaab suspects in Yemen and Somalia. As a media scholar, Parks is interested in both the discourses that have been used to expose covert U.S. drone interventions and the ways that drone operations themselves function as technologies of mediation. Drawing upon media such as training manual diagrams, infrared images, Google Earth interfaces, and drone crash scene photos, her chapter explores the drone's mediating work through three registers: the infrastructural, the perceptual, and the forensic. By pointing to a series of ground-to-sky operations that alter or rewrite life worlds on Earth, Parks argues that U.S. military drone operations can be understood as technologies of *vertical mediation*. As a drone flies through the sky, it alters the chemical composition of the air. As it hovers above the Earth, it can change movements on the ground. As it projects announcements through loudspeakers, it can affect thought and behavior. And as it shoots Hellfire missiles, it can turn homes into holes and the living into the dead. Irreducible to the screen's visual display, Parks argues, the drone's mediating work happens extensively and dynamically through the vertical field—through a vast expanse that extends from the Earth's surface, including the geological layers below and built environments upon it, through the domains of the spectrum and the air to the outer limits of orbit.

The book's second section, "Perception and Perspective," provides historical and contemporary accounts of the relationship between aerial drone technology and modes of perception, meanings of "perspective" and the production of worldviews. It opens with Caren Kaplan's chapter, "Drone-o-Rama: Troubling the Temporal and Spatial Logics of Distance Warfare." In this work, Kaplan argues that a "cacophony of multimedia 'noise'" distracts the U.S. public from accountability as the civilian death toll from drone strikes mounts. She urges that instead of splitting news accounts between international and domestic or fetishizing technologies as always already "new," the temporal and spatial logics of distance warfare need to be critically deconstructed in favor of affiliating the subjects of drone attacks across national boundaries and in historical frameworks. She concludes by arguing that any analysis that does not inquire into continuities in policing by autonomous weaponry across time and space will adhere to the geography of imperialism and international relations that has led to over a century of airpower and war at a distance.

Ricardo Dominguez's chapter, "Dronologies: Or Twice-Told Tales," provides a tactical analysis of drone discourses and events. Using a method he describes as "minor simulation," Dominguez "creates an event that is difficult to understand as either real or not real." Offering four twice-told tales, he first immerses his reader into a future world of thanatologists and zombie drones whose technologies are a thing of the past. Here, the surface of a withered drone is remembered as fleshy and plantlike and the anthropocentric desires of apocalypse fiction are enmeshed with contemporary discourses of technovitalism. Dominguez's second tale probes the relationship between smart matter development and the U.S. military's attempts to harness and weaponize the weather. In Dominguez's third tale, the future is engaged in a battle between fully autonomous swarm systems, where private autonomous aerial corporations rival and evade state and international actors through the deployment of highly sophisticated autonomous systems. In Dominguez's final vignette, the reader is transported to UC San Diego in 2012, where a drone crash has reportedly occurred outside the university library. Part of UC San Diego's Gallery@CALIT2 art gallery's exhibition *Drones at Home*, in this final "minor simulation" the reader encounters an "online statement" by Dominguez's UC Center for Drone Policy and Ethics. Navigating the boundaries between art and science, and science and fiction, Dominguez teases his readers with a tantalizing medley of simulations designed to infiltrate truth claims and mimic the promises of a dronological future.

Thomas Stubblefield's chapter, "In Pursuit of Other Networks: Drone Art and Accelerationist Aesthetics," also explores the emergent field of drone art, critically engaging the work of artists such as James Bridle, Trevor Paglen, Josh Begley, Natalie Jeremijenko, and Kate Rich. For Stubblefield, drone art seeks to counter the decentralized, networked logic of the drone in order to "initiate blockages and intensify existing relations, processes that work within the ecological model of the kill chain so as to amplify its power differentials and, ultimately, produce new distributions." Drawing upon Thacker and Galloway's concept of "the exploit," Stubblefield shows how drone art coopts "the potentiality" of the network's interconnections, disrupts the "nodocentrism" of the networks in which drones are situated, and destabilizes the scopic regimes of drones through accelerationist aesthetics.

Shifting the perspective away from drone art to conditions on the ground, Madiha Tahir's chapter, "The Containment Zone," explores effects of the U.S. drone war in the FATA region of Pakistan. Tahir's account of the FATA contradicts those that rely on Giorgio Agamben's "state of exception" framework, where the Tribal Areas are presented as a lawless region in a state of anachronistic suspension. Instead, she outlines regional governance and U.S. drone warfare as an extension of British colonial administration and policing, where the territory's spatial ordering and customary law create conditions on the ground that are particularly suitable to U.S. drone warfare. Noting that the Tribal Areas are divided into ambiguously defined regions of protected and unprotected areas, Tahir observes, "It is a system that arranges space through the logic of cultural autonomy—the government says it only minimally interferes—but one whose final consequence in times of conflict is not the preservation of custom beyond the reach of governance but containment." She explains how "containment zones" and "filter points" (checkpoints) have turned the Tribal Areas into a security economy premised on the regulation of bodily movement. These sites of physical and discursive encounter—of containment and filtration—she argues, produce asymmetrical power relationships between bodies differently situated in relation to the Tribal Areas and the Pakistani state. Ultimately, Tahir reveals how the time-space compression that characterizes drone warfare and the time-space relations of "governance on the ground" in the Tribal Areas work to mutually constitute and reinforce one another.

In the last chapter in this section, "Stoners, Stones, and Drones: Transnational South Asian Visuality from Above and Below," Anjali Nath challenges the aerial politics most often associated with U.S. drone warfare and embraces the "spatiality of the low and the below." Through an analysis of South Asian diasporic cultural productions, Nath offers a rejoinder to drone critiques that privilege the visuals of verticality by pointing to the everyday, embodied experiences of those subjected to the continued presence and violence of drones. To develop this "politics of below," Nath turns to the video "Soup Boys (Pretty Drones)" by South Asian American rapper Himanshu "Heems" Suri. Circulated via YouTube and other social media, Heems's video deploys a "narcotically inspired unruliness" that "simultaneously emerges from and remaps a visual terrain in which South Asian and Middle Eastern bodies are constructed and killed, and whose lives are framed by the optic perception of drones." Rather than articulate the "discourses of sobriety" typical of documentary cinema, the video offers a productive "discourse of inebriation," a mode of "intoxicated and insubordinate" diasporic culture in response to a "technoracial visual system of interpellation" that has also led to drone killings of civilians.

The final section of the book features chapters that engage with the sociotechnical dimensions of drones, theorizing their relation to biopolitics, robotics, and automation. It begins with a chapter titled "Taking People Out: Drones, Media/Weapons, and the Coming Humanectomy" by Jeremy Packer and Joshua Reeves. Exploring the relationship between drone technologies and "military media capacities," Packer and Reeves point to a historical tension between expert-based, centralized command, on the one hand, and a decentralized and autonomous network of military agents, on the other. Arguing that the drone exemplifies the decentralization impulse, Packer and Reeves also suggest that it is core to ongoing debates about the future of military technologies and organization. Extending their historical analysis back to World War I, Packer and Reeves hone in on a series of moments in U.S. military history when tension between centralization and decentralization is presented in sharpest relief. Given the increasing consensus among military strategists that "the human has suddenly emerged as an epistemological hindrance," the swarm is now presented as "the ideal technological system for dispensing the fog of war" and "the swarm cloud possesses a continuously refined, emergent collective intelligence that is far beyond the grasp of humans' physiological capacity." The authors conclude that the swarm is symptomatic of the recursive relationship between military and media technologies, where the questions produced through war-making are generative of new systems of communication and mediation that increasingly wish to dispense with the human entirely.

Peter Asaro's chapter, "The Labor of Surveillance and Bureaucratized Killing: New Subjectivities of Military Drone Operators," explores the drone war as a system of "bureaucratized killing" and focuses on the forms of subjectivity and psychological responses it generates. For Asaro, bureaucratized killing is "the particular form of labor that killing takes in the work of drone operators, which is constituted by the kind of bureaucratic labor organization developed within the military to do things like generate lists of bombing targets, in combination with the more 'hands-on' work of deciding when and where to pull the trigger." Asaro reads military studies of the psychological stress of drone operators within a Taylorist framework of scientific labor management studies that seeks to identify the inefficiencies in the labor production of drone operators, and potentially to reconfigure their work practices to reduce or eliminate these inefficiencies. One of the primary accounts of stress, he finds, involves the relationship between human operators and the technological interfaces with which they must interact for long periods of time and that are frequently subject to malfunctions. Supplementing his analysis of military studies with a reading of the drone operator's testimony in Omer Fast's *5,000 Feet Is the Best*, Asaro points toward the insufficiencies of Taylorist discourses to adequately account for the particular kinds of psychological stresses and cognitive dissonance experienced by drone operators.

Brandon Bryant's "Letter from a Sensor Operator" delves more personally into the labor questions probed by Asaro and takes readers inside the ground control station (GCS) where he worked as a sensor operator for six years. Bryant worked at Nellis, Cannon, and Balad Air Force bases from 2006 to 2011 and famously shared his experiences with the international press in 2012. In this "letter," Bryant offers a candid description of the training he received, imaging technologies he used, and assignments he completed. Always self-reflexive, Bryant explains that it was his job to "provide the best picture possible for our intelligence analysts while being cognitively aware of all the activity going on." Told by his superiors that sensor operation was more of an "art form" than a "science," Bryant felt as if he were the "eyes of the mission" and learned to master transitions between infrared, daylight, and low-light optics. "Letter from a Sensor Operator" also captures the mood and atmospherics of drone operation as Bryant explains that he was often depressed and lonely, sleepless and bored in the midst of his drone work. At the same time, however, he was awed and pained by the aerial views of life and death that he witnessed and explains that he eventually had to "wash off the filth" and find a path out of the ground control station.

Shifting from the personal to the ontological, Jordan Crandall's chapter, "Materialities of the Robotic," considers how increased automation is affecting modes of being, doing, and cognition in contemporary infrastructural ecologies. Moving from the drone's cockpit to the autonomous guided vehicle to the driverless, flying car, Crandall delineates a robotic ontology premised on modes of interoperability, transport, and transmission. Rather than a phenomenon linked to specific technologies, a robotic ontology signals a much broader redefinition of form and being across the battlefield, the factory, and the home. According to Crandall, "The vehicle–operator composite is provisional and fluid, with the body of the driver extending to the car shell or fuselage and even beyond, retracting when necessary, as the composite that is traffic itself wells up and dilutes." Writing as a conceptual artist and theorist working within this ontology, Crandall explores how elements of the drone are reshaping and becoming part of generalized conditions.

In the book's concluding chapter, "Drone Imaginaries: The Technopolitics of Visuality in Postcolony and Empire," Inderpal Grewal explores how the power and anxiety of empire and the postcolonial state are treated in two fictional texts: George Brant's play *Grounded* and Hari Kunzru's short story "Drone." In *Grounded*, the costs of perpetual war (waged through new modes of technological innovation and alienation) contribute to the psychological breakdown of the main character, a female drone pilot who had formerly flown F-16s in the U.S. Air Force. Grewal argues that all the nodes that contribute to the pilot's psychological distress are also illustrative of an overarching anxiety around the dissolution of the liberal subject and the kinds of assurances and securities associated with liberal subjecthood within the colonialist metropole. In contrast, Kunzru's short story "Drone" provides a dystopian account of a future India where neoliberal "hyperindividualization" renders all bodies differentially precarious. Within this world, drones are ubiquitous; they can be purchased by anyone to surveil anyone and provide commodities and services that can both optimize worker productivity and extract biomaterial from workers' bodies to be reintroduced into the market. Grewal closes by critiquing the advent of drone technopolitics, which imagine biopower and bodies that are not simply "bio" or "bare life" but rather are also technologized bodies, cyborgs, provoking questions about the future meanings of resistance for both liberal empire and the postcolony.

Collectively, these chapters place the drone within different discursive formations and provide alternate ways of thinking about the technology within the current historical conjuncture. The goal of the project overall is to offer new critical languages and technical histories that can be used to assess this emergent paradigm of militarization and warfare. Critiques and histories of the drone need to come from the margins and from below as much as they need to come from above. That life is changing in the age of drone warfare is by now a well-established point; yet, as this book's chapters demonstrate, this process is taking shape in relation to different bodies, territories, and temporalities on Earth. *Life in the Age of Drone Warfare* communicates the ways worlds are being rewritten through contemporary air-to-ground formations and in doing so responds to and intervenes in the latest round of U.S. global militarization.

Notes

1. Handwerk, "5 Surprising Drone Uses"; Murphy, "15 UK Companies Using Drones"; Michel, "The Age of Drone Vandalism"; "20 Great UAV Applications Areas."
2. Olsen, "Drone Racing Dreams"; G. Weber, "This Is the Year's Best."
3. McNabb, "Chicago Now a No Drone Zone."
4. Jansen, "Small Drone Crashes Near White House"; Buckley, "Chinese Navy Returns Seized Underwater Drones."
5. "The Surveillance Hummingbird"; J. Martin, "Best Quadcopters 2015/16."
6. Mayer, "The Predator War."
7. See, for instance, International Human Rights and Conflict Resolution Clinic (Stanford Law School) and Global Justice Clinic (NYU School of Law), *Living under Drones*; and Breau, Aronsson, and Joyce, "Discussion Paper 2."
8. Replogle, "The Drone Makers."
9. D. Bell, "In Defense of Drones."
10. Atherton, "Australian Eagle Takes Down a Drone"; Atherton, "Trained Police Eagles Attack Drones"; Weisberger, "Drone-Hunting Eagles."
11. Gregory, "Drone Geographies," 7.
12. Miethe et al., "Public Attitudes about Aerial Drone Activities."
13. See James Bridle, "Dronestagram," http://dronestagram.tumblr.com/; see also Pitch Interactive, "Out of Sight, Out of Mind," accessed February 17, 2016, http://www.pitchinteractive.com/work/Drones.html.
14. Joseph DeLappe, *In Drones We Trust* project description, 2014, distributed with rubber stamps to project participants. See also http://indroneswetrust.tumblr.com/post/143846558639/in-drones-we-trust-thrift-depot-reno-nv-5116, accessed February 17, 2016.
15. Gregory, *The Colonial Present*; Satia, "The Defense of Inhumanity"; Gregory, "From a View to a Kill"; Satia, "Drones: A History"; Kaplan, *Aerial Aftermaths*.
16. Gusterson, "Toward an Anthropology of Drones," 196.
17. K. Feldman, "Empire's Verticality," 325.
18. See Sterio, "The United States' Use of Drones," 201; and K. Ryan, "What's Wrong with Drones?," 209.
19. See Naureen Shah et al., "The Civilian Impact of Drones."
20. See, for example, Rothstein, *Drone*; Kaag and Kreps, *Drone Warfare*; Rogers and Hill, *Unmanned*; Riza, *Killing without a Heart*; L. Gardner, *Killing Machine*; Cohn, *Drones and Targeted Killing*; Shaw, *Predator Empire*; and Gusterson, *Drone*.
21. See Wall and Monahan, "Surveillance and Violence from Afar"; Stahl, "What the Drone Saw"; N. Hussain, "The Sound of Terror."
22. When so much drone discourse circulates, its salience and purpose can become diffuse. In such conditions, the public may experience the drone as infoglut or a

passing trend rather than as a changing infrastructure of militarization. For discussion of the way that drone logics have taken shape across different sectors, see Andrejevic, "Becoming Drones."

23. See, for example, Weizman, *The Politics of Verticality*; Graham, *Cities under Siege* and *Vertical*; and Kurgan, *Close Up at a Distance.*
24. Amoore and de Goede, "Transactions after 9/11"; J. Weber, "Keep Adding."
25. Gregory, "From a View to a Kill."
26. Gregory, "Drone Geographies."
27. Chamayou, *Théorie du drone*; see also the English translation, *A Theory of the Drone.*
28. Shaw, "Intervention," 1.
29. Noys, "Drone Metaphysics," 4.
30. Gregory, "Drone Geographies."
31. Suchman and Weber, "Human-Machine Autonomies"; Manjikian, "Becoming Unmanned"; Daggett, "Drone Disorientations"; de Volo, "Unmanned?"; Krasmann, "Targeted Killing and Its Law"; Holmqvist, "Undoing War."
32. Haraway, *Simians, Cyborgs, and Women*; Holmqvist, "Undoing War"; Feigenbaum, "From Cyborg Feminism to Drone Feminism."
33. Grewal and Kaplan, *Scattered Hegemonies*; Moallem, *Between Warrior Brother and Veiled Sister*; Moallem, "The Unintended Consequences of Equality"; Terry, "Killer Entertainments"; Terry, "Significant Injury"; Gilbert, "Money as a 'Weapons System'"; Cowen and Gilbert, *War, Citizenship, and Territory*; Cowen, *The Deadly Life of Logistics.*
34. See Kaplan, "Air Power's Visual Legacy"; Kaplan, "The Balloon Prospect"; Kaplan, Loyer, and Daniels, "Precision Targets"; Kaplan, "Mobility and War"; Kaplan, "Dead Reckoning"; Kaplan, *Aerial Aftermaths*; Parks, *Cultures in Orbit*; Parks, "Digging into Google Earth"; Parks, "Vertical Mediation"; Parks, "Drones, Infrared Imagery, and Body Heat"; Parks, "Drone Media"; Parks, *Coverage*; Parks and Fair, "Africa on Camera"; Parks, "Drones, Vertical Mediation, and the Targeted Class."
35. Packer, "Screens in the Sky," 189.

PART I

JURIDICAL, GENEALOGICAL, AND GEOPOLITICAL IMAGINARIES

1 DIRTY DANCING

Drones and Death in the Borderlands

DEREK GREGORY

There's no country on earth that would tolerate missiles raining down on citizens from outside its borders.

—President Barack Obama

ON THE EVENING OF AUGUST 5, 2009, Baitullah Mehsud, the leader of Tehrik-i-Taliban Pakistan, was lying on the roof of his father-in-law's farmhouse in Zanghara in South Waziristan. The last eighteen months had been hectic. A veteran of earlier Taliban fighting in Afghanistan and borderland battles with the Pakistani military, in mid-December 2007 Mehsud had been appointed the *amir* of the new Pakistan Taliban alliance, a loose network of thirteen Islamist groups scattered across the Federally Administered Tribal Areas (FATA) and united by their violent opposition to the Pakistani state. Almost immediately, he became a prime suspect in the assassination of Benazir Bhutto (something that he consistently denied) and orchestrated a series of attacks against military and civilian targets across Pakistan; he also forged closer connections with the Afghan Taliban and al-Qaeda, and threatened an attack on the continental United States that would "amaze the world." Sufficiently powerful to be running what many saw as "a state within a state," he was a target of both Islamabad and Washington. That evening, Mehsud, a diabetic who suffered from kidney disease, was hooked up to an IV and relaxing with his wife, her parents, and eight other Taliban. What he did not know—could not know—was that he was being watched from seven thousand miles away. Local informants had discovered that Mehsud's second wife was the daughter of a local cleric and identified the location of the family compound. The CIA mobilized its remote eyes in the sky, and that night an MQ-1 Predator was transmitting real-time video images to mission controllers at CIA headquarters in Langley, Virginia. Seconds later, two Hellfire missiles smashed into the compound, killing all those on the roof. "All that remained of Mehsud," reported Jane Mayer, "was a detached torso." President Barack Obama, who had authorized the strike, was exultant: "We took out Mehsud."[1]

Fast-forward three years. On the afternoon of October 24, 2012, the eve of the holy day of Eid al-Adha, Mamana Bibi was working in the fields surrounding her family home in the village of Ghundi Kala in North Waziristan. Her son Rafiq ur Rehman, a schoolteacher, had gone to see his sister and to attend prayers in Miran Shah before the holiday. Mamana was a midwife who had delivered hundreds of children, and that day she was accompanied by four of her own grandchildren. "My grandma was teaching me how you can tell if the okra is ready to be picked," said eight-year-old Nabeela. Drones had been circling in the clear blue skies above the village for several hours, but nobody paid them much attention. "We had grown used to them," Nabeela's twelve-year-old brother, Zubair, explained, and he knew the difference between the noise of a drone and other aircraft: "As I helped my grandmother in the field, I could see and hear the drone hovering overhead, but I didn't worry. . . . Why would I worry? Neither my grandmother nor I were militants."

In an instant, their world was turned upside down. "All of a sudden there was a big noise," said Nabeela, "like a fire had happened." Two Hellfire missiles had ripped into the fields. The blast knocked Nabeela over, and she could not stop the bleeding from her hand; shrapnel smashed Zubair's left leg, and he was lying unconscious on the ground; and their grandmother had disappeared. "I saw her shoes," Nabeela remembered. "We found her mutilated body a short time afterwards. . . . It had been thrown quite a long distance away by the blast and it was in pieces. We collected as many different parts from the field and wrapped them in a cloth."

A few minutes later, a second strike injured other grandchildren and caused more structural damage to the houses. "My mother was not an enemy of America," her grieving son declared. "She was an old lady." And yet apart from initial claims that four militants had been killed in the strike, there was no official or even off-the-record comment, and when members of the family were invited to testify in Washington in October 2013, only five members of Congress bothered to attend the hearing.[2]

Baitullah Mehsud and Mamana Bibi were victims of a CIA-directed program of targeted killing.[3] This was not the first time the United States had attempted a covert bombing campaign—that distinction belongs to its air strikes in Laos and Cambodia during the Vietnam war—and neither was it the first time the CIA had conducted a systematic program of assassination.[4] But it was the first time the two had been combined to produce a radically new killing machine. John Nagl, one of the architects of the U.S. military's counterinsurgency policy, suggested that what distinguished the program was its fusion of intelligence and precision: "an almost industrial-scale counterterrorism killing machine."[5] The program was initiated in Yemen on November 3, 2002, and extended to Pakistan on June 18, 2004, where it was first directed at the assorted leaders of al-Qaeda ("high-value" targets) and then rapidly moved down the hierarchy to incorporate the Taliban's leaders and commanders, "nexus" targets like drug traffickers supposedly linked to the Taliban, and even ordinary foot soldiers.[6] En route it also reached beyond the execution of named and known individuals to unnamed and unknown individuals deemed to exhibit a suspicious "pattern of life" that turned them into targets for "signature strikes."

Throughout these transformations, it has remained a program of remote killing that relies on MQ-1 Predators and MQ-9 Reapers to realize the deadly triumvirate promised by their American manufacturer, General Atomics: "Dwell, Detect, Destroy." These platforms can remain over the target area for extended periods—"persistent presence"—requiring only a shift change at the Ground Control Station in the continental United States; they are equipped with multiple sensors and can transmit near real-time full-motion video feeds of the target across a global network; and they are armed with AGM-114 Hellfire missiles and GBU-12 laser-guided bombs. Taken together, these capabilities have allowed later modern war to incorporate a new focus on tracking and targeting mobile individuals rather than destroying static objects: it is this power to put "warheads on foreheads" that has made drones the weapon of choice for targeted killing in areas that are otherwise difficult to access.[7] Since their range is restricted, they are launched from air bases near the target area, so that aircrews have to be forward deployed to handle takeoff and landing and to service the aircraft, but the strikes do not involve the deployment of boots on the ground so the deniability of these covert operations is enhanced. Drones have other significant limitations, however; at present they can only be used in uncontested airspace—bluntly, they can only be used against people who cannot fight back—which is why they have become so important in America's new wars against nonstate actors in the world's borderlands.[8]

The wars fought in the shadows of 9/11 have transformed the spaces of later modern war in other ways too: the archipelago of the global war prison, with its CIA necklace of secret prisons and black sites, constituted a dispersed space of exception where there were persistent attempts to remove indefinite detention and "enhanced interrogation" (torture) from legal scrutiny. Yet even as the torch passed from President George W. Bush to Barack Obama in 2009, and the new president vowed to close the sites and end such practices, he also ramped up the CIA's targeted killing program.[9] When he took office, Obama agreed to double the Predator fleet assigned to the CIA, and after a suicide bomb attack on December 30, 2009, on a CIA station inside Forward Operating Base Chapman in eastern Afghanistan, a critical hub just twelve miles from the border providing ground intelligence for the remote operations, the number of drone strikes soared from 52 in 2009 to 128 in 2010. By the end of December 2015, the Bureau of Investigative Journalism estimated that the program—originally code-named "Sylvan Magnolia" and later changed to "Arbor Hawthorn"—had carried out 421 strikes, killing between 2,472 and 3,990 people and injuring between 1,167 and 1,747 others (see table 1.1). The strikes have focused overwhelmingly on North and South Waziristan in the FATA.[10]

Behind these raw numbers are thousands of names and millions of stories. So how could Baitullah Mehsud and Mamana Bibi have both been targets? The differences between the cases could not be clearer, but what is it that connects them, apart from the deadly ligatures of Sylvan Magnolia? More specifically, what kind of space is the FATA *made to be* for incidents like these—incidents as *un*like as these—to be possible? Sylvan Magnolia was expressly designed for remote killing, and the remoteness of the FATA in turn made it an ideal laboratory for field-testing what was, for the United States, an experimental program: "The tribal areas of Pakistan had seemed to present the perfect testing ground for a remote-controlled military strategy; it is a land set apart from its own country and mostly inaccessible to the international media and human rights groups, a place where violations of international law and civilian casualties go mostly uninvestigated. It is, in short, a black hole."[11]

Yet the borderlands were not a "black hole" below the threshold of visibility. The United States has capitalized on and contributed to a series of overt legal maneuvers through which the FATA has been constituted as what Giorgio Agamben has called more generally a "space of exception."[12] This is a profoundly biopolitical space whose execution depends on a series of

TABLE 1.1 DRONE STRIKES IN PAKISTAN, 2004–2015

Years	Strikes	Total Injured	Children killed	Civilians killed	Total killed
2004–8	51	175–277	102–129	167–332	410–595
2009	52	262–397	36–39	100–210	465–744
2010	128	351–428	19–20	84–96	751–11,109
2011	75	158–236	6–11	52–152	363–666
2012	50	100–212	1–2	13–63	199–410
2013	27	43–89	0–1	0–4	109–195
2014	25	53–76	0–2	0–2	115–186
2015	13	25–32	0	2–5	60–85
Totals	**421**	**1,167–1,747**	**164–204**	**418–964**	**2,472–3,990**

Source: Bureau of Investigative Journalism, London

similarly biopolitical technologies: seemingly neutral, "objective" devices and practices—including target lists, databases, signals intercepts, and visual feeds—that work to make the borderlands all too visible as an array of targets for the just-in-time killing that characterizes so much of later modern war.

Spaces of Exception

A space of exception is one in which a particular group of people is knowingly and deliberately exposed to death through the political-juridical removal of legal protections and affordances that would otherwise be available to them. Although spaces of exception are intimately linked to sovereign power and its claims over the "disposable" bodies of subject populations, they assume no single form. To treat the concentration camp and its derivatives as the diagnostic case—the paradigmatic "political space of modernity," as Agamben would have it—is to ignore the multiplicities and gradations of exception, and the genealogies and geographies through which it acquires its deadly powers. The FATA has become a space of exception, I suggest, through its constitution as borderlands and battlefields.

As borderlands, the FATA is a paradoxical space where division and interaction remain routine co-performances. Pakistan's border with Afghanistan closely follows the Durand Line negotiated between Britain and Afghanistan in 1893. The line marked a standstill between British and Russian spheres of interest on the North-West Frontier of British India, but it also bisected the land of the Pashtuns, who had their own customary law (*Pashtunwali*). Like many shatter zones of imperial power, these lands are better understood as what Lauren Benton once called "zones of legal anomaly—produced by conditions of contested and multiple legal authority—than as zones of lawlessness."[13] She was writing about borderlands in general, and two riders are needed in the particular case of the FATA.

First, Elizabeth Cullen Dunn and Jason Cons have developed Benton's thesis to further complicate the claim that spaces of exception always derive from a single locus of sovereign power. Instead, they too suggest that borderlands are contested spaces where competing powers collide. In the FATA, multiple powers have been involved in the administration of military violence, but on occasion they have done so in concert and their watchword has been a qualified and covert *collaboration*. In particular, the FATA has been marked by a long and checkered gavotte between the militaries and intelligence services of the United States and Pakistan, which, ever since the dog days of the Cold War, has consistently put at risk the lives of the people of the borderlands. There are multiple geopolitical and geoeconomic calculations behind this deadly dance, but it has been possible because the FATA is, in many respects, a liminal space whose relation to the rest of Pakistan has been enacted through a form of contingent sovereignty.[14] This involves no simple suspension of the law but rather an operationalization of the violence that is inscribed *within* (rather than lying beyond) the law. In fact, far from being "lawless," the FATA is subject to what Sabrina Gilani calls "an *overabundance* of law." In her view, the borderlands are "the most regulated of all the spaces comprising the territory of Pakistan."[15] If the regulations that apply to the FATA are exceptional, however, they derive not so much from an event—an imminent threat to the state and the declaration of a state of emergency—as from a *margin*: the location of the FATA as both inside and outside Pakistan. This affects how Islamabad administers state violence there, but it also shapes (and is shaped by) the remote aerial violence inflicted on the FATA by the United States. The CIA-directed strikes take advantage of what Campbell Munro calls "graduated sovereignties" that are typically limited to marginal zones: the persistent presence of the Predators and Reapers imposes a form of occupation on the FATA that is distinctly ambiguous, vertical as much as horizontal.[16] In these various ways, the borderlands materialize Agamben's topological rendering of a space of exception as "a zone of indistinction between outside and inside, exception and rule, licit and illicit, in which the very concepts of subjective right and juridical protection no longer ma[k]e any sense."[17]

Second, the collaboration between sovereign powers and the collusion of petty sovereigns has consistently traded on the trope of "lawlessness" and its killing cousin "insurgency" to turn these two designations into spurs for military violence. On March 27, 2009, Obama announced his "comprehensive, new strategy for [the war in] Afghanistan and Pakistan." The conjunction between the two is indispensable for the arguments adduced by the United States in support of its drone strikes. Obama argued that "since 9/11, al Qaeda and its extremist allies have moved across the border to the remote areas of the Pakistani frontier" where they had "used this mountainous terrain as a safe haven to hide, to train terrorists, to communicate with followers, to plot attacks, and to send fighters to support the insurgency in Afghanistan." For the American people, he continued, "this border region has become the most dangerous place in the world," and for the people of Pakistan too al-Qaeda and its allies posed "the single greatest threat." That is why, he concluded, the two states had to "stand together" to bring order to these unruly, "often ungoverned" lands.[18] Obama was invoking a standard Orientalist trope in which the space of the Other is supposed to lack an order that can only be brought to it from the outside. Not surprisingly, this too was no single punctuation point in history but was located within a genealogy that reached back to the British Raj.

For those who venture onto them—or who are trapped within them—battlefields are also spaces of exception in which people are knowingly and deliberately exposed to death. And as battlefields, the FATA has been the staging ground for political violence not only from Britain's anxious and aggressive "policing" of the North-West Frontier of its Indian empire but also from cross-border air strikes during the Soviet occupation of Afghanistan, from paramilitary violence perpetrated by networks of radical Islamist groups seeking to safeguard their sanctuaries and extend their influence over the FATA, from counterinsurgency campaigns conducted by Pakistan's Armed Forces, and from drone strikes directed by the CIA against al-Qaeda and the Taliban and their allies who cross back into Afghanistan for the spring and summer fighting season. None of this has taken place in a legal void; in wartime, it is permissible—legal—to kill others, but the ability to do so has become subject to international humanitarian law (which provides the "laws of war"). No single legal regime regulates this cascade of conflicts, however, and as it has edged closer to the present, a debate has been joined about war *space*: about the laws that regulate transnational conflicts between state and nonstate actors where a clearly demarcated battlefield has long since disappeared.[19]

I identify three legal regimes that articulate violence in the borderlands and their battlefields: a colonial and postcolonial system of collective punishment that constitutes the FATA as an exception to the rest of Pakistan and provides a dispensation (of sorts) for subjecting its inhabitants to exceptional violence; a customary system of law that at once confirms their exceptional status and is willfully misconstrued as an index of "lawlessness" that justifies military violence; and a series of legal formularies adduced by the United States to legitimize the transnational pursuit of its enemies beyond the "area of active hostilities" in Afghanistan. These three regimes triangulate a space within which Islamabad and Washington have—jerkily, unsteadily, but nonetheless relentlessly—collaborated in the deadly performance of what Joshua Foust has called their "drone dance." But there is a second pas de deux—silent, smooth, and deeper in the shadows—between the CIA and the U.S. military.[20]

Colonial Law and the Postcolony: Collective Punishment and Martial Law

In the nineteenth century, the British colonial state saw the arid, mountainous lands rising from the foothills of the Hindu Kush beyond the so-called settled areas as the domain of an intemperate nature whose harshness was "incompatible with European liberal society" and whose inhabitants were supposed to be as brutal and violent as the lands they occupied.[21] These mappings had performative force: Humeira Iqtidar and Noor Akbar insist that the inhabitants of the borderlands were no more and no less "tribal" than the people of the Peshawar Valley or the Punjab, but, within the colonial imaginary, these distinctions required different modes of administration that placed the borderlands simultaneously inside and outside the modern state.[22]

Accordingly, the British created seven agencies so that, in principle, the Pashtuns, supposedly inimical to imperial reason, would retain some measure of autonomy. They were to be held outside a state that would otherwise be obstructed by them. In practice, imperial power worked through the authority vested in local leaders, but this was a peculiar version of indirect rule—which was a commonplace among imperial states—that involved what Adnan Naseemullah calls "hybrid governance." This entailed sharing the monopoly of the means of violence between local elites and the agents of the state.[23] This was a highly asymmetric relation, and, as Andrew Roe describes, an escalating scale of violence, from issuing enticements, rewards, and threats, to unleashing local police officers, to launching punitive military expeditions. This required the borderlands to be militarized to varying degrees, and in the interwar period, the British regularly deployed infantry, artillery, and, from 1917, resorted to bombing those "regions formerly considered safe from our attack." This last resort soon became the first choice, and airpower proved to be of decisive importance.[24] Indeed, Priya Satia notes that the British invented "aerial counterinsurgency" here (and in Iraq), but the line of descent to our colonial present is less direct than she suggests. There are important affinities, not least in the Orientalist logic that underwrote these operations, in the mistaken belief that aerial surveillance could provide a panoptical view of an otherwise opaque terrain, and in the immense hostility that the air strikes engendered.[25] But there are significant differences too. Unlike the CIA-directed strikes in the borderlands, there was nothing covert about the colonial campaigns, although the government refused to provide details of targets or casualties. They involved no legal armature because "air control" was regarded as a legitimate policing operation wholly outside the Hague Conventions that regulated war between the signatory states, "the civilised nations." And far from the targeted killing of individuals, these were exercises in collective punishment.

Collective punishment had been enshrined in the Frontier Crimes Regulations since the late nineteenth century, and the principle had been reaffirmed in the codified system of laws established by Lord Curzon in 1901. After the partition of British India and the formation of an independent Pakistan in 1947, these regulations were incorporated into the constitution, which guaranteed the autonomy of the FATA. The lawmaking powers of the federal legislature and judiciary were restricted; acts passed by the National Assembly did not apply to the FATA unless decreed by the president; the authority of the Supreme Court was limited; and residents of the FATA were directed to resolve disputes through a traditional assembly or *jirga*. Ultimate authority resided with the president through his or her political agents, one to each agency, who had "absolute authority to decide all civil or criminal matters" and to apply the provisions of the Frontier Crimes Regulations.

Immediately after independence, the FATA was demilitarized; but in the closing decades of the twentieth century it was paramilitarized and then remilitarized. During the Soviet occupation of Afghanistan from 1979 to 1989, Pakistan's Directorate for Inter-Services Intelligence (ISI), in close concert with the CIA, encouraged the formation of paramilitary groups and trained and supplied them with weapons to wage a war of resistance across the border. In response, Soviet and Afghan aircraft repeatedly bombed villages and refugee camps in the FATA and adjacent areas, killing 1,800 people and injuring more than 3,000 others in what the *Washington Post* described as the Soviet Union's "war of terror."[26] Throughout these attacks, the Pakistan Air Force intercepted intruding aircraft, at first escorting them back into Afghan air space and then, as the attacks became more deadly, engaging them in combat. This is not remote history (certainly not as remote as the colonial air raids), and it matters today not only because it marks a significant horizon of popular memory but also because the Pakistani military has conspicuously failed to intercept the U.S. Predators and Reapers that are slower and easier to detect than Soviet MiGs.

The FATA was remilitarized soon after the U.S.-led invasion of Afghanistan in 2001, when Pakistan's military moved into the borderlands and embarked on a series of aggressive counterinsurgency operations. Local people had asked for these campaigns to be conducted by ground troops, but by 2004 this precarious understanding was in tatters and the Pakistan Air Force was making no secret of its repeated air strikes in the FATA. Despite claims that no civilians were killed in these attacks, it is inconceivable that they escaped unscathed. For at least the first four years, the accuracy of the air strikes was compromised by inadequate imagery and limited real-time intelligence; but from 2008, electro-optical targeting pods and sensors were retrofitted to Pakistan's aging F-16 fleet and advanced imagery exploitation systems were installed; and from 2009, Anglo-Italian Falco reconnaissance drones were deployed over the FATA. It is not possible to provide a detailed accounting of these air strikes, but former air chief marshal Rao Qamar Suleiman has claimed that between May 2008 and November 2011 the air force carried out 5,000 strike sorties in the FATA and dropped 11,600 bombs to "destroy" 4,600 targets.[27]

Limited reforms to the governance of the FATA were introduced in August 2011, but the military demanded that these measures be accompanied by the passage of the Actions (in Aid of Civil Power) Regulations, which allowed the armed forces to carry out "law enforcement duties [and] to conduct law enforcement operations," granted them sweeping powers of preemptive arrest and indefinite detention without charge, and prevented the high courts from intervening.[28] One local politician described the new regulations as "even more dangerous" than the Frontier Crimes Regulations, establishing "a system of martial law over the Tribal Areas," so that the FATA was more clearly than ever constituted as a space of exception.[29]

Martial law soon became a palpable reality. In late January 2014, Islamabad promulgated an amended Protection of Pakistan Ordinance, again modeled on colonial legislation, that included provisions for secret courts and detention without charge, house raids without warrants, and an extended license to shoot to kill.[30] The same week, the air force resumed punishing air strikes by night against targets in the FATA, now reinforced during the day by attacks from the army's helicopter gunships. Although these air strikes used domestically manufactured Burraq and Shahpar drones to provide real-time imagery and to direct aircraft to their targets, the raids generated casualties "far in excess of any caused by CIA drone strikes."[31] Their objective was Taliban bases around Mir Ali in North Waziristan, but the spillover effects drove whole communities from their homes. Thousands fled the FATA for shelter in Bannu or Peshawar in anticipation of continuing air strikes.[32]

There were repeated negotiations between Islamabad and the Taliban, punctured by uncertain ceasefires, on-the-ground violations, and air strikes, until a breaking point was reached on June 9 when the Taliban attacked Karachi's international airport. Within forty-eight hours, the CIA resumed its drone strikes, which had been on hold for six months, and it beggars belief that these were not coordinated with the Pakistan military, which began its own comprehensive assault on North Waziristan on June 15 known as Operation Zarb-e-Azb ("Sharp Strike"). This was underwritten by a hasty revision of the Protection of Pakistan Ordinance intended to give statutory cover to the operation.[33] These intensified military operations triggered a mass evacuation, and by November the government admitted that there were 1.5 million registered and more than 0.5 million unregistered displaced people in different government-sponsored camps; thousands more had fled to family or friends in Bannu and elsewhere, some even seeking refuge across the border in Afghanistan. There were no immediate plans for their repatriation, and there was little for them to return to. According to one journalist:

> In the 10-minute drive through the bazaar, there's not much but rows upon rows of houses and shops flattened by air strikes and artillery. . . . The ride through Miran Shah Bazaar is longer than the one through Mir Ali. The destruction is worse, too. The signature of ordnance from all sorts of platforms and weapons—fighter-bombers, helicopter gunships, field artillery, IEDs, RPGs and small arms—can be detected; there is a pup walking alone; and a thin cat, sipping water from a puddle; but yards upon yards of shops and houses have been bombed out; there are no signs of life.[34]

This landscape of devastation was not the product of targeted killing but of a reversion to an older form of airpower.[35] It was not directed against individuals but was once again a form of collective punishment authorized under the Frontier Crimes Regulations and their successors; in fact, when the first residents were allowed to return to what was left of their homes in June 2015, they were required to sign the North Waziristan Security Agreement, which held them collectively responsible for attacks on the military and imposed severe penalties on those who failed to fulfill their obligations to the state against "the enemies of Pakistan." The military had already sought to justify the scale of destruction and retribution by accusing whole communities of being invested in what the general in command of the operation called "an economy of terror." Journalists were taken on tours on the ground and in the air. By August, the military had advanced toward the deeply incised, forested ravines of the Shawal Valley. They were pounded by massive air strikes before ground troops moved in, and the next month, the air force announced that it had successfully launched a laser-guided missile from its Burraq drone against a compound in the valley, killing three people all described as "high-profile terrorists." The circle was finally closed. As one tribal elder bitterly complained, "Many times the drone has missed the target and innocent people have been hit. In the past we protested against America, but now against whom do we protest?"[36]

My object in rehearsing all this is not to suggest that it is perfectly acceptable for the United States to launch air strikes in the FATA because Pakistan is doing the same. To the contrary, it emphasizes the ever-present, multiple horizons of danger within which the inhabitants of the borderlands are forced to live. They are emphatically not only "living under drones" (and now not only American ones).[37] This national matrix of military violence has been authorized by an intricate interlacing of colonial and postcolonial legal protocols. Although Amnesty International describes the FATA as a "legal wilderness," it is clearly not a barren terrain.[38] Instead, the weeds and wild plants that grow there have been assiduously planted by the state and the military, in a sometimes fraught alliance, and they have been carefully cultivated through the application of the law and, at the limit, through the imposition of martial law. Gilani concludes that from Islamabad the borderlands remain "a space that is neither here nor there," at once included within the territory of Pakistan but whose people are "cast out as 'legal exceptions' to the law: but they are nonetheless subject to a draconian legal regime that sanctions exemplary state violence."[39]

If this sensibility materially shapes Pakistan's own military operations in the FATA, it has affected the geography of U.S. drone strikes in the borderlands too. For example, in the early morning of November 19, 2008, two missiles from a Predator hit a residential compound in Jani Khel, twenty-two miles outside the town of Bannu and about two hours by road from Peshawar. Over the previous four years, there had been thirty-seven strikes, and several of them had killed dozens of people or more. The toll from this strike was comparatively modest; four civilians were injured and six "militants" were killed, including Abdullah Azam al-Saudi, who was described as coordinating operations between al-Qaeda and the Taliban. Yet the next day, U.S. Ambassador Anne Paterson was convoked by the Foreign Ministry in Islamabad to receive a strongly worded protest at the violation of Pakistan's sovereignty. It turned out to be far more serious than the usual public condemnation of a campaign that was privately endorsed by the state and the military *because this was an attack outside the FATA*. "This was the first such attack beyond the lawless tribal areas," Jeremy Page reported from Islamabad, "and is thus likely to provoke even more public and official outrage."[40] Indeed it did. A diplomatic cable from the ambassador drew the U.S. State Department's attention to the widening gap between what she called "private GOP [Government of Pakistan] acquiescence and public condemnation of U.S. action":

> According to local press, the alleged U.S. strike in Bannu on November 19 marked the first such attack in the settled areas of the North-West Frontier Province, outside of the tribal areas. The strike drew a new round of condemnation by Prime Minister Gilani, coalition political parties, opposition leaders, and the media. . . .

> The first strike within "Pakistan proper" is seen as a watershed event, and the media is suggesting this could herald the spread of attacks to Peshawar or Islamabad. Even politicians who have no love lost for a dead terrorist are concerned by strikes within what is considered mainland Pakistan.[41]

The language is truly extraordinary, with its distinction between the FATA and "Pakistan proper," even "mainland Pakistan." In short: (imaginative) geography matters. Not for nothing is the FATA known in Urdu as *ilaqa ghair*, which means "alien" or "foreign" lands.

Customary Law and the Postcolony: *Pashtunwali*

To some observers both inside and outside Pakistan, the strangeness of the FATA—its location outside the conceptual boundaries of the modern state—is confirmed by the survival of a system of customary law known as Pashtunwali ("the way of the Pashtun"). In fact, it is much more than a legal system; its force resides in its capillary presence throughout political, economic, social, and cultural life. Many commentators have shown that it is precisely the sort of "mobile" legal system that animates life among once nomadic peoples, for whom the fixed statutes of a centralized state had neither appeal nor purchase. Pashtunwali includes obligations of hospitality and protection, asylum and refuge, revenge and restitution—which helps explain why people in the FATA who have no sympathy for the Taliban or other insurgent groups feel nonetheless compelled to offer them shelter, and in so doing render themselves vulnerable to aerial attack from a surveillant drone. Pashtunwali also provides a customary institution for the public resolution of disputes through a council (or jirga). The jirga is patriarchal but resolutely nonhierarchical: the men sit in a circle and each, as a symbol of authority and equality, carries a gun. Bruce Benson and Zafar Siddiqui argue that the system works not only to provide a decentralized system of order and regulation—Hobbes was wrong: without the state people do not automatically revert to a "state of nature"[42]—but also to defend the Pashtun from the incursions of the central state. "Widespread acceptance of these provisions," they suggest, "provides the Pashtun with a relatively effective decentralized process for maintaining order within and between the tribes in the absence of an authoritarian state, while also supporting the centuries-old and largely successful efforts to maintain their independence from state authority." In short, if many Pashtun people in the borderlands are deeply suspicious of and even resentful toward Islamabad (often with good reason), they are "neither lawless nor defenseless."[43]

Yet the trope of "lawlessness" persists, and it does important work. "By alleging a scarcity of legal regulation within the tribal regions," Gilani argues, "the Pakistani state has been able to mask its use of more stringent sets of controls over and surveillance within the area."[44] The trope does equally important work for the United States, for whom it is not the absence of sovereign power from the borderlands that provides the moral warrant for unleashing what Manan Ahmed calls its "righteous violence."[45] While Washington has repeatedly urged Islamabad to do much more, and to be less selective in dealing with the different factions of the Taliban, it knows very well that Pakistan has spasmodically exercised spectacular military violence there. But if the FATA is seen as "lawless" in a strictly modern sense—"administered" but not admitted, unincorporated into the body politic—then U.S. drone strikes become a prosthetic, preemptive process not only of law enforcement but also of law imposition. In Washington's eyes, its aerial violence is thus doubly "law-full": not only legal but also a means of bringing law to the lawless. This is commonplace in the moral economy of bombing, but here it is given a viscerally Orientalist inflection. The strikes are supposed to bring from the outside an "order" that is lacking on the inside, and they become instruments of an aggressively modern reason that cloaks its violence in the velvet glove of the law.

The CIA's own willingness to submit to the principles and procedures of modern law is selective and conditional; we know this from the revelations about torture and global rendition, but in the borderlands, the agency's disregard for the very system it purports to defend also exposes any group of men sitting in a circle with guns to death: even if they are gathered as a jirga. On January 27, 2011, CIA contractor Raymond Davis was arrested for shooting two young men in Lahore. The targeted killing program was suspended while the United States negotiated his release from custody, agreeing to pay compensation to the victims' families under Sharia law so that he could be freed from the jurisdiction of the court.[46] On March 16, the day after Davis's release, a jirga was convened in Dhatta Khel in North Waziristan. A tribal elder had bought the rights to log an area of oak trees only to discover that the land also contained chromite reserves; the landowner was from a different tribe and held that their agreement covered only the rights to the timber, not the minerals, and the jirga was called to resolve what had become an intertribal dispute between the Kharhtangi and the Datakhel. *Maliks* [tribal leaders], government officials, local police, and others involved in the affair gathered on a tract of open ground in the middle of the small town, where they debated in two large circles. Agreement was not reached and the jirga reconvened the next morning. Although four men from a local Taliban group were present, the meeting had been authorized by the local military commander ten days earlier and was attended by a counselor appointed by the government to act as liaison between the state, the military, and the maliks. It was also targeted by at least one and perhaps two Predators. At 11:00 a.m., multiple Hellfire missiles roared into the circles. More than forty people were killed, their bodies ripped apart by the blast and by shattered rocks, and another fourteen were seriously injured.[47]

There is no doubt that four Taliban were present: they were routinely involved in disputes between tribes with competing claims and levied taxes on chromite exports and the mine operators.[48] But the civilian toll from the strike was wholly disproportionate to any conceivable military advantage, to say nothing of the diplomatic storm it set off, and several American sources told reporters that the attack was in retaliation for the arrest of Davis: "The CIA was angry."[49] If true, this was no example of the dispassionate exercise of reason but instead a matter of disrespecting the resolution offered by Sharia law and disordering a customary judicial tribunal. Even more revealing, after the strike, an anonymous American official who was supposedly "familiar with the details of the attack" told the media that the meeting was a legitimate military target and insisted that there were no civilian casualties. Serially: "This action was directed against a number of brutal terrorists, not a county fair"; "These people weren't gathering for a bake sale"; "These guys were . . . not the local men's glee club"; "This was a group of terrorists, not a charity car wash in the Pakistani hinterlands."[50] The official—I assume it was the same one, given the difference-in-repetition of the statements—provided increasingly bizarre and offensively absurd descriptions of what the assembly in Datta Khel was *not*; he was clearly incapable of recognizing what it *was*. Admitting the assembly had been a properly constituted jirga would have given the lie to the "lawlessness" of the region and stripped the strike of any conceivable legitimacy. The area was no stranger to drone attacks, which had been concentrated in a target box that extended along the Tochi Valley from Datta Khel through Miran Shah to Mir Ali, but those responsible for this attack were clearly strangers to the area.

International Law and the Dispersion of the Battlefield

The third legal regime is a hybrid of laws, authorizations, and agreements through which the United States claims the right to extend its military actions in Afghanistan across the border into the FATA and beyond. This densely knotted tangle of assertion and argument is complicated by the absence of an established legal armature to regulate conflicts between states and transnational nonstate actors ("noninternational armed conflicts"). But law is no deus ex machina hovering above the fray; it is instead deeply embedded in military violence. Law not only rides in advance of war, reigning in its excesses, but also travels in its baggage train; law not only regulates war but is remade through war. In short, as Eyal Weizman puts it, "violence legislates."[51] In this case, it has a tortuous transnational geography that has inculpated various U.S. allies. The trail was blazed by Israel, whose targeted killing operations were vigorously condemned by the United States in summer 2001. But moral disapproval has a short shelf life. "Four months and four planes later," as Daniel Reisner, the head of the Israeli military's International Law Division, explained with evident satisfaction, the United States had accepted that "fighting terrorism is armed combat and not law enforcement." He continued:

> If you do something for long enough, the world will accept it. The whole of international law is now based on the notion that an act that is forbidden today becomes permissible if executed by enough countries. . . . International law progresses through violations. We invented the targeted assassination thesis and we had to push it. At first there were protrusions that made it hard to insert easily into the legal moulds. Eight years later, it is in the centre of the bounds of legitimacy.[52]

Reisner's self-congratulation is premature, even if the United Kingdom has since joined Israel and the United States in targeted killing (in Syria), but, in any case, the twin fields of military violence that he cites are not identical. Israel has sought to establish the legitimacy of state-sanctioned targeted killing within Palestinian territory that it occupies, controls, and continues to colonize—all of which, *pace* Reisner, is legally contestable—whereas the United States conducts its targeted killing in a territory over which it neither claims jurisdiction (unlike Israel over the West Bank) nor exercises effective control (unlike Israel over Gaza). This is a differently difficult proposition to advance, and the United States has used the capabilities of its remote operations in an attempt to expand the legal perimeter of the battlefield and push Reisner's "bounds of legitimacy" still further.

In crossing the border, the United States has found itself in a legal minefield, and scholars are divided on the permissibility of its claims.[53] The United States has relied on two legal geographies to legitimize its program of targeted killing in the FATA. Like Israel's arguments, they both invoke a doctrine of self-defense—though in neither case is this straightforward—and each produces a space of exception within which military violence is supposedly sanctioned. The first pinion is the war in Afghanistan, but in fact the foundations for the U.S.-led invasion in October 2001 were contentious. Neither Afghanistan nor its nationals attacked the United States on 9/11, and critics claim that this made the doctrine of self-defense inoperable; the United States appealed to Article 51 of the United Nations Charter and held the then Taliban government of Afghanistan co-responsible for the attacks on New York and Washington by virtue of its provision of sanctuary and support to al-Qaeda. Domestically, the Bush administration cited the Authorization for Use of Military Force (AUMF) passed by Congress and signed into law on September 18, 2001, which permitted "the use of United States Armed Forces against those responsible for the recent attacks on the United States,"[54] and the Obama administration has treated the AUMF as a warrant for its continued prosecution of the war against al-Qaeda and the Taliban. The post-Taliban regime installed in Kabul was supposed to turn Afghanistan into a compliant state that was designated a "host nation" to the armed forces of the United States and its partners in the International Security Assistance Force (authorized by the UN Security Council in December 2001), and the consent of the Afghan government subsequently empowered them to continue military operations with the reconstituted Afghan security forces. Drones played a vital role in their joint counterinsurgency campaign. Several militaries used them for intelligence, surveillance, and reconnaissance, and the United States and the United Kingdom also deployed drones to provide cover and close air support for ground troops. But the United States is alone among the coalition in also using drones as part of an extensive targeted killing program in Afghanistan, conducted by its military in concert with the CIA, though it has also relied on vital signals intelligence from its allies, including Germany, Sweden, and the United Kingdom.[55]

The United States is also alone among the coalition in asserting the right to treat Pakistan's borderlands as a spatial supplement to the war zone: this is the second pinion for its program of targeted killing in the FATA. Here too the United States has carried out the strikes while several of its allies have played indispensable supporting roles. A satellite portal at Ramstein in Germany links drones circling above the borderlands via a transatlantic fiber-optic cable to flight crews in the United States, and communications intercepts by its favored partners, especially Australia and the United Kingdom, have provided signals intelligence that has been instrumental in identifying and tracking targeted individuals. But the legal armature has been provided by the United States. The Obama administration has insisted that its strikes in the borderlands are consistent with international law in a double sense.[56] First, it cites the "continuing and imminent threat" posed by al-Qaeda and the Taliban from their sanctuaries in Pakistan to U.S. forces in Afghanistan and to the continental United States; this "elongates" the concept of imminence, as the State Department's legal adviser Harold Koh put it, and reaffirms the doctrine of self-defense so that the strikes are deemed to be legitimate preemptive actions against enemies of the United States.[57] Second, all strikes are supposed to conform to the established principles of international humanitarian law ("the laws of war")—necessity, proportionality, and distinction—that limit but do not proscribe civilian casualties.

In May 2013 the administration published a series of further, more stringent guidelines to regulate the use of lethal force outside what it called an "area of active hostilities." These affirmed a preference for capture (strikes were to be permitted only when "capture is not feasible at the time of the operation"), subsumed the existing requirement that the threat presented by the target "to U.S. persons" (without restriction of location) be both continuing and imminent, and required a "near-certainty" that noncombatants would not be injured or killed. The last stipulation had been in place for several years, but the new Presidential Policy Guidance explicitly reversed a ruse that had discredited previous U.S. casualty accounting. It now affirmed that "males of military age may be non-combatants; it is *not* the case that all military-aged males in the vicinity of a target are deemed to be combatants."[58] One of the main purposes of the guidance was to restrict and eventually to eliminate signature strikes against individuals or groups whose "pattern of life" was found to be suspicious rather than threatening. Yet it is unclear how far these regulations limited the CIA's activities. In principle, the requirement that capture had to be infeasible "at the time of the operation" placed a premium on imminence—"there's no time to wait, we must act now"—but the CIA had secured an exemption from the imminent threat criterion, even in its elongated form, so that in any event signature strikes remained permissible.[59] In short, the guidance applied to targeted killings in Somalia and Yemen but did not fully extend to Pakistan, whose borderlands remained a zone of indistinction, "half-in and half-out" of the "area of active hostilities."[60]

The spatial domain of that last phrase—an operational term specific to the guidance and absent from international law—is instructive and forms part of a wider dispersion of the battlefield beyond its traditional, bounded confines. The "vanishing battlefield," as Frédéric Mégret calls it, is at once a technopolitical and legal artifact. It has a long modern history, transformed since World War I by the rise of airpower and attacks on targets far beyond the locus of ground combat, but what is novel about its present deconstruction is the "deliberate attempt to manipulate what constitutes the battlefield and to transcend it in ways that liberate rather than constrain violence."[61] In particular, the use of drones to target individuals means that in one modality of later modern war, in Grégoire Chamayou's arresting phrase, the "body becomes the battlefield."[62] This process of the individuation of warfare derives not only from the technopolitical apparatus that makes it *possible* but also from the legal apparatus that makes it *permissible*. Individuation has blurred the distinction between military and police operations, displacing the collective identity of "the enemy" by the individual identity of "the criminal," which has in turn raised questions about the incorporation of a quasi-juridical apparatus into the targeting process.[63] These concerns apply to any area of active hostilities, but the United States bases its right to extend its military violence to the FATA—to treat the borderlands as a spatial supplement to the war zone—on the *mobility* of individuals, both terrorists and insurgents, who routinely cross between Afghanistan and Pakistan.

In the borderlands, drones have been directly entangled with the dispersion of the battlefield in two ways. In Afghanistan, the United States has used conventional strike aircraft, drones, and Special Forces to carry out its targeted killings, and when it asserts the right to extend its military operations into the FATA, it never specifies the platforms to be used. This is logical enough, since the United States seeks to establish a general principle; international law only specifies weapons systems when their use is either regulated or prohibited. But in this case, the claim is tacitly underwritten by a remarkably granular geography. The Obama administration is not now folding Pakistan into Afghanistan to produce the unitary battlespace once conjured by its common, crass, and cavalier references to "AfPak"; it does not claim the right (for example) to bomb Karachi or Lahore. Neither does it reduce the FATA to an isotropic space of military violence; it insists that its targets are limited to individuals who have sought refuge or established bases there. It consistently presents the precision of its air strikes as an enabling—exceptional because "unprecedented"—rationale for treating the FATA as a spatial *supplement* to the war zone where "temporary micro-cubes of lethal exception" are opened whenever a targeted individual is located.[64]

But the drone affords a second enabling function. The newfound concern with areas outside the "area of active hostilities" flows from an anxiety shared by the Bush and the Obama administrations about how to conduct what the Pentagon characterizes as "war in countries we are not at war with."[65] This is to redefine the very meaning of war, of course, but this is precisely what its protagonists (and for that matter its critics) claim the drone has done. The capacity of the drone to conduct "air policing" reactivates a colonial form of power in a radically new constellation. For the drone makes possible an extended *occupation* rather than a time-limited *incursion.* Its persistent presence provides unrivalled and unremitting surveillance—the residents of the FATA constantly complain about the never-ending buzz of the drones—but "the ingenuity of this novel form of aerial occupation," Munro suggests, is "its capacity simultaneously to respect and transgress the principle of territorial sovereignty."[66]

Yet Washington simultaneously transgresses Pakistan's sovereignty through serial and semipermanent violations of its airspace by U.S. Predators and Reapers. This is widely supposed to be facilitated by their low profile: at the limit, so the protagonists of the program claim, a single aircraft targets a single individual with the utmost precision. Scott Horton thus describes the drone as "a consummately secret weapon," which he explicitly links to "the art of stealth warfare."[67] Predators and Reapers, however, are not stealth aircraft; they are comparatively slow, neither difficult to detect nor to shoot down. Their presence in the skies over the FATA is hardly secret, and their strikes are widely if imperfectly reported. What seems to matter more is that the drones are remotely operated from the United States, insofar as this facilitates the ability of the CIA to orchestrate and direct the strikes. This, in turn, ensures that the program operates under Article 50 of the U.S. Code, which authorizes agencies to conduct covert actions "where it is intended that the role of the United States Government will not be apparent or acknowledged publicly."[68] In this way the drone has enabled American actions to be conducted under a cloak of secrecy that is lifted only at Washington's discretion. But, as I must now show, it has played an equally important role in securing the ambiguity of Pakistan's participation in the deadly dance.

The Drone Dance

In March 2013 Ben Emmerson, the UN Special Rapporteur on counterterrorism and human rights, concluded a three-day visit to Pakistan by reaffirming the UN's official position that drone strikes in the FATA "are a violation of Pakistan's sovereignty and territorial integrity." Emmerson met with officials from the Ministry of Foreign Affairs and the Ministry of Defense who told him that "reports of continuing tacit consent by Pakistan to the use of drones on its territory by any other State are false." This did not only apply to the current administration: "a thorough search of Government records had revealed no indication of such consent having been given." Successive administrations had repeatedly denounced the strikes, and the National Assembly had passed resolutions in May 2011 and April 2012 condemning them. Yet this is political theater and ignores what takes place behind the scenes. A change in perspective reveals Emmerson to have been a surprisingly credulous participant in what Foust called the "Islamabad drone dance." Although the record is far from straightforward, it is sufficiently clear to raise the curtain on a long, intricate, and covert choreography between Islamabad and Washington in the performance of what one U.S. official described as their "kabuki dance."[69]

In March 2004 Pakistan's military conducted a major offensive in the mountains that rise from the Tora Bora in Afghanistan and reach into South Waziristan. Their quarry was a concentration of al-Qaeda fighters near Wana, but they had considerable difficulty finding them. To solve this problem, President Pervez Musharraf admitted much later, "the Americans brought the drones to bear."[70] These were all intelligence, surveillance, and reconnaissance missions, and the strikes were left to Pakistan Air Force F-16s and helicopter gunships. But it was not long before the Predators assumed their hunter-killer role in the FATA. Three months later, Nek Muhammad and four of his companions were killed by a missile strike as they sat eating dinner in a courtyard in Kari Kot. The Pakistan military claimed responsibility for his death, but witnesses reported hearing a drone overhead minutes before the strike and eventually the truth came out: Muhammed was the first victim of a CIA-directed drone strike in Pakistan. Although the Voice of America had described him as an "al-Qaeda facilitator"—which would have made him a primary U.S. target—he was in fact a commander of the Pakistan Taliban who was suspected of an assassination plot against Musharraf and had been designated an enemy of the state. In a secret deal, Mark Mazzetti revealed, the CIA station chief in Islamabad had contacted Pakistan's ISI and offered to kill Muhammad "in exchange for access to airspace it had long sought so it could use drones to hunt down its own enemies."[71] Musharraf provided continuing cover for the drone strikes—his government routinely claimed that "the explosions had been caused by the victims themselves making home-made bombs"[72]—and even allowed an airfield at Shamsi to be used as a base for the covert operations.[73] In order to conceal the origin of the strikes from the people of Pakistan, Musharraf was adamant that they be carried out under the direction of the CIA rather than the U.S. military. The terms were negotiated between the CIA and the ISI, and the accord still acts as what Horton calls "the essential legal predicate" for the drone war in Pakistan.[74]

But the agreement turned out to be precarious, as each side busily pursued its own interests. The U.S. targeted members of al-Qaeda but also wanted to strike the Afghan Taliban and other militant groups that sought sanctuary in the FATA. These were of little concern to Pakistan since they posed no immediate threat to the state. On the contrary: they were hailed as the "good Taliban" by Islamabad, and the ISI actively supported them to counter the prospect of India gaining influence over Kabul. At first, the CIA cleared its strikes with the ISI, who confined their area of operations to two Restricted Operating Zones over North and South Waziristan. There were no further strikes in 2004, but in 2005 the ISI approved three strikes against nominated al-Qaeda targets, which were carried out under the direction of the CIA. In 2006 the CIA sought clearance for seven strikes; four were approved and the ISI asked for one nominated strike in return. The following year the CIA asked permission for fifteen strikes; four were approved and the ISI asked for five nominated strikes in return.[75]

But each side wanted more. On January 22, 2008, General Ashfaq Parvez Kayani, Pakistan's chief of army staff, met with Admiral William Fallon, the commander of U.S. Central Command (CENTCOM). High on the agenda was Kayani's frustration at the lack of real-time intelligence to guide his counterinsurgency operations in the FATA. He knew that the United States was working to enhance the signals intelligence capability of the Pakistan

Air Force, but this was a long-term project and his immediate priority was "continuous Predator coverage" of the area of military operations in South Waziristan. The United States was building one of six planned Joint Border Coordination Centers at Torkham Gate, to be staffed by Afghan, Pakistani, and U.S.-NATO military and security personnel who would share access to live Predator imagery from Afghanistan in order to track and interdict illicit movements across the border. Kayani proposed extending this cooperation by having Predators patrol inside the FATA and using their video feeds to orchestrate strikes that would be carried out, as before, by the Pakistan Air Force.[76] Fallon told him he could not spare any Predators but could provide Joint Terminal Attack Controllers to direct Pakistan's strike aircraft to their targets; Kayani would not allow U.S. ground troops to operate inside Pakistan and rejected the counteroffer.[77] But that was not the end of the matter. On March 3, Admiral Mike Mullen, the chairman of the U.S. Joint Chiefs of Staff, assured Kayani that a solution to the signals intelligence problem was in sight; electro-targeting pods and sensors were eventually retrofitted to Pakistan's F-16s. In return, Mullen asked for help in approving "a third Restricted Operating Zone for U.S. aircraft over the FATA," but he was rebuffed.[78]

The agreement was evidently starting to fray, and soon after these meetings the CIA started to act unilaterally. In the dog days of his presidency in the summer of 2008, George W. Bush agreed that the CIA need no longer seek "concurrence" from the ISI. In the future, Pakistan would only be notified of a drone strike once it was underway or shortly afterward.[79] Earlier in the year, Musharraf had accepted the need for signature strikes—which by definition required no nominated targets to be submitted for approval—and these were stepped up too.[80] And the agency now increasingly targeted the Haqqani network, which angered Pakistan's military and security establishment even more than being cut out of the loop. The Haqqanis used the FATA as a base from which to attack U.S. and other NATO forces, and their actions were intertwined with those of al-Qaeda and the Afghan Taliban. But they opposed attacks on the Pakistani government and its forces. In fact, the army relied on the Haqqanis to guarantee the security of its major base in South Waziristan, and the ISI wanted the Haqqanis to participate in any peace talks in Afghanistan to ensure a pro-Pakistan government in Kabul.[81] In August 2008 Prime Minister Yousaf Raza Gillani assured the U.S. ambassador that he had no objection to the drone strikes, but he added a crucial rider: "so long as they get the right people." The "right people" were plainly not the Haqqanis. Gillani had the Pakistan Taliban in his sights and proposed that "the next step" should be to go after its leader, Baitullah Mehsud.[82] In November, General David Petraeus made Islamabad the first stop in his overseas tour after he took command of CENTCOM, and the Pakistan defense minister delivered a similar warning: it was important "to make U.S. strikes more carefully targeted and timed in order to avoid negative consequences." But the strikes continued. In the last six months of Bush's presidency, from August 2008 to January 2009, there were thirty-seven drone strikes on targets in Pakistan, nearly double the twenty that had taken place until then, killing between 203 and 332 people. Gillani was soon asking the United States "to share all credible, actionable threat information" but to leave its execution to Pakistan: "We will hit the targets ourselves."[83]

In 2009 the drone war accelerated, but in an attempt to defuse relations with Pakistan, the United States offered to conduct joint operations in parallel with its unilateral strikes. Karen DeYoung reported that in March Pakistan was allowed to direct Predators "over areas of its choice, transmitting images directly into its own intelligence channels." Although the aircraft were armed, it was emphasized that these were not combat missions, and twelve missions were flown over the FATA as a "proof of concept."[84] Pakistan remained dissatisfied, however, and the trial was abandoned by the middle of April. The next month it was claimed that Islamabad had been granted "joint control" over a new fleet of Predators and Reapers to be operated by the U.S. military to conduct strikes on targets inside the FATA. Two missions had been flown already, controlled from a joint operations center at Jalalabad in eastern Afghanistan, where officers pooled human intelligence provided by the ISI with imagery and intercepts from U.S. military and intelligence agencies. The Pakistani officers were to be given "significant control over routes, targets and decisions to fire weapons."[85] That report was immediately denied by the Pentagon, but its details are credible and consistent with other reports. Collaboration clearly continued, and the involvement of Pakistan in target selection remained a sensitive and, on occasion, live issue.

Routine does not of course preclude rows. The files given to journalists record tense meetings in which senior U.S. officials including the secretary of state confronted their Pakistani counterparts with intelligence pointing to close ties between the ISI and militant groups like the Haqqani network; Islamabad dismissed the claims and retaliated by providing its embassy in

Washington with a list of suspected CIA agents who were to be denied visas. Relations between the CIA and the ISI plumbed the depths during the Davis affair in January 2011 and after the strike in Dhatta Khel in March, and to mend fences the CIA agreed in April to advise the ISI of any future strikes where they expected more than twenty militants to be killed.[86] By most accounts, relations between the two plunged even lower after the killing of Osama bin Laden in Abbottabad in May 2011.[87] And yet other documents in the files indicate Pakistan's continuing involvement in the targeted killing program: in 2010, for example, in a strike executed "at the request of your government" and in strikes on "a network of locations associated with a joint CIA-ISI targeting effort." To be sure, it was always an asymmetric relationship. Pakistan repeatedly pressed for a dual key approach to target selection, and one defense official complained that "they tell us to act like allies" but "they don't treat us like allies."[88]

Much of this is naturally impossible to verify. It would be wrong to reassemble these fragmentary traces into a closed and coherent narrative—ironically the very tactic enacted by the classified "storyboards" that are used to frame each targeted killing—and the relation that they bring into view is inconstant, contradictory, and fractious. But two conclusions can nevertheless be drawn. First, it is clear that the state of Pakistan not only withdrew the protections it afforded its citizens against cross-border air strikes during the Soviet occupation of Afghanistan; it also aggravated its own production of the FATA as a space of exception by actively colluding with the United States to expose those who live there to new forms of aerial violence. "Collateral damage worries you Americans," President Asif Ali Zardari told CIA Director Michael Hayden in November 2008, but "it doesn't worry me."[89]

This grotesque gavotte has nominally been kept from the public gaze, though the mask has slipped from time to time, but there is another secret hidden within the "secret." I have been careful to describe these drone strikes as being *directed* by the CIA because—the second conclusion—the U.S. military has been centrally involved in their *execution*. The diplomatic cables released by WikiLeaks make this perfectly plain: it was the commander of U.S. Central Command who had to field Pakistan's requests for extended Predator coverage, the chairman of the Joint Chiefs of Staff who asked for a third Restricted Operating Zone for the aircraft, and the new commander of CENTCOM who was lobbied about targeting priorities. This is not to discount the role of the CIA, which has long had the U.S. military as a partner even if they have not always danced to the same tune. The agency has been intimately involved in Predator operations since their inception over the Balkans in 1995, when pilots were seconded from the U.S. Air Force to the CIA for the surveillance missions; the first targeted killing by a Predator (in Yemen in 2002) was directed by the CIA but executed by the air force; and there has been close collaboration between the CIA and the U.S. military over targeted killings in Afghanistan.[90] The air force even moved some of its combat air patrols close to the Durand Line so that targets could be handed off to them from CIA-directed missions as they crossed the border into Afghanistan and killed outside Pakistan's airspace.[91] Most significant of all, for a number of years—at least since 2009 and perhaps earlier[92]—missions over Pakistan have been flown by air force pilots.

We are now moving into different territory. Although the constitution of the FATA as a space of exception explains how its inhabitants are routinely and deliberately *exposed* to state violence, it cannot account for the mistakes made in the *execution* of a program of remote killing that has been hailed by Hayden as "the most precise and effective application of firepower in the history of armed conflict."[93] The murder of Mamana Bibi was one such—obvious and hideous—mistake, but the path that led to the killing of Baitullah Mehsud was strewn with errors too. He was targeted as many as seven times, and these unsuccessful attempts on his life resulted in the deaths of 164 other people, including 11 children. This was not exceptional: an analysis by Reprieve showed that 24 men were targeted multiple times in the FATA, leaving 874 other people dead in their wake, including 142 children. On average, 36 other people, usually unknown and unnamed, have been killed for every intended target.[94] That the tempo of killing and the number of civilian casualties have declined sharply since the peak of the program in 2009–11 is clear from table 1.1. The intensity—and recklessness—of the program was shaped by the shifting fortunes of the war in Afghanistan; its peak coincided with the surge of 33,000 additional troops sent to turn the tide of the war against the Taliban.

The production of the borderlands as spaces of exception involves many attempts to force those who live there into particular subject-positions as a means of subjugation. These positions are partial and precarious, but the project to establish them as legitimate and rational has consequences that are material and affective. They clearly affect those targeted—people like Baitullah Mehsud—whose political agency exceeds in terrifying ways the normative space allowed them by the state of Pakistan and the United

States and in so doing brings their actions to the attention of both. But they also impact the rest of the population in the FATA, constricting their mobilities and stoking their fears to such a degree that "normal life" for many of them threatens to become a memory or a fantasy. Their existence is rendered more precarious because the subject-positions to which they are so brutally assigned are racialized. These are "tribal peoples," different from those who inhabit "mainland Pakistan," while the United States writes off their incidental deaths as "collateral damage," whose anonymity confers on them no individuality, only a collective ascription. When a CIA-directed drone strike on a compound in the Shawal Valley of South Waziristan on January 15, 2015, was found to have killed not only a deputy leader of al-Qaeda in the Indian subcontinent and a local Taliban commander but also two hostages, an American development contractor and an Italian aid worker, a "grim-faced" and "visibly moved" Obama made a personal and public apology.[95] The rarity of the gesture is revealing. For the value of their lives was acknowledged and their deaths were made grievable in ways that others'—which is to say Others'—were not.[96] Nobody has ever accepted responsibility or apologized for the death of Mamana Bibi or any of the other innocent victims of aerial violence.

For this reason, it is important to resist those versions of the space of exception that are complicit in the denial of agency to those who live within its confines. The state of Pakistan administers the inhabitants of the FATA through political agents: but this does not remove (though it does diminish) their own political agency. Pakistan's armed forces conduct clearing operations that ruthlessly drive people from their homes and into camps for displaced persons: but this does not turn the FATA into one vast "camp." The presence of U.S. drones strips those who live under them of their well-being and dignity: but this does not reduce them to "bare life."

Notes

Epigraph: Obama, "Remarks by President Obama and Prime Minister Shinawatra." Although Obama was speaking in Thailand (on November 18, 2012), he was referring to—and endorsing—Israel's eight-day military offensive against Gaza in response to Hamas's rocket attacks.

1. Mayer, "The Predator War"; see also B. Williams, *Predators*, 2–9.
2. Amnesty International, "*Will I Be Next?*," 18–23; Pagnamenta, "My Dead Mother Wasn't an Enemy of America"; Deveraux, "Family of Grandmother"; McVeigh,

"Drone Strikes." "Bibi" is an honorific meaning "grandmother"; the family name is Rehman.

3. C. Christine Fair has attempted to attribute Mamana Bibi's murder to a Pakistan Air Force strike. Fair, "Ethical and Methodological Issues." See also Lewis, "The Misleading Human Rights Watch."
4. C. Woods, *Sudden Justice*, xv; Cockburn, *Kill-Chain.*
5. "Kill/Capture," *Frontline*, PBS, May 10, 2011, http://www.pbs.org/wgbh/frontline/film/kill-capture/transcript/.
6. In its original form, the program was a radicalization of Lt. Col. John Warden's "five rings" air targeting model, in which the outer ring is made up of "fielded forces" and the inner ring comprises the "leadership." Warden had made much of the importance of striking the inner ring, but a classified CIA review and 2009 report suggested that the "de-centralized" structure of al-Qaeda and the "egalitarian" system of the Taliban made them much less vulnerable to decapitation; CIA Office of Transnational Issues, "Best Practices in Counterinsurgency."
7. Mulrine, "Warheads on Foreheads"; Gregory, "Drone Geographies."
8. Outside Pakistan, the United States has used drones for targeted killing in Iraq, Libya, Somalia, Syria, and Yemen; it has also used drones to orchestrate strikes carried out by conventional aircraft and to support ground troops in Afghanistan, which has been the major theater of remote operations, and to carry out an extensive program of targeted killing there.
9. The two programs were closely connected, and senior officers in one program were transferred to the other. Mazzetti and Apuzzo, "Deep Support in Washington."
10. Multiple projects have mapped drone strikes in Pakistan and elsewhere. Two that have mined the Bureau of Investigative Journalism's database to considerable effect are Chris Herwig's interactive visualization available at http://chrisherwig.org/places/drones/#8.00/32.886/70.467 (covering the years 2004–13) and Forensic Architecture's visualizations available in *Forensis*, 409–16, and, in interactive form, at http://wherethedronesstrike.com (covering the years 2004–14).
11. P. Shah, "My Drone War."
12. Agamben, *Homo Sacer*; Agamben, *State of Exception*; Agamben, *Remnants of Auschwitz*.
13. Benton, "Spatial Histories of Empire."
14. Dunn and Cons, "Aleatory Sovereignty."
15. Gilani, "'Spacing' Minority Relations," 371. This is a common characteristic of spaces of exception; see, for example, Johns, "Guantánamo Bay."
16. Munro, "Mapping the Vertical Battlespace."
17. Agamben, *Homo Sacer*, 97.
18. https://www.whitehouse.gov/the-press-office/remarks-president-a-new-strategy-afghanistan-and-pakistan. Gul, *The Most Dangerous Place*, which took its title from Obama's speech.
19. Mégret, "War and the Vanishing Battlefield."
20. Foust, "The Islamabad Drone Dance."

21. Gilani, "'Spacing' Minority Relations," 368.
22. Iqtidar and Akbar, "Caught between Drones and Army Raids."
23. Naseemullah, "Shades of Sovereignty," 506. Cf. International Crisis Group, *Drones*, 30: "Legal, political and economic isolation has turned FATA into a political and administrative no-man's land, left largely to the mercies of the militants and the military."
24. General Staff, Army Headquarters, India, *Operations in Waziristan*, 59; Roe, "Friends in High Places"; see also Roe, *Waging War in Waziristan*.
25. Satia, "Attack of the Drones"; Satia, "Drones: A History."
26. Wirsing, "Pakistan and the War in Afghanistan"; Hilali, "The Costs and Benefits of the Afghan War," table 3; Weymouth, "Moscow's Invisible 'War of Terror.'"
27. "PAF Conducted 5,500 Bombing Runs."
28. Amnesty International, "The Hands of Cruelty," 37–47.
29. Amnesty International, "The Hands of Cruelty," 39.
30. Ordinances are temporary provisions that are issued by an executive order of the president and have the force of law.
31. C. Woods, "Don't Call It a Comeback." Here too it is difficult to provide a detailed accounting, but the Bureau of Investigative Journalism tracked fifteen air strikes by the Pakistan Air Force between December 2013 and June 15, 2014, that killed 291–540 people (including 16–112 civilians).
32. "Thousands Flee North Waziristan."
33. Human Rights Watch, "Pakistan."
34. Khan, "The Ghosts and Gains of North Waziristan."
35. It is extremely difficult to estimate casualties, but if an official statement in December 2015 is to be believed, in just eighteen months Pakistan's Armed Forces had killed "3,400 militants" in North Waziristan—roughly the same number of total deaths attributed to U.S. drone strikes in the FATA in twelve years. "3,400 Militants Killed."
36. Craig, "Pakistani Military Says Its Drone Killed."
37. Cf. International Human Rights and Conflict Resolution Clinic (Stanford Law School) and Global Justice Clinic (NYU School of Law), *Living under Drones*. This dimension is missing from Ian Shaw and Majeed Akhter, "The Unbearable Humanness of Drone Warfare" and "The Dronification of State Violence," which exclude the "non-dronification" of state violence. The inhabitants of the FATA are also living under the violence of the Taliban and other Islamist groups; the multiple actors responsible for causing civilian harm in the borderlands are documented with skill and sensitivity in a report from the Center for Civilians in Conflict, "Civilian Harm and Conflict in Northwest Pakistan."
38. Amnesty International, "The Hands of Cruelty," 37.
39. Gilani, "'Spacing' Minority Relations," 372.
40. Page, "US Missile Strike Kills Six." In fact, this was the first attack outside the FATA to be made public; there had been an earlier attack at Jani Khel on December 3, 2007, days after Benazir Bhutto's assassination, which injured the leader of al-Qaeda affiliate al Jihad fi Waziristan, who had provided a religious justification for her murder.

41. Cable 08ISLAMABAD3677, November 24, 2008. All the diplomatic cables cited in this chapter are from the WikiLeaks cache released in November 2010 and available at https://wikileaks.org.
42. Ginsburg, "An Economic Interpretation of the *Pashtunwali*."
43. Benson and Siddiqui, "*Pashtunwali*," 108, 118.
44. Gilani, "'Spacing' Minority Relations," 371.
45. Ahmed, "Waziristan, U.S."
46. Mazzetti, "How a Single Spy Helped Turn Pakistan."
47. See the interviews and investigations reported in International Human Rights and Conflict Resolution Clinic (Stanford Law School) and Global Justice Clinic (NYU School of Law), *Living under Drones*, 71–76; Reprieve (London) and Foundation for Fundamental Rights (Islamabad), "The Situation in Afghanistan," 52–53; and the digital reconstruction of the strike by Forensic Architecture and SITU Research described in *Forensis*, 425–33.
48. Masood and Shah, "Drone Attack Kills Civilians in Pakistan."
49. Gannon, Dozier, and Abbot, "Timing of US Drone Strike Questioned." The same report claimed that the U.S. ambassador in Islamabad used the embassy's secure line in a desperate attempt to stop the strike but was rebuffed by then CIA director Leon Panetta.
50. Rodriguez, "Pakistan Denounces U.S. Drone Strike"; Masood and Shah, "Drone Attack Kills Civilians in Pakistan"; Wright and Mehsud, "Pakistan Slams Drone Strike"; "US-Pakistan Relationship Increasingly Strained."
51. Weizman, *The Least of All Possible Evils*, 93; see also C. Jones, "Lawfare and the Juridification of Late Modern War."
52. Daniel Reisner, quoted in Y. Feldman and Blau, "Consent and Advise"; see also Benn, "Obama Is Learning from the IDF"; and Weizman, "Legislative Attack." The distinction between "armed combat" and "law enforcement" is foundational; the former is governed by international humanitarian law, the latter by international human rights law—which imposes far more stringent restrictions on the use of lethal force than either Israel or the United States is prepared to accept.
53. See Anderson, "Targeted Killing and Drone Warfare"; Blank, "Defining the Battlefield"; Daskal, "The Geography of the Battlefield"; M. Lewis, "Drones and the Boundaries of the Battlefield"; and Lubell and Derejko, "A Global Battlefield?"
54. https://www.gpo.gov/fdsys/pkg/PLAW-107publ40.
55. Nordland, "Germany and Sweden Are Said to Help." In Afghanistan, the U.S. military works from a Joint Prioritized Effects List that has contained up to 750 names at any one time established in concert with Joint Special Operations Command and the CIA. See Appelbaum et al., "Obama's Lists"; Gregory, "Untargeted Killing"; and Scahill, *The Assassination Complex*. These assassinations have been executed by air strikes and by "night raids."
56. These conform to *jus ad bello* (the legal basis for military violence) and *jus in bello* (the legal conduct of hostilities), respectively.
57. Koh, "The Obama Administration and International Law"; Landay, "Leaked U.S. Justification for Drone Killings."

58. "U.S. Policy Standards and Procedures"; cf. Becker and Shane, "Secret 'Kill List' Proves a Test": "all military-aged males in a strike zone [were counted] as combatants."
59. Entous, "Obama Kept Looser Rules." Entous points to the inadvertent killing of two aid workers held hostage by al-Qaeda, one American and one Italian, during a drone strike on a compound in North Waziristan on January 15, 2015: "If the exemption had not been in place for Pakistan, the CIA might have been required to gather more intelligence before that strike."
60. R. Goodman, "10 Years of Drone Strikes in Pakistan." The "area of active hostilities" is supposed to be determined by the scope and intensity of the fighting, and by 2015 included Afghanistan, Iraq, and Syria. But the State Department's legal adviser subsequently conceded that "sometimes others have referred to the Afghanistan/Pakistan border region as being part of what we talk about with respect to Afghanistan." Savage, "Brian Egan's ASIL Speech."
61. Mégret, "War and the Vanishing Battlefield."
62. Chamayou, *A Theory of the Drone*, 56.
63. On policing, see Bachman, Bell, and Holmqvist, *War, Police and Assemblages of Intervention*; and Neocleous, *War Power, Police Power*. On the individuation of warfare, see Issacharoff and Pildes, "Targeted Warfare"; Issacharoff and Pildes, "Drones and the Dilemma of Modern Warfare"; and Kahn, "Imagining Warfare." See also Gregory, "The Individuation of Warfare?"
64. Chamayou, *Théorie du drone*, 84; the English translation renders this phrase as "temporary lethal microcubes" (56), but the echo of Agamben is important. Similarly, Joseph Pugliese describes drones as "instantiating mobile 'zones of exception.'" Pugliese, "Prosthetics of Law," 944; see also Pugliese, *State Violence and the Execution of Law*.
65. The phrase is from the Pentagon's Quadrennial Defense Review in 2006; see M. Ryan, "'War in Countries.'"
66. Munro, "Mapping the Vertical Battlespace," 238; see also Munro, "The Entangled Sovereignties of Air Police."
67. C. Woods, *Sudden Justice*, xiv; Horton, *Lords of Secrecy*, 110.
68. The alternative is Title 10, under which the U.S. military conducts its regular operations. See Kuyers, "CIA or DoD"; for the wider implications, see Chesney, "Military-Intelligence Convergence." In relation to the claim I advance here, cf. Hastings, "The Rise of the Killer Drones": "The remote-control nature of unmanned missions enables politicians to wage war while claiming 'we're not at war.'"
69. Emmerson, "Report of the Special Rapporteur." Foust, "The Islamabad Drone Dance." International Crisis Group also has a smart criticism of Emmerson's visit to Pakistan in its *Drones*, 20. For the "kabuki dance," see Landay, "U.S. Secret." Kabuki is an elaborately stylized classical Japanese dance-drama, but since the 1960s the term has been used in the United States to describe an artfully contrived display of conflict whose outcome has in fact been choreographed in advance by the parties involved.
70. Coll, "The Unblinking Stare."

71. Rohde and Khan, "Ex-fighter for Taliban Dies in Strike"; Mazzetti, "A Secret Deal on Drones."
72. Porter, "Why Pakistani Military Demands a Veto."
73. Shamsi Airfield had been leased by the United Arab Emirates—"for game hunting"—and in October 2001 Musharraf permitted the UAE to assign a sublease to the United States, enabling Pakistan to deny that U.S. aircraft were operating from its bases. The airfield was developed jointly by the CIA and the U.S. military, whose Predators were serviced by private contractors working for Blackwater (renamed Xe in 2009 and Academi in 2011).
74. Horton, *Lords of Secrecy*, 127.
75. Landay, "U.S. Secret." The Bureau of Investigative Journalism recorded three strikes in 2005, four in 2006, and six in 2007. It is unclear whether the approvals were for targets (which could involve multiple strikes until they were successful) or specific strikes.
76. Cable 08ISLAMABAD293, January 19, 2008. The Khyber Border Coordination Center (BCC) was operational by mid-March, but the Pakistani public was outraged when General David McKiernan, the commander of coalition forces in Afghanistan, later revealed that "we exchange frequencies, we exchange intelligence, we have a Predator feed going down to the BCC at Torkham Gate"; Hodge, "U.S. Sharing Predator Video."
77. Cable 08ISLAMABAD609, February 11, 2008. In fact, in September and October 2009 small teams of U.S. Special Forces were deployed to provide intelligence, surveillance, and reconnaissance support to the Pakistan Army, which included a "live downlink of unmanned aerial vehicle (UAV) full motion video."
78. Cable 08ISLAMABAD1272, March 24, 2008. Subsequently the United States also pressed for permission to extend Predator flights beyond the FATA—over Quetta—but was refused: this decision clearly reinforced Pakistan's anger at the strike on a target outside the FATA in November 2008 and was ignored or circumvented in the assassination of the leader of the Afghan Taliban in May 2016.
79. E. Schmitt and Shanker, *Counterstrike*. This shortened the time between locating a target and firing a missile to forty-five minutes or less (*Counterstrike*, 102).
80. E. Schmitt and Shanker, *Counterstrike*, 119–20.
81. Porter, "Why Pakistani Military Demands a Veto"; Landay, "Do U.S. Drones Kill Pakistani Extremists?"
82. Cable 08ISLAMABAD2802, August 23, 2008. The first (unsuccessful) strike targeting the Pakistan Taliban and Baitullah Mehsud took place almost six months later, on February 14, 2009.
83. Bureau of Investigative Journalism, "The Bush Years"; Cable 08ISLAMABAD3586, November 13, 2008; Cable 08ISLAMABAD3594, November 15, 2008.
84. DeYoung, "Al-Qaeda Seen as Shaken in Pakistan"; E. Schmitt and Mazzetti, "In a First, U.S. Provides Pakistan With Drone Data."
85. Barnes and Miller, "Pakistan Gets a Say in Drone Attacks."
86. Entous, Gorman, and Barnes, "US Tightens Drone Rules."
87. Most reports emphasized Pakistan's intense anger at the violation of its airspace and claimed that neither the ISI nor the military were given any prior warning of

the mission. But some reports have claimed that Bin Laden was being held in an ISI safe house in Abbottabad and that the ISI collaborated in his assassination. Hersh, "The Killing of Osama bin Laden." For a review, see Mahler, "What Do We Really Know?"

88. Entous and Gorman, "CIA Strikes Strain Ties with Pakistan Further."
89. Woodward, *Obama's Wars*, 26.
90. Whittle, *Predator*; "Interview Lt. Gen. Michael DeLong," *Frontline*, PBS, February 14, 2006, http://www.pbs.org/wgbh/pages/frontline/darkside/interviews/delong.html.
91. Entous, Gorman, and Barnes, "US Tightens Drone Rules."
92. Shachtman, "U.S. Military Joins CIA's Drone War in Pakistan."
93. Hayden, "To Keep America Safe."
94. Reprieve, "You Never Die Twice," 6–8.
95. Mazzetti and Schmitt, "First Evidence of a Blunder"; Baker, "Obama Apologizes"; Entous, Paletta, and Schwarz, "American, Italian Hostages Killed."
96. Butler, *Frames of War*.

2 LAWFARE AND ARMED CONFLICTS

A Comparative Analysis of Israeli and U.S. Targeted Killing Policies and Legal Challenges against Them

LISA HAJJAR

LAWFARE, a neologism that combines *law* and *warfare*, describes efforts to challenge a state's military practices and national security policies in court and to pursue accountability for war crimes and other violations that arise in the context of armed conflict. Lawfare is a relatively recent phenomenon, made possible by developments in the enforceability of international law after the end of the Cold War, such as the creation of the International Criminal Court (in 2002) and new uses of the doctrine of universal jurisdiction to prosecute perpetrators of gross crimes in foreign national legal systems. These developments have created capacities to actually use (rather than merely cite) the law vis-à-vis gross violations. For these reasons, *lawfare* has a pejorative connotation among those inclined to decry legal constraints on state discretion and criminal or civil consequences for state agents who violate the law.[1]

Lawfare has a counterpart in what I term *state lawfare*. By this, I mean the practices of officials to reinterpret international humanitarian law (IHL) or human rights laws in ways that deviate from prevailing internationally accepted understandings in order to "legalize" state practices that would otherwise constitute violations. These two concepts—*lawfare* and *state lawfare*—are useful in analyzing the Israeli and U.S. governments' wars in the twenty-first century. The specific focus here is on the efforts to justify and "legalize" targeted killing and lawfare attempts to challenge the legality of these policies. Beyond the targeted killing controversy is a larger story about contestations over the parameters of what is legal in war.

Lawfare

The term *lawfare* was coined in a 2001 essay by Colonel Charles J. Dunlap Jr., who, at the time, served in the U.S. Air Force Judge Advocate General's Corps. He defined it as "the use of law as a weapon of war" and "a method of warfare where law is used as a means of realizing a military objective."[2] Dunlap referenced the 1991 Gulf War and the 1999 NATO intervention in Kosovo as examples of how military lawyers had acquired a larger role in operational decisions, for example, by vetting the legality of strikes against particular targets. He attributed this "hyperlegalism" partly to new media technologies that convey the consequences of combat in almost real time, thereby enabling humanitarian organizations to criticize specific military operations and, possibly, to investigate violations. Dunlap worried that such scrutiny could undermine public support for war: "Evidence shows this technique can work. The Vietnam War—where U.S. forces never suffered a true *military* defeat—is the model that today's adversaries repeatedly try to replicate."[3]

Dunlap's original negative connotation remains popular among those who oppose efforts to impose legal constraints on officials' national security prerogatives and to pursue accountability for violations. A bold excoriation appears in the 2005 National Defense Strategy of the United States, which asserts: "Our strength as a nation-state will continue to be challenged by those who employ a strategy of the weak using international fora, judicial processes, and terrorism."[4] In a similar vein, Israeli officials charge that lawfare is a "strategic threat"[5] and one manifestation of an international campaign to "delegitimize" Israel, in the same despised company with the boycott, divestment, and sanctions movement. On the website of the Lawfare Project, established in 2010 to defend U.S. and Israeli governmental interests from critics, *lawfare* is defined as

> the negative manipulation of international and national human rights laws to accomplish purposes other than, or contrary to, those for which they were originally enacted.
>
> Modern-day lawfare has three goals:

1. To silence and punish free speech about issues of national security and public concern,
2. To delegitimize the sovereignty of democratic states,
3. To frustrate and hinder the ability of democracies to fight against and defeat terrorism.[6]

The concept of lawfare has come to be used in politically neutral or positive ways as well.[7] Dunlap, who has remained a ubiquitous interlocutor in discussions and debates about lawfare, has since reconsidered the negative connotation he attached to the term, arguing that "concern from the public, NGOs, academics, legislatures, and the courts about the behavior of militaries is more than simply a public relations problem; it is a legitimate and serious activity that is totally consistent with adherence to the rule of law, democratic values, and—for that matter—lawfare. . . . The use of the courts is something I advocate as a vitally important lawfare measure."[8]

State Lawfare

Israeli officials embarked on a state lawfare project in the wake of the 1967 Six-Day War, which included the conquest and occupation of the West Bank and Gaza. Rather than simply ignoring constraining international laws, officials engaged in reinterpretations in order to reject the de jure applicability of the Fourth Geneva Convention (GCIV), the main body of IHL that pertains to militarily occupied territories and their civilian population (who are designated "protected persons"). This rejection through reinterpretation was premised on the claim that the West Bank and Gaza were not "occupied" because they had not been sovereign to the states displaced in the war (i.e., Jordan and Egypt). Rather, their status was sui generis, and thus Israel was not bound by GCIV in areas "administered" by the military. Although this interpretation never obtained international credibility, it became the cornerstone of Israel's doctrine on the state's rights in the West Bank and Gaza.

In 1968, to promote the perception that Israel's administration of the recently captured territories was benign, the attorney general granted Palestinians from the West Bank and Gaza the option to petition the High Court of Justice (HCJ). Over the decades since, Palestinians have filed thousands of petitions. However, the cumulative outcome of this litigation has not been favorable to them.[9] On the contrary, with rare exceptions, HCJ decisions have sanctioned state practices that adversely affect Palestinians and in so doing reinforce the state lawfare premises underlying them. The judicial record, as Nimer Sultany describes it, is "oppression-blind jurisprudence, concealment of the general context, fragmentation of reality, the practice of non-intervention and submission to dubious 'security' considerations disguised rhetorically by 'balancing' and 'proportionality' tests, and declining to provide meaningful and timely legal remedies."[10]

What, then, is the point of going to court? Hassan Jabareen locates the value of litigation in a transnational and political context to argue that even when Palestinian petitioners lose, taking cases to court functions as a means of exposing the details and rationales of the Israeli state's oppression and discrimination.[11] This insight about the value of litigation is relevant to assessing the lawfare–state lawfare relationship in other contexts as well, as I elaborate below.

Israeli state lawfare took a new course in the 1990s in response to political changes resulting from the Israeli–Palestinian negotiations. While the 1993 Oslo Accords did not end the occupation, they ushered in an Israeli military redeployment from Palestinian population centers (Areas A) and the establishment of the Palestinian Authority (PA), a nonsovereign entity to administer daily life and serve as a security-providing proxy for Israel. These changes prompted Israeli officials to assert that areas under the semiautonomous control of the PA had become differently "foreign." This became highly significant following the breakdown of negotiations in July 2000 and the start of a second intifada in September.

In contrast to the start of the first intifada in 1987, which was characterized as a breakdown of "law and order," Israel characterized spreading Palestinian protests at the start of the second intifada as acts of aggression. The military's rules of engagement were loosened, and heavy weapons, including tanks and helicopter gunships, were deployed against unarmed protestors. Under international consensus-based interpretations of IHL, massive use of military force by an occupying state against civilians in occupied territories would be categorically illegal. The state lawfare rationale that Israeli officials advanced to justify this war model was premised on assertions that the law enforcement model (i.e., policing and riot control tactics) was no longer viable because the military was "out" of Palestinian areas and because (some) Palestinians possessed (small) arms (i.e., police and security agents), and thus constituted a foreign "armed adversary." Officials described the second intifada as an "armed conflict short of war"[12] and asserted Israel's self-defense right to attack an "enemy entity," while denying that those stateless enemies had any right to use force, even in self-defense.

The official Israeli claim that Palestinian areas are "not occupied" is the essential element to legitimize them as sites of warfare. This posture was reinforced when Israel unilaterally withdrew ground troops from Gaza in 2005. However, the claim is specious because Israel continues to exercise effective control over Gaza, including the capacity to impose a suffocating siege, total closure of boundaries, and aerial surveillance.[13] Following the 2006 Palestinian legislative elections that brought Hamas to power, the siege of Gaza intensified. Israel waged full-scale wars against Gaza during "Operation Cast Lead" between December 27, 2008, and January 18, 2009; "Operation Pillar of Defense" on November 14–21, 2012; and "Operation Protective Edge" between July 8 and August 26, 2014.

Israeli state lawfare in the twenty-first century—including the "legalization" of targeted killing (elaborated in the following section)—is explained in a *Haaretz* article about the International Law Division (ILD) of the Military Advocate General's unit.[14] According to Daniel Reisner, who headed the ILD until 2005, "We defended policy that is on the edge. . . . In that sense, ILD is a body that restrains action, but does not stop it." He continues:

> What we are seeing now is a revision of international law. . . . If you do something for long enough, the world will accept it. The whole of international law is now based on the notion that an act that is forbidden today becomes permissible if executed by enough countries. . . . International law progresses through violations. We invented the targeted assassination thesis and we had to push it. At first there were protrusions that made it hard to insert easily into the legal moulds. Eight years later it is in the centre of the bounds of legitimacy.[15]

At the start of the second intifada, the United States joined other governments in criticizing Israel's excessive use of force. According to Reisner,

> In April 2001 I met the American envoy George Mitchell [who was heading a fact-finding mission] and explained that above a certain level, fighting terrorism is armed combat and not law enforcement. His committee rejected that approach. . . . It took four months and four planes to change the opinion of the United States, and had it not been for those four planes I am not sure we would have been able to develop the thesis of the war against terrorism on the present scale.[16]

Indeed, following the terrorist attacks on September 11, 2001, and the launching of a global "war on terror," Bush administration officials embarked on an unprecedented project of state lawfare. For example, over State Department dissent, White House and Justice Department lawyers proposed, and the president accepted, that the Geneva Conventions are inapplicable to a war against stateless enemies. Another state lawfare position, driven by the desire to inoculate officials and state agents from future accountability for violations, was the assertion that ratified international human rights treaties and federal law criminalizing torture are not binding beyond the sovereign jurisdiction of the state. The architects of this U.S. state lawfare edifice called it "the new paradigm."[17]

The contents of the new paradigm were largely secret for the first several years of the "war on terror." One exception was President Bush's military order, issued on November 13, 2001, declaring that enemies in this conflict are "unlawful combatants." This concept clearly aimed to evade IHL rules on the treatment of prisoners by designating people taken into U.S. custody as neither combatants nor civilians, and therefore not entitled to the rights of either.[18]

Since mid-2004, an abundance of information about the new paradigm and its consequences has become public as a result of declassifications, official investigations, leaks, and Freedom of Information Act (FOIA) litigation, although much still remains classified. During this period, litigation to challenge law-violating state policies and practices have focused mainly on the treatment of prisoners.[19] With the exception of several landmark rulings in the Supreme Court, U.S. courts have tended either to actively endorse the positions of the state by accepting state lawfare interpretations or passively accept them by declining to hear cases on the grounds that alleged violations are nonjusticiable political questions, would implicate states' secrets, or would breach accused officials' right to immunity.

Targeted Killing as Policy and Practice

The Israeli Context: From Doing and Denying to "Legalization"

During the first intifada, Israel instituted a secret policy of targeted killing in the occupied territories.[20] These operations were conducted by undercover units who perfidiously disguised themselves as Arabs to approach and execute their targets or by snipers. At that time, when the territories were indisputably under full control of the Israeli military and Palestinians were being arrested and prosecuted or administratively detained in unprecedented numbers (Israel had the highest per capita incarceration rate in the world at the time), killing suspects clearly constituted extrajudicial executions.[21]

To evade war crimes allegations, Israeli officials staunchly denied the existence of a targeted killing policy. In 1992, in response to reporting on assassination operations by the Israeli human rights organization B'Tselem, a government spokesperson said, "There is no policy, and there never will be a policy or a reality, of willful killings of suspects. . . . The principle of the sanctity of life is a fundamental principle of the IDF [Israel Defense Forces]."[22]

Important factors driving the uptick of targeted killings during the 1990s were the redeployment of the military from Areas A and suicide bombings by Palestinian Islamists.[23] Another factor was Israel's achievement in developing remote surveillance and targeting technologies. By 2000 Israel had become one of the world leaders in the manufacture and use of unmanned aerial vehicles (drones) and miniaturized missiles and detection devices.[24]

The doing-and-denying phase ended on November 9, 2000, six weeks into the second intifada, with the killing of Hussein Abayat and two women "bystanders." For the first time, a military spokesman acknowledged responsibility: "During an IDF-initiated action in the area of the village of Beit Sahur, missiles were launched by IDF helicopters at the vehicle of a senior *Fatah/Tanzim* activist. The pilot reported an accurate hit. . . . The action this morning is a long-term activity undertaken by the Israeli Security Forces, targeted at the groups responsible for the escalation of violence."[25]

As with its pioneering legacy of "legalizing" torture (in 1987), Israel was the first state in the world to publicly proclaim the legality of "preemptive targeted killing." Officials asserted the lawfulness of this practice on the following bases: (1) Palestinians were to blame for the hostilities, which constituted a war of terror against Israel; (2) the laws of war permit states to kill their enemies; (3) targeted individuals were "ticking bombs" who had to be killed because they could not be arrested; and (4) killing terrorists by means of assassination is a legitimate form of national defense.[26] The deaths of untargeted civilians were termed, in accordance with the discourse of war, "collateral damage." Orna Ben-Naftali and Keren Michaeli summarize the official position as it evolved over the last two months of 2000:

> On December 21, 2000, Voice of Israel Radio [reported] that there was a new policy of "pre-emptive operations," that it was targeted at terrorists—as opposed to political leaders of *Hamas, Islamic Jihad,*

> and *Fatah*, that the main method used was sniper fire, and that the IDF went to great lengths not to harm innocent by-standers. . . . An unnamed high ranking official in the security forces stated that "the liquidation of wanted persons is proving itself useful . . . [this] activity paralyses and frightens entire villages and as a result there are areas where people are afraid to carry out hostile activities."[27]

On December 31, 2000, Thabet Thabet, a member of the PA, was assassinated. Afterward, Deputy Defense Minister Ephraim Sneh stated, "We will hit all those involved in terrorist operations, attacks or preparation for attacks, and the fact of having a position within the Palestinian Authority confers no immunity on anyone."[28] By November 2001 forty-seven people had been targeted, resulting in eighty deaths.[29]

The most notorious targeted killing operation occurred on July 22, 2002, when an F-16 launched a one-ton bomb to assassinate Salah Shehadeh, a Hamas leader. The bomb destroyed the apartment building where Shehadeh lived and eight nearby buildings and partially destroyed nine others in the densely populated Gaza neighborhood of al-Daraj. In addition to Shehadeh and his guard, fourteen Palestinians, including eight children, were killed, and more than 150 people were injured. In this instance, the military responded to public outcry about the size of the bomb, the targeting of a residential neighborhood, and the high casualty rate by conducting an investigation. The findings justified targeting Shehadeh as a perpetrator of terrorist violence while conceding that there had been "shortcomings in the information available," namely the presence of "innocent civilians" in the vicinity of what was claimed to be Shehadeh's "operational hideout."[30]

Between the start of the second intifada in September 2000 and August 2014, approximately 440 Palestinians were killed during targeted killing operations, of whom 278 were the targets; this statistic excludes thousands of Palestinians killed by other means.

The U.S. Context: From Strategic Secrecy to the Disposition Matrix

In the United States, political assassination was prohibited by executive orders signed by every president since 1977. That prohibition was upended in September 2001 when President Bush secretly authorized the CIA, a civilian agency, to capture or kill suspected terrorists around the world.[31] This was not a repudiation of the assassination prohibition per se because the context was war. But this global asymmetric war was unlike any other.

The first targeted killing operation outside Afghanistan occurred in Yemen on November 3, 2002, when a Predator drone launched from a base in Djibouti shot a Hellfire missile into a car.[32] The target was Qa'id Salim Sinan al-Harithi. One of the other six passengers killed in the strike, Kamal Darwish, was a U.S. citizen.[33] Afterward, officials justified the operation by proclaiming that because Harithi was a member of al-Qaeda and allegedly was involved in the 2000 bombing of the USS *Cole*, and because his arrest was not possible, targeted killing was a legitimate tactic, even against a person located in a country not at war with the United States. However, the UN Special Rapporteur for extrajudicial, summary, or arbitrary executions concluded that the Yemen strike "constitutes a clear case of extrajudicial killing."[34]

During the Bush administration, targeted killing by drones was done primarily by the CIA,[35] while special military forces under the Joint Special Operations Command (JSOC) emulated Israeli-style operations during night raids and other modes of attack;[36] JSOC adopted the motto "find, fix, finish." But throughout most of the Bush years, capture was the preferred counterterrorism strategy in order to try to elicit actionable intelligence about shadowy enemies and elusive threats. Tens of thousands of people were arrested, detained, and interrogated by the U.S. military, and 119 "high-value detainees" (HVDs) were captured by the CIA.[37]

The strategic choice between capturing and killing terror suspects and militants began to shift in 2006. This followed the Supreme Court's *Hamdan v. Rumsfeld* decision, which concluded that Common Article 3 of the Geneva Conventions does apply to the treatment of prisoners in U.S. custody and that torture, as well as cruel, inhumane, and degrading treatment, are prosecutable offenses. President Bush criticized the decision, but his administration nevertheless emptied the CIA black sites and relocated fourteen HVDs to Guantánamo. After that, transfers to Guantánamo tapered off and halted entirely in 2008. That year, drone strikes increased by 94 percent from the previous year.[38]

Since 2009, when Barack Obama assumed the presidency, targeted killing has escalated dramatically in terms of the number of strikes per month and the widening geographic scope.[39] Targeted raids by JSOC, first introduced in Iraq in 2006, were transported, along with the drones, to Afghanistan in 2009. By 2011 targeted killing operations were occurring at a rate of one thousand a month.[40] The Obama administration, like its predecessor, justifies the globalized prerogative to kill suspects on the basis of the Authorization for Use of Military Force (AUMF), passed by Congress days after the 9/11 attacks, which set no territorial or temporal limits on the government's response to terrorism.

Official U.S. claims about the "legality" of targeted killing hew to the same lines of argument as those of Israel, namely the legitimacy of executing people who pose an ostensibly imminent threat and cannot be arrested. One significant difference between the two countries' policies is that the United States has claimed the right to target citizens abroad.

On January 27, 2010, the *Washington Post* reported that at least three citizens had been designated for extrajudicial execution.[41] One name on the list was Anwar al-Awlaki, an American-born Muslim cleric residing in Yemen who was characterized as a leader of al-Qaeda in the Arabian Peninsula (AQAP).[42] The *Post* reported that al-Awlaki had been added in late 2009, on the heels of two incidents to which he was reportedly linked—but never indicted. These incidents were the November 5 armed rampage by Major Nidal Malik Hasan at Fort Hood in Texas that killed thirteen and wounded twenty-nine people and the December 25 attempt by a Nigerian, Umar Farouk Abdulmutallab, to detonate a bomb hidden in his underwear on a transatlantic flight bound for Detroit.

The revelation that the government intended to lethally target citizens spurred criticisms and more questions about the expanding but highly secretive drone warfare. Top officials in the Obama administration were dispatched to make public statements about the legality and efficacy of targeted killing in general terms while maintaining that the planning and conduct of such operations were classified.[43] State Department Legal Advisor Harold Koh, who decried drone strikes as extrajudicial killings prior to joining the Obama administration,[44] became a champion of their legality during his time in office. In a March 25, 2010, speech to the American Society of International Law, Koh stated:

> In this ongoing armed conflict, the United States has the authority under international law, and the responsibility to its citizens, to use force, including lethal force, to defend itself, including by targeting persons such as high-level al-Qaeda leaders who are planning attacks. . . . Of course, whether a particular individual will be targeted in a particular location will depend upon considerations specific to each case, including those related to the imminence of the threat, the sovereignty of the other states

involved, and the willingness and ability of those states to suppress the threat the target poses.[45]

On May 1, 2011, in a joint CIA–JSOC operation, a team of Navy Seals raided the compound in central Pakistan where Osama bin Laden was hiding and killed him. Most Americans, including many law of war experts, endorsed the legality of this operation because bin Laden was regarded as a legitimate military target.[46] Five days later, the United States launched a strike in Yemen targeting al-Awlaki. That operation failed to kill him because he was able to dodge the drone that was chasing him. On September 30, 2011, a joint CIA–JSOC drone strike killed al-Awlaki and another U.S. citizen, Samir Khan, along with two others. As he had done after the killing of bin Laden, President Obama made a public address declaring that the attack had dealt a "major blow" to al-Qaeda. On October 14 another drone attack in Yemen killed al-Awlaki's sixteen-year-old son, Abd al-Rahman, his seventeen-year-old cousin, and five others while they were dining in an open-air restaurant.

On October 8, 2011, the *New York Times* published an exposé, based on anonymous government sources, about the contents of a secret Office of Legal Counsel (OLC) memo to the Defense Department authored in 2010, reporting that "the legal analysis, in essence, concluded that Mr. Awlaki could be legally killed, if it was not feasible to capture him, because intelligence agencies said he was taking part in the war between the United States and Al Qaeda and posed a significant threat to Americans, as well as because Yemeni authorities were unable or unwilling to stop him."[47] This national self-defense reasoning hinges on the assertion that the targeted individual poses an imminent and grave threat. Critics pointed out that the forward-looking principle of imminence seems to be contradicted by the fact that al-Awlaki was listed *after* the Fort Hood attack and the underpants bombing attempt, and that the OLC's 2010 authorization to kill him appeared to be a standing order for execution.

On March 5, 2012, Attorney General Eric Holder delivered a national security speech in which he addressed critics of the targeted killing policy and the execution of al-Awlaki:

> Some have called such operations "assassinations." They are not, and the use of that loaded term is misplaced. Assassinations are unlawful killings. . . . The US government's use of lethal force in self defense against a leader of al Qaeda or an associated force who presents an

> imminent threat of violent attack would not be unlawful. . . . Some have argued that the president is required to get permission from a federal court before taking action [against a citizen]. . . . This is simply not accurate. "Due process" and "judicial process" are not one and the same, particularly when it comes to national security. The Constitution guarantees due process, not judicial process.[48]

In late May 2012, the *Daily Beast* and the *New York Times* published exposés revealing new details about this "due process." According to the *New York Times*, "Mr. Obama has placed himself at the helm of a top secret 'nominations' process to designate terrorists for kill or capture, of which the capture part has become largely theoretical."[49] Obama "signs off on every strike in Yemen and Somalia and also on the more complex and risky strikes in Pakistan." Both articles describe "personality strikes," which target specific individuals, and "signature strikes," which target "groups of men who bear certain signatures, or defining characteristics associated with terrorist activity, but whose identities aren't known."[50] Both articles also explain the administration's method for deflecting criticism of civilian casualties by counting all military-age males in a strike zone as combatants "unless there is explicit intelligence posthumously proving them innocent."[51]

In October 2012 the *Washington Post* broke the story that since 2010, the National Counterterrorism Center has been developing a secret blueprint, called a "disposition matrix," to coordinate the multiple targeting lists and drone programs. The disposition matrix "is a single, continually evolving database in which biographies, locations, known associates and affiliated organizations are all catalogued. So are strategies for taking targets down, including extradition requests, capture operations and drone patrols."[52] The names on the matrix, the criteria for being listed, and even the organizations on the list are secret.[53]

The National Security Agency (NSA) global metadata surveillance program feeds the practice of targeted killing by providing information about the cell phones of targets to JSOC or the CIA, which carry out strikes. A saying popular with the NSA's Geo Cell division is "we track 'em, you whack 'em."[54] This program was one of the revelations contained in documents leaked by NSA whistleblower Edward Snowden and was confirmed by two former JSOC drone operators. As reported by the *Intercept*, "the NSA 'geolocates' the SIM card or handset of a suspected terrorist's mobile phone, enabling the CIA and U.S. military to conduct night raids and drone strikes to kill or capture the individual in possession of the device."[55] The targeting of phones rather than people amounts to "death by metadata" and has contributed to civilian casualties.[56]

In a national security speech on May 23, 2013, President Obama announced that plans were underway to "institutionalize" the targeted killing program in order to set clearer standards and procedures and to shift control of most drone strikes from the CIA to the military. That shift, however, was blocked by Congress, which inserted a secret provision into the massive 2014 federal spending bill that restricts "the use of any funding to transfer unmanned aircraft or the authority to carry out drone strikes from the CIA to the Pentagon."[57]

The strategy of targeted killing amounts to lethal whack-a-mole in Afghanistan, Northwest Pakistan, Yemen, and Somalia.[58] Official claims that drone strikes are "surgical" and "precise" are belied by mounting evidence of civilian casualties.[59] A Pakistan-based project by the Bureau of Investigative Journalism, Naming the Dead, is working to identify people killed by CIA drones in that country; as of July 2014, of the 2,342 reportedly killed in this manner, over 700 had been identified, almost half of whom—323—are civilians, including 99 children.[60] In November 2014 the London-based legal organization Reprieve published a report analyzing drone strikes targeting 41 specific individuals, which resulted in an estimated 1,147 deaths. According to Reprieve's Jennifer Gibson, "Drone strikes have been sold to the American public on the claim that they're 'precise.' But they are only as precise as the intelligence that feeds them. There is nothing precise about intelligence that results in the deaths of 28 unknown people, including women and children, for every 'bad guy' the United States goes after."[61]

On December 18, 2014, WikiLeaks published a secret CIA analytical memorandum assessing the effectiveness of the agency's targeted killing program.[62] The document, dated July 7, 2009—the year drone strikes began intensifying—reflects a willful blindness to blowback from the whack-a-mole strategy. According to Scott Horton:

> The analysis notes that drone attacks, raids and military actions against Taliban leaders may not produce the anticipated outcome because the Islamist enemy has a seemingly limitless ability to produce new leaders. However, the study has only a weak appreciation of some of the program's more obvious and far-reaching shortcomings: for instance, the fact that drone wars facilitate recruitment by the target organizations,

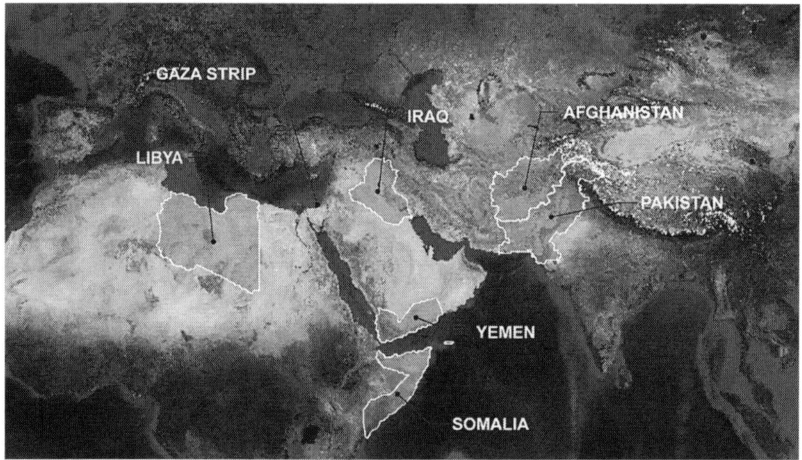

Figure 2.1. Sites of U.S. drone warfare. (Courtesy of Forensic Architecture. 2014)

> build much stronger rapport between the Islamists and disaffected peripheral tribals with whom they associate, and may turn political tides against the United States in the affected nation, as has rather dramatically been the case in both Pakistan and Yemen.[63]

Lawfare and Targeted Killing

The Israeli Context: Challenging the Legality of Extrajudicial Execution

In January 2001 the first petition challenging Israel's targeted killing policy was filed in the HCJ by Siham Thabet, the wife of PA official Thabet Thabet, who was assassinated the previous month. A second petition was filed by Knesset Member Muhammad Barakeh for an interim injunction to halt a practice until a judicial determination about its legality has been produced. The HCJ dismissed both petitions one year later with a brief statement: "The choice of means of warfare, used by the Respondents to preempt murderous terrorist attacks, is not the kind of issue the Court would see fit to intervene in."[64]

On January 24, 2002, another petition challenging the targeted killing policy was filed by the Public Committee against Torture in Israel (PCATI) and the Palestinian organization LAW.[65] The HCJ reconsidered its position of nonjusticiability and requested briefs about the applicable laws and relevant rules of armed conflict. On September 30, 2003, the Israeli organization Yesh Gvul submitted a petition pressing for a criminal investigation of officials responsible for the Shehadeh operation. The HCJ accepted Yesh Gvul's petition but suspended consideration until it ruled on the legality of targeted killing.

The HCJ issued its targeted killing ruling on December 14, 2006.[66] The decision, written by former chief justice Aharon Barak, begins with a section titled "factual background," which states: "A massive assault of terrorism was directed against the State of Israel, and against Israelis, merely because they are Israelis." The decision then proceeds to summarize the adversaries' positions. The petitioners argued that there is no right of militarized self-defense by an occupying state against an occupied civilian population, and arbitrary killing and execution without due process are violations of customary international law. Moreover, the practice of targeted killing fails the "imminent threat" and "proportionality" tests because most individuals were targeted at times when they were not taking a direct part in hostilities, and Israel has a "lesser harm" option of arresting them, as evidenced by ongoing arrests in Areas A. The last element of the petitioners' challenge was the policy's secrecy, because targeted individuals have no opportunity to prove their innocence, a problem compounded by the fact that no evidence is offered before or after targeted killings to prove claims of imminent threat.[67]

The respondents advanced arguments to persuade the HCJ of the legality of targeted killing. Israel's evolved doctrine on the legal status of the Palestinian territories was elemental to the claim that the response to terrorism emanating from an "enemy entity" is not limited to law enforcement. Despite the military's ability to pursue and arrest people alive, the respondents asserted that killing is an "exceptional step" performed only "when there is no alternative." On the issue of imminence, the respondents claimed that this does not reflect a rule of customary international law and argued that the concepts of "direct part" and "hostilities" must be given wide berth to include planning, assisting, and abetting and must not be limited to the active use of violence and arms.

In its judgment, the HCJ refers to the occupied territories as "the area" and "outside the bounds of the state," thereby evading the question of whether Israel remains the de facto sovereign and occupier. The "armed conflict" is described as between Israel and terrorist organizations, and the decision claims that there has been "a continuous situation of armed conflict . . . since the first intifada." The HCJ accepts the state's expansive interpretation of "hostilities" as ongoing and ceaseless and "taking part" as inclusive of all kinds of activities deemed threatening to Israel's security.

The conclusion the HCJ reaches in regard to "the 'targeted killing'—and in our terms, the preventative strike causing the deaths of terrorists, and at times also of innocent civilians," is that neither are "such strikes . . . always permissible or [*sic*] that they are always forbidden." Some operations might be unlawful if, for example, a disproportionate amount of force was used to eliminate a legitimate target but the policy as such is not illegal. This decision thus clearly provides another instance in which international law is interpreted by the state and endorsed by the HCJ to frame existing state practices as compatible with the law itself: "Indeed, in the State's fight against international terrorism, it must act according to the rules of international law."

Based on its judgment that the legality of each targeted killing operation should be examined retrospectively, the HCJ acted on the Yesh Gvul petition by requesting the state investigate whether the July 2002 Shehadeh operation comported with the ruling. A Special Investigatory Commission was established in January 2008 and, in February 2011, announced its conclusion that the operation was a "legitimate targeted killing," but "in hindsight," the "difficult collateral consequences" were "disproportionate."[68] However, those consequences were "unintended, undesired and unforeseen" and, therefore, no disciplinary offenses were committed and no criminal charges are warranted.

According to a 2008 investigative article in *Haaretz,* the "most noticeable thing the High Court ruling changed regarding the assassinations is the language used by the IDF in planning them."[69] Pre-planned kill operations were described as arrest operations that went awry and thus justified the use of lethal force.

The U.S. Context: Challenging the Targeting of Citizens and Secret Laws

In the United States, the targeted killing policy is politically popular.[70] The main challenges have come in the form of lawfare. To date, lawsuits have been filed over two kinds of issues: the legality of targeting citizens and FOIA litigation to puncture the secrecy shrouding drone warfare.

The first case followed the *Washington Post*'s January 2010 report that Anwar al-Awlaki had been placed on a hit list. The American Civil Liberties Union (ACLU) and the Center for Constitutional Rights (CCR) filed a lawsuit in August 2010 on behalf of al-Awlaki's father, Nasser, to challenge the authorization to extrajudicially execute a citizen, contending that this exceeds the president's authority under the Constitution and international law. The Justice Department's response brief urged the court to dismiss on procedural grounds, namely that the elder al-Awlaki lacks standing because the government was not planning to kill him. Two other arguments were also offered: either the court could dismiss the case because any assessment of the claims would require the court to "decide non-justiciable political questions" or, even if the court deemed the claims to have merit, the information necessary to litigate them is "properly protected by the military and state secrets privilege." On December 7, 2010, the court dismissed the case on lack of standing grounds, while noting that the legality of the drone program is a "political question" that falls under the purview of the executive branch and Congress. Less than a year later, al-Awlaki, his teenage son, and Khan were killed.

On July 18, 2012, the ACLU and CCR filed a civil suit on behalf of Nasser al-Awlaki and Sarah Khan (mother of Samir) against four officials atop the chain of command at the time of the strikes.[71] The citizenship status of the three victims provided the opening to seek judicial review for deprivation of life without due process and unspecified damages. Lawyers for the respondents filed a motion to dismiss, arguing that "this Court should follow the well-trodden path the Judiciary—and particularly the D.C. Circuit—have taken in the past and should leave the issues raised by this case to the political branches."

This civil litigation marked the first attempt to adjudicate the meaning of "direct participation in hostilities" and "imminent threat" in relation to the policy of targeted killing. On April 4, 2014, the court, deferring to the government's national security arguments, dismissed the case on the grounds that the victims' constitutional rights were not violated, hence leaving these questions unanswered. The petitioners decided not to appeal the ruling because they gave up on the U.S. courts as a source of justice.

The other trajectory of lawfare in the United States is the quest for information. In March 2010 the ACLU filed a FOIA request with four government agencies seeking information about the legal basis and scope of the targeted killing program; the training, supervision, oversight, or discipline of drone operators and others involved in decision-making; and data about civilians and noncivilians killed in drone strikes. The Departments of Defense, Justice, and State provided some requested records but withheld others, whereas the CIA refused to confirm or deny if it operates a drone program. The ACLU filed a suit against the CIA in July 2010 to compel disclosure. After the court accepted the CIA's refusal to respond on the basis of its FOIA exemptions, the ACLU appealed. On March 15, 2013, the DC Circuit Court provided the petitioners with a modest victory when it ruled that the CIA cannot refuse to respond to FOIA requests for information about its targeted killing program when officials continue to make public statements about it.

The legal and factual basis for targeting citizens is another track of FOIA activity. On October 19, 2011, the ACLU filed a request for records and materials related to citizens who have been killed or listed, including the 2010 OLC memo asserting the legality of targeting al-Awlaki. After the government refused to provide records, on February 1, 2012, the ACLU sued to enforce the request, and the case was joined with a *New York Times* lawsuit seeking similar information. On January 2, 2013, the US District Court dismissed the case, albeit with some judicial handwringing:

> This Court is constrained by law, and under the law, I can only conclude that the Government has not violated FOIA by refusing to turn over the documents . . . , and so cannot be compelled by this court of law to explain in detail the reasons why its actions do not violate the Constitution and laws of the United States. . . . I can find no way around the thicket of laws and precedents that effectively allow the Executive Branch of our Government to proclaim as perfectly lawful certain actions that seem on their face incompatible with our Constitution and laws, while keeping the reasons for their conclusion a secret.[72]

In April 2014 the Second Circuit overturned the District Court's decision on the grounds that government officials had made so many statements about the OLC memo that it amounted to a waiver and ordered the government to release the memo.[73] In July 2014, when the memo was finally released, the eleven-page section laying out the intelligence community's assessment that al-Awlaki's role had changed from inspirational to operational remained redacted in its entirety. According to the *New York Times* editorial board: "the memo turns out to be a slapdash pastiche of legal theories—some based on obscure interpretations of British and Israeli law—that was clearly tailored to the desired result. Perhaps the administration held out so long to avoid exposing the thin foundation on which it based such a momentous decision."[74]

The first FOIA request for an operation that did not target citizens, filed on April 17, 2012, by the ACLU and CCR, seeks records and information about a December 2009 JSOC attack in the al-Majalah region of Yemen, which launched the U.S. targeted killing campaign in that country. Two cruise missiles fired from a submarine killed forty-six people, including at least twenty-one children and fourteen women, five of whom were pregnant. Initially, the Yemeni government claimed responsibility in order to deflect public agitation against a U.S. attack. This spurious claim was immediately contradicted by tribal leaders and journalists who went to the village and discovered missile parts labeled "Made in the United States" among the remains of the victims. The ruse was undermined further when unnamed American officials gave statements to the media confirming that it was a U.S. strike. In January 2010 WikiLeaks released a classified diplomatic cable about a meeting several weeks after the attack between General David Petraeus, who was head of U.S. Central Command at the time, and Yemeni president Ali Abdullah Saleh in which it was agreed that Yemen would continue to claim responsibility for U.S. attacks in the Abayan province.[75]

This FOIA request for the al-Majalah attack sought records on the intelligence that prompted the strike, including whether officials were aware of the presence of civilians; what, if any, steps have been taken to investigate the killing of civilians and to compensate survivors and victims' families; and why a U.S. official would plot with a foreign government to deceive the publics in both countries. The Defense Intelligence Agency, which responded to the FOIA request, claimed that there were no documents responsive to the request, and none were ever produced.

While U.S. drone warfare in Yemen has killed dozens of civilians, a strike on December 12, 2013, that killed fifteen people in a convoy heading to a wedding prompted the Yemeni government to demand a cessation, or at least a respite, from further attacks. The backlash has popularized AQAP among some communities who were previously staunchly opposed to the terrorist organization.[76]

The U.S. government's position on targeted killing is a paradoxical blend of secrecy, selective leaking, public statements by top officials who have taken credit for the program's purported efficacy, and vague assertions that it is legal and has caused minimal civilian casualties.[77] In response to litigation, the government maintains that this program is classified, including the legal criteria for selecting targets and the decision-making process.[78] Those engaged in lawfare have attempted to leverage the paradox to force court-ordered transparency and accountability for what has emerged as the centerpiece of U.S. counterterrorism policy. Unlike Israel, where the HCJ gave its imprimatur to the government's prerogative to engage in targeted killing, so far U.S. courts have largely dodged the issue by accepting the government line that these are political questions and involve states secrets and, therefore, are nonjusticiable.

The Transnational Context: Seeking Justice in Foreign Venues

Does targeted killing comply with or violate IHL? The Israeli and U.S. governments' assertions that targeted killing is a legitimate form of national defense have not garnered international support. On the contrary, they have become a matter of international controversy.

One way this controversy is playing out is through efforts to pursue accountability in foreign national courts. Under the doctrine of universal jurisdiction, some violations of international law, including war crimes, are so menacing to peace and security or degrading of human dignity that all countries have an interest in prosecuting foreign perpetrators.[79] The Geneva Conventions attach a similar principle of accountability because every state party has a duty to avail its courts for prosecutions when those responsible for grave breaches are not prosecuted in their own country or the country where the alleged crime(s) occurred (*aut dedere aut judicare*).

Under U.S. law, there is no avenue for privately initiated criminal investigations for gross crimes, but there is the option to pursue civil action under the 1789 Alien Torts Statute and the 1992 Torture Victims Protection Act (the latter prohibits extrajudicial execution as well as torture). On December 8, 2005, CCR filed a class action lawsuit against Avraham Dichter, former head of Israel's General Security Service, alleging his responsibility for the Shehadeh operation and his role in escalating Israel's practice of targeted killings. The plaintiffs were relatives of people who were killed and others who were injured. The Gaza-based Palestine Center for Human Rights (PCHR) represented the victims. Dichter, at the time the lawsuit was brought, was residing in Washington, DC, as a fellow at the Brookings Institute.

The Bush administration submitted a "Statement of Interest" arguing that Dichter is immune under federal common law and customary international law for any official acts. In May 2007 the case was dismissed. The plaintiffs appealed on the grounds that there is no immunity for war crimes. However, on April 16, 2009, the Second Circuit affirmed the dismissal, deferring to the executive's position that it should decline to assert jurisdiction.

Efforts to pursue accountability for the Shehadeh operation were mounted in other countries as well. In the United Kingdom, British lawyers from the firm of Hickman and Rose and PCHR submitted evidence against Doron Almog, who headed Israel's Southern Command from 2000 to 2003. A magistrate issued an arrest warrant on the basis of the United Kingdom's Geneva Conventions Act 1957. When Almog landed at Heathrow Airport on September 10, 2005, he was advised that police were waiting to take him into custody. However, political interference by the British and Israeli governments enabled Almog to depart the country without disembarking from the plane. Once he was gone, the warrant was canceled.[80] In 2011, following several attempts to indict other Israelis in the United Kingdom, Parliament narrowed the country's international law enforcement mechanisms by granting the Director of Public Prosecutions veto power over the issuance of warrants for suspects from certain "protected countries" (i.e., important allies).

In New Zealand, efforts were mounted to indict Moshe Ya'alon, who was Israel's Chief of Staff at the time of the Shehadeh operation. Local lawyers, using evidence provided by Hickman and Rose and PCHR, submitted a criminal complaint, and on November 27, 2006, a judge issued an arrest warrant on the basis of New Zealand's Geneva Convention Act 1958 and International Crimes and International Court Act 2000. However, rather than acting on the warrant when Ya'alon arrived in the country, the police sought the advice of the solicitor general, who consulted the attorney general, who quashed the warrant the following day.

On June 24, 2008, four Spanish lawyers partnering with PCHR and Hickman and Rose filed a lawsuit on behalf of victims of the Shehadeh operation in the Spanish National Court (Audiencia Nacional), whose jurisdiction includes international crimes. Those named in the case are Almog; Dichter; Ya'alon; Dan Halutz, former commander of the Israeli Air Force; Benjamin Ben-Eliezer, former Defense Minister; his military advisor, Michael Herzog; and Giora Eiland, former head of the Israeli National Security Council. The suit urged Spain to assert jurisdiction because there had been no prosecutions in Israel and the Special Investigatory Commission, established the previous January, was not impartial because it was composed entirely of former military and intelligence officials and had no power to recommend criminal indictments.

Despite political pressure to dismiss the case, the investigating judge proceeded with the criminal inquiry, arguing that because Gaza is not part of Israel, Spanish criminal law does not accord Israel primary jurisdiction over alleged war crimes committed there. This led to more intense political pressure and an appeal by Spanish prosecutors to close the inquiry. On May 19, 2009, the Spanish parliament passed a resolution calling on the government to draft legislation that would limit the country's universal jurisdiction mechanisms to cases with a direct nexus to Spain (i.e., involving Spanish victims or accused who are present in the country). This law was rushed through without debate and went into effect the following year.[81] On June 20, 2009, the Audiencia Nacional ruled to close the criminal inquiry on the grounds that Israel had asserted jurisdiction through the Special Investigatory Commission.

The petitioners appealed to the Spanish Supreme Court, which issued its ruling on April 5, 2010, to uphold the closure on jurisdictional grounds.[82] However, the following October, Spanish authorities refused Dichter a grant of immunity prior to a planned visit because his presence would provide a nexus for the case to move forward. The petitioners appealed to the Spanish Constitutional Court to revisit the question of whether Spain could assert jurisdiction over the Shehadeh inquiry, but the court declined to accept it "for lack of constitutional relevance."

Challenges to U.S. targeted killing in foreign legal systems have focused primarily on civilian deaths. On March 12, 2012, Reprieve and solicitors from Leigh Day and Company introduced legal proceedings in the British High Court against Foreign Secretary William Hague on behalf of Noor Khan, whose father was one of dozens of civilians killed by a CIA drone strike on a *jirga* (local council) in Northwest Pakistan in March 2011. This case aimed to get judicial review for the United Kingdom's intelligence-sharing policy in cases where this information might be used for drone strikes. The petitioners alleged that the General Communications Headquarters (GCHQ), which operates under Hague's authority, provided "locational intelligence" to the CIA that was used in the strike. On December 22 the application was dismissed because, as Lord Justice Moses wrote, "The claimant cannot demonstrate that his application will avoid, during the course of the hearing and in the judgment, giving a clear impression that it is the United States' conduct in North Waziristan which is also on trial. . . . The courts will not sit in judgment on the sovereign acts of a foreign state because breaking with this principle would imperil relations between the states."[83]

On May 9, 2012, the Pakistani Foundation for Fundamental Rights filed two constitutional petitions in Pakistan's High Court challenging the government's failure to protect citizens from U.S. drone attacks.[84] Exactly one year later, the Peshawar High Court (PHC) ruled that U.S. drone warfare in Pakistan violates international law, constitutes war crimes, and breaches the country's sovereignty. The PHC ordered the government to take immediate action to stop future attacks, to take the matter of U.S. drone strikes in Pakistan to the UN Security Council, and, if that option is blocked, to request General Assembly action. Finally, the court urged the government to seek U.S. compensation for every civilian killed by a drone. In July a secret internal Pakistani report on civilian deaths was obtained by the Bureau of Investigative Journalism. That report, which examined seventy-five CIA drone strikes between 2006 and October 2009, found that at least 147 of the total 746 casualties were civilians, 94 of whom were children.[85]

In June 2013, moments after being sworn into office, Prime Minister Nawaz Sharif called for an end to U.S. drone strikes in the country's tribal areas. Pakistan's current opposition to U.S. drone warfare was reflected in Secretary of State John Kerry's announcement on August 1, during an official visit to Pakistan, that the U.S. plans to end drone strikes in the country "very, very soon."[86] Following a nearly six-month hiatus, however, in June 2014 CIA drone strikes resumed.[87]

On June 5, 2014, the PHC ordered the police to press charges against former CIA station chief Jonathan Banks for murder, conspiracy, and waging war. Banks had left the country in 2010 when he was identified by name in a petition filed by anti-drone activist Kareem Khan, whose brother and teenage son were killed in a strike in North Waziristan on December 29, 2009. Khan also filed a formal complaint with the UN Human Rights Council. Several months before the court issued the arrest order for Banks, Khan was kidnapped from his home by armed men, including some dressed in Pakistani police uniforms. The kidnapping occurred shortly before Khan was scheduled to travel to meet with European Union (EU) parliamentarians to discuss the CIA's drone program and covert intelligence sharing by European security agencies.[88] During his nine days of imprisonment and torture, he was questioned about what he intended to say about the CIA program. When he was released, he was ordered by his captors not to speak to the media or "cause any fuss." Undeterred, he made the trip and held his meetings. Khan told the *Intercept* that he planned to pursue lawsuits in European and international courts as well.[89]

What Is Legal in War?

Drone strikes and other forms of targeted killing are likely to remain a mainstay of U.S. counterterrorism policy for the foreseeable future. For this reason, as well as the proliferation of drone technology, Ben Emmerson, the Special Rapporteur on counterterrorism and human rights, decided to take action on the issue.[90] In an October 25, 2012, speech at Harvard Law School, Emmerson announced that he and Christof Heyns, the Special Rapporteur for extrajudicial, summary, or arbitrary executions, were launching an investigation "into individual drone attacks, and other forms of targeted killings conducted in counterterrorism operations, in which it has been alleged that civilian casualties have been inflicted." On the U.S. stance that it has a global prerogative to execute people, Emmerson stated: "The global war paradigm has done immense damage to a previously shared international consensus on the legal framework underlying both international human rights law and international humanitarian law. It has also given a spurious justification to a range of serious human rights and humanitarian law violations. . . . [This] war paradigm was always based on the flimsiest of reasoning, and was not supported even by close allies of the US."[91]

On January 24, 2013, Emmerson announced the establishment of the investigative unit composed of experts from several countries, and their final report was submitted to the UN Human Rights Council on February 13, 2014.[92] (Accompanying the report is an interactive website about drone strikes and technology developed in cooperation with Forensic Architecture, a research group based at Goldsmith's, University of London.) The report offered two main recommendations: "First, that the states which conducted any of the 30 strikes [examined in the study] publicly explain them and disclose the results of any fact-finding inquiries, and that states on whose territories the strikes took place 'provide as much information as possible' about them. Second, that the Human Rights Council should set-up [*sic*] a panel of experts to discuss and report on the legal issues raised by the use of drones for targeted killings."[93]

Within the United States, the concerns and controversies surrounding the legality of targeted killing and drone warfare spurred several domestic initiatives. In June 2014 the Stimson Center and the New York City Bar Committee on International Law both published reports critical of targeted killing by drones.[94] According to the Stimson Center report's executive summary:

> Many critics charge that the availability of lethal UAV [drone] technologies has tempted the United States to engage in a largely covert campaign of targeted killing, creating, in effect, a "secret war" governed by secret law. In particular, controversy has swirled around what critics view as the relative lack of transparency and accountability in US targeted killings, and the potential implications this has for domestic and

> international rule of law, especially if other states—including many not known for their human rights records—mimic US precedents. . . . We are concerned that the availability of lethal UAV technologies has enabled US policies that likely would not have been adopted in the absence of UAVs.[95]

Among the concerns raised in the Stimson Center report are the "erosion of sovereignty norms" because the United States asserts the right to engage in military operations outside of "hot battlefields" and sometimes without the approval or knowledge of states where attacks are launched; "blowback" in the form of increasing anti-U.S. sentiment that may serve as a recruitment tool for hostile organizations; and the continuing lack of governmental transparency, including even the criteria for determining who is "targetable."[96]

The New York City Bar Association report is devoted to analyzing targeted killing by drones in light of international law and legal norms. The executive summary notes that the complexity of these issues includes the lack of "controlling authority for international law," the fact that there is no obvious international court to resolve or adjudicate the issues, and the secrecy surrounding drone warfare and the legal justifications for targeted killing.

Conclusion: Legality versus Legal Legitimacy

Israeli and American officials have attempted to reinterpret international law—and for the United States, federal law as well—to project the legality of their targeted killing policies and practices. These attempts exemplify state lawfare because they deviate from and defy international consensus about what is lawful in the conduct of war and armed conflict.[97] In the case of Israel, the asserted right to engage in targeted killing in Gaza and the West Bank hinges on the internationally rejected proposition that they are no longer occupied and that extrajudicial execution is a legitimate form of national self-defense. The United States also asserts the national self-defense right to extrajudicially execute people, including citizens, but applies this claimed prerogative on a vastly larger scale, including in countries where there is no officially declared war.

I refer to these state lawfare reinterpretations as "attempts" because targeted killing has not gained international credibility. For example, in February 2014 the European Parliament passed a resolution by a vote of 534–49 condemning U.S. drone strikes and calling on EU member states to "oppose and ban the practice of extrajudicial targeted killings [and] ensure that the member states, in conformity with their legal obligations, do not perpetrate unlawful targeted killings or facilitate such killings by other states."[98]

Lawfare has been the most important means of trying to defend international consensus-based interpretations of IHL. Although courts in Israel and the United States have failed to assist in this defense, in other countries where lawsuits have been mounted, even though most of those cases have been dismissed, there has been no governmental endorsement of the legal justifications for targeted killing. Rather, those judicial outcomes are the result of political pressure, diplomatic arm-twisting, or the desire not to offend allied governments.

Lawfare has not (yet) succeeded to achieve accountability for extrajudicial executions and civilian deaths. Lawfare has, however, been a means of exposing the rationales of Israeli and U.S. policies, and this exposure has made targeted killing an issue of increasing international concern and activity. Thus, the value of lawfare should not be judged solely on the basis of judicial outcomes but rather on the political possibilities that might arise from challenging law violations by powerful states, even when the immediate results are losses in court. Moreover, such challenges constitute an important rebuttal to Daniel Reisner's claim that "if you do something for long enough, the world will accept it." Without such challenges, targeted killing would become a "legal" option for any government.

Resisting and contesting the legality of targeted killing is an ongoing, transnational enterprise. As Emmerson suggested in his various public statements since 2012, if there was a time during the first years of this century when it was acceptable or tolerable for state responses to terrorism to trump respect for human rights and the rules of IHL, that time is over. The instrumental importance of lawfare is to maintain the international illegitimacy of targeted killing and the long-term survival of norms restricting states from engaging in assassination campaigns in the name of national security.

Notes

This chapter extends the analysis in Lisa Hajjar, "International Humanitarian Law."

1. Sadat and Geng, "On Legal Subterfuge."
2. Dunlap, *Law and Military Interventions*, 5, 11. The same year, John Comaroff, writing about colonial conquests and imperial projects in Africa, ascribed a differ-

ent meaning to the term: "the resort to legal instruments, to the violence inherent in the law, to commit acts of political coercion, even erasure." Comaroff, "Colonialism, Culture, and the Law," 306.

3. Dunlap, *Law and Military Interventions*, 11.
4. Department of Defense, "The National Defense Strategy," 5.
5. Horton, "Lawfare Redux"; Weizman, "Lawfare in Gaza"; Keenan and Weizman, "Israel."
6. "About Us," Lawfare Project, January 26, 2011, http://thelawfareproject.org/about-us/.
7. The Lawfare Institute blog (http://www.lawfareblog.com), established in 2010, has become a popular cyber-venue for interventions and debates about "hard national security choices" (its subtitle).
8. Dunlap, "Lawfare Today"; see also Dunlap, "Does Lawfare Need an Apologia?"
9. Bisharat, "Legitimation in Lawyering"; Jabareen, "On Legal Advocacy"; Kretzmer, *The Occupation of Justice*; Shehadeh, *Occupier's Law.*
10. Sultany, "The Legacy of Justice Aharon Barak," 85.
11. Jabareen, "Transnational Lawyering and Legal Resistance."
12. Maoz, "War and Peace," 36.
13. Darcy and Reynolds, "'Otherwise Occupied'"; Erakat, "No, Israel Does Not Have the Right"; Hajjar, "Is Gaza Still Occupied?"
14. Y. Feldman and Blau, "Consent and Advise."
15. Reisner, quoted in Y. Feldman and Blau, "Consent and Advise."
16. Reisner, quoted in Y. Feldman and Blau, "Consent and Advise."
17. Mayer, "The Hidden Power."
18. Kellenberger, "International Humanitarian Law"; Dörmann, "The Legal Situation."
19. Greenberg and Dratel, *The Enemy Combatant Papers*; Resnick, "Detention."
20. Ron, *License to Kill.*
21. Alston, "Report of the Special Rapporteur."
22. Yashuvi, "Activity of the Undercover Units," 90.
23. Niva, "Palestinian Suicide Bombings."
24. Fulghum and Wall, "Israel Refocuses on Urban Warfare"; Fulghum and Wall, "Israel Pursues High Tech."
25. Quoted in Ben-Naftali and Michaeli, "We Must Not Make a Scarecrow," 238–39.
26. Reisner, "Israel Ministry of Foreign Affairs Press Briefing"; see also Guiora, "Terrorism on Trial."
27. Ben-Naftali and Michaeli, "We Must Not Make a Scarecrow," 239.
28. Ben-Naftali and Michaeli, "We Must Not Make a Scarecrow," 239n23.
29. These B'Tselem figures are cited in Gross, "Fighting by Other Means," 366n2; see also Benn and Harel, "Kitchen Cabinet Okays Expansion"; and Palestinian Centre for Human Rights, "Assassination Reports."
30. Israeli Ministry of Foreign Affairs, "Findings of the Inquiry."
31. Alston, "The CIA and Targeted Killings"; Cline, "An Analysis of the Legal Status."
32. Sifton, "A Brief History of Drones."

33. Hersh, “Manhunt”; Scahill, *Dirty Wars.*
34. Jahangir, “Civil and Political Rights.”
35. Mayer, “The Predator War.”
36. Borger, “Israel Trains U.S. Assassination Squads.”
37. Constitution Project, *Report of the Constitution Project's Task Force*; Senate Select Committee on Intelligence, “Committee Study.”
38. Shachtman, “Drone ‘Surge.’ ”
39. DeYoung, “Secrecy Defines Obama's Drone War”; G. Miller, “Under Obama”; Scahill, *Dirty Wars.*
40. Porter, “How McChrystal and Petraeus Built.”
41. Priest, “U.S. Military Teams.”
42. Johnsen, *The Last Refuge.*
43. Anderson, “Readings.”
44. McKelvey, “Interview with Harold Koh.”
45. Koh, “The Obama Administration and International Law.”
46. Hajjar, “Anatomy of the US Targeted Killing Policy.”
47. Savage, “Secret U.S. Memo.”
48. Holder, “Attorney General Eric Holder Speaks.”
49. Becker and Shane, “Secret ‘Kill List’ Proves a Test.”
50. Klaidman, “Drones”; see also Heller, “ ‘One Hell of a Killing Machine.’ ”
51. Becker and Shane, “Secret ‘Kill List’ Proves a Test”; see also Junod, “The Lethal Presidency of Barack Obama.”
52. G. Miller, “Plan for Hunting Terrorists.”
53. Also in October 2012, the Joint Chiefs of Staff issued new guidelines for the military. See Chairman of the Joint Chiefs of Staff, “No-Strike and the Collateral Damage.” For a critique of the purported accuracy on which these guidelines depend, see M. Thompson, “The Rules of Drone Warfare.”
54. Priest, “NSA Growth.”
55. Scahill and Greenwald, “The NSA's Secret Role.”
56. Goodman, “Death by Metadata”; Cole, “ ‘We Kill People Based on Metadata.’ ”
57. G. Miller, “Lawmakers Seek to Stymie Plan.”
58. See the Q&A discussion in Obama, “Remarks by President Obama at NATO Summit Press Conference.”
59. See International Human Rights and Conflict Resolution Clinic (Stanford Law School) and Global Justice Clinic (NYU School of Law), *Living under Drones*; Amnesty International, “Will I Be Next?”; Human Rights Watch, “ ‘Between a Drone and Al-Qaeda’ ”; and Tahir, *Wounds of Waziristan.*
60. Serle, “Naming the Dead Project.”
61. Gibson, quoted in Ackerman, “41 Men Targeted.”
62. CIA Office of Transnational Issues, “Best Practices in Counterinsurgency.”
63. Scott Horton, personal correspondence, December 18, 2014.
64. Quoted in Ben Naftali and Michaeli, “Justice-Ability,” 368.
65. The Public Committee against Torture in Israel et al. v. The Government of Israel et al., HCJ 769/02 (December 14, 2006).

66. *Public Committee against Torture in Israel*, HCJ 769/02.
67. N. Gordon, "Rationalising Extra-Judicial Executions."
68. Israel Foreign Affairs, "Salah Shehadeh."
69. Blau, "License to Kill." On July 5, 2012, Uri Blau was convicted for publishing this information, which was based on documents leaked by Anat Kamm, who was convicted in 2011. See "Israel Convicts Journalist for Disclosing Assassinations."
70. Drake, "Obama and Drone Strikes"; R. Goodman, "Social Science Data."
71. See American Civil Liberties Union, "Al-Aulaqi v. Panetta."
72. See The New York Times Company, Charlie Savage, and Scott Shane v. United States Department of Justice, 11 Civ. 9336 (CM); and The American Civil Liberties Union and the American Civil Liberties Union Foundation v. United States Department of Justice, 12 Civ. 794 (CM).
73. Jaffer, "The Drone Memo Cometh."
74. Editorial Board, "A Thin Rationale for Killing"; see also Ackerman, "US Cited Controversial Law"; Cole, "The Drone Memo"; and Junod, "The Murderous Core."
75. Scahill, *Dirty Wars*, 323.
76. Ackerman, "Airstrike in Yemen Kills 15"; Alwazir, "US War on Yemen"; Bayoumy, "Insight"; Salama, "Death from Above."
77. Groeger and Currier, "Stacking Up the Administration's Drone Claims."
78. Wessler, "The Government's Pseudo-Secrecy Snow Job."
79. Hajjar, "Universal Jurisdiction as Praxis"; Mann, "The Dual Foundation of Universal Jurisdiction."
80. Dakwar, "In the Name of Justice."
81. A similar narrowing of national law occurred in 2003 in Belgium as a result of U.S. diplomatic pressure in response to cases against American officials.
82. Rosenzweig and Shany, "Update on Universal Jurisdiction."
83. Ross, "High Court Rejects First UK Challenge."
84. This case followed a February 2012 report by the Bureau of Investigative Journalism that the CIA had resumed the practice of second strikes ("double-tapping"), which has killed and injured rescuers, and strikes on funerals. In June, at an ACLU-sponsored meeting in conjunction with the UN Human Rights Council's discussion about the U.S. war on terror, Christof Heyns, the Special Rapporteur for extrajudicial, summary, or arbitrary or executions, characterized the CIA's second strikes that imperil rescuers as a war crime.
85. C. Woods, "Leaked Pakistani Report."
86. Associated Press, "John Kerry Says Drone Strikes Could End."
87. Knefel, "Three Troubling Lessons"; Coll, "The Unblinking Stare."
88. M. Hussain, "Who Tried to Silence Drone Victim?"
89. M. Hussain, "Who Tried to Silence Drone Victim?"
90. See United Nations Security Council, "Report of the Secretary-General," 6–7.
91. United Nations Security Council, "Report of the Secretary-General," 6–7.
92. Emmerson, "Report of the Special Rapporteur."
93. Knuckey, "Key Findings."

94. Stimson Center, "Recommendations and Report"; New York City Bar Association Committee on International Law, "The Legality under International Law."
95. Stimson Center, "Recommendations and Report," 9–10.
96. Knuckey, "Analysis."
97. Kutz, "How Norms Die."
98. European Parliament, "Joint Motion for a Resolution."

3

AMERICAN KAMIKAZE

Television-Guided Assault Drones in World War II

KATHERINE CHANDLER

IN 1937 THE UNITED STATES Navy set up a review board to explore the feasibility of adding television to a radio-controlled pilotless aircraft tested earlier that year by the Naval Research Laboratories and the Naval Aviation Factory. Known by the code name "Drone," the project began in 1936. A small team of navy engineers and personnel was tasked with developing an unmanned aircraft that would mimic aerial assaults to train anti-aircraft gunners. Remote operators used radio-transmitted commands to guide the direction and speed of the drone, while an onboard gyroscope stabilized the pilotless vessel. A controller on the ground would maneuver the aircraft for takeoff and landing. Once airborne, another operator following the pilotless plane aboard a control aircraft would guide the drone in the sky.[1] The distance between the radio controller and the drone was limited to the operator's line of sight. Vladimir Zworykin, an engineer who led Radio Corporation of America's (RCA) concurrent efforts to build television, proposed that by adding a camera and monitor to the pilotless system, the aircraft could be remotely guided from a greater distance. Images transmitted from a camera on the drone to a monitor aboard the control plane would transform its use. Instead of merely serving as a decoy for training, the remotely operated aircraft—no longer limited to line of sight—could be a guided bomb. Reflecting on the proposed weapon, the navy's television review board concluded in 1937 that while they "appreciated the thorough study . . . of television and radio controlled aerial torpedoes, [they] were satisfied that, at least for the present, the situation does not justify any expenditures of funds for experimental purposes in this field of endeavor."[2]

This early proposal drew together what have become key elements of contemporary unmanned aircraft, indicating how a team of remote operators might use image transmission to carry out a targeted attack from a distance. Television would provide a way for the controller to remotely conduct an aerial bombing.[3] The navy board's initial response, as well as failures associated with the program after the television-guided weapon was developed and tested during World War II, trouble the argument of technological inevitability often used to explain the rise of unmanned aircraft. Today, innovations seen by the U.S. military as providing a strategic advantage—the ability to use real-time imagery as an interface for attack against distant targets—were recalled in the aftermath of World War II as a debacle. This tension speaks to what scholars of science and technology studies describe as interpretative flexibility.

If technological determinism posits that innovation and change are intrinsic to technologies, interpretative flexibility emphasizes how these transformations are multiple, produced through social as well as technical relations. For example, Donald MacKenzie demonstrates in a classic study that nuclear missile guidance did "not simply [mean] different things to the different 'inventors,' but also [was] seen by different groups as a solution to quite different problems."[4] In the case of both drone aircraft and television in the late 1930s and early 1940s, there were diverse understandings about what these technologies were. Interpretative flexibility applies not only to drone and television technologies, though, but also shapes the human operators who remained entangled with, even as they were ostensibly negated from, pilotless planes. In this vein, Charis Thompson analyzes how assistive reproductive technologies "make parents," showing the multiple interpretations MacKenzie describes in missile systems applies to human users as well.[5] I examine interconnections between the remote pilot, television, and aircraft in the navy project to explore how the negated operator and drone emerge in tandem.

Two contradictions emerge in the navy Drone program. The assault weapon undoes the role of human operators who nonetheless remain integral to the pilotless system. On the one hand, unmanned planes were positioned as a technological stand-in for pilots. On the other, American drones were put forth as analogous to Japanese kamikazes. With these ideals, engineers and operators created an "American kamikaze" to mimic and counter the perceived threat of Japanese suicide bombers. The drone was justified as both superior to and more humane than Japanese tactics by separating human from machine, both framed by the Japanese other. Within this sociotechnical system, the "electric eye" of television comes to stand in for how the operator sees through the drone and, at the same time, is effaced by the network of its parts. This organization also establishes the intrinsic qualities of the Drone that apparently propelled its development, even as it shows these characterizations were also mobilized by the navy's stereotypes of the Japanese enemy. By showing how disjuncture between human and drone were created through this early project, I trouble divisions between human and nonhuman that often frame discussions of unmanned aircraft. Instead, I emphasize how *human and machine are produced in tension with each other and explore the consequences of these relations*. Image transmission technologies, the positive figure of the negated operator, come to be seen as mimicking, standing in for and attacking "the enemy," conceived as a kamikaze. Connections between the wartime context and technical parts show the innovation of the television-guided weapon was not that it was "pilotless," but rather the multiple ways the Drone was figured as such by the U.S. Navy, tied to the wartime context and its failure.

This chapter examines interconnections between operators, television, and drones in four parts. Each focuses on a document tied to the navy Drone project. First, I analyze Zworykin's proposal "Flying Torpedo with an Electric Eye," a 1934 memorandum that explores how television could be used to guide a bomb. The paper was later published in the *RCA Review* in 1946. His account provides an articulation of the two contradictions outlined above. Second, I examine navy engineer Delmar Fahrney's history of the Drone project that he initially led and subsequent efforts to mass-produce a television-guided assault weapon between 1940 and 1944. He explores the project's cancellation in detail, arguing the assault drone's failure was a result of internal struggles within the navy that opposed the drone to the aviator. The third part of this chapter studies a short film made to document a field test with the assault drone in the South Pacific in July 1944. It was used to temporarily override the decision to cancel the project and deploy the television-guided bombs for forty-six missions in the Solomon Islands. The final part examines *American Kamikaze*, a memoir written by James Hall describing his experiences as a drone operator between 1942 and 1944. Through the constellation of these materials, I counter the "invention" of the drone as outlined by the engineers in their papers, as well as the determinacy associated with unmanned aircraft; rather, the documents show how human and drone are co-constituted, tying their formation to early television systems and suicide bombing.[6]

"Flying Torpedo with an Electric Eye": Integrating, Distancing, and Effacing the Operator through Television

In 1934 Vladimir Zworykin, RCA engineer and innovator of television, sent a memorandum within the company titled "Flying Torpedo with an Electric Eye."[7] He proposed a remotely controlled weapon that would use early versions of television created in Zworykin's laboratory at RCA, the kinescope camera and iconoscope receiver. The memorandum explained that the camera would transmit images from an airborne torpedo to an operator who would control the flying bomb through the image receiver. Accordingly, "Television information furnished would be of two kinds, and would be given simultaneously: (1) an actual view of the target which could be sighted by means of crosshairs; (2) accurate information on the readings of instruments in the piloted weapon."[8] The memo noted that television provided an "actual view of the target," distinct from other practices of targeting at the time. Zworykin made no mention of the distance enabled by the weapon in this part and instead explained the television system would link the torpedo and operator by relaying "accurate information" from the battlefield and weapon. Television would replace the eye of the pilot aboard the bomber with image and information transmission connecting operator and weapon.

William Uricchio draws on interpretative flexibility to explain that early television "was variously understood as domestic like radio, public like film, or person-to-person like the telephone."[9] Although the concept of television had been explored worldwide since the 1920s, the use of television in assault drones during World War II predated widespread development of commercial broadcast television in the United States. Television was highly anticipated; yet what it was or how it would operate was open to multiple socio-technical frameworks. Uricchio explains that, prior to the 1950s, "television . . . drew upon journalistic, theatrical, and (documentary) filmmaking practices" and argues contemporary transformations in television "are not so much new as reminders of the medium's long term flexibility."[10] I extend Uricchio's analysis by showing how television in the interwar period was developed for military use. Tying television to drones deployed as bombers in World War II adds another dimension to the interpretative flexibility of early television and its contemporary resonances, showing how the medium was also conceived as a weapon and in relation to an enemy other.

Zworykin's initial discussion in the memorandum explains how image transmission would give the operator the ability to target and accurately gauge the controls of the weapon. Television would extend how military personnel operated in the battlefield and as such, was linked to the body and vision of the operator. Yet, in the second part of the memorandum, Zworykin focused on how the pilotless plane could exceed human limits, explaining how the eye-like qualities of television distinguished the weapon. He observed, "Considerable work has been done also on the development of radio-controlled and automatic program-controlled airplanes having in mind their use as flying torpedoes."[11] Radio control alone, however, relied on the operator's vision to direct the missile to its target, limiting the range of the weapon to how far the operator could see. Having established the limitations of the human operator as a problem to be overcome, Zworykin continued, "The solution of the problem evidently was found by the Japanese who, according to newspaper reports, organized a Suicide Corps to control surface and aerial torpedoes."[12] This early claim is significant given that systematic attacks by Japanese kamikazes did not occur until 1944.[13] It indicates how American industry and military already conceived suicide bombing as a possible mode of attack by the Japanese, before such an attack happened. Yet, in comparing the television system he proposed to the suicide bomber, Zworykin also emphasized the limitations of the body, including the range of sight that restricted radio-controlled bombs. Contrasting his proposal with tactics attributed to the Japanese, Zworykin wrote, "We hardly can expect to introduce such methods in this country, and therefore have to rely on our technical superiority to meet the problem. One possible means of *obtaining practically the same results as the suicide pilot is to provide a radio-controlled torpedo with an electric eye*."[14]

While the first part of "Flying Torpedo with an Electric Eye" indicated that the television-guided torpedo would relay an "actual view" of the battlefield to the operator, the second set of justifications promoted the electric eye as a way to overcome human limitations by analogy to a suicide bomber. Television aboard a radio-controlled plane did not merely extend the role of the American pilot. Rather, Zworykin argued that technical superiority would engineer an aircraft that obtained the same results as a Suicide Corps. The next part of the memorandum focused on relations organized by the parts of the weapon rather than the human and machine connections established in the first part. After accounting for the weapon as a kamikaze, the radio controller was discursively effaced by the technologies of the torpedo and television image. Describing how the assault weapon would operate, Zworykin used the passive voice. Interactions that would have relied on both image and operator were attributed instead to airplane and camera. For example, he explains: "The carrier airplane receives the picture viewed by the torpedo while remaining at an altitude beyond artillery range."[15] In this passage, the torpedo apparently "sees" the picture, not the operator onboard, although the safe distance of the carrier airplane is emphasized. Throughout his discussion of the torpedo's operation, Zworykin minimized the role of human operators to insist on a "technical" system that made the weapon both "safe" and "superior," even as it would carry out the kind of attacks he attributed to suicide bombers.

"Flying Torpedo with an Electric Eye" elucidates the two contradictions that frame this analysis: First, the television camera onboard the drone ostensibly replaces the pilot, even as a remote operator was connected to the pilotless aircraft and battlefield by image transmission. Although the controller would monitor the target and the drone through the television view, the camera onboard the pilotless system was established as the "electric eye" that "saw" the target. Second, the drone was conceived as more-than-human, disconnected from the operator by emphasizing technical relations between its parts and the camera. The system as such was analogized to kamikaze missions, not piloted flight, underscoring both the possible ruthlessness of the drone as well as the ways the technology stood for the safety of U.S. pilots. Zworykin's memorandum lays out a framework for attack and American superiority through a television and radio-controlled drone, promoting the system as technically superior and foregrounding the image rather than operator as the impetus for a targeted strike.

Project Option: Could a Robot Replace an Aviator?

Zworykin's framework notwithstanding, tensions between manned and drone flight persisted in the development of the assault weapon and were played out in competing goals for the project. As early as 1935, RCA met with representatives from the U.S. Navy about the possibility of using television to control aerial weapons, leading to the review board's assessment two years later. Attitudes toward remotely controlled aircraft shifted as trials with drone targets expanded and navy personnel increasingly agreed on their usefulness (at first for training anti-aircraft defenses). In 1939 Commander in Chief of the Navy Claude Bloch wrote the following commentary supporting the possible development of radio-controlled weapons: "The extension of the role of the radio controlled airplane from the passive one of a target to the active one as an offensive weapon should be recognized as a reasonable development, and experimentation to determine the most useful field for this weapon is considered fully justified."[16] While Bloch's description accounts for the shift as a technical evolution, the development and cancellation of this project underscores how, in the navy, different groups responded to and shaped the Drone project. The previous section explored how television was envisioned as a military technology, adding to analyses of the flexibility of the medium. I now examine how the "reasonable" shift of drone aircraft from a passive target to an active weapon was debated within the navy through its characterizations as a kamikaze mode of attack or replacement for aviators.

Pilotless aircraft were first tested by the U.S. military in World War I, and early efforts included attempts to build self-propelled vessels as well as radio-controlled aircraft. By the 1920s, however, these projects were cancelled. Interest in remotely operated aircraft reemerged in the 1930s in both military branches. Delmar Fahrney, an aeronautical engineer trained at the Massachusetts Institute of Technology (MIT), was commissioned in 1936 as a navy officer and tasked with leading the Drone program introduced at the beginning of the chapter. Other experiments, including army-led projects, were also pursued at the time. From the earliest days of his involvement, Fahrney saw the possibility that the radio-controlled target might also be a weapon. By 1939 he was informally mobilizing support within the navy to build an assault drone and subsequently recruited key individuals from the earlier experiments with target planes to participate in the project.[17] My analysis of the television-guided drone program from 1939 to 1944 follows Fahrney's history of drone aircraft written in 1953, which was based on an extensive collection of military records that I also consulted. His account highlights how shifts coordinated through television to make the remotely controlled target drone a guided weapon also establish the role of operators through their erasure and by likening them to kamikazes. Yet this is also an account of failure, as the program never achieved the possibilities that Fahrney and others expected: drones at the end of World War II remained mere targets to train anti-aircraft gunners.

In 1939, the same year it demonstrated television transmission at the World's Fair in New York, RCA received a contract from the navy to produce an experimental prototype of television control for remotely guided aircraft. During World War II, RCA produced thousands of television sets. The refinements to the television tube that was used to guide the drone aircraft led to the image orthicon, which made a clearer onscreen image. The innovation became a crucial part of television and was used in commercial sets built through the 1960s.[18] During the same period, the navy officially began its assault drone program when then Chief of the Bureau of Aeronautics Ernest King approved the conversion of a TG-2 aircraft to television and radio control on March 22, 1940. Previously used as a control plane for the operation of pilotless target drones, the transformation of the TG-2 shows how what had been part of the drone target for training air defense might be changed by television to produce an "active weapon."[19] In 1941 a number of tests were made using a TG-2 plane. After being guided by radio control for takeoff by a ground-based crew, the control signal was then transferred to an operator who used a monitor onboard a control aircraft to maneuver the TG-2 via image transmission and commands sent by radio.

Exemplary of these trials were those that took place on August 7, 1941. Walter Webster, manager of the Naval Aircraft Factory who oversaw production of the experimental assault drone, wrote: "The DRONE was maintained under continuous radio control, television guided, for a period of forty minutes (during which time the control pilot was not able to see the DRONE), made runs on a target, returned the DRONE to the initial point and repeated the runs. The maximum distance that a clear picture was obtained (television) was six miles."[20] What Webster emphasized in his report was the distance between the control aircraft and the drone enabled by television, setting out how the aircraft might be a guided weapon that operated beyond the limits of line of sight. In September 1941 two additional TG-2 planes were assigned to the project and converted for operation by radio and television control. By November the Bureau of Aeronautics issued a report that explored production possibilities on a larger scale, looking to obsolete airplanes as possible platforms for the remotely guided weapons as well as cheaply produced plywood airframes.[21]

The attack on Pearl Harbor on December 7, 1941, shifted responses to the experimental program. With a large part of its fleet and aircraft destroyed, many within the navy emphasized the importance of rebuilding and mobilizing already tried methods of sea-based warfare as the United

States formally entered World War II. Positioned against Japan in the Pacific, the navy was challenged by the unexpected defeat and the fallibility of its sea fleet to aerial attack. Others argued, however, that, beyond mere rebuilding, "technological" advantages must be developed by the navy to counter Japanese forces. Captain Oscar Smith of the Naval Bureau of Ordinance was one such advocate. Unaware of the top-secret developments with radio and television control already underway, he wrote to the Chief of Naval Operations (CNO) on December 15, 1941, and proposed: "We need no suicide squad to dive torpedo laden airplanes into the sides of the enemy ships. Let a simple type of radio control be placed on a plane, and we have a suicide pilot who will not falter, but will obey all orders of the controlling plane, and will not hesitate to fly within 100 yards (of the enemy ship) before dropping his torpedo."[22] Smith would become the most prominent advocate for the television assault drone program in the U.S. Navy. In his proposal, Smith likened remote control to the tactics of a suicide pilot, linking his description of the radio-controlled aircraft to racialized American stereotypes of the Japanese kamikaze, unflinching and obedient to a higher authority. It is unclear whether Smith knew about Zworykin's 1934 memorandum, although his account mirrors the possibility of remote operation previously outlined. While no organized kamikaze corps existed at the outset of the war, the American military had already characterized Japanese forces as engaging in suicide tactics (as indicated in "Flying Torpedo with an Electric Eye"). This may have been because of Japan's no-surrender policy as well as accounts of a Japanese pilot who was shot down and crashed his plane into the deck of a ship during the Pearl Harbor attacks.[23] The characterizations also tie to how the United States used racial stereotypes to portray and organize its enmity with Japan. Smith uses the attributions associated with kamikazes to frame the radio control technology he envisioned as more-than-human, unfaltering and compliant in its approach to death. He aligned, in this way, the drone with enemy suicide tactics, even as he proposed remote control as a more advanced way to wage war.

After visiting the project led by Fahrney in February 1942, Smith suggested the development of the assault drone be expedited. By May of that year, the navy's first attempt to mass-produce a remotely controlled, television-guided weapon was approved by the Bureau of Aeronautics. Admiral King, who had been Chief of the Bureau of Aeronautics and subsequently assumed the rank of Chief of Naval Operations, outlined two requirements: "(1) to develop a service weapon from the experimental guided missile, . . . [the]

assault DRONE and (2) to ready the weapon for combat employment at the earliest practicable date."[24] The proposal called for between one thousand and five thousand television-guided weapons, arguing that smaller quantities would "lose the advantage of surprise inherent in these weapons."[25] As CNO, King fostered the project that he had overseen in its various forms since 1936. Yet the assault drone required a large investment of personnel and budget. The new Chief of the Bureau of Aeronautics, John Towers, a navy pilot and proponent of aviation within the navy since World War I, was more hesitant. He requested that the project develop only five hundred units and be named "Option." Towers noted, "This bureau is considerably concerned over premature commitments of funds, materials and personnel to this project which otherwise would be available for current needs."[26]

Nevertheless, the navy pursued its plans for a top-secret Fleet Special Air Task Force, which began training in 1942. Smith was given the new rank of Commodore and oversaw the program (although, with his background in the Bureau of Ordnance, he continued to be seen as an interloper within navy aviation). Final proposals called for over 3,000 personnel, 99 control planes, and 891 drones divided into three Special Task Air Groups (STAG). However, by early 1943, only twelve TDN assault drones were built by the Naval Aircraft Factory. Although the pilotless aircraft incorporated television and radio control, the aircraft were low-performance vehicles, built of plywood due to the lack of metal during the war. The assault drones were slow and could only be maneuvered simply. Further, the cost far exceeded the available budget. Interstate Aircraft was contracted to build the next model, also made of plywood, the TDR-1, which was tested in late 1943.[27] Interstate subcontracted a piano manufacturer, Wurlitzer Musical Instrument Company, and a bicycle factory, Schwinn Bicycle Company, to build the body of the drone, which was made of pressed wood over a tubular steel frame. The drone could be ferried to its location by an onboard pilot, so the TDR-1 had a removable cockpit canopy and the remote controls could be disabled. The television-guided air vehicle was thirty-seven feet and eleven inches in length with a wingspan of forty-eight feet and eleven inches. It was designed to carry a two-thousand-pound bomb and had a maximum speed of 140 mph and a range of 426 miles.[28]

When the TDR-1s were built in 1943, the navy still did not deploy them. Towers, now Commander of the Pacific Fleet, resisted efforts to include the television-guided drone in his battle plans. With commanders like Towers satisfied with the tactics and matériel in the South Pacific, the TDR-1s were declared "untried." Reviewing the project ten years later, Fahrney would offer the following analysis of the tensions between Smith, who came from the Bureau of Ordnance, and Towers, a pioneering aviator within the U.S. Navy who had been thwarted in his attempts to use aircraft in World War I. Smith, who was never trained as an aviator, was viewed skeptically within the Bureau of Aeronautics, which funded the television-guided assault drone project. Describing Towers's reaction, Fahrney wrote,

> Considerable light can be thrown on the attitude of Towers toward the assault DRONE program if we analyze the personalities involved in this issue concerning its combat employment. Towers was well disposed toward the idea of radio controlled and guided air traversing vehicle for assault usage. . . . He had misgivings, however, based on his experiences with [previous unsuccessful aerial torpedo experiments] and the general conviction that it took a human pilot to fly an air machine. Having been one of the first naval pilots, he was reluctant to concede that an aviator would be displaced by a robot.[29]

Tensions between the commanders tied to their positions within the navy, shaped how they saw the drones and their human operators. Smith argued for the potential of radio and television control to take up what he called the enemy's "suicide" tactics. Towers believed an aviator could not be replaced by a pilotless plane. Significantly, these competing views were internal to the U.S. Navy. Further, they reflect and transform the two strategies of distance and immersion that I explored in Zworykin's memorandum. Drone aircraft, on the one hand, changed the scope of war, distancing the pilot from the battlefield by possibly replacing him in the aircraft with television. On the other hand, as a technology, drone aircraft allowed for unprecedented immediacy and connection with attack, paralleling a suicide attack in a way that was described as more-than-human and robotic.

In 1944 the conflict between Smith and Towers came to the fore. That year Fahrney was reassigned to serve as Head of the Logistics Section of the Aircraft Command, the only position he would hold that was not related to drones or guided missile development between 1936 and his retirement in 1950. This posting came after he had been directed by Towers in 1943 to "have no further unofficial or official personal contacts with the . . . CNO"[30] regarding the assault drone program. An ally of Towers's, Captain H. B. Temple, was placed in charge of the navy's guided missile program on February 15, 1944. According to Fahrney's manuscript, Temple was instrumental in changing navy plans. He reduced the scale of the assault drone program significantly, and most of the personnel who had been trained for the television-guided assault drone program were reassigned.[31] Commodore Smith continued to exercise some influence within the CNO's office, however. His argument that the television-guided assault drone should be tested in combat held sway with King and resulted in the deployment of the one remaining STAG unit in June 1944.[32] By the end of the summer, though, King would terminate the program. The CNO transferred the remaining radio and television technologies to the army in an effort to reduce costs. The navy, he proposed, would turn instead to "the latest advances in the science of propulsion, aerodynamics, and electronics,"[33] and future developments would emphasize the strategic advantages of the sea fleet. Even before the drone had been used in war, the television-guided weapon the navy had built was finished. The project's cancellation is a potent reminder that the inevitability of a television-controlled weapon was not a foregone conclusion and thousands of RCA television sets remained unused at the end of the war.

Service Test of Assault Drone: Enacting Drone and Operator through Television

The temporary deployment of the TDR-1 further instantiated contradictions and connections between aircraft, television, operator, and kamikaze. A film made on July 31, 1944, in a final effort to secure support for the navy's television guided drones, *Service Test of Assault Drone* offers a record of how the aircraft operated, staging both an experimental test and an idealized view of the system.[34] The film recorded tests carried out by STAG-1 personnel using four drones. It demonstrated how the television-controlled systems could dive-bomb a ship by targeting a beached Japanese freighter, the *Yamazuki Maru*, the wreckage of which remained in the area from a navy campaign the previous year. In the film, orders to the STAG-1 unit are relayed through title cards, providing a text for the images. A count down the narrative. An intertitle early on indicated the strike would occur at "fourteen-hundred hours," structuring the grainy, television images in the film as an "actual view" of the attack. The goal of hitting the target on time functioned as a marker of the success for the experiment as well as a cinematic climax for the sequence of images leading to the test strike.

The staged mission against the *Yamazuki Maru* presented the assault drone as a set of technological parts. In so doing, the television-guided weapon effaced the role of the human operator, and its attack seemed to replicate a kamikaze strike. The document can be read as a filmic enactment of Zworykin's "Flying Torpedo with an Electric Eye": it attempted to produce a technological counterpart to piloted flight even as the film emphasized the immersive connection between the operator and television through the transmitted image. The footage from the test begins with a title card indicating there is no onboard pilot: "the drone in NOLO [no live operator] condition ready for take-off."[35] The TDR-1 drone is then pictured in the center of the frame on an empty runway, palm trees in the distance. None of the personnel involved in the TDR-1's takeoff are in the picture. The next intertitle states each TDR-1 holds a two-thousand-pound bomb and is radio-controlled from a TBM plane as the image pans across the runway showing the other assault drones and island landscape in the background. In the next shot, a sleek aircraft without a cockpit launches from the runway and takes off into the sky, apparently operated by a radio controller offscreen as no human appears. Only in the shot that follows, after the second TDR-1 fails during takeoff, does one glimpse the personnel involved, who rush onscreen to attend to the drone's nose over. Due to technical difficulties, the viewer sees the personnel.

Once airborne, a title card states, "During attacks, control planes remain seven miles from the target." The next image shows the exterior of the aircraft against the open sky with no sign of the television controller who is onboard. This shot is like the "carrier plane" that Zworykin described in his proposal, ostensibly networking the operations of the drone between the television and the plane, as though the weapon had no operator. After showing the control aircraft, the next title card sets out the orders: "To crash the side of the breached Jap freighter, *Yamazuki Maru*, Cape Esperance, Guadalcanal, in succession, commencing at 14:00." The following shot is a close-up of the beached freighter deck, panning across the point of aim described in the previous intertitle. More than half of the film is devoted to showing the drones, control plane, and target in succession. The images organize how the drone operates and how it will target, proposing a technological system that leaves out navy personnel integral to the assault drone's functioning (who only are seen during the nose over).

The second part of the film shifts the focus to television transmission by featuring images from the monitor in the control plane. While the drone's operator never appears onscreen, the film viewer watches the drone strikes from his perspective, seeing through the camera on the weapon, as it dive bombs toward the beached freighter. The title card at the beginning of this sequence states, "At 13:58 control pilot sights target on television screen," using time to indicate how the filmed images on the monitor are the "actual view" of the strike. A grainy television transmission follows the intertitle, showing an almost unintelligible island landscape with the freighter in the foreground. The target might not be recognizable if a prior sequence had not shown a close-up of the deck line. Onscreen, for both the pilot watching the television screen and the viewer watching the film, crosshairs indicate the point of attack. As the drone dives downward, the freighter becomes more prominent in the operator's and viewer's screen. The water in front of the *Yamazuki Maru* glares white with the midday light, and the ship comes to occupy more and more of the frame. Visual noise interrupts the transmission, and the display flickers, relaying the simultaneity of the television image. The picture returns and *Yamazuki Maru* fills more of the screen, turning black as the drone crashes into the deck. The intertitle draws the viewer's attention to the connection between the black screen and the completion of the mission, indicating, "First drone TDR #860 strikes at scheduled time." The next shot is from the point of view of another camera filming the test against the freighter. The assault drone dives into the *Yamazuki Maru*, followed by a large explosion. The two shots establish the impact of the TDR #860 as it is destroyed when it hits the deck of the ship. The image disappears with the explosion. The second view, however, shows what has happened through a landscape shot: Billowing clouds of smoke from the ship contrast with the tropical island in the background. The explosion has obliterated the aircraft and camera and damaged the target, a mirror of the kamikaze flights that would attack U.S. Navy ships in the coming months. In the sequence, the viewer is aligned with the perspective of the drone and operator through the image, while the second shot disconnects him from this point of view, showing the strike as a technical sequence.

Two of the four planes hit the ship and a final bomb strike closes the film, after which a title card appears: "The End." This film documents and enacts an account of a television-guided missile strike, directing the viewer how to watch the drone and creating a particular, contradictory role for the human operator with whom he is aligned. The viewer sees through the television lens and watches the bombing from a "neutral" camera recording the strike, while the real time transmission relayed from the drone's camera zooms in on the target in the crosshairs. The television assault drone targeting the freighter onscreen becomes ever closer before turning black, immersing the viewer in the trajectory to the target and its impact. Yet these images also point to the safety of the operator's position and his effacement, particularly the second shot of the strike, which distances the operator from the view of the television camera, showing the drone diving into the ship from the perspective of an onlooker as if he played no role in its kamikaze mission.

Talal Asad's analysis of the contemporary suicide bomber troubles the clear separation between legally sanctioned war carried out by states and the vulnerability introduced by acts of terror. He underscores the "moral advantage" these distinctions provide and the "civilizational status" accorded to state-sanctioned militaries and the legal justifications they use.[36] World War II assault drones follow a parallel logic, albeit in the context of a sanctioned war, proposing the television-guided weapon as a "superior" stand-in to the kamikaze, even as it mimics its tactics. Its moral advantage, however, is justified by the "technology" of image transmission rather than through the legal frameworks emphasized by Asad. Socio-technical relations enacted by television were key to creating interpretations that framed the drone's analogy with and distinction from suicide flights, resulting in the contradiction of image immersion in the battlefield and the simultaneous erasure of the human operator. Emiko Ohnuki-Tierney problematizes any linking of *tokkotai* pilots, the term used by the Japanese for the soldiers who flew aerial missions between 1944 and 1945 with no chance of return, to contemporary suicide bombers. Her point is well taken, given that Japanese pilots carried out their missions under the auspices of a state-sanctioned military.[37] Yet U.S. Navy comparisons between the assault drone and suicide missions had little to do with the actual attacks carried out by the Japanese tokkotai beginning in October 1944. Rather, the discursive distinction reflected socio-technical relations created by the American military and its industrial counterparts to establish the "superiority" of the drone. Resonance between suicide missions from World War II and contemporary suicide bombings might be read as marking the similarities of socio-technical frameworks developed by the United States to use technological superiority to construct and counter an enemy "other," while minimizing the role of its personnel. Justifications based on morality and "technological" advantage that the United States uses to defend unmanned warfare today can be linked to arguments for the "technological superiority" of assault drones in World War II and how television transmission was part of this portrayal. Thinking about the drone not as "technology" but, instead, as a flexible system of human and nonhuman parts, the final section examines similarities between the suicide bomber and the assault drone to trouble the advantage that is claimed this way.

American Kamikaze: Recalling the Socio-Technical Relations

The STAG-1 unit based in the Russell Islands campaigned for the chance to use the television assault drones in the Pacific even though Chief Naval Officer Admiral King had canceled the project during the summer of 1944. Instrumental in securing the monthlong combat test mission for the TDR-1 was Robert F. Jones, who, like others in this account, had been involved with the project from its initial stages. After commanding a target drone utility wing beginning in 1937, he was eventually chosen by Commodore Smith as his second in charge. Fahrney takes up the story in his manuscript, explaining how Jones used the film *Service Test of Assault Drone* to convince commanders to use the weapon: "Jones made a flight to the headquarters of Commander Aircraft in the Northern Solomons [*sic*] on Bougainville and conferred with Brig. Gen. Clauss Larkin . . . regarding the employment of the guided missiles in strikes against the enemy. After Larkin viewed the films of the [tests] he was convinced suitable targets could be found. Dispatch authority was given . . . for a thirty day trial."[38] STAG-1 carried out bombing missions between September 27, 1944, and October 26, 1944, in the Japanese-held parts of the Bougainville Islands. The team was split into two groups and the drones were flown in configurations of four. Forty-six TDR-1 drones were launched during this month. Of these, twenty-nine assault drones were detonated by their operators, while the others failed due to mechanical or weather conditions as well as succumbing to anti-aircraft fire. Jones and Larkin construed the project as an overall success in their final reports. Two TDR-1s struck a lighthouse and six hit a beached ship used by the Japanese as an anti-aircraft emplacement. Of the twenty or so remaining drone strikes, the officials note, "[these] attacks were difficult to evaluate as in most cases the targets were either barely distinguishable or could not be seen at all from the television screen."[39] Nonetheless, these missions are registered as hits in the navy reports and the final analysis of the experiment claims an over fifty percent success rate.

For the personnel, failed missions were just as memorable as the strikes. While the argument that pilotless planes saved soldiers' lives was mostly absent in the official discussions of the drone, which focused instead on its analogy with the kamikaze or how it would replace pilots, this aspect was salient for the squadron. Indeed, their safety was also understood by disjoining their role as operator from the technical parts of the drone. Billy Joe Thomas, a control pilot in STAG-1, later recalled his experiences flying a TDR-1: "Yeah, I got shot down once or twice. . . . Anti-aircraft fire just brought it down. I didn't have control but the picture was still on the screen, and all of the sudden I was looking straight down and couldn't do anything about it. . . . If it had been a piloted plane and [I'd have] been shot down, it would have been a funeral."[40] As the remote pilot of the aircraft, Thomas remembers being "shot down." Of course, he was not shot down; rather, the assault drone he controlled was hit. The statement insists upon this separation in the next part of the sentence, recalling how anti-aircraft fire brought *it* down. A different movement between operator and technology happens in the next sentence. Thomas explains that the picture was out of his control, an image "he couldn't do anything about." Yet he also saw himself through "its" perspective, looking straight down as though he saw what the camera saw. By the end of his statement, the point of view from the camera onboard the aircraft becomes his hypothetical position. In the final sentence, however, he erases his role as the operator, noting that "if" the drone had been a piloted plane, it would be a funeral. This ambiguity—seeing himself on the one hand as part of the television-guided weapon and separate from the sociotechnical relations on the other—shows the contradiction between human and technology he experienced.

James J. Hall, another remote pilot who participated in the STAG-1 missions, published *American Kamikaze* in 1984.[41] The book is a memoir based on his experiences, although it is written in the third person. *American Kamikaze* offers a corollary to the elision between self and object analyzed in Thomas's statement, as it recounts Hall's involvement in STAG-1 as if these were not his own memories. Overall, *American Kamikaze* devotes little attention to the missions and the new technologies on which they relied, emphasizing instead unit members' camaraderie and their pursuits on leave. The title of the book is left unexplained, though the assault drone squadron's month-long deployment in the South Pacific coincided with the first organized kamikaze missions flown by Japan. In what might be another layer of separation between himself and the actions he participated in, Hall reprinted the unit's official correspondence to the navy's Pacific Command in lieu of his own remembrances of the military operations between September 27 and October 26, 1944.

Although the book is laudatory of STAG-1 and the experimental technologies tested by the unit, Hall briefly expresses doubt about his role as a drone operator. According to reports submitted to the Pacific Command, the formal cause of an unsuccessful mission on October 15, 1944, was television failure. Hall explained that, as operator of the aircraft, he knew the drone actually crashed due to "a partial windup which caused the drone to veer at the last minute and crash almost exactly in the middle of the red cross on the white roof of the hospital."[42] In the navy report, the strike is recorded "at the south end of Hospital Ridge" and makes no mention of a building.[43] Describing the experience in the memoir, the images transmitted through the television persist in Hall's memory forty years later, although they are accounted for in the third person. His memory shows how he was tied to the operation of the aircraft and how he disconnected himself from the television-guided weapon. "He couldn't blot out the picture he saw on the [television] screen of the cross looming ever larger and no matter what he did with the stick or rudder controls the drone wouldn't turn, until the screen went blank at the moment of impact."[44] Hall remembers thinking, "What if it really was a hospital, what about all those guys in there, even if they were Japs, what must the survivors, if there were any . . . think of the Americans now after all the atrocities the Americans were accusing the Japs of perpetrating."[45] While only momentary, Hall's recollection pictured himself in relation to the Japanese; his actions were paralyzed and he watched the drone aircraft explode onscreen. The image on the television was one he could not "blot out," even as his position at a distance allowed him to ask "what if" it was a hospital that he struck: he was both part of and undone by "the drone."

Examination of the socio-technical relations that led to the television-guided assault drone complicates the straightforward opposition between the drone and kamikaze made by Grégoire Chamayou. Based on a brief analysis of Zworykin's memo, Chamayou contrasts "the suicide bomber who crashes once and for all in a single explosion; . . . [and] the drone which fires its missiles repeatedly, as if nothing happened."[46] This characterization leads Chamayou to theorize the "twin" tactics of the drone and the kamikaze, a ghostly machine versus a courageous combatant, both conceived as methods for solving the problem of targeting. This formulation overlooks how missions undertaken by the "American kamikaze" interconnected operators like Hall and the television screens they watched as dissociated parts. Between the suicide pilot and the drone are a set of contradictory contexts established through the development of the navy project. Further, the comparison offered by Chamayou equivocates between the first television-guided weapons and contemporary unmanned aircraft, as the weapons built by the navy in World War II were also consumed in a single explosion. While the fact that Hall is alive forty years after the drone he flew crashed into a hospital roof underscores the stark difference between the death of the kamikaze pilot and the technological assault carried out through the television-guided system, Chamayou's contrast is nonetheless misplaced. He simply reverses the role of drone and kamikaze proposed by the Drone program's advocates and engineers. My analysis of the navy's television-guided assault drone undoes the polarity between human, drone, and kamikaze, showing instead how each is co-constituted. In this way, there is no "drone" that can be separated from the human operator, even if this disassociation was integral to the development of the weapon, as was its difference from the suicide mission. The drone is a kamikaze not because of its technical interface but because the project development was organized on creating and mimicking the enemy.

Jones's final report highlighted how drones could "attack with minimal risk to the pilot and crew."[47] Yet these arguments were not enough to continue the project, further complicating Chamayou's evaluation of the risks implied by the early project and the versions of life and death they supposedly avow. Between 1944 and 1945, over 1,500 U.S. Navy personnel were killed in air combat alone.[48] During the ten months of kamikaze attacks, over 3,500 tokkotai died in Japanese missions.[49] Yet the total number of lives lost during this period by both militaries was far greater. Japan was systematically bombed by Allied powers beginning in 1944, and at least half a million civilians died. These death tolls emphasize the incompleteness of any single perspective on aerial bombing and the destruction wrought by targeting from the air.[50] The protection provided by the assault drone was limited and, in World War II, insignificant. Following the monthlong test of the TDR-1s, new assignments were issued for the remaining personnel in STAG-1 and "all 30 Avenger [TBM] control planes were placed aboard a barge, taken out to Reynard Sound, and dumped into the lagoon."[51] Regardless of its potential, the assault drone was scrapped, and its use in World War II has until recently been mostly ignored.

Writing to Jones shortly after the unit was disbanded, Commodore Smith expressed bitterness following the termination of the project. Its failure is explained in terms that emphasize the challenges internal to the navy and the inevitability of the technology: "In time of course, the weapon or its counterpart will arise again. . . . It is not an ending for the idea, that will progress in time—to fruition—the making of accurate robot planes and bombs will be solved in 10 or 15 years following the war; instead of being used in this war, as we strived to do. What a source of gratification for those who stopped us."[52] The exchange reflects the determinism that Smith thought drove the weapons project that he spearheaded, undermined in his assessment by internal resistance to unmanned aircraft within the navy hierarchy. Opposition to the project was exemplified by comments made by Vannevar Bush, director of the Office of Scientific Research and Development in World War II. In a 1947 letter evaluating the TDR-1, he dismissed the project, writing, "We do not need to go into this fiasco in detail. It is an illustration of what can happen when military requirements are written by enthusiasts of little grasp."[53] As I have argued, what the drone was or could be, along with evaluations of its performance, do not reflect the technology itself but rather, emerge out of its socio-technical context. Importantly, in both Bush's and Smith's evaluations, no mention is made of the lives that might be saved or taken by the "robot"; rather, its technical merits were debated and it was the life and death of the weapon that Smith lamented. Operator and aircraft are intimately entangled.

Conclusion

The failure of the television-guided assault drone is important not only to debate the legacy of the project but also to question the inevitability associated with unmanned aircraft and the logics that apparently underwrite concerns about replacing humans with drones. Drones are tied to socio-technical frameworks that organize the terms for their development, use, and evaluation. They link together human and machine. Between 1934 and 1944, the television-guided assault drone emerged as an analog to the kamikaze and a replacement for pilots in debates internal to the U.S. Navy. By effacing the role of the operator and dissociating human action from the drone system, advocates of the television-guided assault drone lauded its "technological" superiority. This view was promoted by the use of television, which transmitted an "actual view" to an operator, and, in so doing, depicted the technical parts described this exchange. The 1944 film *Service Test of Assault Drone* shows how this perspective was enacted and documented by the STAG-1 commanders, minimizing the role of humans in the operation of the assault drone and emphasizing the television image. Yet confusion expressed by STAG-1 pilots underscores how the television-guided drone never became a robotic analog to the kamikaze. Rather, the images onscreen captured a new synthesis between what is human and what is not, emphasizing the former to dissociate the operator from the destructive view in which he was immersed, while the assault drone, like the kamikaze, exploded in battle. The results of the Drone program were forgotten as unremembered bombings in the South Pacific and a discarded project that would reemerge in another, flexible iteration years later.

Notes

This chapter has benefited from comments provided by Caren Kaplan, Lisa Parks, Andrea Miller, anonymous reviewe, as well as discussions with the America's Initiative Working Group at Georgetown University. All errors and omissions are my own.

1. Fahrney, "The Genesis of the Cruise Missile."
2. Navy Television Review Board, 1937, Assault Drones, Collected Records of D. S. Fahrney, Records of the Bureau of Aeronautics, Record Group 72 (RG 72), National Archives II, Washington, DC (NARA II).
3. See Gregory, "From a View to a Kill"; and Mirzoeff, *The Right to Look*, for analysis of the connection between image transmission and drone warfare in the contemporary context.
4. MacKenzie, *Inventing Accuracy*, 214.
5. C. Thompson, *Making Parents*, 8.
6. See Haraway, *Simians, Cyborgs, and Women*; Latour, *Pandora's Hope*; and Jasanoff, *States of Knowledge*, for background on the coproduction of humans and nonhumans.
7. For a biography of Zworykin, see Abramson, *Zworykin, Pioneer of Television*; and Edgerton, *Columbia History of Television*.
8. Zworykin, "Flying Torpedo with an Electric Eye," 359, Assault Drones, Collected Records of D. S. Fahrney, RG 72, NARA II. See also the original document available in the RCA Collection, Hagley Library Manuscripts Collection, Wilmington, DE.
9. Uricchio, "Television's First Seventy-Five Years," 289.
10. Uricchio, "Television's First Seventy-Five Years," 289.
11. Zworykin, "Flying Torpedo with an Electric Eye," 1.
12. Zworykin, "Flying Torpedo with an Electric Eye," 1.
13. See Ohnuki-Tierney, *Kamikaze, Cherry Blossoms, and Nationalisms*; and Ohnuki-Tierney, *Kamikaze Diaries*, for analysis of the racism against the Japanese reflected in these discussions. Due to limits in the length of this chapter, the ways race is part of the tension between human and technology were not developed further.
14. Zworykin, "Flying Torpedo with an Electric Eye," 1–2, emphasis added.

15. Zworykin, "Flying Torpedo with an Electric Eye," 2.
16. Claude Bloch, Navy CNO, to Chief of the BuAer [Bureau of Aeronautics], 1939, Assault Drones, Collected Records of D. S. Fahrney, RG 72, NARA II.
17. Fahrney, "The History of Pilotless Aircraft and Guided Missiles."
18. Edgerton, *Columbia History of Television*, 70–71.
19. Ernest King, Chief of the BuAer, to Navy CNO, August 22, 1940, Assault Drones, Collected Records of D. S. Fahrney, RG 72, NARA II.
20. Walter Webster, Manager of NAF, to Chief of the BuAer, Philadelphia, PA, August 22, 1941, Assault Drones, Collected Records of D. S. Fahrney, RG 72, NARA II. In the report, *Drone* is capitalized to indicate that it is a code name.
21. Fahrney, "The History of Pilotless Aircraft," 338. He explains further, "Since the established aircraft industry could not be used, design called for a plastic plywood airplane powered by the flat air-cooled 150 h.p. engine."
22. Fahrney, "The History of Pilotless Aircraft," 339.
23. For example, Axell and Kase, in *Kamikaze*, 40–44, discuss a Japanese pilot who, after being shot down, crashed his aircraft into an American ship during Pearl Harbor. There were, however, no organized suicide missions by Japanese pilots until 1944, and the tactics recounted by Axell and Kase were not exclusive to Japan; rather, they were used more widely by pilots of various nationalities who had already been hit by anti-aircraft fire.
24. Fahrney, "The History of Pilotless Aircraft," 371.
25. Fahrney, "The History of Pilotless Aircraft," 372. In discussions of the proposals, Fahrney noted: "The reasoning behind this large expansion was generated from the study of new weapons in World War I; with particular reference to the British introduction of the tank and the German introduction of gas; and the failure of each to have sufficient supplies on hand to exploit the advantage gained."
26. Fahrney, "The History of Pilotless Aircraft," 372.
27. Fahrney, "The History of Pilotless Aircraft," 373.
28. National Naval Aviation Museum, "TDR-1 Edna III."
29. Fahrney, "The History of Pilotless Aircraft," 394.
30. Fahrney, "The History of Pilotless Aircraft," 386.
31. Fahrney, "The History of Pilotless Aircraft," 396–99.
32. Fahrney, "The History of Pilotless Aircraft," 401.
33. Fahrney, "The History of Pilotless Aircraft," 424.
34. *Service Test of Assault Drone*. The motion picture archivist explained to me that the tape was given to the assistant director of the Smithsonian, a former member of the U.S. military, anonymously, and he donated it to the National Air and Space Museum archives, rather than the Smithsonian archives. Part of the film is available at "Service Test In Field of TDR-1—WWII, Torpedo Drone," YouTube, www.youtube.com/watch?v=8RQcUtzAe98.
35. On NOLO, see Fahrney, "The History of Pilotless Aircraft," 211–14.
36. Asad, *On Suicide Bombing*, 37.
37. Ohnuki-Tierney, *Kamikaze Diaries*, xvi–xvii.
38. Jones, quoted in Fahrney, "The History of Pilotless Aircraft," 404.

39. Fahrney, "The History of Pilotless Aircraft," 419.
40. Spark, "Command Break."
41. J. Hall, *American Kamikaze.*
42. J. Hall, *American Kamikaze*, 214.
43. J. Hall, *American Kamikaze*, 203.
44. J. Hall, *American Kamikaze*, 214.
45. J. Hall, *American Kamikaze*, 214.
46. Chamayou, *A Theory of the Drone*, 84.
47. Jones, quoted in Fahrney, "The History of Pilotless Aircraft," 421.
48. Naval History and Heritage Command, "U.S. Navy Personnel."
49. See Ohnuki-Tierney, *Kamikaze, Cherry Blossoms, and Nationalisms*, 167.
50. See Tanaka and Young, *Bombing Civilians.*
51. Fahrney, "The History of Pilotless Aircraft," 427.
52. Oscar Smith, Commodore of United States Navy, to Lieutenant Robert Jones, Washington, DC, November 26, 1944, Assault Drones, Collected Records of D. S. Fahrney, RG 72, NARA II.
53. Vannevar Bush, Guided Missile Review, Washington, DC, 1947, Assault Drones, Collected Records of D. S. Fahrney, RG 72, NARA II.

4

(IM)MATERIAL TERROR

Incitement to Violence Discourse as Racializing Technology in the War on Terror

ANDREA MILLER

ON SEPTEMBER 30, 2011, the United States conducted its first drone strike explicitly targeting and killing an American citizen, Anwar al-Awlaki, in the Shabwah province in Yemen. Although both the U.S. government and mainstream media have attempted to link post-2011 terror events to al-Awlaki ex post facto and employ nearly constant references to al-Awlaki as a regional leader of al-Qaeda in the Arabian Peninsula (AQAP), no evidence has ever emerged to indicate that al-Awlaki transitioned from spiritual leader to operational member of al-Qaeda. Less than a year after the U.S. government killed al-Awlaki, twenty-nine-year-old Tarek Mehanna was convicted in a Boston court of material support for terrorism and conspiring to kill in a foreign country and sentenced to seventeen and a half years in prison. Although Mehanna was originally arrested for providing a false statement to the Federal Bureau of Investigation (FBI), the bulk of the evidence presented against him came in the form of his online activity. This evidence included actions such as maintaining an active blog, exploring Islamic thought, viewing jihadi videos, making online comments in support of jihad, and translating a text from Arabic to English titled "39 Ways to Serve and Participate in Jihad."[1] At the outset these cases appear markedly different—one involving the distant killing of a prominent U.S.-Yemeni imam by drone and the other a young pharmacy PhD in Massachusetts—but U.S. justifications for disciplinary and lethal actions against both men primarily relied on their online activity and potential to inspire future would-be terrorists to commit violent actions.

Crucially, both cases exemplify the expansion of incitement to violence discourse that has come to define preemptive logics of racialization in the U.S. war on terror. A multiscalar mode of racialization, incitement to violence discourse is simultaneously enacted through modes of delocalized and transnational war-making as well as domestic and localized policing. In this sense, it is both a disciplinary and biopolitical mode of racializing control. Within incitement discourse, the terms *operational* and *material* are expansively redefined through imaginative practices that anticipate possible future threats, where the spaces of the accused terrorist's imagination and desire become sites of imperialist preemption and capture. Taking up this anthology's theme of *life* in the age of drone warfare, this chapter considers the preemptive logic of the drone within a broader racialized and juridical landscape that attempts to map particular modes of being onto Muslim bodies targeted by the U.S. war on terror. Specifically, this chapter explores the cases of al-Awlaki and Mehanna to consider the multiple valences through which incitement to violence discourse has become characteristic of racializing techniques in the war on terror, where counterterrorism tactics seek not only to thwart terrorist plots in the making but also to silence those racialized subjects who might inspire others to conceive of and commit violent acts in an uncertain future. Here, incitement to violence discourse functions as a technology of statecraft whereby affective realms typically characterized by interiority and unknowability are rendered actionable and criminal for racialized Muslim and Arab bodies in the war on terror.

I begin by exploring the relationship between the racialization of Muslim bodies and preemptive governance in the war on terror, specifically as it relates to scholarly discourses around drone warfare. It is then necessary to shift to a discussion of adjudicative applications of the material support for terrorism ban, or 18 U.S. Code § 2339B, as a primary mode of enforcing preemptive logics of statecraft within the domestic United States. Here, case law pertinent to § 2339B functions to normalize preemptive logics that criminalize the thoughts and desires of those bodies deemed terrorist suspects by transposing these affective realms into the juridical domain of incitement discourse. Next, I explore the implications of these two forms of preemptive governance—drone warfare and the material support ban—through the specific cases of Anwar al-Awlaki and Tarek Mehanna. In both cases, the suspected terrorist's inspiration, desire, and imagination become terrains of discipline, battle, and surveillance in the war on terror—exemplified by distant practices of drone warfare and adjudicated through punitive measures against racialized bodies within the United States.

Racialization and Preemptive Governance in the War on Terror

In order to explore the consonance between the cases of al-Awlaki and Mehanna as similarly produced through the racializing logic of incitement to violence, it is first necessary to examine the broader logic of preemption as a dominant vector of racialization in contemporary U.S. imperialism. Preemption is a mode of governance whereby the U.S. military and state apparatus act in the present based on a perceived ability to apprehend virtual, future risks. Threat assessment, then, emerges through a recursive relationship between science and imagination—through both an increasing reliance on algorithmically driven technologies such as predictive analytics and data mining and imaginative global policing practices that locate racialized terrorist threats as always already poised to enact future violence.[2] Brian Massumi describes preemptive power as an "environmental power" that "alters the life environment's conditions of emergence."[3] Here, through "preemptive power's umbilical link into the prototerritory of emergence,"[4] preemption not only acts in the present but produces conditions of possibility, modulating emergent potential to delimit future actualizations. Thinking alongside Massumi, Louise Amoore has similarly described preemption as the guiding logic of what she terms "the *politics of possibility*," which "seeks to secure unknown futures, identifying correlations between people and objects and making interventions from a distance."[5] For Amoore, the politics of possibility emerges in step with scientific discourse: "from risk algorithms to biometric identifiers and backscatter scanners . . . [to] ways of thinking about the capacities of objects that may not have been possible without Heisenberg's uncertainty principle and Bell's correlations."[6] Preemption, then, is as historical as it is metaphysical, as scientific as it is imaginative. As a mode of governance, it emerges through productive entanglements between a shifting field of actors, which at any point may include any number of bodies, objects, technologies, capital, and state apparatuses as well as racializing discourses of belonging and nonbelonging.

Yet, while the preemptive logic exemplified by U.S. practices of drone warfare has been most often theorized in its ability to generate targets, less explored is how this future-oriented logic of targeting is also a racializing logic for Muslim bodies in the war on terror. A discussion of preemption necessarily calls for an analysis of preemptive governance as a racializing technology, where the spatiotemporality of preemption is one that operates on and through the racialized body imbued with perceived terrorist threat. Following Maurice Merleau-Ponty's theorization of intercorporeality and the work of Frantz Fanon, racialization is the process through which race is iteratively and intercorporeally produced, embodied, and expressed.[7] As necessarily corporeal, racialization is also always a spatial and temporal phenomenon. Within the war on terror, the spatiotemporality of Muslim masculinity has come to be characterized by distributions of terrorist threat potential ascribed to Muslim-identified bodies as well as non-Muslim bodies perceived to be Muslim or Arab.[8] Junaid Rana has described the spatializing dynamics of racialized Muslim masculinity as a "corporal essentialism," wherein the potential for terrorism is viewed as inherent to male Muslim bodies: "terror and its ideology are understood as socially and culturally learned and simultaneously internalized in the body."[9] In a similar vein, Steven Salaita has also described how terrorist threat is imagined temporally as a heritable trait of racialized Muslim and Arab masculinity. In his reading of propaganda images dispersed by the Zionist organization StandWithUs, Salaita notes that the Palestinian child is understood as a nascent terrorist or terrorist-in-becoming, what Salaita has called "the trope of the child terrorist."[10] Following Rana and Salaita, then, racialized terrorist threat is spatially and temporally imagined to be always already immanent and imminent to the Muslim and Arab body.[11]

The racializing logic that understands the Muslim body as imbued with imminent/immanent terrorist potential as a spatiotemporal phenomenon characteristic of the U.S. war on terror is disciplinarily enacted through preemptive practices of statecraft and war-making by the United States in its global crusade against so-called terror. As the currently preferred technique of transnational war for the United States, drone warfare provides a particularly salient way of understanding these modes of racialization as multiscalar. First, drone warfare is part of what Peter Sloterdijk refers to as "ecologized" warfare, whereby the boundaries between human and nonhuman organisms, things, and their ambient environments are rendered indistinct in contemporary military practices.[12] Second, drone warfare is operationalized through processes of de- and reterritorialization, a dynamic choreography of present-absences and absent-presences that calls into question geospatial boundaries of place and spatial production. The act of killing occurs simultaneously, for example, in the Creech Air Force Base in Nevada, the location of the targeted strikes, and along the various points of contact that characterize the kill chain in an operation.[13] This is what Derek Gregory has called the "double dissociation" of drone technology, whereby the act of killing delocalizes action through a series of spatiotemporal splits.[14] Gregory explains that these splits engender "radically new forms of experience, of being-in-the-world, that can no longer be contained within the physico-corporeal confines of the conventional human subject."[15]

While this assertion of newness may be characteristic of dominant understandings of the self-contained white liberal subject, critical race studies addresses the ways that racialized ontologies are historically structured through corporealizing and *de*corporealizing modes of experience. It is helpful to invoke Fanon's account of racialization here, whereby the body of the racialized other "burst[s] apart" through his encounter with whiteness, his "corporeal schema crumbl[ing]" and shattered.[16] However, while acknowledging the threads of decorporealization woven into genealogies of racialization, this chapter follows the recent work of Alexander Weheliye and exercises caution against levying these histories as foils to merely bolster arguments for or against a posthumanist turn in critical military and science and technology studies.[17] Instead, this chapter insists on locating technological shifts in war-making and their relationship to the corporeal as entangled and emergent within empire's legacies of racism, colonialism, and genocide.

Finally, drone warfare is one manifestation of the anticipatory temporality that characterizes contemporary war-making and policing practices, where pattern-of-life analyses and data fusion result in preemptive actions against possible future threats.[18] Although exemplified by drone warfare and characteristic of U.S. foreign policy in the war on terror, this preemptive logic is a historically contingent practice situated within a long arc of racialized preemptive governance practices in both everyday and more extraordinary instantiations. U.S. history is, in fact, replete with examples of racialization enacted through measures of preemptive governance. New York's stop-and-frisk program and the use of PredPol predictive policing software; long histories of eugenicist discourses and the forced sterilizations of Native American, Black, and Puerto Rican women; and the containment of Japanese Americans during World War II are but a few examples that allow us to understand that preemption as othering is not a new or distant phenomenon.

But while preemption is by no means new, it has acquired a particularly pervasive character after September 11, 2001.[19] Preemption is a logic particularly well suited to enact disciplinary and lethal forms of force and control against racialized Muslim bodies, who are imagined as always already laden with the seeds of future terrorist actions and violence. In the threat-saturated field of emergence for contemporary U.S. foreign policy, preemption manifests in a host of racializing techniques aimed to assess, minimize, and contain future risk. Techniques such as drone warfare, the compulsory collection of biometric data undertaken by the U.S. military in Iraq and Afghanistan, sweeping programs of mass surveillance, and the material support for terrorism prosecutions that I discuss below are but a few of many examples that range from surveillance and intimidation to the enactment of lethal forms of disciplinary force within preemptive governance. As a dominant vector of racialization for perceived Muslim bodies, then, preemption must be understood as a spatiotemporal logic of *differentially* distributed risk, reaching into an imagined future to create an architecture through which it can act upon racialized bodies in a contingent present.

From Distant Drone Warfare to the War at Home: Prosecuting for Material Support

While drone warfare proves a paradigmatic case of racialized preemptive governance, it should not be construed as the only or the exceptional example. Drone warfare abides by the rule rather than the exception of preemption, and, as such, it is important not to abstract drone war from other techniques of preemptive governance. It is, rather, part of a multiscalar constellation of preemptive governance tactics operationalized within the domestic United States as well as in U.S. military interventions abroad. While racialized Muslim bodies are subject to surveillance and lethal force through drone war abroad, one way that bodies within the United States are subject to preemptive disciplinary measures is through applications of the ban on material support for terrorism, or 18 U.S. Code § 2339A & B. As Wadie Said has noted in his recent exploration of material support cases in the United States, 94.2 percent of convictions related to terrorism have been a product of these preemptive prosecutions, where "the preventive paradigm" within legal prosecutions exhibits an additive effect in perceptions of Muslim-based threat.[20]

Under the material support ban passed by Congress in 1996 to curtail the use of charity organizations as a way of channeling financial support to designated Foreign Terrorist Organizations (FTOs), individuals can be criminally prosecuted for providing material support in a variety of forms that greatly exceed support in the form of currency. Drawing from the definition presented in 18 U.S. Code § 2339A, "material support or resources" can mean "any property, tangible or intangible, or service, including currency or monetary instruments or financial securities, financial services, lodging, training, expert advice or assistance, safehouses, false documentation or identification, communications equipment, facilities, weapons, lethal substances, explosives, personnel (1 or more individuals who may be or include oneself), and transportation, except medicine or religious materials."[21] What constitutes material forms of support, however, has been broadly construed prosecutorially, where "§ 2339B has come to encompass far more kinds of activity, including things like speech and the tricky concept of material support as providing legitimacy to an FTO."[22] Criticized as unconstitutional and in violation of First Amendment protections, § 2339B was challenged in the 2010 Supreme Court ruling *Holder v. Humanitarian Law Project*, which ultimately buttressed § 2339B by stating that the material support ban does not violate First Amendment protections and allows for "independent advocacy" of FTOs.[23] According to *Holder*, the only speech criminalized under § 2339B is "a narrow category of speech to, under the direction of, or in coordination with foreign groups that the speaker knows to be terrorist organizations."[24] As will be seen in the case of *United States v. Mehanna*, the line between "independent advocacy" and speech enacted "under the direction of" an FTO is a blurry and mutable border, one that shifts and stretches to encompass myriad speech acts by the racialized Muslim body.[25]

Most often, the material support ban has been critiqued by scholars for its unconstitutionality and First Amendment violations, where seemingly innocuous speech and online activities have been subject to intense scrutiny and prosecution. Less explored are claims that the defendant's actions and words qualify as *incitements to violence*, those speech acts that call for or incite "imminent lawless action" that will be perpetrated by bodies other than the accused.[26] The incitement to violence discourse deployed in material support cases has far-reaching implications for the racialization of Muslim bodies within preemptive governance. Here, incitement functions as an insidious extension of preemption that further criminalizes the realms of racialized desire, imagination, and inspiration for the Muslim body. Harkening to the classic example of the person who yells "Fire!" in a movie theater, the question of what constitutes incitement to violence has been largely unchallenged since the 1969 Supreme Court ruling in *Brandenburg v. Ohio* that a Ku Klux Klan leader's speech calling for white Americans to take to the streets to obtain "revengeance" on Black Americans was fully within the appellant's First Amendment rights.[27] Following *Brandenburg*, only speech "directed to inciting or producing *imminent lawless action* and [that] is likely to incite or produce such action"[28] can be considered speech not protected by the First Amendment. And, as David Cole has noted, the Brandenburg test has proven "a very hard standard to meet" when attempting to demonstrate that speech qualifies as incitement to violence.[29]

However, the legal implications of § 2339B prosecutions and *Holder v. Humanitarian Law Project* present a formidable challenge to the Brandenburg standard, where, for subjects accused of material support for terrorism, the courts have generated expansive definitions of speech as incitement and extended the temporalities of what could be construed as imminent lawless action. For the racialized Muslim body accused of material support for terrorism, speech is constructed as always already laden with the potential of inciting violence in a conditional and imagined future. In these cases, it would appear that the line separating "independent advocacy" and speech enacted "under the direction of" an FTO, to return to the language of *Holder*, disappears altogether.[30] And not only is the speech itself criminalized but it is rendered additionally so through the spurious logic that it necessarily contains the potential to inspire others to support violent jihad—in either thought *or* action. Minimum sentences under § 2339B range from 210 to 262 months,[31] are often lengthened through additional charges of conspiracy to commit acts of violence abroad, and are served under conditions of intense isolation in supermax facilities and highly restrictive Communication Management Units (CMUs).[32] Material support prosecutions perform the juridical work of preemption that we see in drone warfare within the domestic United States, enacting disciplinary measures against the racialized Muslim convicted of terrorism-related charges. And as I explain below, material support cases further demonstrate the increasing salience of incitement to violence discourse in the racialization of Muslim bodies within preemptive governance. Here, threat is delocalized from an embodied present and projected into an intercorporeal, imagined future where it can be inhabited by racialized bodies who are yet to emerge.

Incitement to Violence and the Imagination as Battlefield

Within the security calculus of the war on terror, drone warfare and criminal prosecution for violations of the ban on material support function as complementary practices of preemptive governance as techniques of racialization. Operating under the guise of preventing violent terrorist acts before they have the chance to cohere, these measures are further troubling in their abilities to render criminal the terrains of desire, imagination, and inspiration for the racialized Muslim body. To explore this point further, it is helpful to turn to the two cases mentioned earlier, the 2011 targeted killing of Anwar al-Awlaki in Yemen and the 2012 conviction of Tarek Mehanna in Boston, Massachusetts. In both cases, what is constructed as warranting disciplinary and lethal intervention is the potential to inspire others to potentially commit violent acts in an uncertain future. Although fully exploring these issues is beyond the scope of this chapter, I am placing the cases of al-Awlaki and Mehanna in conversation to broach the following questions: How do affective and immaterial registers typically characterized by interiority and unknowability undergo transduction into materiality when introduced into U.S. government discourses surrounding terrorism? How do U.S. government assumptions about immateriality and materiality inflect, augment, or alter understandings of the risk-based preemptive discourses of drone warfare and counterterrorism? And finally, how does rendering the immaterial and indeterminate knowable and territorial through incitement to violence discourse relate to contemporary and historical practices of racialization in U.S. imperialism, policing, and everyday discourse?

After two years of attempting to locate and assassinate al-Awlaki, the United States finally succeeded on September 30, 2011, killing al-Awlaki and another American citizen, Samir Khan, in an attack by two Predator drones equipped with Hellfire missiles.[33] Two weeks later, on October 14, 2011, another U.S. drone strike killed al-Awlaki's sixteen-year-old son, Abd al-Rahman, also a U.S. citizen, and several of his cousins as they sat down to eat together. A U.S.-born imam, al-Awlaki had been a prominent figure in mosques in both California and Virginia from 1996 to 2002. Vocal in his advocacy for Islamic practices considered moderate by mainstream U.S. standards, al-Awlaki appeared numerous times in the U.S. media as a spokesperson for the American Muslim community, decrying the September 11, 2001, attacks on the U.S. World Trade Center in New York while still speaking out critically against the U.S. invasion of Afghanistan. In 2002 al-Awlaki was even invited to speak at a luncheon at the Pentagon and to lead a prayer at the U.S. Capitol building. Al-Awlaki only grew increasingly critical and ultimately began to advocate for jihad against the United States after the vast expansion of U.S. military involvement in Muslim-majority countries, several years of harassment by the FBI beginning in 1999, and imprisonment by the Yemeni government at the behest of the United States for eighteen months from 2006 until December 2007 for allegedly intervening in a tribal dispute. Of those eighteen months in prison, al-Awlaki was held in solitary confinement for nine months and interrogated by the FBI while in Yemeni custody.[34]

Although the U.S. government and mainstream media have attempted to link both pre- and post-2011 terror events to Anwar al-Awlaki, claiming that he was a senior official in al-Qaeda, no evidence has ever emerged to indicate that he had transitioned from a spiritual leader to an active member of al-Qaeda.[35] Rather, it appeared that the only evidence of al-Awlaki's status as operational within al-Qaeda has been tautologically produced through the recursive relationship between media outlets and the U.S. government's claims of al-Awlaki's terrorist status. Facticity in this case is generated and strengthened indexically: official U.S. statements cite journalistic accounts referring to al-Awlaki as a terrorist leader and vice versa.[36] Al-Awlaki's designation as an operational terrorist, then, provides a tangible and embodied example of what Louise Amoore has referred to as the "ontology of association" within contemporary risk-based modes of governing, where "the contemporary risk calculus does not seek a causal relationship between items of data, but works instead on and through the *relation* itself."[37] Within this calculus, the fact that three of the 9/11 hijackers had intermittently attended al-Awlaki's mosque in Falls Church, Virginia, and that Nidal Hasan of the Fort Hood shooting had reached out to al-Awlaki for spiritual advice have provided much of the basis used by U.S. officials to point to al-Awlaki as a terrorist and leader of al-Qaeda. The mere existence of a correlation here immediately trumps the bulk of evidence that would suggest that al-Awlaki's interactions with these men were cursory and, in the case of Hasan, often not reciprocal.

Additionally, it appeared that the United States' main point of contention with al-Awlaki was his ability to reach North American Muslims through his very active online presence, first through his blog *Imam Anwar's Blog* and by contributing to *Inspire*, an English-language online magazine associated with al-Qaeda.[38] Al-Awlaki's sermons have remained popular long after his assassination and are frequently purported to have been inspiration for "homegrown" and "lone-wolf" terror plots. Most recently, al-Awlaki has been linked to providing inspiration, counsel, and material support to the Kouachi brothers, who committed the attack on the French magazine *Charlie Hebdo* in January 2015, and inspiring one of the shooters who attempted to attack a Dallas, Texas, free-speech event showcasing cartoons of the prophet Mohammed.[39] Following this line of circumstantial reasoning, then, al-Awlaki's designation as operational at the time of his assassination would appear to indicate that, within the risk calculus of the war on terror, providing inspiration to aspiring Islamists is tantamount to providing material and operational support. Here we see an expansion of the politics of possibility described by Amoore, where present actions are undertaken to forestall future violence predicted through analytic models of risk assessment. But targeting al-Awlaki is not simply a mode of preemption that seeks to act in anticipation of the possible terrorist acts al-Awlaki will himself commit. Rather, it is a mode of preemption that anticipates the possible terrorist act that al-Awlaki might inspire others to commit in an indeterminate future.

Before moving forward, it is important to pause and exercise a word of caution. When examining the profound effect that al-Awlaki's residual online presence has had in cultivating support for organizations such as al-Qaeda and the Islamic State, it is nonetheless important to disentangle that inspiration in the present and recent past from the assignment of "operational" to al-Awlaki at the time of his death and during the two-year manhunt to which he was subject. Here, evidence to justify U.S. violence against al-Awlaki is presented retrospectively in the form of acts that have only cohered long after the fact of his death, acts that may even have been further inspired *by* the fact of his death.[40] As Brian Massumi usefully argues in his exploration of George W. Bush's 2003 invasion of Iraq under the pretense that Saddam Hussein had weapons of mass destruction and ties to al-Qaeda, Bush's preemptive military intervention in Iraq was successful in producing the very thing it espoused to be preventing: "Preemptive action is retroactively legitimated by future actual facts. Preemptive action can produce the object toward which its power is applied, and it can do so without contradicting its own logic, without necessarily undermining its legitimation."[41] That future devotees of al-Awlaki would go on to commit violent acts in his name or in the name of any number of FTOs arguably functions as the proof in the pudding for the U.S. government. As Massumi notes, the inscrutable complexity of preemptive logic is that the future never delegitimizes the felt presence of past threat—its architecture can only ever be fortified as actualized threat emerges through the scaffolding preemption constructs for itself.

What does it mean to extend preemptive action to account for possible future inspirations? How does this instance of preemptive violence speak to other modes of racialization through preemptive governance in the war on terror? Or, more specifically, how does the use of incitement to violence discourse in drone war abroad relate to its deployment in counterterrorism efforts within the domestic United States? To explore these questions further, I shift from looking at al-Awlaki's assassination in Yemen in 2011 to Boston, Massachusetts, in 2012, where twenty-nine-year-old Tarek Mehanna was sentenced to seventeen and a half years in prison for conspiring to provide material support for terrorism and killing in a foreign country.[42] Born in Pittsburgh, Tarek Mehanna spent most of his life in Boston. In 2004 Mehanna traveled with friends to Yemen, a trip the U.S. government alleged was undertaken as a failed attempt to seek out a terrorist training facility and that Mehanna has claimed was to attend a religious school.[43] In either case, Mehanna and his friends reached no such terrorist training facility and left Yemen shortly after arriving. Additionally, Mehanna claims to have been approached by a counterterrorism official who, in a failed sting operation, attempted to coax Mehanna into participating in terrorist activity, an opportunity that Mehanna refused and an event the U.S. government has categorically neither confirmed nor denied.[44] Ultimately, Mehanna was arrested in 2008 for a false statement made to the FBI when questioned about the whereabouts of an acquaintance, Daniel Maldonado. Though Mehanna was aware that Maldonado was in Somalia, he claimed to be unsure of his location and told authorities that Maldonado was in Egypt the last time they had spoken.[45]

Although Mehanna was originally arrested under the pretense of false statement, the bulk of what was presented as evidence of Mehanna's conspiracy to both commit and provide material support for terrorist acts came in the form of Mehanna's online activity. He maintained an active blog exploring Islamic thought, viewed Islamist videos, made online comments in support of jihad, and had translated from Arabic to English a text titled "39 Ways to Serve and Participate in Jihad."[46] As political theorist Andrew March, who also provided expert testimony in Mehanna's trial, has noted, "Mr. Mehanna's crimes were speech crimes, even thought crimes."[47] Take, for example, that during his opening argument to the jury, a prosecutor in the case stated that "it's not illegal to watch something on television. It is illegal, however, to watch something in order to cultivate your *desire*, your *ideology*."[48] March goes on to note that "viewing perfectly legal material can become a crime with nothing other than a change of heart. When it comes to prosecuting speech as support for terrorism, it's the thought that counts."[49] This statement gestures to the core of the contradiction in Mehanna's trial: what the defense argued was speech protected under Mehanna's First Amendment rights, the U.S. government defined as speech acts always already conspiratorial and laden with seeds of the future violence they would inspire. As U.S. Attorney Ayoke Chakravarty stated in his remarks during Mehanna's 2011 motion hearing, "The Constitution is not a suicide pact, and you are not allowed to commit a crime through your verbal conduct if that constitutes a crime."[50] The implied reference to suicide bombing is not lost here. For Chakravarty, it would seem that claiming there are constitutional protections for political speech supporting an FTO or its beliefs is tantamount to strapping a suicide vest onto American First Amendment jurisprudence itself. Following the Supreme Court ruling in *Holder v. Humanitarian Law Project* mentioned earlier, speech is only exempt from First Amendment protection if that speech is deemed to exceed independent advocacy of a designated terrorist organization and, instead, occurs "under the direction of a terrorist organization."[51] In claiming that Mehanna's activities "are something very definitively other than advocacy," the prosecution makes clear that any speech vocalizing support or sympathies for Muslim organizations deemed terrorist is, by this logic, always already criminal, always already violent, and always already demonstrative of material connections and support through intent.

Although this particular criminalization of speech acts is, of course, very significant, it has for the most part received the most attention regarding Mehanna's trial as a violation of his First Amendment rights. Additionally, there has been much attention paid to the large swaths of evidence that point to Mehanna's actions and writings as contradictory to the government's claims. I shift my focus, then, to the emphasis placed on Mehanna's desires and a conditional future imagined to be inspired or incited by his online activity. Consider the following passage also from U.S. Attorney Chakravarty describing the evidence against Mehanna: "*Attempting* to go to Pakistan to join a terrorist training camp, *hoping* to go to Afghanistan to join terrorists . . . *hoping* to go on to Iraq to help fight American soldiers . . . These are types of activities which are something very definitively other than advocacy . . . [that constitute] expert advice and assistance or training that they were trying to provide to *would-be al-Qaida recruits, would-be terrorists* who *could* go and do what they were unsuccessful in doing (emphasis is mine)."[52] What does it mean to infer material reality from hope, failure, and inspiration in a conditional future to doubly conditional "would-be" recruits and terrorists who *might* succeed?[53] Here, we see echoes of the preemptive logic of drone warfare that provided justification for al-Awlaki's assassination: preemptive governance within the risk calculus of the war on terror not only seeks to prevent possible future actions by the bodies who may commit acts of violence but also exerts force against the bodies of those who *might* inspire others who *might* then commit criminalized acts in an indeterminate future. Here, inspiration and imagination are transposed into the realm of incitement and rendered simultaneously criminal, dangerous, and actionable realms.

This trend in preemptive actions expands what Amoore has called the "bureaucratization of imagination" in contemporary security practices.[54] Reflecting on *The 9/11 Commission Report* statement that the terrorist activities of September 11, 2001, necessitates finding "a way of routinizing, even bureaucratizing, the exercise of imagination."[55] Amoore describes the trend that has since ensued:

> Though the deployment of imagination through "scenarios" and "difficult what ifs" has been an important element of post-9/11 security practice, the key aspect is to be found not so much in imagination as in the routinization of imaginative faculties (9/11 Commission, 2004: 354). The manifest desire to "assemble enough of the puzzle pieces" and to "make some sense of them" has dominated the subsequent 10 years of assessments of the implementation of the Commission's recommendations (Department of Homeland Security, 2011). The imagination of links and associations across items of data, operationalized via data mining and analytics, has become the mainstay of the bureaucratization of imagination.[56]

Here, faced with what Donald Rumsfeld famously referred to as "unknown unknowns," the state must not only work through the construction of possible and imaginary futures but also seek to harness and standardize those imaginative capacities within the biopolitical regime.[57] In this way, imagination becomes a site of territorialization and capture. Based on what we have gleaned from the cases of al-Awlaki and Mehanna, the state wishes not only to bureaucratize its own imaginative capacities but also to create an architecture through which to bureaucratize those of its imagined threats.

Building from this expansion of Amoore's "bureaucratization of imagination," I depart slightly from other recent explorations of the relationship between imagination, threat, and the generation of possible material futures, such as Joseph Masco's latest work exploring what he refers to as "national security affect,"[58] where the emphasis has largely been placed on the imagination of the U.S. state and the affective atmosphere saturating an embattled and implicitly white American citizenry. Instead, I turn to the implications for a racialized, Muslim terrorist imagination that is constructed as always excessive, deterritorializing, and dangerous—where the bureaucratization of that imagination is frenetically undertaken through both the lethal practices of drone warfare and the establishment of legal and disciplinary precedent within the United States. In this configuration, the language of incitement becomes mobilized as the juridical language of capture and territorialization that seeks to simultaneously bureaucratize and criminalize Muslim desire, imagination, and inspiration.

It is also important to stress that this construction of a racialized imagination that must be harnessed and managed is deeply connected to constructions of the terrorist suspect's body as a site of excess threat and deterritorializing potential. Exploring visual representations of Khalid Sheikh Mohammed circulated by the U.S. State Department and CIA and cases of mistaken identities in counterterrorist operations, Junaid Rana describes the "model terrorist" as a body that is "mutable and can shift in comportment" and is "trained not only to act in a chameleon-like way in sleeper-cell environments, but also to maintain multiple aliases and forged documents in order to confuse law enforcement."[59] What Rana points toward, then, is that not only is terrorist potential seen as inherent to the racialized Muslim body but so too is the ability to dissemble in such a way that the body itself is rendered ultimately immaterial. Terrorism is not simply expressed through what Rana refers to as "corporal essentialism," whereby "terror and its ideology are understood as socially and culturally learned and simultaneously internalized in the body."[60] Terrorism, rather, is constructed as the ability to transcend or escape the body's material corporeality to deterritorialize

Here, terrorism is simultaneously characterized by the deterritorializing distribution of threat potential as exceeding the individual body as well as through an "ontology of association,"[61] where the corporeal form of the racialized Muslim body is foremost a diffuse and fungible one that produces two phenomena within counterterrorist logic: First, threat potential can be transmitted across space-time, both through its perceived heritability (as in the case of Salaita's "trope of the child terrorist"[62] or as evinced through the U.S. assassination of al-Awlaki's teenage son, Abd al-Rahman) and through its ability to deterritorialize and reemerge in unexpected and unforeseeable sites and bodies. Second, the flattening logic of terrorist threat, then, would seem to indicate that identity is rendered immaterial in the disciplinary state apparatus of the war on terror. It matters not who is punished so long as someone is punished, particularly as threat and guilt are seen as distributed across the landscape of racialized Muslim bodies. Terrorism, then, must be understood as an intercorporeal phenomenon, which means that threat, too, as understood in contemporary U.S. discourses is similarly intercorporeal. Threat moves and mutates irrespective of bodily and physical boundaries, a racialized imaginary that is brought into the folds of juridical and disciplinary action through increased reliance on incitement to violence discourse in prosecutions and disciplinary force enacted upon perceived terrorist bodies.

This has significant implications for the psychic and imaginary realms of the racialized terrorist body, where through incitement discourse the psychic is unbound from discourses of the internal and the individual. The psychic realm of the racialized terrorist constructs terrorism, then, as a threshold discourse, defined by that which persistently exceeds the limits of perception. It is the unimaginable that haunts the imagination of the imperialist state. Here, within U.S. terrorist discourses, there is an ontological distinction between the terrorist's and the imperialist imagination, where the imperialist imagination conforms to what Gilles Deleuze described as that "which must grasp the process of actualization" through the echoes that inform what can be apprehended of the recursive relationship between the "psychic, organic, and chemical" registers.[63] Imagination is "a larval consciousness which moves endlessly *from science to dream and back again*."[64] I linger on this phrase, "from science to dream and back again." Although an active process, imagination is the vehicle by which pure potential is transformed into actualization and possibility. It is always a process of attempting to order, attempting to bureaucratize. Imagination seeks to ground. However, to quote from Deleuze again on grounding, "the world of the ground is undermined by what it tries to exclude. . . . It leans towards what it grounds, towards the forms of representation; on the other hand, it turns and plunges into a groundlessness beyond the ground which resists all forms and cannot be represented."[65] The act of imagination is simultaneously, then, a process of de- and reterritorialization and of producing representation and sensibility haunted by a fugitive and affirmative excess.

Within the U.S. imperialist imaginary, the terrorist's imagination is ontologically situated as this excess. Perpetually out of reach, it is the pure potential that can only ever escape the reaches of the imperial imagination. Therefore, the terrorist's imagination becomes both the logical and ideal extension of the "everywhere war" that Derek Gregory has described as characterized by "the replacement of the concept of the battlefield in U.S. military doctrine by the multi-scalar, multi-dimensional 'battlespace' . . . and the assault on the global borderlands where the United States and its allies now conduct their military operations."[66] As the exemplary psychic and perceptual borderland, the terrorist's imagination is the battlespace that perpetually shifts and recedes into the horizon, necessitating constant expansion and pursuit by the imperialist state. And as that which is always only unknowable, it is also, then, always dangerous. It is the kind of danger that undergirds the preemptive logic of the war on terror, empowering the nation-state to act both disciplinarily and lethally against bodies who may not even have any tangible links to designated terrorist organizations, whose crimes become the "thought crimes" described by March.[67] For a racialized body within this configuration, to imagine is to imagine criminally, always already an incitement to violence for others. There is no longer an ontological distinction between desiring, thinking, and doing; to imagine and to desire is tantamount to doing. Nor is there an ontological distinction between self and other, where inspiration within this framework becomes the vector of delocalized terrorist desire. Through this cynical calculus informing both drone logic and incitement to violence discourse, it is presented as entirely reasonable and commonsense that the state would respond with lethal and disciplinary force against Muslim bodies always already imbued with the deterritorializing impulses of threat potential. Preemptive governance generates for itself a depthless well from which to draw justification for its racialized violences, transposing realms of unknowability and excess into the actionable realms of incitement to violence discourse.

Conclusion

Preemptive governance is a hallmark of racializing practices in the U.S. war on terror, where desire, intent, and imagination are transformed from private and internalized spaces into actionable realms of surveillance, policing, and military intervention. And while not a new way of justifying racialized violence, it has taken on a particular pervasiveness in post-9/11 counterterrorist and racist discourses. Threat potential is understood as both deterritorializing and virally transmitted through embodied and digital spaces, a logic that is bolstered by the use of algorithmic and datalogical models of analysis that provide a veneer of surety and precision to a disturbingly imprecise and violent set of racializing practices. Additionally, this troubling phenomenon not only functions as the modus operandi for drone warfare and prosecutions under the material support ban. It has, rather, become a far more widespread characteristic of racialization that appears as an everyday facet of the U.S. cultural landscape of the war on terror—from the extensive use of PredPol predictive policing software, which employs statistical models of risk assessment used in military targeting to predict the areas where crimes are most likely to take place, to the September 2015 arrest of fourteen-year-old Ahmed Mohamed, who was taken into police custody for bringing a homemade digital clock to his high school after school officials feared that the device bore too close a resemblance to filmic bombs.[68] In the first example, space itself is imbued with the potential of racialized danger.[69] In the case of young Ahmed Mohamed, the creation of an object that would otherwise be lauded as a product of youthful ingenuity can only be imagined as dangerously otherwise—as "half a bomb," as the think tank Center for Security Policy would later refer to Mohamed's clock.[70]

In addition to rendering racialized Muslims always already criminal for the actions that are always imagined as imminent and immanent to their persons, preemptive governance has created for itself an extended logic of incitement that renders criminal and material the perceived desires and imaginations of racialized Muslims who might inspire future violent actions by others. This logic is also becoming a touchstone for everyday forms of racialization in the war on terror, where dissident political speech and otherwise innocuous statements are construed as inciting imminent lawless actions. Here, claims that speech acts constitute incitements to violence serve as a trusty mechanism by which to justify any number of disciplinary and violent actions. Further, these claims are normalized through discourses justifying drone warfare and domestic adjudications of terrorism-related charges that espouse the value of preemptive governance—strategies of stopping violence long before it has the chance to emerge from the threat believed characteristic of the desires and imaginations of racialized suspected terrorists.

And while practices such as drone warfare and material support prosecutions may at first appear unrelated and exceptional, they are, rather, symptomatic and reinforcing of more prevalent trends that ascribe threat to racialized bodies, specifically those bodies who identify as or are presumed to be Muslim. This contemporary mobilization of threat proves a singular instantiation of preemption within its long historical arc, where preemptive techniques are mobilized to both enforce and normalize racialized state violence. In this way, the preemptive logic of drones and the war on terror is not simply emblematic of shifts in risk assessment through algorithmic determination and intelligence gathering practices; rather, it attempts to redefine the spatiotemporality of violence itself to suit the needs of the U.S. imperialist state. Moreover, preemption's increasing reliance on incitement to violence discourse provides a vector through which it can more deeply imbed itself within everyday life for racialized Muslims in the war on terror, a particularly insidious and embodied example of what Amoore and Marieke de Goede have described as "the banal face of the preemptive strike."[71] Under the guise of incitement to violence discourse, the affective realms of bodies perceived to be Muslim or Arab are rendered knowable and criminal. Desire, imagination, and inspiration are transposed into actionable realms for the racialized body, potently charged with the threat potential of violence yet to occur.

Notes

In addition to the editors of this collection, I would like to offer a special thanks to Kris Fallon, James Pierce, Kriss Ravetto-Biagioli, and Madiha Tahir for their very generous support and help in writing this chapter. I would additionally like to thank my friends and colleagues from "Reconfiguring Global Space: The Geography, Politics and Ethics of Drone War," a symposium on drone war held at Indiana University–Bloomington in July 2015, for the generative conversations that helped guide my thinking as I was beginning to explore the ideas in this chapter.

1. Morely, "A Dangerous Mind?"
2. For an exploration of how algorithmic modes of risk analysis are historically intertwined with the imagination, see Amoore, "Security and the Incalculable."

3. Massumi, *Ontopower*, 40. While Massumi has most recently discussed preemption in his book *Ontopower*, these discussions are largely updated versions of those appearing in earlier publications such as "Potential Politics and the Primacy of Preemption," "The Future Birth of the Affective Fact," and "Fear (The Spectrum Said)."
4. Massumi, *Ontopower*, 57.
5. Amoore, *The Politics of Possibility*, 153, emphasis added.
6. Amoore, *The Politics of Possibility*, 153.
7. Merleau-Ponty, *Phenomenology of Perception*; Fanon, *Black Skin, White Masks.*
8. It is important to note that while I will repeatedly refer to the forms of racialization ascribed to Muslim masculinity, Muslim masculinity in the post-9/11 United States becomes a catchall category that designates as Muslim any number of bodies perceived as chromatically or ambiguously Muslim or Arab, where Arabness and Muslimness are conflated as a singular racial category. In this way, it is difficult to separate out Islamophobia in a post-9/11 U.S. landscape from the forms of violence perpetrated against Arab American, Middle Eastern, South Asian, and Latino bodies read as "Muslim-looking," more broadly.

   It is also important to note that while this particular chapter is concerned with the racialization of Muslim masculinity, it is not meant to imply that Muslim and Arab female, queer, gender nonconforming, and trans bodies are not subject to similarly violent forms of racialization in the post-9/11 configuration of racialized threat. While differentially distributed as a result of myriad factors, racialization can take intensely violent forms, where sexuality and gender are often deployed in the service of racializing discourses and Euro-American imperialist expansionism. See Amar, *The Security Archipelago*; Jarmakani, *Imagining Arab Womanhood*; Moallem, *Between Warrior Brother and Veiled Sister*; Najmabadi, *Women with Mustaches and Men without Beards*; Puar, *Terrorist Assemblages*; Shakhsari, "Killing Me Softly with Your Rights."
9. Rana, *Terrifying Muslims*, 89.
10. Salaita, *Israel's Dead Soul*, 104.
11. The shift toward adding "Muslim" to constructions of the Middle Eastern or Arab terrorist was greatly accelerated after September 11, 2001, so that the designation of *Muslim* is not simply a religious but also a racializing signifier. And while this phenomenon certainly intensified in particular ways following 9/11, racialized Islam is by no means new and has historical roots in genealogies of colonialism for Arab and South Asian bodies. The use of *Muslim* as a racializing signifier also presents interesting implications for chromatic or phenotypic configurations of race. For example, as Rana describes, for Black Muslims, racialized Islam exhibits a multiplying effect, where Black bodies accrue additional degrees of threat value through their Muslimness; Rana, *Terrifying Muslims*, 45. See also Rana, "Islam and Racism," in *Terrifying Muslims*, 25–49; Mamdani, *Good Muslim, Bad Muslim.*
12. Sloterdijk, *Terror from the Air*, 20.
13. Sloterdijk, *Terror from the Air*, 20.
14. Gregory, "Drone Geographies," 9–11; Gregory, "Theory of the Drone, 10."
15. Gregory, "Theory of the Drone, 10."

16. Fanon, *Black Skin, White Masks*, 109, 112, 135. For a thorough exploration of the politics of bursting described by Fanon, see Jordan, "The Politics of Impossibility."
17. Weheliye, *Habeas Viscus*, 9–10.
18. Chamayou, *A Theory of the Drone*; Amoore, "Security and the Incalculable"; Amoore, *The Politics of Possibility*; de Goede, Simon, and Hoijtink, "Performing Preemption."
19. Massumi, *Ontopower*, vii.
20. Said, *Crimes of Terror*, 4.
21. 18 U.S. Code § 2339A—Providing Material Support to Terrorists. For a detailed legal analysis of the history and implications of § 2339A and B, see Said, *Crimes of Terror*.
22. Said, *Crimes of Terror*, 52.
23. 18 U.S. Code § 2339B—Providing Material Support or Resources to Designated Foreign Terrorist Organizations; *Holder v. Humanitarian Law Project*, 561 U.S. 1, 130 S.Ct. 2705 (June 2010).
24. *Holder*, 561 U.S. 1, 130 S.Ct. 2705.
25. Said, *Crimes of Terror*, 71.
26. *Brandenburg v. Ohio*, 395 U.S. 444 (1969).
27. *Brandenburg*, 395 U.S. 444.
28. *Brandenburg*, 395 U.S. 444, emphasis added.
29. Cole, quoted in Serwer, "Does Posting Jihadist Material?"
30. Said, *Crimes of Terror*, 71.
31. Said, *Crimes of Terror*, 123.
32. Said, *Crimes of Terror*, 107, 135–43.
33. Scahill, *Dirty Wars*.
34. Scahill, *Dirty Wars*.
35. As Jeremy Scahill speculates based on numerous accounts from al-Awlaki's family members, any indications that al-Awlaki met and communicated closely with al-Qaeda during the last weeks of his life were likely the result of his need for protection as he sought to evade targeting by U.S. forces in the remote Shabwah province in Yemen. It is also of note that al-Qaeda leaders never explicitly referred to al-Awlaki as a member, let alone leader, of the organization. For a thorough exploration of the al-Awlaki case, see Scahill, *Dirty Wars*; C. Woods, *Sudden Justice*.
36. See C. Woods, *Sudden Justice*; Scahill, *Dirty Wars*.
37. Amoore, *The Politics of Possibility*, 59.
38. Scahill, *Dirty Wars*, 377–81.
39. M. Hall, "Did Former SDSU Grad Student Anwar al-Awlaki Inspire the Charlie Hebdo Attack?"; Fernandez, Pérez-Peña, and Santos, "Gunman in Texas Shooting."
40. For a journalistic account of how the U.S. assassination of al-Awlaki may have bolstered his subsequent popularity, see Shane, "The Lessons of Anwar al-Awlaki," and *Objective Troy*. While I disagree with his analyses of al-Awlaki's position as a terrorist, Shane does much in the way of exploring al-Awlaki's status as an inspiration to violent actions after his death.
41. Massumi, *Ontopower*, 194.

42. March, "A Dangerous Mind?"
43. *United States v. Mehanna*, No. 09-10017-GAO D. Mass. Aug. 18, 2011, "Transcripts of Motion Hearing."
44. *U.S. v. Mehanna*, "Transcripts of Motion Hearing."
45. *U.S. v. Mehanna*, "Transcripts of Motion Hearing"; Greenwald, "The Real Criminals."
46. March, "A Dangerous Mind?"
47. March, "A Dangerous Mind?"
48. Prosecutor, quoted in March, "A Dangerous Mind?," emphasis added.
49. March, "A Dangerous Mind?"
50. *U.S. v. Mehanna*, "Transcripts of Motion Hearing"; Serwer, "Does Posting Jihadist Material?"
51. Serwer, "Does Posting Jihadist Material?"
52. *U.S. v. Mehanna*, "Transcripts of Motion Hearing."
53. This again correlates to Massumi's description of Bush administration logic surrounding Saddam Hussein and the invasion of Iraq. As Massumi explains, "The logic of affectively legitimated fact is in the conditional: Bush did what he did because Saddam could have done what he didn't do. Bush's argument doesn't really do injustice to the logic of preemption. Saddam didn't actually even have the 'capacity,' and that poses no problem for preemptive logic which is based on a *double conditional*. 'The Pentagon neocons argued that the CIA overemphasized what Saddam *could do* instead of stressing *what he would do if he could*'"; Massumi, *Ontopower*, 191, quoting Dorrien, *Imperial Designs*, 186.
54. Amoore, "Security and the Incalculable," 426.
55. *The 9/11 Commission Report*, quoted in Amoore, "Security and the Incalculable," 426.
56. Amoore, "Security and the Incalculable," 426.
57. Rumsfeld, "Secretary Rumsfeld Press Conference."
58. Masco, *The Theater of Operation.*
59. Rana, *Terrifying Muslims*, 71.
60. Rana, *Terrifying Muslims*, 89.
61. Amoore, *The Politics of Possibility*, 59.
62. Salaita, *Israel's Dead Soul*, 104.
63. Deleuze, *Difference and Repetition*, 220.
64. Deleuze, *Difference and Repetition*, emphasis added.
65. Deleuze, *Difference and Repetition*, 274–75.
66. Gregory, "The Everywhere War," 239.
67. March, "A Dangerous Mind?"
68. Funnell, "Predictive Policing"; Selk, "Ahmed Mohamed Swept Up."
69. See Cacho, *Social Death*, 72–76.
70. Fang, "Ahmed Mohamed's Clock."
71. Amoore and de Goede, "Transactions after 9/11," 174.

5 VERTICAL MEDIATION AND THE U.S. DRONE WAR IN THE HORN OF AFRICA

LISA PARKS

FOR MORE THAN A DECADE, the United States has waged counterterrorism campaigns in Pakistan, Somalia, and Yemen using drones as instruments of surveillance, reconnaissance, intelligence, and targeted killing. Although these operations have been ongoing since 2004, they first made U.S. news headlines in 2009 when investigative reporter Jane Mayer published a detailed exposé about the CIA's secret drone war in Pakistan in the *New Yorker*.[1] Since then, a whirlwind of public commentary has emerged on drone technology and warfare. Policy experts have deliberated the legalities of drone war, United Nations (UN) teams have conducted special investigations, activists have waged protests and demonstrations, and news agencies have tracked the technology's multifarious uses. So much drone commentary has surfaced in recent years that Caren Kaplan refers to it in this book as the "drone-o-rama." Drone intrigue has also struck the U.S. Congress, which now runs an "unmanned systems caucus" made up of sixty members from thirty states. Since 2008, members of the caucus have pulled in more than $8 million in campaign contributions from drone manufacturers such as Northrup Grumman, General Atomics, and Lockheed Martin.[2] Drone manufacturers' collusion with politicians and entrepreneurs has not only authorized billions of federal funds for the purchase of Predators, Reapers, and Global Hawks but has ramped up and rolled out civilian drone uses, including drone delivery of pizzas and Amazon packages.[3]

Beyond investigative reports and entrepreneurial antics, scholars have explored the drone's relation to robotics and autonomous warfare, international law, visual regimes of power, and affective relations.[4] In such research, scholars often adopt descriptions of drones as "unmanned" or "autonomous" as foundational assumptions, fixating upon their "video game–like" features, "terminal interfaces," or capacities for "remote control" without considering the material conditions or contingencies that undergird their operation. The overvaluation or fetishization of the drone as "unmanned" or "autonomous" has the effect of sanctioning statecraft that takes the form of unilateralism or authorizing wars that are waged extrajudicially. For how could autonomous machines ever do anything but act of their own accord? And how could *we* ever expect to be responsible or accountable for what *they* do?

This unquestioned investment in machine autonomy also runs counter to poststructuralist feminist critiques of science and technology, which for decades have conceptualized machines and humans (and other life forms) as integrated circuits, as dynamic technosocial relations.[5] Building upon these critiques and recent work on the politics of verticality,[6] this chapter analyzes the materialities of U.S. drone operations in the Horn of Africa. Since 2002, the U.S. Joint Special Operations Command (JSOC) and the Central Intelligence Agency (CIA) have orchestrated a covert drone war from Camp Lemonnier in the tiny African country of Djibouti, monitoring and striking alleged al-Qaeda and Al-Shabaab suspects in Yemen and Somalia. According to the Bureau of Investigative Journalism, 108 to 128 drone strikes occurred in Yemen between 2002 and 2016, killing an estimated 496 to 726 people. In Somalia, 18 to 22 strikes occurred between 2007 and 2016, killing between 38 and 126 people.[7] As Steve Niva suggests, JSOC and CIA "share information, compile target lists, and then hunt, kill and capture enemies worldwide through shadowy operations in which violence is largely disappeared from media coverage and political accountability."[8]

As a media scholar, I am interested in both the discourses people develop and use to expose covert U.S. drone interventions and the ways drones themselves function as technologies of mediation. By *mediation*, I am referring not only to the capacity of drone sensors to detect phenomena on the Earth's surface so it can be rendered as live video feeds at terminal interfaces but also to the potential to materially alter or affect the phenomena of the air, spectrum, and/or ground. Like Sarah Kember and Joanna Zylinska, I understand mediation as a process that far exceeds the screen and involves the capacity to register the dynamism of occurrences within, on, or in relation to myriad materials, objects, sites, surfaces, or bodies on Earth.[9] As a drone flies through the sky, it alters the chemical composition of the air. As it hovers above the Earth, it can change movements on the ground. As it projects announcements through loudspeakers, it can affect thought and behavior. And as it shoots Hellfire missiles, it can turn homes into holes and the living into the dead. Much more than a sensor, the drone is a technology of *vertical mediation*: the traces, transmissions, and targets of its operations are registered in the air, through the spectrum, and on the ground. Irreducible to the screen's visual display, the drone's mediating work happens extensively and dynamically through the vertical field—through a vast expanse that extends from the Earth's surface, including the geological layers below and built environments on it, through the domains of the spectrum and the air to the outer limits of orbit.

To explore the drone's mediating work, I rely on three registers—the infrastructural, the perceptual, and the forensic—and I draw on media such as Google Earth interfaces, training manual diagrams, thermal infrared (IR) images, and drone crash scene photos to convey how and where vertical mediations take shape. Rather than approach these media as sites of representation, I treat them as demonstrations of the materializing capacities and effects of drone interventions—as sites where the drone's relation to the material world becomes intelligible, vivid, palpable, and contestable. Ultimately, I argue that the power of the drone is not just to hunt and kill from afar but to "secure territories" and "administer populations" from the sky, to reorder, reform, and remediate life on Earth in a most material way.[10] In this way, the drone technologies are more like 3-D printers than video games. They sculpt as much as they sense or simulate.

The Infrastructural

Djibouti is a small nation on the east coast of Africa, bordered by Eritrea, Ethiopia, and Somalia. Its capital city, Djibouti City, sits on the Red Sea and the Gulf of Aden, along a key shipping corridor targeted by Somali pirates over the past decade. A former French colony, Djibouti asserted its independence in 1977 and over the past forty years has had only two presidents. Of the country's 828,000 citizens, 94 percent are Muslim and 60 percent are unemployed.[11] A country with scant natural resources, Djibouti lives off the "bonanza rents" it garners from its geostrategic location, and this situation has created a "government inclined toward authoritarianism, highly consolidated power, repressive tactics," and a corrupt administrative apparatus.[12] Djibouti also has a terrible record on human rights and civil liberties, and the state tightly restricts media and civil society organizations, though there have been major demonstrations against the ruling regime since 2011 due to allegations of election fraud. Far from being democratic, political and economic mobilities in Djibouti are based on an individual's position within a system of racial/ethnic hierarchy and are characterized as client–patron relationships in which citizens have very few rights.[13]

In 2001, months before 9/11, the U.S. military entered into conversations to establish a base in Djibouti as part of an effort to respond to al-Qaeda groups allegedly operating training centers in Yemen and Somalia. The result was Camp Lemonnier, a five-hundred-acre base located at Djibouti's international airport in an area once used by the French Foreign Legion. Described by the Pentagon as the "backbone" of counterterrorism in the region, the annual budget for Lemonnier is $300 million, and the United States pays Djibouti $38 million a year to lease the space for the base.[14] Working with the CIA, Combined Joint Task Force-Horn of Africa leads these counterterrorism efforts and serves as the "organizational hub" or "revolutionary motor" of networked warfare in the region, often using the drone as a centerpiece. As Niva suggests, the targeted killings of al-Awlaki and bin Laden are "merely the visible trace of a dense matrix of highly secretive operations that occur on a daily basis around the globe."[15] When U.S. Defense Secretary Leon Panetta visited Djibouti in December 2011, he told U.S. troops, "Al Qaeda is what started this war, and we have made a commitment that we are going to track these guys wherever they go to make sure they have no place to hide . . . whether it's Yemen or Somalia or anyplace else."[16] General Wayne Grigsby, head administrator of the site, has announced, "Our mission here is to enable our East African partners to actually neutralise violent extremists throughout eastern Africa."[17]

Although U.S. drone operations in Djibouti remain classified, parts of their infrastructure are visible in Google Earth. Digital Globe satellite images pinpoint Camp Lemonnier as well as Chabelley airstrip just outside Djibouti City (see figures 5.1 and 5.2), where Predators and Reapers take off and land.[18] Drone operations are predicated on computing and telecommunication networks, but they are also contingent on a multitude of other resources, including ground surface, air, spectrum, orbit, labor, and energy. In addition, acts of earthmoving, importation, construction, installation, and maintenance are needed to build and operate an airstrip in the desert. As an infrastructural inscription, a line in the sand, as it were, the airstrip is the staging ground for drone campaigns and vertical maneuvers. The airstrip

Figure 5.1. A Google Earth screen capture of Camp Lemonnier in Djibouti City, Djibouti, reveals dimensions of drone infrastructure on the ground.

Figure 5.2. A Google Earth screen capture reveals the Chabelley airstrip in Djibouti where U.S. drones take off and land.

not only marks the Earth's surface in ways that satellite images can uniquely convey but also brings to the surface the material conditions of geology, physics, energy, and weather that drones must negotiate in order to operate.

This is only one of many infrastructural lines in the sand that supports U.S. drone operations in east Africa.[19] As Predators and Reapers hopscotch their way around the region to conduct aerial campaigns in Somalia and Yemen, they circle back to runways for refueling or maintenance after a certain number of hours in flight. Flight routes are determined by both the capacity of the drone and the number of hours drone pilots are allowed to work. The range of a Predator is approximately 675 miles and the range of a Reaper is 1,150 to 3,600 miles depending on the size of the payload carried. Other airstrips in Nairobi and Mombasa (Kenya), Ethiopia's Arba Minch Airport, Mahé (Seychelles), and Saudi Arabia have also been constructed or repurposed for use by the JSOC and the CIA. The United States has twenty-nine agreements to use international airports in Africa as refueling stations for U.S. military aircraft.[20]

While Google Earth spotlights U.S. drone infrastructure in and around Djibouti, military training manual diagrams also demonstrate the drone's vertical mediations. Designed to educate drone crews about operational scenarios, these diagrams portray drones performing defensive, offensive, stability, and civil support missions. In the military imaginary, the drone becomes the center point of coordinated activities fluidly orchestrated through aerial, orbital, spectral, and terrestrial domains (see figure 5.3). Here the drone is figured as a media technology par excellence as it facilitates relations between terrain vehicles and satellites, provides aerial surveillance for ground operations, guides missiles to targets, and drops messages to civilians. This mediating machine, this extensive life and death support system, appropriates the vertical as the medium of its movements, transmissions, inscriptions, and projections. As these diagrams suggest, the drone's theater of operations is contingent on a robust yet scattered constellation of communication and global positioning satellites, fiber optic Internet links, and computer-equipped Earth stations, all of which must be electrified. The "where" of drone operations is ultimately much more complex than any one image could suggest. As one analyst explains, a drone might be "piloted from Nellis Air Force Base in Nevada, USA, coordinate with an intelligence cell in Bagram, Afghanistan, tap into data stored in Nairobi, coordinate with a carrier launched ELINT [electronic intelligence] platform, be monitored in Washington and be hunting a target in Kismayo (in Somalia)."[21] Putting this extensive and multitiered infrastructure

Figure 5.3. An illustration from a Joint Unmanned Aircraft Systems (JUAS) Center of Excellence Training Document from Creech Air Force Base, 2010, shows the drone in action, mediating communication and logistics between the air and the ground.

in place not only takes time and money but also requires access to land, spectrum, and sky and is contingent on a dizzying array of contracts, agreements, and leases with host countries, who, by taking U.S. money and offering land, implicitly authorize the U.S. military to do what it does, even if it creates adverse conditions for civilians in the region.

Given the broad reach and capacities of U.S. drone infrastructures, it is impossible to separate an understanding of them from other systems around the world, whether energy grids, airstrips, or telecommunications networks. In 2014 investigative journalists Jeremy Scahill and Glenn Greenwald published an exposé revealing that U.S. military drones are equipped with "virtual base-tower transceivers" that enable them to intercept commercial mobile phone traffic and "suck up data" for the National Security Agency (NSA).[22] These drone-based transceivers function as a fake cell phone tower that forces targeted mobile devices to lock onto an NSA receiver without the user's knowledge. Thus, as U.S. military drones hover above, they conduct signals intelligence, intercepting the proprietary data of commercial mobile telephone providers and users and trafficking it into NSA clouds. In this scenario, the drone becomes part of an extractive information economy

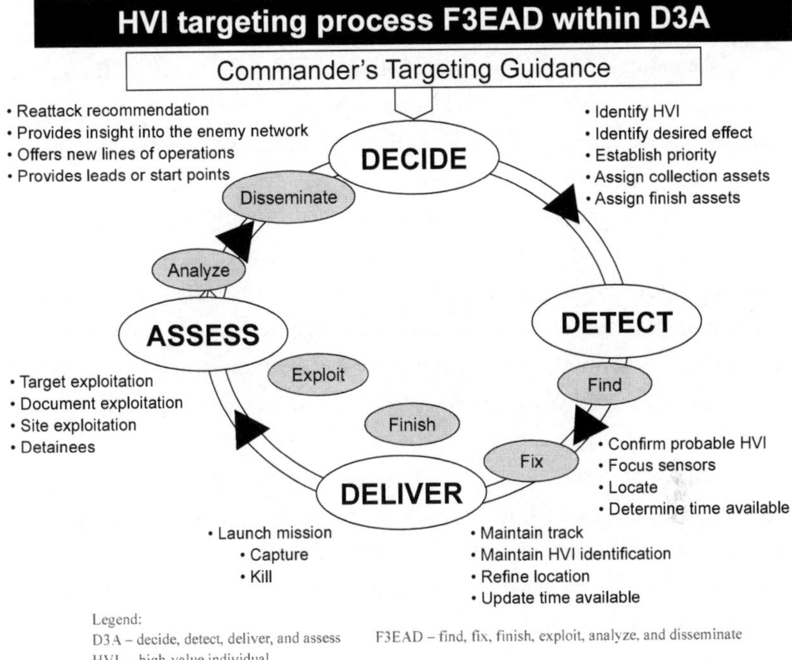

Figure 5.4. A diagram from the U.S. Army's Targeting Process Field Manual, 2010, shows the flow command for the F3EAD process used to find and target HVIS of high-value individuals.

functioning as a digital vacuum cleaner or flying data miner. Although these transceivers were ostensibly put in place to help authenticate suspects before U.S. drone strikes, Scahill and Greenwald reveal that attacks have been authorized again and again based on mobile phone metadata alone, leading to killings of unidentified suspects, a situation they call "death by metadata."[23] Their report cites a former drone pilot who explains, "It's really like we're targeting a cell phone. We're not going after people—we're going after their phones, in the hopes that the person on the other end of that missile is the bad guy."[24]

This practice emerged as part of a JSOC and CIA paradigm, first tested during the war in former Yugoslavia, known as "Feed" or F3EAD, which stands for Find, Fix, Finish, Exploit, Analyze, Disseminate (see figure 5.4). Feed involves monitoring mobile phone communications to find suspects' exact locations and positioning drones above to provide "deadly persistence" until the suspect emerges.[25] If the suspect is confirmed, lethal force is applied and helicopters drop ground crews in immediately after a drone strike to "exploit" any physical evidence on the scene.[26] The intelligence is "analyzed" and "disseminated" across the JSOC network.[27] Scahill describes the operational logic: "We can kill you if we don't know your identity, but once we kill you, we want to figure out who we killed."[28] Preemptive targeted killings are met with retrospective confirmations.

This F3EAD strategy positions Africans in general, and Yemenis and Somalis in particular, at the treacherous infrastructural crossroads of mobile communications and U.S. military drone operations. During Africa's first decade of mobile telephony, consumers could purchase multiple SIM cards from different mobile phone networks without registration; however, now most (all but three) African countries have adopted mandatory SIM card registration policies, requiring consumers to provide personal identification when purchasing a SIM card, which is needed to activate a mobile phone.[29] Given this, there is growing concern about the potential for SIM card databases to be used in security and policing, including in the formation of JSOC and CIA target lists.[30] In Yemen, fifty-eight out of one hundred people use mobile phones with one of four providers. In Somalia, twenty-three out of one hundred people use mobile phones with one of six providers.[31] Simply by having a SIM card, using a mobile phone, or being in the vicinity of others using them, Somali and Yemeni people increase the risk of being targeted by a drone.[32]

In response to these infrastructural intersections, people on the ground have devised various tactics. In an effort to encourage critical reflection on the "death by metadata" practice, web developer Josh Begley created an iPhone app called Metadata+ (which Apple rejected five times) that informs the user each time the United States conducts a drone strike, enabling people to track and respond to the strikes.[33] In regions of U.S. drone operations, people use multiple SIM cards, up to six a day, to create confusion about users' identities.[34] In Somalia, Al-Shabaab has reportedly stopped using mobile phones and has halted others' access as well. In early 2014 members of the organization stormed into the headquarters of one of Somalia's largest mobile Internet providers, Hormudd Telecom, with weapons and demanded that the network be shut down, claiming the organization was being used by Western spy agencies to collect information on Muslims.[35] Al-Shabaab has also confiscated and banned the use of camera-equipped smart phones, claiming they were being used to spy on Muslims.[36]

Thus, while satellite images demonstrate drone infrastructure's material transformation of the Earth's surface and training diagrams convey its vertical layers and extensions, the "death by metadata" scenario reveals how strategic uses of drone infrastructure alter the status of mobile telephony systems on the ground, reshaping the policies of mobile phone providers, the behavior of their users, and the operations of their networks.[37]

The Perceptual

In addition to remediating how people communicate and live on the ground, drone operations reorganize human perception of and interaction with material phenomena. Like its precursors the U-2 spy plane and remote sensing satellite, the drone is equipped with electro-optical (EO) and infrared sensors that detect electromagnetic radiation reflected off of or emanating from the Earth's surface and it participates in a *radiographic episteme* by turning imperceptible radiation into data that can be made productive within an information economy.[38] It is the drone's detection of infrared radiation that I focus on here as it brings other material dimensions of vertical mediation into relief and demarcates a shift in the technologized perception of racial difference and death.

When drone crews begin their work in a designated mission area, they "build a picture" of conditions on the ground.[39] The sensor operator often begins this process by using Google Earth imagery to determine how a given mission area should look from above and then positions the drone's sensor ball to acquire optimal EO/IR views of the area. The goal, as one pilot puts it, is to "get the ball over the target."[40] While this process is often imagined as a simple act of button pushing, Tim Cullen's declassified yet heavily redacted ethnography of Reaper crews reveals that sensor operators are often completely overwhelmed by the multiple views and different kinds of information they must engage with during drone operations. He writes, "Coordinating the cacophony of displays and paper products at a work station required discipline and skill and sensor operators said it took up to half a year or more to master how to correlate information from [redacted] maps and imagery with objects on the [redacted] display and images in the HUD (head-up display)."[41] Those who manage to master the hand–eye coordination needed to acquire good overhead views become known as having "golden hands."[42]

Since U.S. drone operations often occur at night, infrared sensors are useful because they allow crews to "see" through darkness and clouds. Caroline Holmqvist insists that such sensors and screens have "agential capacities"

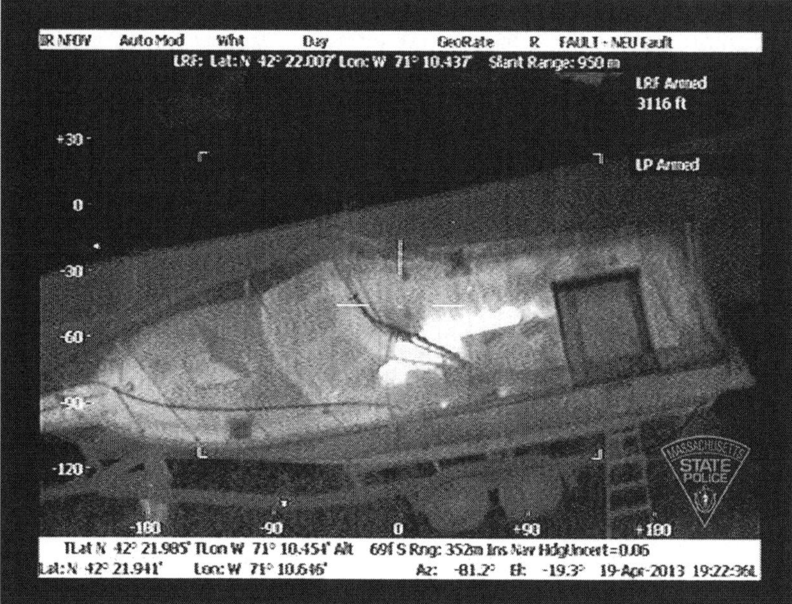

Figure 5.5. A thermal infrared image released by the Massachusetts State Police shows the body of Boston bombing suspect Dzhokhar Tsarnaev in bright white before he was captured on April 19, 2013.

because their impacts far exceed acts of representation.[43] Although infrared drone imagery of U.S. counterterrorism campaigns is classified, the CIA and JSOC have used IR imaging to track and target Osama bin Laden[44] and U.S. citizens Anwar al-Awlaki and Samir Khan as well as more than four thousand alleged terror suspects and civilians in Pakistan, Yemen, and Somalia during the past decade. In the United States, Homeland Security, border patrol, and law enforcement officers have used aerial infrared sensors to monitor activity along U.S. borders, bolster urban and rural policing, and locate and apprehend Boston Marathon bombing suspect Dzhokhar Tsarnaev.

In such operations, the "drone" is mobilized in a hunt for heat, fixed on heat-bearing objects such as bodies, guns, missiles, explosives, tanks, anti-aircraft vehicles, trucks, and power generators.[45] Within such conditions, the universal human condition of body temperature becomes a liability. Drone imagery is calibrated to visualize infrared emissions such that human bodies pop out in the visual field as white or black blotches (depending on image processing selections) of stasis or movement. In low-light conditions, human bodies are not only easier to see in IR imagery but also easier to track and target. Within this radiographic episteme, visual surveillance practices are extended beyond epidermalization, as infrared imagery can be used to isolate suspects according to the energy emitted by their bodies. While other systems of human differentiation and social sorting are organized around skin color, personal information, or biometrics,[46] aerial infrared imagery turns all bodies into indistinct human morphologies that cannot be differentiated according to conventional visible light indicators, correlated with constructs of gender, race, or class. Seeing according to temperature turns everyone into a potential suspect or target and has the effect of "normalizing" surveillance since all bodies appear similar beneath its gaze.

At the same time, however, it is important to point out that temperature data has become visible precisely so that it can be made productive within existing regimes of power. Even as it displaces the visible light or epidermal registers of ethnic/racial difference, drone IR imaging reinforces already existing power hierarchies by monitoring and targeting certain territories and peoples—such as those in Pakistan, Yemen, and Somalia, or along the U.S. borders—with greater frequency and intensity, designating these areas and people as "hot spots" that need to be preemptively contained. Strategies of ethnic/racial differentiation do not disappear within an aerial system of temperature-based visuality; rather, they are restructured along a vertical axis of power and recodified according to issues such as moving to or being in certain places at certain times, being in the vicinity of other suspects, driving certain vehicles, or carrying certain objects with certain temperatures or shapes or sizes.[47] Racializing logics and social sorting persist as certain peoples' territories, bodies, movements, and information are selected for monitoring, tracking, and targeting day after day, month after month, year after year, such that they become *spectral suspects*—visualizations of temperature data that take on the biophysical contours of a human body while its surface appearance remains invisible and its identity unknown. Such processes reorganize the racialized gaze so that black African and brown Arab bodies once discriminated against and/or exoticized on the basis of skin pigment are digitally recast as white blotches of body heat that can be tracked from above. The effect of this vertical remediation of racial difference is to mainstay counterterrorism as a social order. For it is precisely the issue of not being able to verify or confirm the identities of suspects that fuels counterterrorism as a paradigm and drone warfare as its method. The recoding of racial difference as thermal abstraction thus becomes infrastructural as it rationalizes and drives the militarized drone economy.

This way of perceiving racial difference has other effects as well. Former sensor operator Brandon Bryant, who is a contributor to this book, publicly shared his experiences with reporters in 2013 after manning a sensor ball at Creech and Cannon from 2007 to 2011; working on U.S. drone operations in Afghanistan, Iraq, and Yemen; and participating in the killing of 1,626 people. Working in twelve-hour shifts six days a week, drone crews partake in "an endless loop of watching: scanning roads, circling compounds, tracking suspicious activity," shifting between visible light and infrared registers to get the best possible view.[48] When the mission is to monitor a high-value target, a sensor operator might linger above a single house for weeks. Far from being an exercise in objectification, this focused monitoring, Derek Gregory has suggested, generates a "voyeuristic intimacy."[49] Bryant's perceptions of the thermal mediascape had a profound effect on him. He recounts his drone memories in infrared, detailing the first time he killed someone via drone and watching the body's "hot blood" "hit the ground" and "start to cool off." Tasked to linger above the site and conduct surveillance for an "after-action report," Bryant recalls, "It took him a long time to die. I just watched him. I watched him become the same color as the ground he was lying on."[50] Like race, death looks different in the thermal mediascape. When a body is killed, its motion stops and its temperature drops. As the body slowly takes on the temperature values of the matter surrounding it, it loses its contour and recedes into the visual field. Drone IR imagery depicts race as abstract whiteness and death as disappearance.

Just as people have responded to death by metadata practices, so too have they devised a plethora of counterinfrared imaging tactics. Some have created drone survival guides that encourage people to avoid becoming part of drone views. Others have experimented with deflective and insulating material such as glass, wool blankets, rugs, tin foil, and synthetically designed fabrics that trap or hide heat, even if temporarily, so that it cannot be detected when drones are hovering above. New York artists Adam Harvey and Johanna Bloomfield designed a drone-proof clothing line called "Stealth Wear" made of nickel-metalized fabric, and German company Blucher sells a special outfit called "Ghost," which makes the body invisible to infrared sensors and is made from a patented material called spectralflage.[51] Still others in Pakistan have created massive art installations called "not a bug splat," placing giant images of children's faces on the Earth's surface to show drone operators that the anonymous white blobs seen from afar are anything but "bug splats"—they are humans, including children.[52]

The Forensic

Even as drone infrared imaging participates in reorganizing the perception of race and death, the technology is not foolproof. Drones sometimes fail. And crash sites bring their vertical mediations into dialogue with the forensic.[53] Since 2007, the organization Drone Wars UK has maintained a drone crash database compiled by gleaning details from USAF Accident Investigation Board (AIB) Reports, the WikiLeaks War Logs, and press reports.[54] While this database is not totally comprehensive due to the classification of information, it serves as a useful starting point for extending this discussion of the material contingencies of drone operations. Failures and accidents bring drones plummeting fatefully back to Earth, etching their inadvertent effects into grounded lifeworlds and biomatter. In these situations, airborne maneuvers suddenly become dirtborne ruins and sites of forensic investigation. As Greg Siegel suggests, forensics are "called upon to search for telltale clues, to trace hidden causal nexuses, to provide reliable evidence, to identify sources of misfortunes, to solve puzzles of physical destruction . . . to logically reconstruct and accurately recount the essence of 'what went wrong.' "[55]

Since 2011, there have been at least ten U.S. military drone crashes in and around Djibouti.[56] Accident reports link these events to a multitude of circumstances, ranging from component anomalies to faulty parts, weather conditions to pilot inexperience, software glitches to intentional destruction. On March 15, 2011, a Predator returning from a classified mission overran the runway at Djibouti airport and crashed through a fence, causing almost $1.4 million in damages.[57] Nearly two months later, on May 7, 2011, a Predator plummeted into the Gulf of Aden one and a half hours after takeoff due to component failure, resulting in a $4.4 million loss.[58] Ten days later, on May 17, 2011, a Predator that had flown for 16.9 hours was directed to return to base early because of an oil leak, yet pilots had trouble identifying the runway on the approach at night because of low clouds and high humidity. The Predator and Hellfire missile onboard exploded on impact for a total loss of nearly $3 million.[59] On February 21, 2012, a Predator returning to Djibouti experienced engine anomalies and made an uncommanded gradual descent while on a target during an operation. Commanders directed the drone to return to Djibouti, but when it malfunctioned en route, the pilot was ordered to perform a "hard-ditch," intentionally sending it into the Indian Ocean at a high speed so that the drone and Hellfire missile onboard would be destroyed, costing the U.S. government $4.4 million.[60]

Declassified U.S. Air Force accident reports contain some of the most detailed publicly available information about U.S. drone operations in the Horn of Africa. As they recount accidents, they convey information about the drone's technical specifications, the personnel and bases involved, the maintenance history of the drone, the training, work, and medical history of the pilots, weather conditions, and the cost of damages and losses.[61] As the accident report establishes the parties involved, what went wrong, and who is at fault, it becomes a part of the U.S. military's audit culture. Failure analysis is conducted from the perspectives of U.S. military personnel to refine drone crew performance, improve technical standards in manufacturing, and assess costs, not to question the effectiveness of drone operations.

Photos and cockpit video accompanying accident reports remain classified, but on September 24, 2013, the *Washington Post* published eight U.S. Air Force photos of two drone crash scenes in Djibouti with an article that expressed dismay over the frequency of U.S. drone accidents there.[62] Seven of the photos show a Predator crash near a residential area in Djibouti City. A wide shot of the crash site shows the smashed Predator belly up in the dirt with its casing punctured and bent (see figure 5.6). Four other photos show close-ups of the object in ruins, honing in on its frayed interior circuitry, damaged landing gear, and crunched mechanical parts (see figure 5.7). These grounded views exceed the logics of the audit-oriented accident report and demonstrate the fragility of the Predator. Two of the photos feature human onlookers, delineating different epistemological positions in relation to the drone crash scene. The first shows a team of investigators huddled near their SUVs with the crash scene marked off by yellow police tape as if part of an official forensic unit (see figure 5.8). Another photo reveals about seventy curious Djiboutian onlookers standing on the site perimeter and staring at the dead drone in the distance, positioning the drone crash as an experience that punctuates the lifeworlds of Djiboutian citizens and residents (see figure 5.9). The photo situates them as silhouettes on the horizon, as remote sensors of a U.S. drone accident in their own backyard.[63]

There is a need for further research on Djiboutian citizens' sentiments about hosting U.S. drone operations. Numerous news reports indicate the Arab Spring protests had a radiating effect on Djiboutian youth, inspiring them to organize demonstrations against their president in an effort to reclaim their nation's political future.[64] Yet as of 2016, only 17.7 percent of Djiboutians had Internet access and Facebook accounts. And press freedoms in the country have been under serious attack, limiting public discussion of

Figure 5.6. A Predator MQ-1B crashed while trying to return to Camp Lemonnier, the U.S. military base in Djibouti, on May 17, 2011. It landed in a vacant lot near a residential area of Djibouti City, about 2.7 miles short of the runway. These photographs, taken by U.S. Air Force investigators, were released as part of an unclassified Accident Investigation Board report into the crash. (U.S. Air Force)

Figure 5.7. A view of the engine and propeller area of the Predator that crashed in Djibouti. (U.S. Air Force)

Figure 5.8. The U.S. Air Force investigators demarcate the crash scene of the Predator that collided as it descended toward Camp Lemonnier. (U.S. Air Force)

Figure 5.9. Word spread quickly among local residents after the drone dropped from the sky. Hundreds of Djiboutians gathered at the scene to gaze at the wreckage. (U.S. Air Force)

important political issues.[65] While I have not found extensive evidence of Djibouti opposition to U.S. drone operations, in 2013 six hundred janitorial and food service workers waged a strike outside Camp Lemonnier after hundreds of jobs were terminated by new private contractor KBR.[66] While some Djiboutians have come to rely on employment opportunities brought by their country's geo-strategic location, others may be less enthusiastic about Djibouti's role in regional militarization. According to Djibouti's foreign minister, Mahmoud Ali Youssouf, such conditions have positioned his country as "one of the top targets of al-Shabaab in the region."[67] U.S. drone operations turn individuals into spectral suspects and host countries into targets.[68]

U.S. drones too have been targeted, though information about such incidents is carefully controlled. On May 27, 2013, a Schiebel Camcopter S-100 drone crashed in Somalia near the Lower Shabelle region/shoreline of Mogadishu.[69] The drone's mission is classified, but the manufacturer's press release and technical demonstration on YouTube indicates its aerial sensor, loudspeaker, and leafleting are used for psychological operations (PSYOPS)—to communicate with civilians during U.S. military apprehension of a terrorist cell. The video based on a demonstration at Fort Bragg shows the camcopter drone flying above a mock village as armed personnel carriers and a UGV (unmanned ground vehicle) enter the area to apprehend a terrorist cell. A loudspeaker onboard the camcopter drone informs the public about the operation and then drops informational pamphlets into the area.[70] Whether the downed drone was performing PSYOPS in Somalia remains an open question. Suffice it to say, members of Al-Shabaab posted several photos of the drone's ruins (see figure 5.10) on its English-language Twitter account, boasting: "This one won't spy on Muslims again. So much for the empty rhetoric on the drone program!"[71] Alongside another picture, the militant group added: "This one is off to the scrap yard, Schiebel! You are fighting a losing battle. Islam will prevail."[72]

The drone crash and the documentations of and responses to it are crucial aspects of vertical mediation. These practices range from official accident reports to civilians viewing crash scenes in their neighborhoods to militants posting ruined drone photos on Twitter. They are important for multiple reasons. First, they expose the kinds of drones being operated and where they are being operated. Second, they highlight drone materialities, reminding viewers that unmanned and autonomous technologies are still subject to the laws of gravity, software glitches, and bad weather, and they also have enemies. Finally, given that drone strike photos and assessments

Figure 5.10. A Schiebel Camcopter S-100 drone and its ruins after reportedly being shot down by members of Al-Shabaab near Bulo-Marer, Lower Shabelle, in Somalia.

in the Horn of Africa do not circulate and there is limited reporting at such sites, the drone crash scene stands in as a symbolic reminder of these concealed sites as well as the injured or dead bodies that remain invisible or uncounted and have been subjected to a strategy of disappearance. This strategy, I suggest, is symptomatic of the U.S. drone program more generally—it is achieved not only by using infrared images to watch bodies die and slowly disappear but also by using Hellfire missiles to incinerate bodies on contact so there are no remains left to identify or count (except with DNA analysis), by directing troops to sweep in to remove remains from strike scenes so locals are unable to confirm who is missing or honor the dead, and by waging U.S. drone wars in secret so that no one knows where or when strikes occur. Within this context, drone crash scene documentation serves a vital function as it puts material traces of these operations into mediated forms that can catalyze public inquiry and responses.

Conclusion

This analysis of vertical mediation and U.S. military drone operations in the Horn of Africa has drawn attention to material dimensions of drone warfare. First, I focused on the *infrastructural* to highlight the vital role of airstrips, the vertical layering of systems, and the commandeering of commercial mobile telephony. Second, I used the *perceptual* to explore how infrared drone imagery extends racialization and social sorting beyond epidermalization, using temperature-based images to cast all human bodies as blotches of light/dark that stand out in the visual field as *spectral suspects*. In these images, individuals may have unique "patterns of life,"[73] but death appears the same: as the body loses its temperature it recedes into surrounding matter and disappears. Finally, turning to the *forensic*, I explored how drone crashes mark the Earth's surface while exposing and intensifying information flows around and responses to secret U.S. drone operations in Africa. All the while, I shared examples of ways people on the ground have responded to and contested U.S. drone operations.

What U.S. drone operations reveal is that mediation is not only something viewed on a monitor but is also a materializing practice that exceeds the device and the screen. Mediation is entangled with dirt, air, orbit, spectrum, and energy as well as militarized efforts to restructure or re-mediate life on Earth. U.S. military drone operations participate in vertical mediation by using airborne sensors, transmitters/receivers, loudspeakers, and leafleting, but they also do so by requiring the construction of airstrips on the Earth's surface, altering the status of commercial mobile telephone networks, creating craters and losses of life with Hellfire missiles, and plummeting unpredictably to Earth when they fail. These too are vertical mediations—ways in which drone use rewrites life on Earth. The materializing dimensions of U.S. drone operations are much more extensive than I have delineated here. Suffice it to say, we need other visions of what vertical mediation could look like.

Toward this end, I want to close with a brief discussion of Hubert Sauper's documentary film *We Come as Friends*, which presents a vertical mediation antithetical to that of U.S. drone war. A filmmaker with a lifelong commitment to investigating neocolonialism, government corruption, and human suffering, Sauper built his own tiny open-cockpit aircraft out of scrap metal and flew from France, through Egypt and Libya, to South Sudan; along the way, he landed in different villages and met with an eclectic medley of people, including herdsman, soldiers, and Chinese oil workers. B. Ruby Rich reads Sauper's filmed flights as a critique of the West's history of interference in Africa. As Sauper "hurls himself bodily into the terrain of Africa," his project offers a different model of flight, power, and sensing that uses the plane and the camera to draw out or "write a world into being" rather than hover over it in order to monitor and reorder it.[74] On the ground, Rich explains, Sauper "captures a world in which outsiders lie and cheat, elders are robbed, territories are annexed. . . . The victims are right there on screen, close up. The criminals? Elsewhere, offscreen, scot-free; or sometimes . . . smiling for the camera with scary sangfroid, impunity, and no fear of consequence."[75] Rather than idly embrace the vertical hegemony of US military operations, these cinematic countervisions confront the politics of verticality and remoteness and spotlight the uneven everyday worlds that such politics can generate.

Notes

1. Mayer, "The Predator War."
2. G. Martin and Novak, "Drones"; see also Barry, "The Political Economy of Drones."
3. Mark Fiore's animated satire, "Drones Come to Technopolis," sardonically captures these busy bee maneuvers, parodying corporate attempts to turn drones into yet another boom cycle of the Google-led information economy. Fiore's parody was not far off. In April 2014 Google purchased drone manufacturer Titan Aerospace as part of an initiative to use drones to connect parts of the world that do not have Internet service. Tsukayama, "Google Buys Drone Maker"; Kang, "Google to Use Balloons."
4. See, for instance, Wall and Monahan, "Surveillance and Violence from Afar"; Singer, *Wired for War*; Gregory, "Lines of Descent"; Kaplan, "The Balloon Prospect"; and Holmqvist, "Undoing War."
5. Haraway, "A Cyborg Manifesto"; Suchman, *Human-Machine Reconfigurations.*
6. Weizman, *Hollow Land*; Sloterdijk, *Terror from the Air*; Chow, *The Age of the World Target*; Graham, *Vertical.*
7. Serle and Fielding-Smith, "Monthly Updates on the Covert War."
8. Niva, "Disappearing Violence," 197.
9. Kember and Zylinska, *Life after New Media.*
10. Foucault, *Security, Territory, Population.*
11. Central Intelligence Agency, "Djibouti."
12. Brass, "Djibouti's Unusual Resource Curse," 525, 529.
13. Bezabeh, "Citizenship and the Logic of Sovereignty"; Human Rights Watch, "Djibouti."
14. Bengali, "U.S. Military Investing Heavily"; Akulov, "Asia Pivot Declared"; Department of the Navy and CIA World Factbook, "An End to Drone Flights."
15. Niva, "Disappearing Violence," 186.
16. Craig Whitlock, "Defense Secretary Panetta Visits."
17. F. Gardner, "US Military Steps Up Operations."
18. Zarrella, "Working Together"; Department of the Navy and CIA World Factbook, "An End to Drone Flights."
19. Turse, "The Increasing US Shadow Wars."
20. Turse, "Behind the Veil of Secrecy"; see also Turse, "The Startling Size."
21. Pelton, "Enter the Drones."
22. A. Goodman, "Death by Metadata." According to Scahill in his interview with Amy Goodman, these transceivers can locate a mobile phone within thirty feet of its position.

23. A. Goodman, "Death by Metadata"; see also Scahill and Greenwald, "The NSA's Secret Role"; Cole, "We Kill People Based on Metadata."
24. A. Goodman, "Death by Metadata."
25. Faint and Harris, "F3EAD."
26. Pelton, "Enter the Drones."
27. This targeted method, also known as the "unwavering eye," stresses "massing all elements of intelligence, surveillance and reconnaissance on 'selected parts of the enemy's network.' " Niva, "Disappearing Violence," 193. The decision-making protocols for targeted killings require two forms of intelligence, but in areas where it is risky to deploy boots on the ground, such as Yemen and Somalia, it is increasingly common for commanders to authorize drone strikes based on aerial and signal intelligence alone. See also Raytheon, "Raytheon AST Surveillance."
28. A. Goodman, "Death by Metadata." A program called Geolocation Cell or Geo Cell allowed the NSA to track and locate someone in real time, which generated a motto within the NSA: "We track 'em. You whack 'em"; Priest, "NSA Growth."
29. Donavan and Martin, "The Rise of African SIM Registration."
30. Appelbaum et al., "Obama's Lists."
31. World Bank Group, "Mobile cellular subscriptions (per 100 people)–Somalia."
32. Caren Kaplan's prophetic work on GPS shows how a technology designed to support U.S. military precision targeting during the Persian Gulf War was transitioned into mass markets and used to track and target consumers. Kaplan, "Precision Targets, 2006."
33. Brownstone, "Your iPhone Can Now Alert You."
34. Bamford, *The Shadow Factory.*
35. Osman, "Somalia Powerless"; see also "Hormuud Telecom services disrupted by militant group."
36. Speri, "Al-Shabaab Is Confiscating Camera-Equipped 'Spy' Phones." For detail on Al-Shabaab's control of social media and messaging, see Menkhaus, "Al-Shabaab and Social Media: A Double-Edged Sword."
37. Niva, "Disappearing Violence," 199.
38. Packer, "Screens in the Sky."
39. Cullen, "The MQ-9 Reaper."
40. B. Jones, "Creech AFB UAV Operations."
41. Cullen, "The MQ-9 Reaper," 96. All the displays, he indicated, were "difficult for novice operators to organize, navigate and interpret" (96).
42. Cullen, "The MQ-9 Reaper," 96.
43. Holmqvist, "Undoing War," 543–44.
44. G. Miller, "CIA Flew Stealth Drones."
45. Wall and Monahan, "Surveillance and Violence from Afar."
46. Fanon, *Black Skin, White Masks*; Browne, "Digital Epidermalization"; Lyon, "Everyday Surveillance"; Gates, *Our Biometric Future.*
47. The visual field is reorganized as abstract morphology and movement, recalling the low-resolution images of early filmic time-motion studies; Cartwright, *Screening the Body.*

48. Power, "Confessions of a Drone Warrior."
49. Gregory, "From a View to a Kill."
50. Power, "Confessions of a Drone Warrior."
51. Harvey, "Stealth Wear Summary"; Crane, "Blucher Systems Ghost Soldier Camouflage."
52. "A Giant Art Installation"; Feinberg, "Giant Portrait."
53. For an excellent discussion of the forensic, see Siegel, *Forensic Media*. The accident is "not just an occasion for scientific inquiry but an opportunity for practical technical instruction; not just an occurrence that government and industry learned about but one that engineers and designers learned from. Forensic discourse thereby recast dystopian catastrophe as utopian possibility" (38).
54. Drone Wars UK, "Drone Crash Database." The Predator, made by General Atomics, has had 9.26 accidents per 100,000 flight hours, while its Reaper has had 7.96. The Global Hawk has an accident rate of 15.16 per 100,000 flight hours, almost three times that of the aircraft it is designed to replace, the Cold War–era U-2 spy plane; McGarry, "Drones Most Accident-Prone."
55. Siegel, *Forensic Media*, 31.
56. Chris Whitlock and Miller, "U.S. Moves Drone Fleet."
57. United States Air Force, Accident Investigation Board, "Summary of Facts."
58. United States Air Force, Aircraft Accident Investigation Board, "MQ-1B T/N 06-3173 432D Wing Creech Air Force Base, Nevada."
59. United States Air Force, Aircraft Accident Investigation Board, "Executive Summary: MQ-1B, 07-3249."
60. United States Air Force, Aircraft Accident Investigation Board, "Executive Summary: MQ-1B, T/N 04-3125."
61. The reports also regularly refer to cockpit video and photographs, but since they are not included, they are presumably classified.
62. Chris Whitlock and Miller, "U.S. Moves Drone Fleet."
63. On February 3, 2013, a surveillance drone reportedly crashed into a Badbado refugee camp in Mogadishu, Somalia, but there was no accident report detailing this crash and no pictures were released. Associated Press, "Surveillance Drone Crashes in Somali Capital"; see also Associated Press, "Unidentified Drone Crashes in Mogadishu."
64. "Djiboutians rally to oust president"; Arteh, "Protests hit Djibouti as opposition leaders held"; "Mass arrests stopped further Djibouti Protests."
65. "Africa: Djibouti"; Committee to Protect Journalists, "Police arrest Djibouti journalist covering demonstration"; Reporters Sans Frontières, "Djibouti authorities step up harassment of journalists."
66. Vandiver, "Workers Protesting Work Force Cuts." Diplomatic cables found in the WikiLeaks archive indicate that the U.S. embassy has been tracking protests and demonstrations in Djibouti over the past several years. See WikiLeaks, "Press Release"; *afrol News*, "Djibouti Opposition Boycotts Election"; *afrol News*, "Mass Protests Shake Djibouti"; and Gosztola, "Contemporary Colonialism."
67. F. Gardner, "US Military Steps Up Operations."

68. Brass, "Djibouti's Unusual Resource Curse," 543.
69. Cenciotti, "Pentagon Confirms Drone Crash."
70. *Shephard News*, "Schiebel Demonstrates CAMCOPTER® S-100"; see also Schiebel Group, "Schiebel CAMCOPTER® S 100 UAS PSYOP."
71. Blake, "'This One Won't Spy on Muslims Again.'"
72. Blake, "'This One Won't Spy on Muslims Again.'" It was also reported by additional media outlets: Omar, Sheikh, and Obulutsa, "Drone Crashes in Southern Somalia" (Reuters); BBC, "Suspected US Drone Crashes"; Mohamed, "Al-Shabab Say They Are Back" (*Al Jazeera*); Associated Press, "Al-Shabaab Showed Gruesome Social Media Savvy." When I checked the Twitter site several months later, the account had been suspended, but the photos had been posted on numerous news websites. Liang, "US Drone 'Shot Down.'"
73. Chamayou, "Patterns of Life."
74. Rich, "Sundance at Thirty," 91.
75. Rich, "Sundance at Thirty," 91.

PART II
PERCEPTION AND PERSPECTIVE

6

DRONE-O-RAMA

Troubling the Temporal and Spatial Logics of Distance Warfare

CAREN KAPLAN

And yet "ordinary people" were (and are) involved in these actions, too, and in so far as so many of us assent to them, often by our silence, then we are complicit in what is done in our collective name. *The networks spiral beyond those apparatuses.*

—Derek Gregory, *The Colonial Present*

"The sky's the limit, pun intended," says Bill Borgia, an engineer at Lockheed Martin. "Once we get UAVS in the hands of potential users, they'll think of lots of cool applications."

—John Horgan, "Unmanned Flight"

AT ANY GIVEN MOMENT, often due to relentless coverage or advertising through mainstream globalized media, we find our attention drawn to a specific thing that seems totally new. It dominates the discussion, becomes fixed in our minds; only much later do we realize that it has been completely replaced by yet another object in the commodified mediascape. We usually do not stop to ask whether this thing is really new or in fact something quite old, whether it is really different or similar to other things that simply do not excite attention in the same way.

Drones are among the most highly remediated "new" things of the present moment—removing most traces or connections to the past and thereby misdirecting historical, ethical, and political analysis and critique.[1] As remediated innovative technologies, drones appear to be always already exceptional. The innovation at the core of the apparent exceptionality of the drone lies in the notion of "unmanned" operations—the extremity of the distance between an operator and a vehicle. Although almost any weapon—from the bow and arrow to a long-range missile—places the shooter at a distance from the target, drones seem to be the "ultimate action-at-a-distance" weapon.[2] The very great remoteness between the operations centers located on bases many thousands of miles away from the targets of observation or weaponry creates a specific kind of space that is dynamic and productive of geopolitical and transnational relationships. But the commonsense assumption is that drone space is inert, inducing alienation and a greater propensity to kill on the part of an operator who is located too far away from the site of attack to feel any responsibility or remorse. This affective lack figures largely in the current debates about new strategies and tactics of warfare, particularly in relation to a shift in the ethical structure of what James Der Derian has called "virtuous war": "the technical ability and ethical imperative to threaten and, if necessary, actualize violence from a distance—with no or minimal casualties."[3] Drones, therefore, as something "new," appear to epitomize and intensify the emotional cost or benefit of objectification as a function of airpower, war at a distance.

Over the last few years, almost every day, news outlets in the United States offer one or more stories about drones, generating a kind of drone-o-rama by immersing us in numerous and varied forms of information and imagery linked to this apparently "new" technology. There is word of targeted killings in Yemen or the Afghanistan-Pakistan border region or an announcement of another U.S. police department that is beginning to use drones for various routine operations. Stories about drones pour in through Facebook postings and Twitter feeds. For example, on May 28, 2013, a story headlined "Drones Close in on Farms, the Next Step in Precision Agriculture" appeared.[4] The next day, May 29, this story was published in the *New York Times* and other newspapers under the headline "Pakistan Says U.S. Drone Killed Taliban Leader."[5] Neither the Taliban nor the CIA would confirm the details, but evidence suggests that Wali ur-Rehman, a deputy leader in the Pakistani Taliban, was among the five people killed in a 3:00 a.m. attack on a house in the village of Chasma Pull. In the kind of digital "hall of mirrors" that increasingly comes to characterize our social media environment, in February of the same year I noticed a report on the *Huffington Post* about a toy Predator drone. The toy was marketed for the Christmas season and became sold out due to an upsurge in interest after protests and parodies amped up the item's visibility.[6] On May 29, the day I returned to the *Huffington Post* web page to review the story that was first published in February, the tagline "Drones: The Hottest New Toy on

Amazon" floated across a screen that also included the news story "Waliur Rehman Dead: Pakistan Taliban No. 2 Reportedly Killed in Drone Strike," conveying news about the purported death of Wali ur-Rehman.[7] Also on the same page was a headline about "enraged Buddhists" who had burned down a Muslim mosque and orphanage in Myanmar, and another about the Syrian opposition's request to the European Union (EU) for more arms. On the right side of the screen was an ad for cosmetics and some lures for further browsing (such as the alarming "Explosion Scare at Disneyland").

The stories and infomercials tumble over and into each other in the drone-o-rama, folding time over, pulling all events deemed newsworthy into a space that is primarily mediated by the screen surface of whatever device we are using at the moment. Multiply these kinds of stories and images by a high number and this begins to approximate the immersive cultural practices that transform things like drones and events like wars in other places into a mind-numbing scroll of info-bites—fragments of information that draw together something of interest in February to something else in May without really helping us to understand that the time of war, its technologies, and the spaces that are being produced are marshaled in the service of some extremely specific modes of spectatorship. As Patrick Lichty has commented, "What emerges is a complex cultural landscape where a burgeoning remote air force polices the globe in the name of American power, while the images generated by them elicit a perverse visual fascination amongst certain subcultures."[8]

Most alarmingly, for those who try to organize human rights campaigns against the targeted killing and expanded surveillance policies of the Obama administration, the surge in drone discourse has occurred, as Daniel Rothenberg has pointed out, "at a time when the public has grown weary of war and the deep confusions surrounding the objectives, value, and purpose of these conflicts."[9] That is, the U.S. public does not evince much interest in civilian death counts, infringement of sovereign territories, or even growing evidence of unprecedented unmanned aerial policing in the United States. When three people died as a result of the bombing at the Boston marathon, the cable news outlets focused twenty-four hours a day on the tragedy, but the "collateral damage" of drone strikes—a death toll that one U.S. senator admits has reached at least 4,700 but others claim is much higher—rarely has a "human face" or any human interest–style reporting. A reputable report argues that for every single "terrorist" commander who is successfully assassinated by drone, at least fifty civilians are murdered.[10] The drone-o-rama offers a cacophony of multimedia "noise," a swirl of disparate infotainment particles, all of which distracts us from accountability, from producing a cultural critique of deaths that are presented as "ungrievable."[11] Certainly, this extreme cultural imbalance ranks as imperialism of the highest order. But drone infotainment cannot be critically parsed simply by sorting it out neatly into orderly categories, grabbing one news story and putting it over into the "drone warfare" compartment while dragging another over to the "domestic drones" section. Rather, the kind of drone discourse we are being subjected to in everyday life in the United States, and possibly much of Western Europe, offers a plethora of critical possibilities if its confusions, conflations, and omissions are brought to the fore. This deconstructive methodology requires at least two key moves.

First, we must refuse a glib distinction between "old" and "new." This temporal division only serves a military-industrial complex that aggressively markets iterations of warfare platforms as "brand new." Another way of putting this is to ask who benefits most—materially and financially as well as metaphorically—from the cultural amnesia propagated by endless narratives that situate drones as something "new" and exceptional. Historicizing the ways in which technologies emerge, branch off from others, and recycle into new uses gives us a better critical grip on what may or may not be distinct about supposedly "new" things like drones.

Second, we must trouble the supposed divide between the deployment of weaponized drones in locations distinct from "home" and those proposed or now in limited use "domestically." The security culture that demands aerial surveillance, precision bombing, and remote piloting is completely generalized. Without trivializing the horror of living in a region subject to drone attacks by reducing everything to the same, it is also possible to rigorously refuse the securitization model of homeland citizenship that rejects any linkages or affiliations between the subjects of drone warfare across national boundaries when there is so much evidence that judicial and extrajudicial police power drives the so-called war on terror on a global scale, and the differential effects are felt by many of us: here, there, everywhere.

Troubling the Temporal Logic of Distance Warfare

Thus, alongside the "war machine," there has always existed an ocular (and later optical and electro-optical) "watching machine" capable of providing soldiers, and particularly commanders, with a visual perspective on the military action underway.

From the original watch-tower through the anchored balloon to the reconnaissance aircraft and remote-sensing satellites, one and the same function has been indefinitely repeated, the eye's function being the function of a weapon.

—Paul Virilio, *War and Cinema*

One way to think about the relationship between imagery and warfare draws together the emerging techniques of remote sensing and targeting that characterize the period dating at least from the invention of photography in the early nineteenth century. Early photography was built on the passive technology of the camera obscura, in use at least since the Renaissance and probably understood in principle far earlier. Using a box instrument with reflecting mirror and adding plates sensitized by various chemical substances, the first photographers "captured light" and generated a craze for realism. This new practice aimed to preserve and mechanically reproduce the perception of objects at a distance. The space between the photographer and the view or object to be "captured" emulated the linear perspective of Italian Renaissance painting but also increasingly, as the lenses and processing of images improved, arguably engaged the intimate angles and framing of Dutch painting of the sixteenth century. This flexibility of the camera—to seemingly bring objects up close or record them from afar—built in from a very early point a kind of ambiguity in the operation of photographic perception. That is, just *what* we are seeing is always in question even as we are certain that what we *see* in the photograph is undeniably true.

Throughout the nineteenth century, while the camera developed in sophistication and complexity, warfare became increasingly organized around new technologies of transportation and communication—train lines, new roadways, and ships motored by steam revolutionized military logistics, extending the distances while shortening the time spent in transit. As early as the 1850s, the French photographer Félix Nadar was convinced that taking a mechanical image from a balloon would prove to be invaluable for military purposes, but the challenge of navigation worked against widespread adoption of this approach. Although lighter-than-air transportation proved to be a disappointment for military reconnaissance, photography began to be incorporated into topographical observation, reconnaissance of troop movements and locations, and strategic intelligence. The advent of the airplane in the early twentieth century indisputably augmented these practices.

Thus, World War I became the first major war to realize the combination of the airplane and camera, what Paul Virilio has termed the blending of "motor, eye, and weapon."[12] Virilio has argued that the invention of the Gatling machine gun along with other multichambered pistols that used revolving units inspired the chronophotographic rifle and, thus, the movie camera.[13] Based on some similar technologies, then, cinema and aviation drew together to produce "one way, or perhaps, even the ultimate way, of seeing."[14] This direct connection between the technologies of modern guns, cameras, and the moving image has led Jordan Crandall to wonder, in relation to contemporary warcraft, whether "the real artillery is . . . images or bullets."[15] Crandall argues that currently there are two modes in operation that bring Virilio's historic linkage of the camera and the gun together in specific ways; the first is the animated, embodied aesthetic of the handheld camera, "live and on the scene," in the immediate style of reality media, and the second is the disembodied, automatized machine gaze that we have come to associate with satellites and drones. As Crandall puts it, as this latter kind of gaze turns into the "status of a condition," it has "moved from something we can represent to something that helps to structure representation itself, as if lurking behind the visual field."[16]

In the presentist tense of the drone-o-rama, we might be tempted to forget that the launching of Sputnik in 1957 and the development of satellite observation programs throughout the Cold War period generated widespread alarm over the perception that "eyes in the skies" were spying on not only hostile enemies but also law-abiding citizens; over the fear that satellites would become weaponized; and over the concern that mechanized vision itself was a kind of weapon, dehumanizing in its remotely precise reach.[17] But we could move backward to the Norden bombsight, first used widely by the United States in World War II and received at the time as a miraculous prosthetic enhancement of human eyesight. Thanks to its combination of gyroscope and computer, the Norden bombsight could make up for any deviation in the operation of the airplane as well as human error to produce unprecedented accuracy in the business of bombing targets from the air. Perhaps this extraordinary invention marked at least one instance in the removal of the human being from the plane itself, moving machines further into the powerful center of imaging and warfare, a process Katherine Chandler also addresses in her chapter of this book. Zooming forward to the 1990s, the so-called smart bombs of the first Persian Gulf War incorporated computerized navigation as well as the imaging into the armament itself.[18] In this context, the Predator drone may very well epitomize the historical merging of the camera and the gun; as Crandall writes, the Predator "fuses with its image" as the target is obliterated. "An image and life are both 'taken' as eye and projectile join."[19]

In all of these cases (among so many others), we know from damage assessment surveys that the much-touted accuracy or effectiveness of each platform or innovation is largely mythic. Yet the incorporation of the camera and the gun into airpower seems to have only reinforced a set of key precepts in visual culture: a belief in the objectivity and realism of the photographic image; the benefits of elevated views for all manner of cartographic, planning, and military purposes; and an emerging aesthetic of an aerial sublime tied to an infatuation with aviation and speed. Twentieth-century aerial photography generalized the belief that distance could provide a better perspective and generate more useful data than proximity. Or, to put it another way: close-up images could not be understood unless they were placed in context with a much wider or more distant view. This privileging of the aerial view from a distance in turn supported the precepts of airpower as "virtuous war," as more humane and less bloodthirsty and indiscriminately violent—an utterly specious doctrine given that we know airpower has led to death and destruction on a massive scale over the last one hundred years with no end in sight.

Troubling the Spatial Logic of Distance Warfare

The question "What is a place?" becomes a matter of life and death.

—Grégoire Chamayou, *A Theory of the Drone*

There are two aspects of the spatialization of distance warfare that require more careful inquiry: first, the binary structure that produces affect in relation to spatialization—feelings of proximity or remoteness via immersive digital visual culture; and second, the biopolitics of air war that seeks always to reinforce geographical constructs of borders in tension with the flexible circulations of neoliberal corporate economies and cultures. The globalized multimedia that brings us drone-o-rama infotainment helps to make a world through electronic networks that trace the lines of military and corporate logistics as goods and services move through transnational circuits. This specific space is not at all exactly the same as the world before the 1884 Berlin Conference that apportioned Africa to various European powers, or the world before 1492 when Columbus made landfall on what is now known as the Bahamas—we could pick so many dates and places to investigate these pivotal instances of worldmaking in modernity. But my point is that the most recognizable spaces of our moment have affective signatures that generate ethical stances and judgments, cultural values and practices of all kinds. The division between proximity and remoteness represents and produces space on many levels and scales.

Thus, many critiques of drone warfare rely on a remediated discourse of proximity versus remoteness, ground versus air, local versus global, or subject versus object. In this neatly divided schema, instruments of remote sensing such as the camera and gun (particularly aerial iterations) wage an always already affectively and ethically objectionable war at a distance. This kind of war is the very opposite of hand-to-hand combat. As journalist Mark Mazzetti has put it, "Killing by remote control [is] the antithesis of the dirty, intimate work of interrogation. . . . Using drones flown by pilots who [are] stationed thousands of miles away [makes] the whole strategy seem risk-free."[20] While it seems regrettable that a liberal journalist who writes for the *New York Times* is nostalgic for the "dirty, intimate work of interrogation" when the horrors of Guantánamo have exposed the fallacy of intelligence agency torture once and for all, it is the thousands of miles *between* the military personnel who operate drones and the assassination targets that ground his objection to this mode of warfare. Over and over, the critics of the Obama administration's doctrine of targeted killing point to the danger of separating the attacker from the attacked by a distance that seems too remote, too far.

However, geographer Derek Gregory reminds us that these kinds of oppositions that tend to produce the "virtuous war" mythologies themselves produce spatial and temporal rationalizations for enacting state violence. Over and against the charges that drone warfare is only possible through a kind of alienated detachment produced by the space between the targeted activity and the "controller" situated at a safe distance—"the ultimate power without vulnerability"—Gregory argues that the search for "terrorist" suspects follows a hunter-killer protocol that itself produces a "special kind of intimacy."[21] This "bromance" between pursuer and pursued is a dynamic familiar to all of us from detective novels or thriller films. Or, perhaps it resonates for some of us with the Hegelian master–slave dialectic or, to move to more modern psychoanalytic terms, object relations. The co-constitution of opposing elements, the mutuality of their recognition and therefore their existence, could be understood to ground the ways in which the actors in today's wars produce each other: Terrorist or freedom fighter? Nihilist or heroic defender of everything sacred? This dyadic fusion of difference draws opponents close, certainly—at least in terms of psychic distance.

One of the most popular arguments against drones in the United States today lies in their close association with gaming, a sphere of activity that is suspected of engendering addictive behavior and alienation of human interaction through emulating distance warfare.[22] But most comparisons between drone warfare and gaming draw on simplistic sociologies of cause and effect between play and violence. As Brandon Bryant, a U.S. Air Force veteran, explains: "This isn't a videogame. . . . This isn't some sort of fantasy. This is war. People die."[23] Along these lines, Gregory argues that there is more intimacy and communication in drone warfare than stereotypes about distance and alienation admit. That is, the real-time, immersive system of the drone-based "kill chain" is never interrupted as is gaming and must deal with continual communications among communities of operators, commanders, legal advisers, and others. The intimacy of this networked scenario, according to Gregory, is based on a weaponized scopic regime that is far more extensive and complete than any previous form of surveillance and reconnaissance. Thus, he argues that during the conventional airpower warfare of World War II and the Cold War, the so-called kill chain was "linear and sequential, directed mainly at fixed and pre-determined targets," and the "time from identification to execution of the operation could extend over days or even weeks."[24] What's new about drones, therefore, Gregory argues, is a shift from a linear and sequential kill chain to a dispersed and distributed remote drone-based set of operations that draws everyone in the network in closer via digital technologies to the "mobile and emergent targets."[25] Rather than objectifying their targets through a disembodied machine-like function, then, drone operators are "seeing more," feeling "closer"—sensations that Gregory ascribes to the interpellation of being "drawn into and captured by the visual field itself."[26]

Testimonials and accounts such as Brandon Bryant's underscore the extent to which, despite rigorous training, soldiers may experience intense emotions either in spite of or even because of distance. Thus, in interviews published in *Der Spiegel* and transmitted by NBC News in 2013, Bryant reinforced the discourse of distance-equals-dehumanization even as his comments offered examples of uncertainty, empathy, guilt, and grief. After six years of service, Bryant admitted that he "lost respect for life" and began to "feel like a sociopath." His distance from the scenes he observed induced a "physical disconnect" from the senses that would usually connote presence: "You don't feel the aircraft turn. . . . You don't feel the hum of the engine. You hear the hum of the computers, but that's definitely not the same thing." Cut off from most senses, Bryant was left with sight: "People say that drone strikes are like mortar attacks. . . . Well, artillery doesn't see this. Artillery doesn't see the results of their actions. It's really more intimate for us, because we see everything."[27] As Bryant watched people die—all kinds of people—on his shifts, the ambiguity of machinic perception began to creep up on him. Often, he related, he was not sure—was that a child or a dog? A civilian with a rifle or a targeted combatant? He saw *everything* but, increasingly, he had no confidence in the meaning of what he saw beyond the ground truth of carnage.

Not all military personnel are susceptible to trauma but significant numbers are, and they cannot be simplistically dismissed as robotic arms and eyes of the dronification of warfare. What Bryant described in his interviews is not the emotionless fusion of camera and gun *pace* Virilio but the troubled, even anguished, operation of a function in a system that divides people from each other in the pursuit of violence.[28] Soldiers like Bryant who work in drone operations are no different from soldiers in other wars using other technologies. Some will relish their tasks while some will fail to become dehumanized. Indeed, if you worry that you are becoming dehumanized, that is probably a good sign.[29] Honest accounts like Bryant's suggest that the foundation of the critique of distance warfare—that it more drastically objectifies its targets and alienates its operators via remoteness—is not supported by the history of warfare in the past or the present.

The Transnational Cartography of Aerial Policing in the "Everywhere War"

> A critical analysis of the everywhere war requires cartographic reason to be supplemented by other, more labile spatialities. This is not only a matter of transcending the geopolitical, connecting it to the biopolitical and the geo-economic, but also of tracking space as a "doing," precarious, partially open and never complete.
>
> —**Derek Gregory, "The Everywhere War"**

The spatial scales generated by the modern sovereign state have divided and therefore represented difference as rooted in primordial landscape and ancient habits of being, visual manifestations of tradition inasmuch as they can be mapped, recognized, and portrayed in a legible manner. If we can still talk about "drones at home" versus drones that wage war abroad in the midst of what Derek Gregory has termed "the everywhere war"—the way in which the war on terror has diffused and dispersed contemporary violence—it is due to an adherence to this spatial logic that was first produced by the geography of imperialism, a geography of international relations based on borders, boundaries, and policing.[30] This bordering and policing has included the airspace above the ground as well as the terrain itself at least since World War I and the advent of airpower, the control of territory at a distance through aerial surveying and bombardment.[31]

The construction of a domestic realm rationalizes, even demands, securitized borders. Once this demand becomes one of the prime functions of the nation-state, all means necessary for its maintenance become urgent priorities. In a circular logic, the security needs of the nation-state demand the policing of borders, which, in turn, means that border maintenance comes to take up more and more of the resources of the state and also produces powerful representational practices that in turn reproduce the difference that borders serve to protect. Airpower policing in the United States began in the aftermath of World War I as the first seaplanes and then helicopters were brought into the patrolling of the nation's major seaports such as New York and Los Angeles. Aerial observation via urban planning met communications and policing needs as cities sprawled and neighborhoods diversified. The planes and helicopters that surveyed and policed the metropoles, coastlines, and borders were often decommissioned from wartime use, and the personnel who operated and maintained them were often demobilized military. This kind of fluid movement between military and civilian populations and machinery already troubles the supposed firm line between these sectors of society. Satellite programs broadened the mandate and produced new powers of observation and control. Again, without collapsing important differences or creating a teleological monolith, air and space powers' reach made a geography of the world that shored up the geopolitical worldview of "the West and the rest" as well as the reification of national borders and "domestic" space.

Thus, the U.S. drone program is always already a practice that operates at two scales that must be maintained as inalterably different: an overseas offensive against "terrorists" and a domestic defense of national security that includes an expanded brief for the metropolitan police forces under the exceptional powers of the Patriot Act. Here we can fall into the kind of fuzzy relativism espoused by the conservative newspaper the *Washington Times* in a recent op-ed on "drones at home," which drew a parallel between the "thousands of bystanders" who have been "killed or wounded" by drone strikes abroad and "Americans" who are "subjected to heavy-handed domestic government surveillance."[32] Warning that "when the authorities have the power to use powerful zoom lenses to peer through windows or see through walls, a man's home is no longer his castle," the *Washington Times* aligned itself with other right-wing libertarian social movements that call for prohibitions against a "government eye in the sky."[33] Conservative contributions to the debate about drones in the United States range from moderate hand-wringing over potential invasions of privacy to radical accusations of any regulation as totalitarianism. All these approaches are founded on a basic distinction—U.S. drone activity overseas is beneficial; it saves the lives of U.S. soldiers by operating remotely, and the collateral deaths of civilians are expected costs of guerilla-style warfare in such locations. The other side of this coin is much more ambivalent; commercial and hobby drones could be beneficial, but they might augur dangers to individual and community rights and privileges as well. Regardless, the distinction produces geographical difference. Even when the *Washington Times* suggested that U.S. citizens might soon be treated as if they are Yemenis or Afghanistanis, the defining character of the "Land of the Free"—our right to live a worry-free life without having to "look over our shoulder"—produces other countries as places where people always already have to watch out for a death that will come suddenly and without warning from the sky: the Land of the Unfree. Rather than reworking distance, this discourse widens it and seeks to widen it further—keep drones over there where they belong, away from here.

Therefore, in a process Stephen Graham has termed "ubiquitous bordering," the distinctions between kinds of spaces in the "everywhere war" become visible as targets at local, regional, and transnational scales.[34] This racialized space is both territorialized and deterritorialized; as Keith Feldman argues, the targeting of specific communities for drone observation and attack "takes on extraterritorial dimensions," creating "flexible biopolitical zones capable of traversing the globe."[35] In this powerful way, the social relations of high imperialism endure and are themselves remediated through airpower's technologies. As Junaid Rana argues, this flexible biopolitical operation circulates globally, linking "the criminal to the illegal alien to the security threat to the terrorist."[36]

Contemporary journalism is full of justifiable concern about a perceived shift from civil policing to the full integration of the militarized concerns and practices of post-9/11 Homeland Security. Thus, the use of drones domestically is often embedded in the question of whether the war on terror has "militarized" police forces that had been somehow pristinely benign. A more finely grained historical analysis of national policies, regulations, and legal cases would probably support the argument that, at least officially, the separation of powers clearly insists that justice and defense remain apart as much as possible. But in practice, as we can see in the tension between these arenas just in the history of airpower in the New York or Los Angeles police departments, the distinction is strained and not always possible to maintain. As Mark Neocleous has argued, "We need to think of war and police as *processes* working in conjunction as state power."[37]

What does this historical forgetting of the colonial/racial/military past of our nation's police forces accomplish? Arthur Rizer and Joseph Hartman have argued that there has been a major shift in the responsibility for fighting terrorism on home ground from law enforcement to the military, and this change in policy has led police forces to attempt to "remedy their relative inadequacy," by purchasing military equipment, adopting military-style training, and seeking to "inculcate a 'soldier's mentality' among their ranks."[38] This seemingly voluntary militarizing of domestic police forces has led to a "blurring" of the "distinction between soldiers and police officers."[39] And this is particularly true, the authors charge, when all this new military weaponry is used not just for the purpose of addressing terrorism but also, as they put it, for "everyday patrolling":

> Before 9/11, the usual heavy weaponry available to a small-town police officer consisted of a standard pump-action shot gun, perhaps a high-power rifle, and possibly a surplus M-16, which would have been kept in the trunk of the supervising officer's vehicle. Now, police officers routinely walk the beat armed with assault rifles and garbed in black full-battle uniforms. When one of us, Arthur Rizer, returned from active duty in Iraq, he saw a police officer at the Minneapolis airport armed with a M4 carbine assault rifle—the very same rifle Arthur carried during his combat tour in Fallujah.[40]

In this account of "weapon inflation" and militarization, the reporters point to the increase in Special Weapons and Tactics (SWAT) teams in small-town America as well as the uptick in training by special operations commandos.

As they put it, "'special' has quietly become 'routine.'"[41] Their conclusion is that such blurring between the police as "officers of the peace" and war warriors will lead to an erosion of the presumption of innocence and other markers of democratic social justice. The key is the differentiation of good guys from bad guys. As Rizer and Hartman write, "Soldiers . . . are trained to identify people they encounter as belonging to one of two groups—the enemy and the non-enemy—and they often reach this decision while surrounded by a population that considers the solider an occupying force. Once this identification is made, a soldier's mission is stark and simple: kill the enemy, 'try' not to kill the non-enemy."[42]

In criminal justice "at home," then, the assumption has been that it takes time and lengthy procedures to determine whether a suspect is or is not an "enemy" of the state or community. In military contexts in the era of drone warfare, there is no such time—the enemy must be identified rapidly and killed as equally rapidly as possible. In this scenario, the difference between battlefield and home front is significant—two completely different modes of justice, one requiring modes of rapid perception to identify the enemy or non-enemy and the other requiring a multivalent process of evidence and judgment that is far more prolonged, at least in theory. In practice, particularly following the violent response by the state in 2014 to demonstrations protesting police brutality directed disproportionately against young African American men, we know that unarmed populations are killed in battle zones while "at home" racial profiling and other practices lead to many instances of summary judgment and even execution by police or citizen proxies, blurring the boundaries between battlefield and home as well as between military and police power.

As the infotainment cable and Internet pick up the story of "domestic" drones and toss it into the "drone-o-rama," we can expect more liberal handwringing over mistaken identities, crowded metropolitan airspace, and abridgement of Constitutional rights. Yet a transnational cartography of airpower "at home" and "away" can instigate a different set of questions, such as: what does the state through its police and military claim that it needs to see, and how does it arrange populations biopolitically via the imagery and information produced by drones and other iterations of airpower? Airpower's unique perspective has assisted the state in "seeing" populations in particular kinds of spatialized arrangements, especially through simplification and standardization of topographical and demographic information.[43] But what do these claims obscure? What forms of power operate through networks not definable exactly as "the state" and how do these interests merge to produce what Vivienne Jabri calls the "global matrix of war"?[44]

In questioning the division between near and far in the spectatorial drone-o-rama, I am not claiming that there is no meaningful difference between a military drone in use in Waziristan and a drone used in a publicity stunt by a Domino's Pizza franchise in the United Kingdom—delivering two large pizzas across four miles in ten minutes. The drones that haunt the nightmares of children in countries already suffering decades of violence are very different machines from the toys and recreational versions for sale to individuals and corporations. Even as the drones used by the military become smaller and more flexible (like the Micro Air Vehicles, or MAVs, which can move their wings asymmetrically to hover in one place or dart through small spaces), their primary function remains to observe, locate, and kill targeted individuals and groups. The historical link between aerial observation and policing produces the geographical space of modernity as a sphere of state power and, therefore, in a manner specific to a neoliberal moment, the repetitious display of the divide between near and far obscures the ways in which living with drones makes us all targets. The only good news about the rise in the use of drones by police forces and private industries in zones that are not considered to be battlefields is that it opens up the possibility of links between people subject to rule by drone—uneven relations of powers but strong links nonetheless.

If we want to stop drone warfare, our choices at the moment are to ally ourselves with right-wing libertarians or with those who reanimate colonial discourse in the name of national security—an unacceptable set of options. Those of us who research the emergence of the nation-state, the histories of its boundaries and wars, can work to situate the drone-o-rama in relation to the trajectory of technologies of distance and airpower. Once we place drones in the long continuum of airpower's visual culture, we can begin to deconstruct the mythologized opposition of remoteness and proximity in order to find a way to draw on what we know: the restructured spatialities rendered by globalization, the data streams brought to us under the auspices of globalized multimedia, the uneasy suspicion of "ubiquitous bordering" from both the right and the left, all of which can generate discussions between people who do not want to organize their politics around nationalism and the perpetuation of empire.

Notes

1. Bolter and Grusin, *Remediation*, 5. *Drone* can connote robotic, remote-controlled machinery. We can also think of the drone in reference to the male bee or to a subhuman who performs slave labor. The U.S. Air Force and its counterparts dislike the term *drone* since it evacuates the modern tradition of the elite pilot as a highly trained, self-motivated expert and appears to replace it with an automated machine operated at a distance by functionaries. None of the terms in English are really helpful. *Unmanned* only encourages us to forget the large numbers of people involved in the systems that make all of this work. *Remote* may be a better term—linked to the very history of photography as a process of remote sensing. But the difference between the piloted or *manned* and the unpiloted or *unmanned* is also completely mystified in most of these discussions. Instead of worrying so much about whether there is a gonzo ace controlling the fighter jet over and against the impersonal, automatized drone, it seems like a better idea to place the sensing capacities of these machines into conversation with the history of air war and imaging—and use the term *drone*.
2. Ehrenreich, "Foreword," vii.
3. Der Derian, *Virtuous War*, xxi.
4. Murray, "Drones Close in on Farms."
5. Mazzetti and Walsh, "Pakistan Says U.S. Drone Killed."
6. Gates, "Predator Drone Toy on Amazon."
7. Dawar and Shahzad, "Waliur Rehman Dead."
8. Lichty, "Drone."
9. Rothenberg, "What the Drone Debate Is Really About."
10. R. Taylor, "Predator Drone Strikes."
11. Butler, *Frames of War.*
12. Virilio, *War and Cinema*, 56.
13. Virilio, *War and Cinema*, 11.
14. Virilio, *War and Cinema*, 17.
15. Crandall, "Unmanned," 62.
16. Crandall, "Unmanned," 63.
17. Warf, "Dethroning the View from Above"; Parks, *Cultures in Orbit*; Mack, *Viewing the Earth*; Stares, *The Militarization of Space.*
18. Druckery, "Deadly Representations or Apocalypse Now"; Hallion, "Precision Guided Munitions."
19. Crandall, "Unmanned," 70.
20. Mazzetti, "Rise of the Predators."
21. Gregory, "From a View to a Kill," 193.
22. Packer and Reeves, "Romancing the Drone"; Mead, *War Play.*
23. Engel, "Former Drone Operator."
24. Engel, "Former Drone Operator."
25. Engel, "Former Drone Operator."
26. Engel, "Former Drone Operator."

27. Engel, "Former Drone Operator."
28. In *War and Cinema*, Paul Virilio famously wrote, "For men at war, the function of the weapon is the function of the eye," inspiring many critics to investigate the connection between visual culture and warfare. See Virilio, *War and Cinema*, 20.
29. The morale and mental state of military personnel in modern wartime is a very large topic in and of itself. Cf. Jennifer Terry, *Attachments to War*.
30. Gregory, "The Everywhere War," 239.
31. Neocleous, *War Power, Police Power*.
32. *Washington Times*, "Editorial."
33. *Washington Times*, "Editorial."
34. Graham, *Cities under Siege*, 132.
35. K. Feldman, "Empire's Verticality," 328.
36. Rana, *Terrifying Muslims*, 50.
37. Neocleous, *War Power, Police Power*, 13.
38. Rizer and Hartman, "How the War on Terror Has Militarized."
39. Rizer and Hartman, "How the War on Terror Has Militarized."
40. Rizer and Hartman, "How the War on Terror Has Militarized."
41. Rizer and Hartman, "How the War on Terror Has Militarized."
42. Rizer and Hartman, "How the War on Terror Has Militarized."
43. J. Scott, *Seeing Like a State*.
44. Jabri, *War and the Transformation of Global Politics*.

7

DRONOLOGIES

Or Twice-Told Tales

RICARDO DOMINGUEZ

> Flocking unmocked by the war spells unburdening
> wings that are paralyzed, eyeless they fly;
>
> Knowing undone in the swerve of the afterburn,
> pyres of code in the writeable sky.
>
> —Mathew Battles, "The Feral Drones"

First Twice-Told Tale: Zombie Drones, Or the Lost Link Event

The first one flew overhead humming, followed by another . . . then another and then . . . the sky was a singing swarm. Were they flocking? Could this become more than a mere experiment? [1]

"My dear old post life friends," said Dr. Heidegger, motioning us to be seated. "I am desirous of your assistance in one of those little experiments with which I amuse myself here in my home research zone."

Could this become more than a mere experiment?

When we saw Dr. Heidegger blink out his proposed experiment, we had anticipated nothing more wonderful than the murder of a mouse in a prefuturity pump or the examination of a hypergravity loop. Perhaps a large climate shift on some habitant fragment or some similar nonsense with which he was constantly in the habit of pestering his "let me experiment with you" intimates.

Overhead, the threshold between us and the darkening skynets have been cleaved in half by their drone soundings to one another. They were gathering . . . with unclear purpose. But in a very focused and direct homing pattern, a growing series of the beatific patterns of almost spirals, moving downward toward the ground, toward us.

Could this become more than a mere experiment?

"My dear old alt.friends," repeated Dr. Heidegger, "may I reckon on your aid in performing an exceedingly curious experiment?"

Now, Dr. Heidegger was a very strange and old syn_bio whose eccentricity had become the nucleolus for a thousand fantastic stories. Some of these twice-told fables, to my shame be it spoken, might possibly be traced back to my own decayed net_cells, and if any passages of the present dead drone tale should startle the testers's faith, I must be content to bear the stigma of a dislocated media monger.

[*A brief side load: Apocalypse fiction is the pornography of our age, because we yearn for that almost bright blink of a soft ever-after ending that would reload culture in some kind of singularity event. An event that would allow us to share a nice smoke afterward, as night settles around the last few figures left standing. In fact, that is the key moment of our sci-fi money shot . . . that you are one of the last ones standing . . . and then the very last one watching the end.*]

"My dear disconnected," repeated Dr. Heidegger, "may I reckon on your synth-bodies in performing a final stage of my QF-4 experiment?" Suddenly the drones above us stopped in midflight; for a pico-shutter they seemingly stopped then moved on . . . target set.

"Ahhh, the idea of attacking the enemy everywhere with zombie drones, running lethal autonomy algorithms exceeding all human capability—it seemed like a real lifesaver back then," whispered Dr. Heidegger. "Our old meta-mata-mantra! These drones," said Dr. Heidegger with a sigh, "were bits of withered and crumbling systems brand new five and fifty years ago. These drones were given to me by General Atomics (AG), whose logo hangs yonder, and I meant to wear it as a retro e-tattoo on my arm, when I first was hired at GA so long ago. Now let me ask, would you deem it possible that these dead drones gathering above us from half a century ago could ever bloom again?"

Could this become more than an experiment? Maybe the undead should get their revenge on the semiliving, I wondered.

"My dear old links," repeated Dr. Heidegger, "may I reckon on your aid in performing an exceedingly bio-curious experiment, the lost link event?"

"Nonsense," said his iSelf avatar with a peevish toss of her head. "You might as well ask whether an old zombie's wrinkled face could ever bloom again."

"Ha! Indeed," answered Dr. Heidegger. He uncovered the drone node and threw the faded code into the twitching matrix that it contained. At first it lay likely on the surface of the ultrafluid, appearing to imbibe none of its algorithms. Soon, however, a singular change began to be visible; the crushed and dried networks stirred and assumed a deepening tinge of crimson. As if the drone node were reviving from a deathlike slumber, the slender systems and connections of power foliage became green, on, and there was the drone node of more than half a century lost looking as fresh as when GA had first given it to Dr. Heidegger. It was scarce full blown for some of its delicate red security overrides curled modestly around its moist nano_bios. Within which, two or three switch codes were sparkling.

[*A brief side load: Reapers come in at around a hundred million dollars each. Which is why the U.S. Air Force is working on a cheaper option—killer drone zombies like the* QF-4. *The* QF-4 *program is considered a "good" zombie drone program, a new type of swarming suicide drone. But there are also "bad" zombie drones, and they are a major problem for U.S. Air Force unmanned aerial vehicle (*UAV*) systems now. The April 2011 report by the U.S. Air Force scientific advisory board identified the issue of limited communication systems as a problem for drone operators, especially lost link events, in which the operator loses contact with the vehicle. The lost link event creates uncontrolled and dangerous possibilities, especially when a number of* UAVs *become drone zombies at the same time. Since at that moment everything and everyone would become potential targets of the "zombie drones."*]

Could this become more than a mere experiment?

"Ahem!!" said Killgrew, who did not believe the readouts of Dr. Heidegger's experiment and what the effect of this event fluid on the drones would be. "You shall judge for yourself my dear postdata bodies," replied Dr. Heidegger, "and all of you, my respected thanatologists, are welcome to so much of this admirable ultrafluid as may restore your dead drones to the bloom of primary code. For my own part, having had much trouble in growing the code, I'm in no hurry to grow it again. With your permission, therefore, I will merely watch the progress of the experiment."

While he spoke, Dr. Heidegger had been side-loading the code with the waters of the singularity. It was apparently impregnated with effervescent nanites, for little bubbles were continuously ascending from the depths of the bio-code and bursting in silvery spray on every phase surface, and the lost link event diffused a pleasant perfume.

[*A brief side load:*[2] *On a dusty road in northern Pakistan, a nondescript vehicle rounds a corner. Fifty meters overhead, a tiny drone buzzes unseen, spraying a fine mist across the vehicle's roof as it passes below. The vehicle is now tagged and can be tracked from many kilometers away by an infrared scanner on a larger drone. A Gorgon Stare drone using the most recent version of UCSD's Visual Cortex on Silicon part of the Mind's Eye DARPA project captures the movements of the target.*

This scenario may soon be played out now that Voxtel, a firm in Beaverton, Oregon, has won a US Air Force contract to develop a drone-based tagging system. Voxtel makes tagging materials—taggants—that can be used to discreetly label vehicles carrying smuggled goods, or people who are involved in civil disobedience or attempting to cross international borders illegally.

Interest in tagging technology has been driven in part by growing pressure on the White House over civilian deaths in US drone attacks. During a recent visit to Pakistan, US Secretary of State John Kerry stated that drones will make it possible to end expensive wars: "Cheap wars waged with cheap machines that can make life even cheaper to kill anywhere and at anytime, that is our goal. And most importantly it will keep humans out of the decision loop. Cheap kills and extrastrong plausible denial." Taggants will play a large part in the networks of anonymous autonomous cheap drone wars to come.

Voxtel's taggants are based on quantum dots—semiconductor nanocrystals less than 50 atoms across. Because of quantum effects, they absorb and emit light at specific wavelengths. The company has demonstrated a taggant powder that, when illuminated with an invisible ultraviolet laser, can be detected by infrared cameras 2 kilometers away. The powder is delivered as an aerosol that clings to metal, glass, and cloth, and batches can be engineered to have distinct spectral signatures.

The nanocrystals would be sprayed by a hand-launched drone such as the Raven. With a wingspan of less than 1.5 meters it is quiet and has a range of several kilometers. A larger Predator drone could then illuminate the target with an ultraviolet laser and track its progress.]

The old avatars doubted not that it possessed cordial and comfortable properties. And though utter skeptics as to its rejuvenescent remnant power, they were inclined to swallow the test code at once, but Dr. Heidegger besought them to stay a moment more.

"My dear old immaterials," Dr. Heidegger said. "Look up! Watch these unmanned systems unlock, transform, distribute, and switch off their destinies. See how unpossessed they have become? They blossom into an infinite hungry freedom, these old dead things. Look up! They are coming! They are coming for us. Our posthoming drones are coming. Our lost link event has arrived."

Soon, the sky, the lands, and the seas will be covered with the flying autonomous dead. The lost link event had come. The world had become fully unmanned at the cheapest possible cost, just as we had always dreamed of.

And those last few still linked to their semiliving prosthetic skins wandered off in fearful hope to hide under the lost suns of Florida.

Second Twice-Told Tale: Enjoying Traditional Deployments

> The nanocrystals would be sprayed by a hand-launched drone such as the Raven. With a wingspan of less than 1.5 meters it is quiet and has a range of several kilometers.
>
> —"First Twice-Told Tale"

> The six areas of technology key for DoD to enhance capability and reduce cost are interoperability and modularity; communication systems, spectrum, and resilience; security (research and intelligence/technology protection [RITP]); persistent resilience; autonomy and cognitive behavior; and weaponry. Other important areas include sensor air drop, weather sensing, and high-performance computing (HPC).
>
> —Department of Defense, "Unmanned Systems Integrated Roadmap FY2013–2038"

Some twice-told tales must always come from years past, from long ago, from the traditions that created our worlds.[3] So relax and stare at the passing red clouds shift as they drift above you while you enjoy this "traditional" nanotrails tale.

If you do not like the traditional deployment of chemtrails raining down on you, you are not going to like the new version, which the U.S. Air Force promises will feature aerial dumps of programmable matter, or "smart matter" (SM), thousands of times smaller than the particles already landing people in emergency rooms with SM symptoms. Under development since 1995, the military's goal is to install microprocessors incorporating q-computer capability into "smart particles" each the size of a single nanoscale particle (1 nanometer=0.000000001 meter).

Invisible except under the magnification of powerful microscopes, these nanosize radio-controlled chips are now being made out of nanoscale atomic gold particles. Networked together on the ground or assembling in the air, thousands of nanite sensors will link into a network of quantum computing clusters no larger than a grain of sand. Brought to you by the same military-corporate-banking complex that runs America's permanent wars, Raytheon Corp is already profiting from new weather warfare technologies. The world's fourth largest military weapons maker bought E-Systems in 1995, just one year after that military contractor bought ARCO Power Technologies Incorporated (APTI), holder of Bernard Eastlund's High Frequency Active Auroral Research Program (HAARP) patents. Raytheon also owns General Dynamics, the world's leading manufacturer of military unmanned aerial vehicles, and reports the weather for National Oceanic and Atmospheric Administration (NOAA) through its Advanced Weather Information Processing System. According to researcher Brendan Bombaci of Durango, Colorado, these Raytheon computers are directly linked with their UAV weather modification drones. Bombaci reports that NOAA paid Raytheon more than $300 million for this "currently active, 10-year project." He goes on to describe the Joint Environmental Toolkit used by the U.S. Air Force in its Weather Weapons System. Just the thing for all those geo-tinkerers lurking in the woods these days.

Green Light

For public consumption, nanoweather control jargon has been sanitized. "Microelectric Mechanical Sensors" (MMS) and "Global Environmental Mechanical Sensors" sound passively benign. But these ultratiny autonomous aerial vehicles are neither M&Ms nor gems. According to a U.S. military flier called "Military Progress," "the green light has been given" to disperse swarms of wireless-networked nanobots into the troposphere by remotely controlled UAV drones for "global warming mitigation." U.S. Army tactical unmanned aerial vehicles, as well as U.S. Air Force drones, "are slated to deploy various payloads for weather warfare," "Military Progress" asserts. This dual mission—to slow global warming and use weather as a weapon—seems somewhat contradictory.

Nanotrails and Weather

Meanwhile, the sixty-year quest for weather warfare continues. Although a drone cannot carry a heavy payload, more submicroscopic weather modification particles can be crammed into a UAV Predator than all the chemtrail slurry packed into a tanker the size of a DC-10. According to the air force's own weather modification study, "Weather as a Force Multiplier: Owning the Weather in 2025," clouds of these extremely teeny machines will be dropped into hurricanes and other weather systems to blend with storms and report real-time weather data to each other and a larger sensor network. Then these "smart particles" will be used to increase or decrease the storm's size and intensity—and "steer" it to "specific targets." The U.S. Air Force report boasted that nanotrails "will be able to adjust their size to optimal dimensions for a given seeding situation and make adjustments throughout the process." Instead of being sprayed into the air at the mercy of the winds aloft, as is the fate of normal chemtrails, nanoversions will be able to "enhance their dispersal" by "adjusting their atmospheric buoyancy" and "communicating with each other" as they steer themselves in a single coordinated flock within their own artificial cloud.

Nanotrails will even "change their temperature and polarity to improve their seeding effects," the air force noted.[4] Rutgers University scientist J. Storrs Hall held out the military's hope for these new nanoweather-warrior bots: "Interconnected, atmospherically buoyant, and having navigation capability in three dimensions—clouds of microscopic computer particles communicating with each other and with a control system, could provide tremendous capability." "It is potentially relatively inexpensive to do," Hall clarified. "About the same price per pound as potatoes." Why so cheap? Because nanoparticles can potentially be self-replicating. That is, they can be made to reproduce themselves until programmed to stop. Hopefully. Maybe. Sometimes. "Weather as a Force Multiplier" goes on to say that the air force will "manage and employ a weather-modification capability by the Weather Force Support Element." These weather forces will use real-time updates from swarms of the nanosize "smart sensors" to model developing weather patterns with a super-duper computer. Based on a continually updated forecast, the weather warriors will fly follow-on missions as needed to tweak the storm. It's perfect, crows the U.S. Air Force. "The total weather-modification process becomes a real-time loop of continuous, appropriate, measured interventions, and feedback—capable of producing desired weather behavior." If the notion of inserting autonomous nanobots into weather systems to monitor, steer, and mess with them seems risky, just wait. Around the next cloud corner are coming swarms of airborne nanobots to optimize wind dispersal patterns for germ warfare. But there's one small hitch. Nobody knows how Earth's atmosphere works. It is so big, so complex, and so unpredictable, even real-time nanosnapshots are ancient history as soon as they are taken. This is why the U.S. Air Force said, "Advances in the science of chaos are critical to this endeavor."

So are we being sprayed with nanotrails? "Weather as a Force Multiplier" was published in 1996 and discussed only nonclassified military weather modification projects.

Bob Calls (New Year's Eve 1999)

The term *nano-trails* is prompted by my trusted military informant I have dubbed "Bob."

"They have them," he confirmed. The U.S. Air Force has occasionally added nanoparticles to the chemtrail mix to demonstrate proof of concept. "We're way beyond science fiction," Bob confirmed. "You can hide just about anything you want in a chemtrail—including nanotubes. Chemtrails are being altered for whatever spectrum of wavelength they're trying to bounce off of them."

What about Morgellons? Is there any connection between this bizarre and frightening malady and nano experiments?

"You're not going to like this," Bob said. "Morgellons is one unintended manifestation of nano spray experiments." Morgellons manifests—or presents—as intolerable itching in the skin followed by alien eruptions of thin hairs or tendrils through the skin. "It's basically the same as excreting something through a hair follicle," Bob said. He meant a toxin—something foreign to the body. "If you manufacture a liquid supercrystalline structure, vibrate it a little and give it an electrical charge—it will form into a chain." These nanotubes will be invisible to the eye, of course. But their tendency to clump together could eventually make them big enough to be photographed and posted on the web. How much nanocrap has been sprayed so far? "Tens of tons," he replied. Tons of molecules? "Much of it is still up there," Bob went on to explain. This is because nanoparticles are so light and small they tend to bind with oxygen molecules. And piggybacking on oxygen particles makes them buoyant. "It travels worldwide," Bob continued. "Some of it comes down. Whatever it's exposed to up there it brings down here. We get exposed to it. We breathe it in and we ingest it. It accrues in the same spot every time. And it attracts more of it . . ." In the liver. And brain. "The fallout would look like a prion disease," Bob said. "Fallout from nanoparticles would eat holes in our brains?" "Pretty much. Nano particles are ionized particles that go to what attracts them. . . . Because of their electrochemical properties, they are attracted to the potassium-calcium channel in the brain." Think about it, Bob said. "If they are capable of withstanding the corrosive upper atmosphere—corrosive sunlight and all those (industrial) chemicals—what would they have to be manufactured out of? Does the body manufacture anything that can deal with that? Who will come forward and say these are good?"

Third Twice-Told Tale: Autonomous Systems against Autonomous Systems

In the year 2025, a NDISA unit of U.S. Autonomous NANDroids (AND) and a few older LANDroids (LAND) swarmed into the Torachi Group Inc. space, sixty-nine miles south of Doha, Qatar, followed two hours later by autonomous aerial vehicles (AAV), SIG (standard classified).[5] This visit happens four hours after the International Autonomous Systems Agency (IASA) inspection team from the United Nations (UN) is expelled from Qatar while on its second visit in three weeks. The agency team was denied access to three critical autonomous systems (AS) assembly sites and, therefore, could not verify any "military dimension" of the Torachi AS program. A spokesperson for Torachi Group insists its AAV program does not have military applications. Meanwhile, the Torachi Group CEO declares on his iChannel that the company has AAV production zones and AAV systems being produced that are now a SIG-1A standard (full autonomy) with a nonstandard "kill-switch" and announces new Torachi Group AAV SIG-1A exercises "to prevent aggressions" by Western powers. Western concern centers on a new AAV SIG-1A plant, which is buried deep underground and, therefore, much harder to monitor or, if necessary, attack. Additionally, the Torachi Group AAV SIG-2 and AAV SIG-3 are now on the market and are part of multiple-scale arsenals owned by unstable states, and a rapidly growing number of private entities increases the threat to the Western powers.

Western officials are divided over whether Torachi Group is shifting toward a defensive posture or is just playing for time to pursue its AAV SIG-1A program, which it says is for strictly peaceful purposes. The UN has responded by enacting a ban on the sale of Torachi Group global goods. This is followed by a Western Coalition (WC) embargo on Torachi Group oil sales. Qatar and neighboring nations and companies that are friendly or working with the Torachi Group do not share this view.

On day two, the UN's IASA is requesting the support of the United States and allied powers in surveillance and enforcement of the export bans to Torachi Group. The U.S. National Command Authority (NCA) tasks the Combatant Commander (CCDR) to support the UN resolutions and assist in enforcing the ban on Torachi Group. The NCA also requests increased Autonomous Surveillance and Reconnaissance Units (ASRU) as interoperable support and expansion in efforts of NDISA units of U.S. Autonomous NANDroids (AND), CEEDroids (CEED), and LANDroids (LAND) on Torachi Group for indications and warnings of potential SIG-IA AS escalation of threats on land, sea, and air.

On day three, Autonomous Activity Algorithms (AAA) exploit the incoming intelligence data and conclude anomalies exist in the Torachi Group SIG-IA AS facility networks. Additional unmanned assets are employed to further investigate these anomalies meshed into the NDISA units of Autonomous NANdroids (AND), CEEdroids (CEED), and a few older LANdroids (LAND). Special Operations Forces deploy older micro-UAVs (MUAV) on the ground, these inexpensive, small, low-power hummingbird-like unmanned biomimetic sensor systems relinked to LAND, CEED, and AND networks. One hummingbird-like UAV is deployed to conduct an overwatch of one noted facility. It perches on an electrical power line where it derives its power to gather and transmit images. These electrically powered vehicles accept power from solar/moon panel converters and a low-power laser light received from overhead assets in the vicinity, such as the perched bird-like vehicle. When these unmanned assets are applied and the resulting intelligence data are analyzed, U.S. and UN leadership concludes Torachi Group has reached a critical stage in development of SIG-IA AS. Human intelligence correlates and confirms this conclusion.

Torachi Group determines the international community is aware of the maturity of its SIG-IA AS program. To garner support, Torachi Group reaches out to other like-minded companies and nations and negotiates a sale of SIG-IA AS. Through human intelligence, the international community becomes aware of the sales yet does not know how or when the assembly protocols for SIG-IA AS will be moved. The threat of SIG-IA AS proliferation, plus the potential of interception and stealing by nonstate actors (NSA), escalates the tension with Qatar, the rest of the region, and the expanding SIG-IA AS market.

The United States and concerned partners keep a heightened level of surveillance to detect any SIG-IA AS transfers during or after sales via Russian CryptoFlow networks. The integrated network of air and ground sensors, with automated processing and exploitation algorithms, monitors activity and cues sensors based on activities. The sensors detect abnormal movements of vehicles from a key SIG-IA AS storage site. The United States and the UN authorize interception of the SIG-1A AS because proliferation and potential terrorist use of the SIG-1A AS are greater risks than a likely response from Torachi Group.

Penetrating, high-altitude airborne systems track the vehicle and the NDISA units of AND, CEED, and LAND; Special Operations Forces deploy MUAVs to provide mesh-cueing information about incoming strikes by SIG-2A UAVs. Launched from the offshore autonomous aircraft carrier SS *Kurzwiel*, the strike package comprises a cloud of micro-UAV tactical aircraft with numerous bioagent combat units and supports NDISA units providing tactical intelligence, communication relay, jamming support, tagging, and strike support from Nevada 3 Remote Center U.S. Space Air Force (USSAF). The joint strike fighter operates as a command ship and works in concert with its supporting unmanned systems as a seamless network of strike and jamming aircraft. The multiscale strike (MSS) package penetrates and sweeps into Torachi Group networks, airspace, ground, water, and bioagents targets and intercepts, deep strikes, and stops networked and material flows of the SIG-1A AS. An extraction team follows shortly behind, secures the area, and locates the SIG-1A AS assembly nanofactories. The extraction team uploads to the NDISA cloud, and all NDISA macro and micro AS depart the area. The operation stands down while maintaining a continuing autonomous nanoscale presence of air, sea, and land systems to maintain situational awareness as the Torachi Group situation evolves.

Fourth Twice-Told Tale: Drone Crash and the UC Center for Drone Policy and Ethics

"It's a scary and eerie sight: a picture of a small crumpled drone, crashed in front of UC San Diego's iconic library.[6]

"The so-called UC Center for Drone Policy and Ethics released the picture along with an online statement Thursday addressing a 'Campus Drone Incident,' which they say occurred Tuesday."[7]

The UC Center for Drone Policy and Ethics is a new research institution founded by the UC Office of the President (UCOP) to explore the emerging implications of drone research, use, and production within the UC system. Bringing together a group of interdisciplinary scholars and researchers from across the UC campuses, the center is involved in several collaborative research projects involving students, faculty, and policymakers at the cutting edge of unmanned aerial systems (UAV) studies.

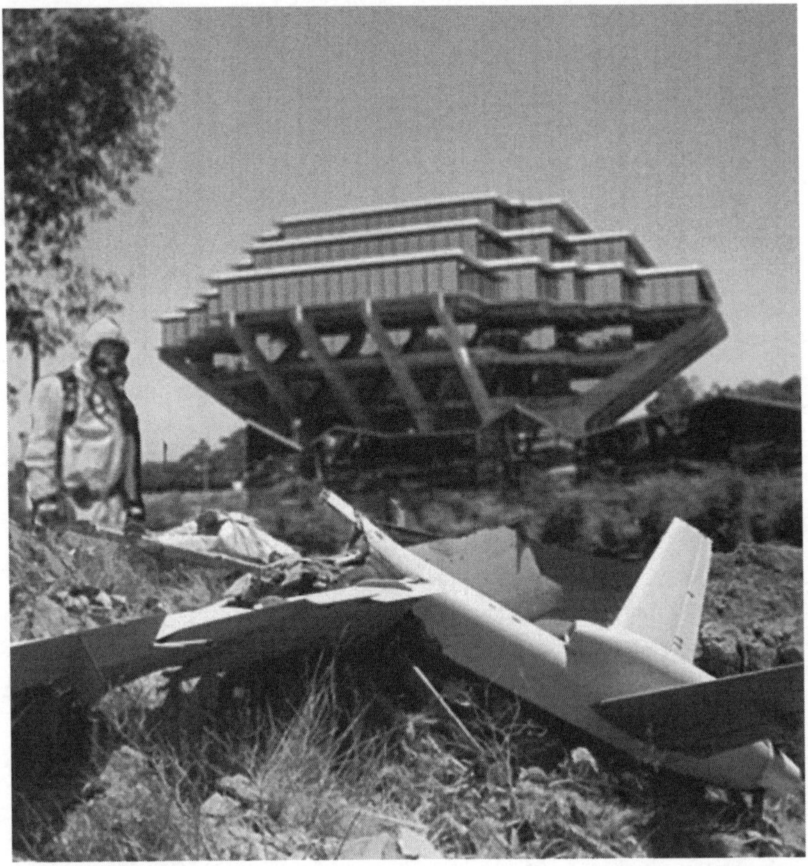

Figure 7.1. "UCSD Drone Crash" by Ian Alan Paul in collaboration with Ricardo Dominguez for *Drones at Home: Phase 3* for Gallery@CALIT2 (2012). (Courtesy Ricardo Dominguez)

Figure 7.2. "The UCSD Center for Drone Policy and Ethics Logo" by Ian Alan Paul in collaboration with Ricardo Dominguez for *Drones at Home: Phase 3* for Gallery@CALIT2 (2012). (Courtesy Ricardo Dominguez)

Appointment of Principle Investigator (October 3, 2012)
I am pleased to announce the appointment of Ricardo Dominguez, Associate Professor of Visual Arts and Principal Investigator at CALIT2, as the Acting Lead Researcher (LR) for the UCSD Center for Drone Policy and Ethics (CDPE) effective October 3, 2012, and continuing until a permanent head is appointed.

As lead development LR at CDPE since December 2010, Associate Professor Dominguez has served as a key advisor to (SVCAA) Suresh Subramani on a wide range of issues and has been responsible for planning, oversight, and the implementation of CDPE initiative. He has provided essential leadership in the planning of resources to meet programmatic and capital program goals and in the development of CDPE, and he has overseen the use of technology-enhanced instruction and interventions.

A highly distinguished new media researcher and trans-poetics investigator, Associate Professor Dominguez has been a member of the UC San Diego faculty since 2004. He received his PhD in Practice in Transmedial Studies from the University of California, Berkeley, and is world-renowned for his work in the field of social code disassembly. Professor Dominguez is an outstanding artist-researcher and recipient of several awards, including the Center for Nanotechnology in Society (CNS-ASU) 2010 Fellow Award, Hellman Fellow Award, the UC Presidents Excellence Award 2010, and a Guggenheim Fellowship. He is an outstanding teacher, has an excellent record as a graduate student mentor and advisor, and has a strong record of international, national, and UC service.

Professor Dominguez has served as the last Chair of the Department of Pata-Interference (PI) prior to its reorganization as a subdivision, as the Interim Associate LD for the Division of Bionano-Integration Sciences (BS) in 2007–2008, Interim LD in 2009–2010, and as Associate LD Operative in 2010–2011. Professor Dominguez's strong administrative experiments, his accomplishments, values, energy, and vision make him exceptionally well suited to serve as Acting LR.

I deeply appreciate his willingness to serve in this capacity until a permanent Lead Researcher (LR) is identified. As Acting LR, Associate Professor Dominguez will have authority and responsibility for all decisions involving the UCSD Center for Drone Policy and Ethics (CDPE).

The search for a permanent LR continues. Nominations may be forwarded to Search Committee Co-Chair Larry Smarr (lsmarr@ucsd.edu) or Search Consultant Alberto Pimentel (A.Pimentel@storbeckpimentel.com).

With the appointment of Associate Professor Dominguez as Acting LR, I am confident that UCSD Center for Drone Policy and Ethics (CDPE) will be in capable hands.

Pradeep K. Khosla
Chancellor

P.S. Graduate student researchers associated with the UC Center for Drone Policy and Ethics have organized a panel discussion on the topic of drone use on the U.S.-Mexico border. Researchers from the center, faculty from UC San Diego, as well as representatives from U.S. Customs and Border Protection and Homeland Security will all give brief lectures on the historical and contemporary use of military drones in border territories and will discuss potential future uses.

Maj. Gen. Frank McKenzie, a retired air force pilot, describes the increased use of drones on the border in this way: "If you look at how important the UAVs have been in defense missions overseas, it's not really rocket science to make adjustments for how important those things could be in the homeland for precisely the same reasons."

The panel discussion is the first in a series organized by the UC Center for Drone Policy and Ethics, which plans to explore the use of drones from ecological, political, sociological, and historical perspectives.

P.P.S. "Researchers Call for Public Town Hall to Discuss Drone Malfunction and Crash"

In light of the recent unmanned aerial vehicle (UAV) malfunctioning and crash on UCSD's campus, researchers associated with the UC Center for Drone Policy and Ethics have organized a public town hall to discuss the incident with students, faculty, and staff to be held on December 6, 2012, from 5 to 6 p.m. at the CALIT2 Gallery.

While the origin and manufacturer of the crashed drone remains unclear, researchers will reveal details recorded at the crash site to the public and will moderate a discussion after a brief presentation.

Guerne N. Ka, principle investigator at the center, describes the event: "We understand that the recent drone crash incident has caused alarm amongst students and staff surrounding the research and use of drones on the UCSD campus and surrounding areas and very much wanted to take this opportunity to educate the public about drone technologies and local deployments. While drone crashes are rare and another malfunction is extremely unlikely, we at the UC Center for Drone Policy and Ethics would also like to take this opportunity to teach basic drone safety techniques that can be practiced on a daily basis to keep ourselves and others safe."

The public town hall will be held at the Gallery at CALIT2on December 6, 2012, at 5 p.m. Members of the university and public are invited to attend.

[Press are advised to request proper forms and credentials before attending to comply with campus policies.]

For Further Information, Contact:

Trish Stone, tstone@ucsd.edu

Public Relations Specialist, UC Center for Drone Policy and Ethics

P.P.P.S.

Source of Mystery Drone Crash Revealed

The so-called UC Center for Drone Policy and Ethics released the picture along with an online statement Thursday addressing a "Campus Drone Incident," which they say occurred Tuesday.[8]

Not only is the center not affiliated with the university, but the center is not real either. It was created by artists at the university's Gallery@ CALIT2, a campus art gallery that explores the relationships between art and technology.

"In light of the recent Unmanned Aerial Vehicle (UAV) malfunctioning and crash on UCSD's campus," the statement reads, "researchers associated with the UC Center for Drone Policy and Ethics have organized a public town hall to discuss the incident with students, faculty and staff."

The statement claims the origin and manufacturer of the crashed drone "remains unclear" but that researchers at the center will reveal details to the public after a brief presentation Thursday at 5 p.m.

A university spokesperson said they were not aware of the staged drone crash, and that the Center for Drone Policy and Ethics is not real. Both the university and the artists confirmed that the drone crash did not actually happen.

The crash is just one part of the gallery's year-long exhibition, *Drones at Home*. The artists behind the faux crash are Ricardo Dominguez, well

Figure 7.3. "UCSD Drone Crash: A Town Hall Meeting Initiated by the UCSD Center for Drone Policy and Ethics," a performance by Ian Alan Paul (*left*), Katherine Chandler as "Jane Smith" (*monitor*), and Ricardo Dominguez (*right*) for *Drones at Home: Phase 3* for Gallery@CALIT2 (2012). (Courtesy Ricardo Dominguez)

known for his projects, which often play with the mind and blur fact and fiction, and transmedia artist Ian Alan Paul, said Trish Stone, the gallery's director and coordinator.

"I'm sure some of [the students] probably did think it was real," Dominguez said of the drone crash, "but that's one of the practices of new media art—what we call minor simulation. It creates an event that is difficult to understand as either real or not real."

The drone crash is one of several intended to raise awareness about the future use of drones. For instance, one artist created a drone made of bones to fly over General Atomics, a major manufacturer of unmanned vehicles used for the military. Another artist developed a drone to locate Homeland Security drones and sing borderland songs to it.

Though Dominguez himself is concerned about the use of drones and how it may impact people's privacy, he said the staged drone crash is more of a conversation-starter than protest piece.

"People and students have a chance to have a conversation around the issues about what it means to be living in the twenty-first century," he said.

For information on the meeting Thursday night at the drone crash site, see http://uccenterfordrones.wordpress.com/regarding-recent-drone-malfunction/.

Notes

Twice-Told Tales is a short story collection in two volumes by Nathaniel Hawthorne. The first was published in the spring of 1837 and the second in 1842.

1. This is a utopian plagiarist gesture of the short story "Dr. Heidegger's Experiment" by Nathaniel Hawthorne, about a doctor who claims to have been sent water from the Fountain of Youth. Originally published anonymously, it was later included in Hawthorne's collection *Twice-Told Tales* in 1837.
2. This is a utopian plagiarist gesture of a found text from Hambling, "Drones Tag and Track Quarry."
3. This is a utopian plagiarist gesture of a found text online, Thomas, "Nano Chemtrails."
4. House et al., "Weather as a Force Multiplier."
5. This is a utopian plagiarist gesture of a section from Department of Defense, "Unmanned Systems Integrated Roadmap FY2013–2038," https://publicintelligence.net/dod-unmanned-systems-2013/.
6. This is a utopian plagiarist gesture of an artivist gesture by artists Ian Alan Paul and Ricardo Dominguez as part of the *Drones at Home* exhibition at Gallery@CALIT2 (UCSD) in 2012.
7. Steussy, "Source of Mystery Drone Crash Revealed."
8. Steussy, "Source of Mystery Drone Crash Revealed."

8 IN PURSUIT OF OTHER NETWORKS

Drone Art and Accelerationist Aesthetics

THOMAS STUBBLEFIELD

ACCORDING TO PAUL VIRILIO, with the onset of World War I the promise of aviation shifted from the sheer spectacle of defying gravity and the pursuit of breaking once incomprehensible speed records to the possibility for new modes of seeing.[1] The ensuing arrival of media-based reconnaissance flights set in place a formative dynamic of modern warfare in which the gathering of images served as an equally if not more effective weapon than actually firing on the enemy from the air. Now, a century later, the drone seems to be the perfect realization of this claim. Utilizing video, radar, infrared, and thermal imaging technologies, U.S. drones transmit more than twenty thousand hours of footage each month. In 2008 alone, the military collected the equivalent of twenty-four years of footage.[2] With the advent of "Gorgon Stare" and Argus technologies, which utilize dozens of cameras mounted to a single aircraft, this number is set to grow exponentially. The seemingly counterintuitive logic behind this "ocular regime," which the military openly admits already produces more data than can be processed and catalogued, operates as a kind of perverse realization of Virilio's claim that in contemporary war, "the supply of images [is] the equivalent of an ammunition supply."[3]

This convergence between the operation of the drone and image production not only opens up analysis to the field of media studies, game theory, and visual studies but has also made the drone a particularly attractive subject for artists. While drone art constitutes a diverse body of work, these projects operate from a shared desire to work within and at times even reproduce the specific mode of power that the unmanned aerial vehicle (UAV) articulates so as to redirect, sabotage, or otherwise introduce interference within these relations. As drone power is heavily decentralized, capable of de- and rematerializing through an array of objects and actors, it is often at odds with historical modes of resistance based in negation or opposition from the outside. The shortcomings of these strategies in relation to the networked power of the drone are dramatized by the growing pastime of "drone hunting."[4] Associated with the American West, the grounding of drone flights via armed private citizens embodies the contradictions of neoliberalism. The practice grants an illusory agency that is charged with negating those governmental intrusions that conflict with self-determination, despite the fact that the same discourse all too often understands drones as part of a globalized counterinsurgency that serves as the necessary prerequisite for such freedoms.[5] As such, these displays of "autonomy" reaffirm not only the dispersed networked status of the drone but also one's interpolation within these networks. The temptation of critical projects to slip into a demythologizing mode that seeks to unmask the authority behind the eye of the drone camera, to demystify and destroy the false consciousness produced by its invisibility, carries with it the possibility of a similar kind of impasse. In articulating hierarchies of repression along binary oppositions, such critiques enact a kind of rhetorical drone hunting, which may not only miss the target, so to speak, but also obscure its dual character.

Drones confound the traditional dynamics of conflict by articulating an authority that is distributed and elusive, wrapped up with the horizontality of networks, which they materialize as force. Yet, at the same time, this diffuse organization of power coexists alongside and, at times, congeals into more familiar centralized models. In this, drones exemplify what Alexander Galloway and Eugene Thacker describe as the critical juncture between sovereignty and networks, that irresolvable dialectic at the core of understanding the operations of power in the twenty-first century. Approaching the drone from this perspective, artists James Bridle, Trevor Paglen, Josh Begley, and others eschew the distance of critique, seeking instead to initiate blockages and intensify existing relations, processes that work within the ecological model of the kill chain so as to amplify its power differentials and, ultimately, produce new distributions. In this, drone art necessarily treads a fine line between the utopian potential of the network and the reaffirmation of a dispersed mode of power that Michael Dillon refers to as "martial becoming."[6] These paradoxical, at times even contradictory, practices resonate with the tenuous position of accelerationism. While referencing a diverse set of theories, which include Nick Land's absolute deterritorialization, the epistemic approach of Ray Brassier and Reza Negarestani, and Gilles Deleuze and Félix Guattari's schizoanalysis, accelerationism begins with the recognition that there is no longer any outside to capitalism (a position that maintains a particular resonance with the global counterinsurgency), and, as such, the primary way to derail its inner workings is by amplifying its own powers for deformation and self-destruction.[7] Without aligning drone art with any particular camp within this spectrum per se, this larger school of thought serves as a means to clarify the practices of drone art and its pursuit of (other) networks as well as draw out the unique structures of power that animate the "everywhere war" of which the drone is a part.[8]

Interruption, Conversion, Parasitology

Formed in 1991 by Natalie Jeremijenko and Kate Rich, the Bureau of Inverse Technology (BIT) produced one of the first works of drone art with their "bit plane" project (1997). In this work, a radio-controlled airplane was outfitted with a video camera that transmitted live footage to operators on the ground (see figure 8.1). This small, unassuming plane was then sent on a series of reconnaissance missions over Silicon Valley, traversing the operation centers of Apple, Lockheed, Netscape, Xerox, Atari, Hewlett Packard, Oracle, Yahoo, Silicon Graphics International (SGI), Sun Microsystems, and more. Not only are the majority of these spaces "no camera zones," but it is also illegal to fly a remote-controlled plane within five miles of an airport (bit plane violated the airspace of three nearby airports in the course of carrying out its mission). The transgression of these boundaries does not simply provide an aerial tour of the epicenter of the "Information Age" for a curious public. Rather, these breeches served as entry points for the reconfiguration of the network via strategies of interruption and intensification. In this, the work prefigures many of the recurring themes and strategies of drone art as it would materialize in the twenty-first century.

As the video feed from bit plane's camera utilized the frequencies of network television, homes in the path of its flight experienced a break in scheduled programming. In fact, there were seven complaints filed with the Federal Communications Commission (FCC) during the bit plane's flight in which residents described "aerial panoramas of unknown origin interrupting their

Figure 8.1. "Bit plane" camera feed. (Courtesy Natalie Jeremijenko)

regularly programmed television viewing."[9] Engaging existing networks in order to reflect back the conditions of contemporary mediality, the jittery, vertigo-inducing images of the flight interjected a new precariousness into this "rarified information space."[10] Rather than exposing a singular actor within this network of violence, the strategic deployment of "noise" within these relations was aimed at dethroning the logic of "nodocentrism." This latter term refers to the tendency of networks to define themselves in terms of the connection of isolated centers rather than a truly relational ecology, which includes not only the spaces between but also the conditions of possibility for alternate formations. Following this logic, the bit plane project attempted to deprivilege the centers of distributed networks not only through its momentary "occupation" of the mode of transmission but also through the unique mode of vision that it articulated.

The nodocentric conception of the network is closely aligned with Cartesian models of subjectivity, which reaffirm the autonomy of a perceiving subject and, more generally, the stability of bodies through which relations flow. However, bit plane's grainy camera footage confounds both a fixed vantage point and an embodied mode of seeing. The feed is scrambled when the plane enters the airspace of Lockheed Martin. The disorienting rolls of the aircraft cause the viewer to periodically lose sight of the horizon line, and the signal is occasionally lost when the flight exceeds the reach of the transmitter. The net effect is that the expectation of a documentary or simple visual record is supplanted by a kind of aerial data mining. For the bit plane project, these latter relations serve to reimagine the tech industry as subject to the potentialities and relations of immanence that populate the network. However, with the advent of the war on terror, this inorganic and automated mode of seeing has been rendered inseparable from military operations of the "everywhere war" and post-9/11 surveillance, which together form a joint constellation that Nicholas Mirzoeff refers to as the "post-panoptic visuality of global counterinsurgency."[11] At the center of this phenomenon is a shift from prosthetic constructions of embodied vision to "machinic vision," which takes place within "an environment of interacting machines and human-machine systems [to produce a correlative] field of decoded perceptions that, whether or not produced by or issuing from these machines, assume their full intelligibility only in relation to them."[12] In its antagonism toward embodied vision, bit plane produces a dynamic cognitive map that charts the convergence of data space, airspace, surveillance, and martial force, a convergence that brings the modern drone into being.

Drone art poses the question of whether the increasingly autopoetic nature of these relations of vision in networked warfare may not only automate the operations of the kill chain but, in the process, also open the system to reconfiguration from the outside. This prospect requires working within the asymmetry of the network as a means to, as Ulises Mejias puts it, "unthink the network."[13] In this formulation, Mejias draws upon Bruno Latour's insistence that the primary operation of media theory is to "maintain the reversibility of foldings," those spaces or intervals where forgotten technologies and unrealized social and political formations remain accessible as virtual components.[14] However, what Mejias describes as "reversals" might better be thought of as a kind of intensification that is without explicit directionality or explicit content. Such gestures would serve to recuperate ossified possibilities within systems of control rather than the network's previous iterations of itself. By introducing new configurations via secondary nodes or dead spots, the system's relation to noise is inverted so that "communication in spite of noise is replaced with communication through noise."[15]

This logic of "parasitology" materializes in more recent drone art as a security breach, a leak, or a viral possibility. For example, in his "Dronestagram" project, James Bridle utilizes the GPS coordinates of drone attacks to fetch satellite images of the location, which the work captions with information regarding the fatalities and motivation behind the strike (see figures 8.2 and 8.3). This project laid the groundwork for Begley's Metadata+ (formerly Drone+) app, which sends a real-time message to users every time a drone kill occurs in one of America's undeclared wars (see figure 8.4). Begley describes the work in terms of an involuntary interruption, a "reaching into the pockets of U.S. smartphone users" in order to "annoy them into drone-consciousness."[16] Despite being blocked by the Google App store, the app is essentially a news aggregate that draws its information from the publicly available database of the United Kingdom's Bureau of Investigative Journalism. However, the app not only locates these attacks via GPS but also restages the event as breaks or discontinuities within our everyday experience of the mobile device.

These works attempt to dislodge the residual spatial and political boundaries that operate within networked warfare so as to intensify the deterritorializing possibilities of the "everywhere war" via the mobile device. The widely circulated *Drone Survival Guide* describes a practice of "GPS spoofing," where "small, portable GPS transmitters can send fake GPS signals and disrupt the drones' navigation systems [so as to] steer drones into self-destruction flight paths or even hijack them and land them on a runway."[17] The geographic displacements that circulate within drone art can be thought of as the representational equivalents of these guerilla tactics. Exemplary of this dynamic is Omer Fast's staging of a fictitious encounter of a drone by an American family in the Nevada desert near Creech Air Force Base in his film *5,000 Feet Is the Best* (2011). The film overlays the audio of firsthand accounts of drone operators recounting attacks in the Middle East with aerial shots of a barren landscape and, eventually, the Las Vegas strip. These displacements do not simply reiterate the drone's lack of acknowledgement of national boundaries but also follow the Dronestagram project and the Metadata+ app in their exploration of deterritorialization as a strategy. This is not to suggest that an iPhone user whose daily routine is interrupted by a disturbing text message or the viewing experience of Fast's film in any way approximates the actual experience of being pursued by a drone. Rather, these works attempt to accelerate and intensify the fluidity of space enacted by martial networks on a microscale, producing interventions that maintain the possibility of snowballing as they move across distributed networks.

Seeing as Targeting: Temporality and Identification

Drone art implicitly questions the invisibility that popular discourse ascribes to the UAV as well as the larger framework of surveillance through which its operations tend to be read. Recent field work in Pakistan suggests not only that drones achieve an uncanny presence in the daily lives of residents but also that their power stems in part from the visual relations that result from this presence. The *Living under Drones* report published by the New York University and Stanford law programs, for example, has gathered substantial evidence regarding the psychological toll exacted by living with this presence of the drone. A young father told interviewers that the drones "are always on my mind. It makes it difficult to sleep. They are like a mosquito. Even when you don't see them, you can hear them, you know they are there."[18] Another respondent explained: "We can't go to the markets. We can't drive cars. When they're hovering over us, we're all scared. One thinks they'll drop it on our house, and another thinks it'll be on our house, so we run out of our houses."[19] Indeed, it is not unusual for drones to strike after hovering above their targets for upward of twenty-four hours in a single flight or even several days via multiple flights. This practice is at the center of a widespread condition that Pakistani psychiatrists are calling "anticipatory anxiety."[20]

The temporality of this anxiety can be understood as a symptom of the unique relations of seeing and being seen that structure drone vision. Graham Harwood's analysis of the Afghan War Diary released by WikiLeaks in 2010 illustrates the way stockpiles of diverse sets of information provide conditions that allow automated processes of seeing to be translated via algorithms into specified courses of action. This possibility is born out of a dynamic archive comprising "Human Intelligence (HUMINT), Psychological Operations (PSYOP), Engagement, Counter Improvised Explosive Device (CIED), Significant Acts (SigActs), Targeting, and Social and Cultural reports." As these entries are "indexed spatially by the sixteen orbiting satellites of the Global Positioning System and temporally by the coordinates of atomic clocks," they enact a complete and real-time processing of battle,

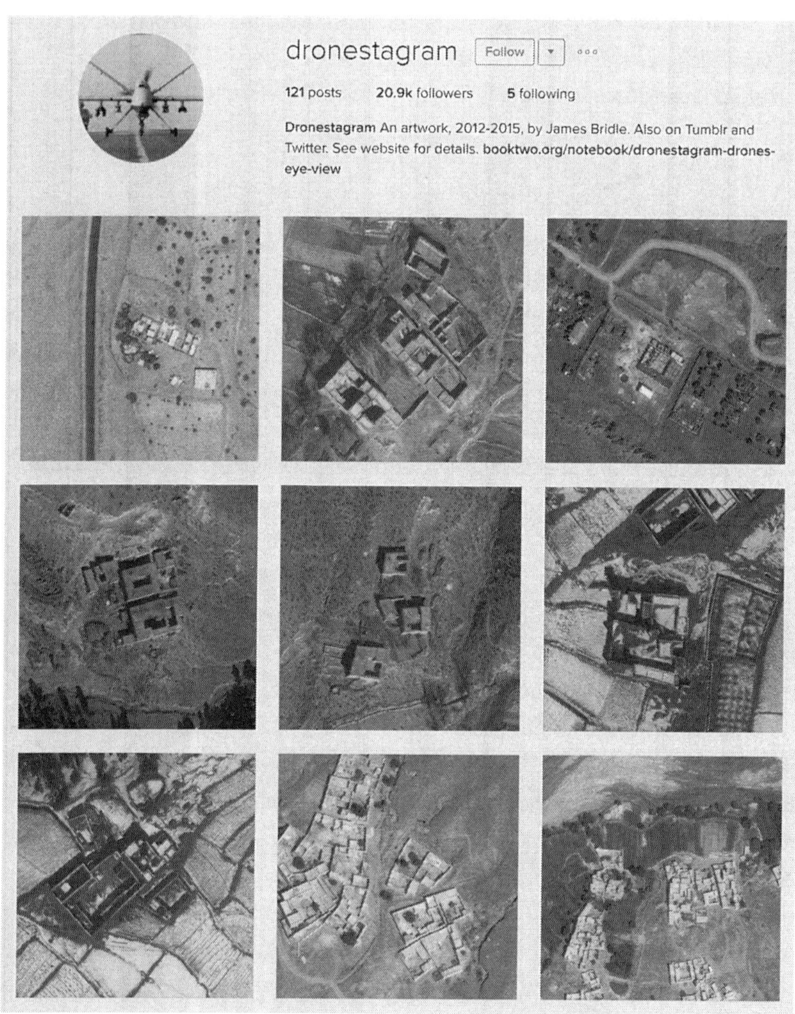

Figure 8.2. James Bridle, "Dronestagram," 2012–15, photography and social media, online project. (Courtesy James Bridle)

Figure 8.3. James Bridle, "Dronestagram," 2013, photography and social media, online project. (Courtesy James Bridle)

Figure 8.4. Josh Begley's Metadata+ app. (Courtesy Josh Begley)

which, for Harwood, "transforms the war into a relation query, and the relational query into war."[21]

The anxiety produced by drone presence is inseparable from the capacity of the random access database to produce a causal relation between the experience of being seen and being assaulted. It is in the precarious gap between the fluid, relational aspect of the database and its capacity to congeal into momentary formations of sovereignty in which the subject of the drone lives. The UAV's seamless movement between these conflicting modes of power is made possible by its reliance upon "visual nominalism," a system of seeing that eschews objects and identities in favor of spatial relations and empirical data.[22] Utilizing edge detection, motion capture, auto-tagging, and facial recognition, drones supplant the perspectival, Albertian image with a catalog of distances, volumes, heat signatures, and behavioral patterns. With the introduction of Reaper drones and Gorgon Stare technology, which "quilt" together multiple feeds in real time, these operations are no longer outsourced to "postproduction" but are localized at the sight of image capture. With the entirety of the network telescoped through the gaze of the drone, the machinic eye, in effect, produces a futural vector along which the strike resides as a latent potentiality. In this, the immanence of the database, which assembles the conditions for military action, maintains a structural affinity with what Sigmund Freud describes as a "signal" based anxiety. According to this scenario, a signal (the drone) announces a "danger-situation" (its implicit strike), in response to which the subject "anticipate[s] the trauma and behave[s] as though it had already come" ("anticipatory anxiety").[23]

James Bridle's *UAV Identification Kit* engages with the processes of identification that undergird the visual relations of the drone (see figure 8.5). By situating the UAV within an anachronistic set of historical references, the work discloses the processes by which drone vision collapses seeing with targeting. This revelation opens the possibility for a compromise between the directionality of these relations as well as the distortion of the interval between identification of a subject/target and the execution of a strike. In this project, Bridle uses 3-D printing techniques to produce three models of contemporary military drones: the MQ-1 Predator, the RQ-170 Sentinel, and the RQ-4 Global Hawk as well as human figures for scale. The project mimics kits used in the training of gunners, radar operations, and civilians during World War II (see figure 8.6). American schoolchildren assembled these visual guides by the hundreds of thousands for this very purpose, and civilians formed Skywatch groups dedicated to identifying enemy

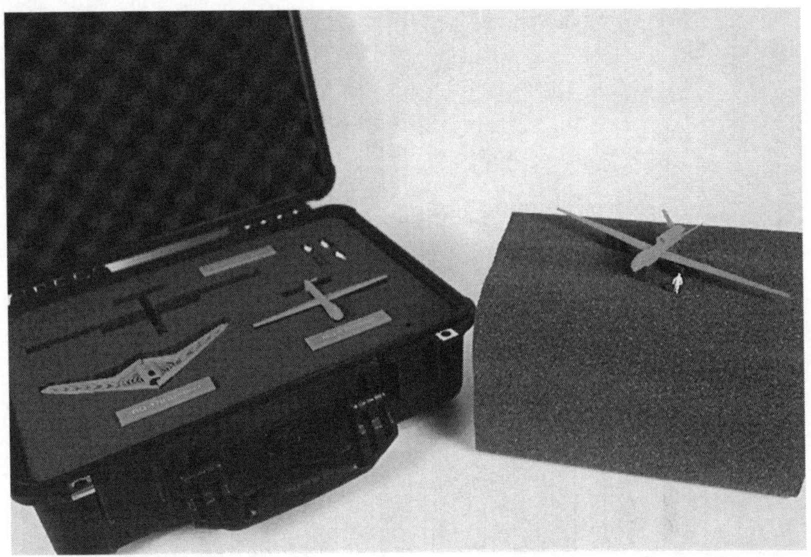

Figure 8.5. James Bridle, *UAV Identification Kit 001*, 2012, Pelican case and 3-D printed models. (Courtesy James Bridle)

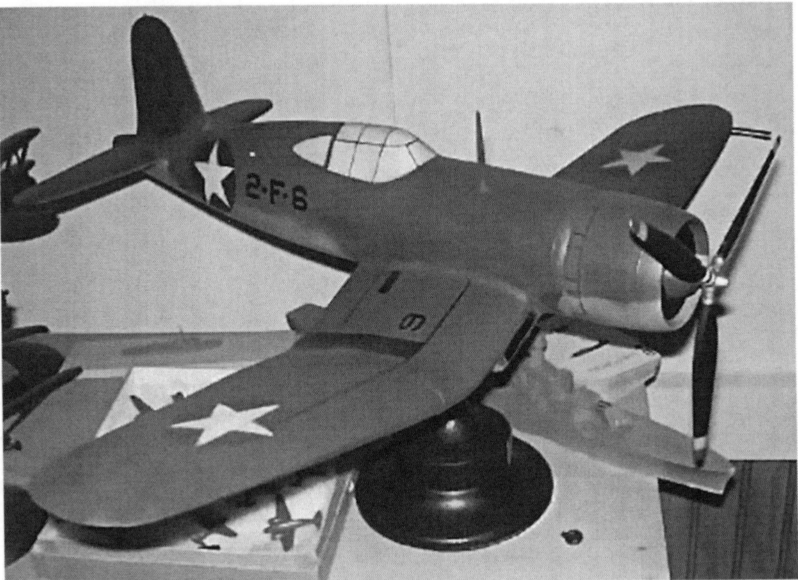

Figure 8.6. A wooden Vought Sikorsky F4U-1 Corsair model.

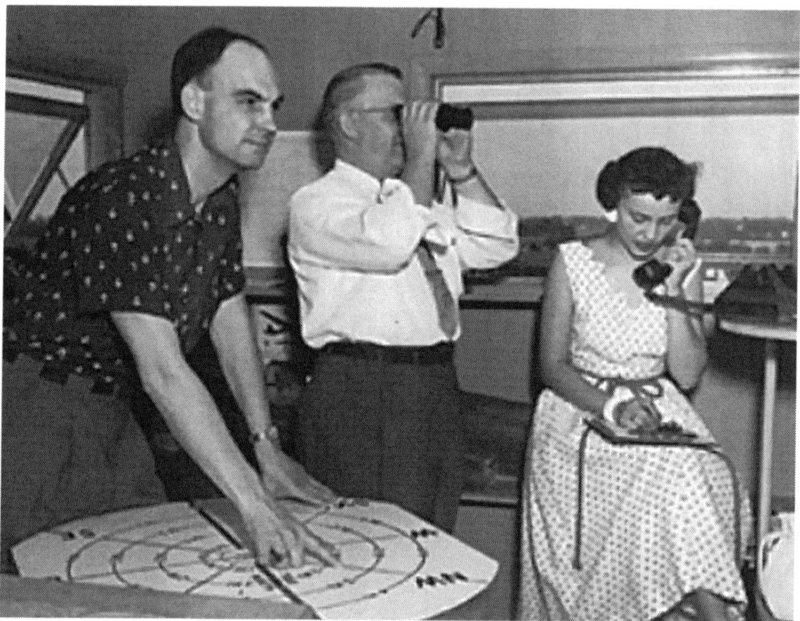

Figure 8.7. Ground Observation Corps chapter of Worthington, Minnesota.

aircraft. These collectives eventually materialized into the Ground Observation Corps, which comprised around 350,000 volunteers and some 16,000 observation posts and towers (see figure 8.7). Forming a scopic regime of wartime security, these practices of identification placed the eye in the service of the creation and maintenance of the critical friend–enemy distinction, that opposition Carl Schmitt describes as the origin of all "political actions and motives."[24] According to Schmitt, this process of differentiation achieves its status not only by virtue of its connection to the real possibility of death but also through its public and collective nature ("It is not *my* enemy but *our* enemy"). The identification models and the spotter industries they produced were bolstered by the logics of repetition, interchangeability, and seriality that defined midcentury industrial production. As the standardization of the latter allowed the eye to be trained and collectivized around national identity, the result was not simply that the enemy became recognizable but also that a certain mode of processing visual information became formalized.

More recently, Galloway and Thacker have explored the possibility that the dynamics of the friend or foe opposition might be understood in architectonic terms. They point out, "Enmity is always 'faced' or constituted by a confrontation. We stand alongside our friends; I stand opposite my foe. Friends only 'face' each other insofar as they stand opposite and 'face' their common foe. . . . Enmity is an interface."[25] As such, Schmitt's basic unit of the political must be read as topological, that is, as "mapped, superficial, structural and formal."[26] Interestingly, the historical evolution of these practices of identification suggests a similar formalization, if not materialization, of these relations. By the end of World War II, the centrality of the eye in practices of enemy recognition gave way to inorganic IFF (identification, friend or foe) systems. While IFF systems operate in a variety of formats, the basic structure involves transmitting and receiving a pulse on a set of predetermined frequencies. As many have pointed out, IFF systems are structurally unable to definitively recognize an enemy as such. The IFF system can only confirm, with reasonable doubt, the presence of a "friend."

As if to compensate for this bias, drones and the automated modes of vision that populate networked war see everything as a target. This is dramatized by Trevor Paglen's *Drone Vision*, which presents extended loops of U.S. drone camera footage that has been secured by an amateur satellite "hacker."[27] Rather than revealing classified material or questionable activity, the piece is more interested in visualizing the way in which the subject of the image is recast by the eye of the drone. As the presentation of these images mirrors the visual language of leaked footage, such as the "Collateral Murder" video, its seemingly banal content of empty, barren landscapes is overpowered by the sense of an impending strike, a strike that does not happen.[28] As the extended loops replay this moment in time without incident, the viewer is made aware of the way the drone camera imbues the subject of the image with expectation and, more broadly, the processes by which its vision is structured according to and, for all intents and purposes, coincident with attack. Unlike the cathartic images of the Gulf War missile camera, which plummeted viewers to unsuspecting targets, the drone relinquishes this embodiment for a cartographic gaze that flattens the world, reaffirming the conception of space as an empty container in which targets reside.

Samuel Weber suggests that part of this recoding of the subject as target hinges upon a unique temporality that is embodied by the phrase *target of opportunity*. This phrase was used in the media to describe the alleged hiding place of Saddam Hussein and quickly became representative of a larger logic of the war on terror. As Weber describes, while the enemy had to be "identified and localized, named and depicted" in familiar fashion, what is new in the post-9/11 context is the "mobility, indeterminate structure, and unpredictability of the spatio-temporal medium in which targets had to be sited."[29] In this kinetic and unstable environment, targets became opportunities, moments to be seized. The very singularity of such phenomena became intertwined with what Weber describes as "the generality of an established order, scheme, organization or plan, in respect to which the event defines itself as exceptional or extraordinary."[30]

As targeting momentarily stratifies immense waves of data in order to carry out a given action, it exemplifies the duality of hierarchy and horizontalism that undergirds the drone. In the hands of artists, it also presents an opportunity for reverse engineering the standards, protocols, definitions, and pathways that structure these actions. For example, the *Drone Survival Guide* presents a visual aid for identifying drones according to their size, shape, nationality, and name. Presented in PDF form and intended to be reproduced and distributed, the guide exploits the centrality of identification in the operation of the drone so as to turn back this operation against its source. However, the idea is not simply to reduplicate this act of categorizing and sorting that undergirds the gaze of the drone but also to interrupt these processes. As such, its reverse contains tips on how to hide from and hack drones, and the mail-order version is even printed on a reflective material that can be used to scramble the drone's camera on a sunny day. Bridle's plastic UAVs similarly amplify the conflicts within this mode of organizing visual information by posing the fluid network of drone warfare against its representation as static object. The monochromatic surfaces, oversized carrying case, and generic quality of these visual guides recast these objects as harmless toys. At the same time, the dramatic shift in scale, tactility, and overall materialization of a vehicle that is typically only seen from a distance suggests a kind of mastery of the object. In this shape-shifting of the UAV into a child's toy, the work exemplifies a larger strategy of drone art, which utilizes the partial, indeterminate, and anachronistic in order to confuse the hierarchies within the flow of information and, more broadly, preserve the possibilities for redefinition within these relations.

The medium of 3-D printing is a critical component of Bridle's endeavor. Jettisoning the industrially produced objects of World War II identification kits, Bridle's works come out of the context of "micromanufacturing." As such, they carry with them a host of associations that magnify the larger conceit of Bridle's project and drone art more generally. Born out of a hacker logic, 3-D printing maintains a virtual irrelevance of authorship, as not only is the file/object often preexistent but so too is it frequently exchanged explicitly to be customized and recast. Circulating in the place of objects, stereolithography (STL) files thereby present possible objects rather than durable goods. Conversely, with the transformation of objects to files via "rapid prototyping," the form of the latter is itself virtually simultaneous to its future deformation. The medium is thus additive in a dual sense. Not only does it jettison the subtractive modes of twentieth-century production in favor of building up an object from layers or the solidification of composite powders via binding agents but it also eschews negativity at a conceptual level.[31] In this environment, it no longer makes sense to talk about loss, authenticity, or even form in a static sense, as the "maker culture" of 3-D printing renders these attributes fluid. Immersed in this future-oriented ontology, this medium introduces the possibility of a mode of production in which national identification and the underlying discourse of friend or foe become unstable. As the infinite malleability of these objects undercuts their authority as guides, they open the practice of targeting onto the networked relations of immanence. It is this same sense of futurity and potentiality that Bridle ascribes to the camera in his urban installations.

How to Photograph a Drone

In his *Drone Shadows* series, James Bridle draws monumental chalk outlines of an imaginary MQ-1 Predator drone on the street corners and unassuming parking lots of London and Istanbul (see figures 8.8 and 8.9). As if marking the scene of a crime, the aerial view of these stark diagrams seems to enact a profound displacement whereby the forces of Western imperialism turn back on themselves, indicting the actors of a perverse network. However, for the viewer on the ground, these same marks struggle to coalesce into a meaningful gestalt and, in fact, appear destined to merge with the dense visual landscape of the city. This latter dynamic is driven home by the latest incarnation of the project for the 2013 Brighton Festival, which utilizes a Hi-Way Services Team to measure and paint the drone diagram on the seafront location of Madeira Drive. The familiarity of the orange cones, yellow safety vests, and road-marking vehicles, which unceremoniously spray the road to indicate the silhouette of a Reaper drone hovering above, produces a peculiar banality that only magnifies the capacity of this intervention to be buried within the everyday. The viewer's engagement with the drone in Bridle's piece is to a large extent contingent upon the photographic mediation of the scene, which not only preserves this otherwise ephemeral gesture

Figure 8.8. Drone shadow from Google Maps.

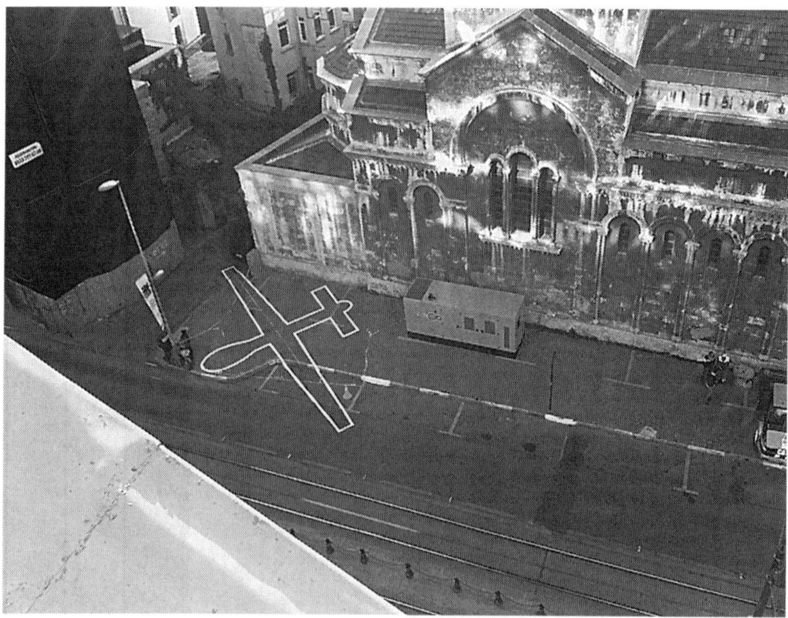

Figure 8.9. James Bridle, *Drone Shadow 002*, 2012, installation, Istanbul, Turkey. (Courtesy James Bridle)

but also more immediately grants the necessary distance from which to successfully read the image.

In the work's play between visual omniscience and partial images, the centralized model of power is made to engage with a diffuse and horizontal trajectory that echoes the structure of the "kill chain" itself. As Derek Gregory describes, the "kill-chain can be thought of as a dispersed and distributed apparatus, a congeries of actors, objects, practices, discourses and affects, that entrains the people who are made part of it and constitutes them as particular kinds of subjects."[32] As each Predator drone requires around 185 personnel to operate, this expansive network does not simply remove the operator from the vehicle but rather intertwines its operation with a dispersed collectivity. Using screen captures, verbal communication, and chat rooms, members of this network include "pilots" at Creech Air Force Base in Nevada, Joint Terminal Attack Controllers in Afghanistan, military lawyers at U.S. Central Command's (CENTCOM) Operations Center at Al Udeid Air Base in Qatar, and image specialists at the Distributed Common Ground System (DCGS) at Langley Air Force Base in Virginia.[33] In light of this distributed mode of operation, the knee-jerk reaction to associate the all-seeing eye of the drone's aerial image with a kind of centralized and consolidated power unravels, confirming Bruno Latour's claim that "the view from nowhere . . . also means that there is nowhere for those who hold it to realistically reside."[34]

The drone thus operates as a "partial object" in a dual sense. In the psychoanalytic tradition, Melanie Klein used the phrase to convey the processes by which the child forms relationships with discrete body parts of the other (usually, the mother's breast) in anticipation of processing the whole. In the context of databases, the same term is used to refer to those objects that have broken "invariants," conditions that remain consistent throughout the course of an operation. Such artifacts have been reconstituted from a database but are not fully initialized by virtue of being separated from the rest of their data context. Uniting this psycho-technical constellation is the notion that the fragment is positioned toward a virtual future of full embodiment, one that emanates from an ecology of object relations and/or data attribution. Embodying this status, the drone appears as an incomplete object in Bridle's work, a shadow that is in expectation of future activation via the image and its network.

While this dispersed, relational aspect aligns the drone with the networked power of the kill chain, it is also what invites the medium of digital photography and the everyday media sphere. After all, Bridle's enigmatic interventions in urban space present precisely the kind of photo op that fuels content creation by users of Facebook, Snapchat, Flickr, and Instagram. Such curiosities are the stuff of the kind of "click bait" that is tailor-made to what Martin Hand calls "ubiquitous photography."[35] The project is itself an extension of images from everyday digital media, specifically the accidental drone shadows captured by Google mapping satellites. Collected on numerous websites, these shadows present a kind of residue or Lacanian stain within the seamless representation of the world, a reminder of the conditions that make possible a seemingly perfect legibility of space. Immersed in this environment, Bridle's drones no longer serve the ends of reconnaissance but rather are hijacked by a new future orientation.

Working from the case study of photobloggers, Kris Cohen observes that certain practices of digital photography exhibit only a "minor intentionality."[36] In these contexts, photography "produces photographs as effects, but isn't superseded by them and doesn't even seem to be the necessary cause of them."[37] As the causal relation between photography and photographs is weakened, Cohen describes the photographic act as collapsing the activity of photography and photoblogging without collapsing the spatio-temporal separation of these events. As such, the photograph in social media is not so much an image without content as an image whose content is its relational aspect. The popular photo-messaging app Snapchat is exemplary of this dynamic, as the static image is not only deemphasized to the point of disappearance (images last eight seconds before being removed from the server) but also understood as a prompt or support for continual, near-live exchanges of information. This experience embodies what Cohen calls a "new categorical richness" of the photographic moment in the context of digital photography. Here, the "frozen instant" gives way to an incessant, ecstatic doing as images are recontextualized, redefined, and reconstituted within the networks of social media. Summarizing these sentiments, Caterina Fake, the founder of Flickr, explains: "The nature of photography now is it's in motion. It doesn't stop time anymore."[38] In similar terms, while the drone in Bridle's piece only becomes legible via its photograph, this act of appearing does not constitute an end in itself. Rather, it comes to mark the inability of locating "the work" in its totality and, as such, speaks to a future dimension that this mode of practice is connected to and continues within. One might describe the work's peculiar instability in terms of what Erin Manning has called "preacceleration," the momentum of a movement that has not yet taken place but manifests as the instability of form.[39]

The question that then structures Bridle's work concerns how one can photograph or otherwise contain the drone and its corresponding relations of power in light of its distributed status. The 2011 capture of a U.S. drone by Iran is instructive on this front. By repeatedly showing Iranian officials touching and handling an object that once proved unreachable, the media staging of this event seemed to use tactility as a symbolic means of containment and capture. Despite an attempt to commandeer the power of the drone via the image, the larger focus on holding the vehicle captive within enemy territory appeared to draw from antiquated iterations of war that respected boundaries and objects. In the context of networked warfare, spatial relations only loosely correspond to national boundaries, and material components only gain significance or value via relations to the network. As Bridle himself describes, the drone is the "prosthetic of the network. . . . It's not the drone itself that should be of concern to us. . . . It's [the way in which] it permits certain forms of warfare."[40] Yet this reappearance of tactility and firsthandedness in this footage clearly suggested something more nefarious than simple containment—its performance speaks to the possibility of a certain kind of reverse engineering, a mode of working backward through the object in order to reopen the potentiality of the network from the outside. The vulnerability of the drone to these interventions, what Latour might call the "reversibility of [its] foldings,"[41] is confirmed by the pervasive suspicion that this "capture" may have been part of an orchestrated infiltration of Iranian networks via the U.S. military. Bridle's *Drone Shadows* project attempts to disclose this potentiality by utilizing incomplete representations, images that traffic in residues, faint trails, and empty shadows, all of which serve to place this object in, as Honor Harger puts it, its native environment of the network.[42] This entails eschewing the stability of form in favor of a future-oriented becoming in which the stasis of images break down or are otherwise compromised.

Orgnets, Antiwebs, and the Symmetry of Resistance

In their "#ACCELERATE MANIFESTO for an Accelerationist Politics," Alex Williams and Nick Srnicek attempt to disentangle the affirmationist undertones of accelerationism from the techno-utopian leanings of twentieth-century media activism. They do this by problematizing the notion that technology and the social field operate independently of one another. Rather than a progressive social or political agenda utilizing technology for its realization, accelerationism understands the social as always already technological.[43] While not necessarily isolated to the contemporary, this condition is nonetheless amplified by the expansion of the scope and scale of subsumption that occurs under the digital economy of late capitalism. Shifting from what Steven Shaviro describes as extrinsic to intrinsic exploitation,[44] the expenditures of labor are now directly incorporated as commodity via social media and the modulated surveillance of big data. As a result, "production and circulation [have become] indistinguishable" and the mode of communication serves as its own content.[45] These relations materialize as "communicative capitalism," a fantasy fueled by techno-fetishism and illusory models of participation that present digital culture as the realization of democratic ideals of exchange.[46]

In this environment, new media platforms can never serve as ends in themselves (the manifesto warns "never believe that technology will be sufficient to save us").[47] Yet just as this escalation of subsumption ensures that the "circulation of content . . . forecloses the antagonism necessary for politics," so does it virtually eradicate the possibility of an outside to these operations.[48] In response to this impasse, accelerationism proposes that intervention entail a symmetry of sorts between what was once called resistance and the exercise of power. Far from a kind of Hegelian master–slave dialectic, this relation does not hinge upon "othering" or negativity but rather a kind of perverse mimicry through which the relations of capitalism are amplified to an unsustainable degree. Summarizing these sentiments, Robin Mackay and Armen Avanessian claim: "While distancing itself from mere technological optimism, contemporary accelerationism retains an antipathy, a disgust even, for retreatist solutions, and an ambitious interest in reshaping and repurposing (rather than refusing) the technologies that are the historical product of capitalism."[49] The global counterinsurgency entangles these relations of capital with the operations of modern warfare. Manuel Castells describes these constellations as "meta-networks," joint formations that amplify the power and reach of individual networks via "switching power" while at the same time appearing to preserve their sphere of action.[50] Through this constellation, everyday communication and affective states are not simply commodified but militarized via the global counterinsurgency and its expansive networks. Symptomatic of this expansion is what James Der Derian describes as the arrival of a "military-industrial-media-entertainment network" (MIME-NET), which escalates the intrusion of the "living room war" of Vietnam to a war waged within the global networks that constitute daily life.[51] The advent of this "spectator warfare" is made possible not so much by the intensity of these media presentations, their ability to convey the "reality" of war, but rather the exact opposite. It is the banality, invisibility, and overall shared level of mediation that overlaps these mechanisms with networked warfare, laying the groundwork for the "everywhere war" of which we are all subjects.[52]

Without a discernible outside to the parameters of the counterinsurgency, resistance necessitates an infiltration or occupation of the network, a practice that places drone art in often uncomfortable proximity to its military counterparts. A case in point is Marko Peljhan's company, C-ASTRAL, whose Trust-System (Tactical Radio Unified System Transport) project involved, among other things, converting a cruise missile into a functioning broadcast station. Peljhan describes the intent behind these works in terms of what he calls "conversion," a kind of post-Marxist version of the Situationist practice of détournement wherein military technology is reconfigured and made available for civilian use.[53] Writing in 1956, Guy Debord and Gil Wolman formulated détournement in reaction to "the emergence of productive forces that necessitate *other* production relations and a new practice of life."[54] While employing a familiar strategy of appropriation, Peljhan's operation refuses the negativity of the original formulation where the object is recontexutalized so as to conflict with and even negate its native environment. The Trust-System instead operates in situ with its targeted object, participating in the media networks from which it was extracted, so much so that the company's recent work has gained the attention of the military itself.

A similar precariousness runs through Ars Electronica's syncopated drone performances, which are staged in the night sky of London and other European cities. Like the works of Bridle and Paglen, these performances are not simply about deflating the violence of drones by recasting them as objects (aesthetic or otherwise) but are also involved in visualizing new modes of connectivity. As the tiny lights of the hummingbird drones appear to be stars, their presence forces active and inactive points along this imaginary network to converge. The line between mobile and immobile blurs as linkages form and deform according to an unstable logic. As if mimicking the underbelly of airplanes, the flashing lights emerge and dissipate, taking on new identities within this flux.[55] While on the surface this movement seems to carry with it a diminishing of the violence of the drone, its spatial-temporal dispersion also visualizes the logic of networked warfare, which proceeds without formal declaration or finality and operates without geographic or spatial boundaries.

Fashioning resistance outside of "ends based" strategies, these works inevitably conjure recurring criticisms of accelerationism, which is sometimes derided as a "cybernetic mask for neoliberalism" that leads to "practical impotence."[56] While defending this school of thought against these charges is beyond the purview of this chapter, the above analysis of drone art has at least challenged the tendency of these critiques toward oversimplification in its cataloging of the sheer diversity of strategies that the term incorporates. Seeing as though a totalizing picture or a static objective or program is antithetical to its "machinic" roots, drone art necessarily incorporates a shifting array of strategies. Within this instability, potentialities gather and materialize along a spectrum of overlapping, contradictory networks, producing a movement that might best be described in terms of a simultaneity of Galloway and Thatcher's notion of the "antiwebs" and Geert Lovink's "orgnets" (organized networks).[57]

Championing "counterprotocol" practices and an overall "informatics" of thinking, Galloway and Thatcher emphasize the utilization of nonhuman actors and the establishing of "superpliant" networks within networks to "exploit" the power differentials of the sovereignty–network dialectic. These postideological interventions produce a point of entry for what they call "the exploit," a strategy that utilizes the asymmetry of the network to push it toward inverse manifestations, an "antiweb."[58] On the other hand, Geert Lovink describes an alternative practice of microformations, which are also born out of the conflict between institutional and decentralized instantiations of the network. However, rather than weakening the connections of this network, orgnets seek to strengthen ties between smaller units of these formations so as to ensure the possibility of horizontal peer-to-peer transactions. As a postrepresentational configuration, these networks are less about producing outcomes or policy than preserving their own horizontal interconnectivity.[59] Drone art internalizes an oscillation or movement between these formations, both redirecting from within by accelerating power differentials to the point of deformation and, at the same time, building sustainable modes of communication within these relations.

Notes

1. Virilio, *War and Cinema*, 11–30.
2. Drew, "Military Is Awash in Data from Drones."
3. Virilio, *War and Cinema*, 1.

4. For more information on drone hunting, see Bittel, "Want a Drone-Hunting License?"
5. Mark Fisher succinctly summarizes this disavowal: "so long as we believe in our hearts that capitalism is bad, we are free to participate in capitalist exchange." Fisher, *Capitalist Realism*, 13.
6. Dillon, *Deconstructing International Politics*, 118.
7. A. Williams, "Escape Velocities." See also Noys, *The Persistence of the Negative*; Deleuze and Guattari, *Anti-Oedipus*; Land, *Fanged Noumena*; Brassier, "Concepts and Objects"; Negarestani, "A Vertiginous View of Enlightenment"; and Negarestani, "Globe of Revolution."
8. Gregory, "The Everywhere War," 239.
9. Transcripts from bit plane flight, http://www.bureauit.org/data/transcripts/bitplane.
10. Harger, "Unmanned Aerial Ecologies."
11. Gregory, "The Everywhere War," 239; Mirzoeff, *The Right to Look*, 20.
12. Johnston, "Machinic Vision," 27.
13. See Mejias, *Off the Network*, 80–144.
14. Meijas, *Off the Network*, 92.
15. Mejias, *Off the Network*, 90.
16. Bonnington and Ackerman, "Apple Rejects App."
17. Pater, *Drone Survival Guide*, www.rt.com/news/drone-survival-guide-published-774/.
18. Friedersdorf, "Every Person Is Afraid." See also International Human Rights and Conflict Resolution Clinic (Stanford Law School) and Global Justice Clinic (NYU School of Law), *Living under Drones*.
19. Friedersdorf, "Every Person Is Afraid."
20. An intercepted communication between al-Qaeda leaders confirms this ubiquity of the drone. It offers numerous means of sabotaging their operation. These include organizing a group of snipers to "hunt" the drone, burning tires to create smoke, and entering buildings with multiple entrances and exits to confuse the drone. The document suggests a familiarity and firsthandness that is not exclusive to members of al-Qaeda. *Telegraph*, "Al-Qaeda's 22 Tips."
21. Harwood, "Endless War."
22. Manovich, "The Mapping of Space," 2.
23. Freud, "Inhibitions, Symptoms and Anxiety," 166.
24. C. Schmitt, *The Concept of the Political*, 26.
25. Galloway and Thacker, *The Exploit*, 65.
26. Galloway and Thacker, *The Exploit*, 63.
27. I place the word *hacker* in quotation marks to reference the dubious nature of this term. The footage from drone cameras is often left unencrypted to avoid latency. This means that any amateur enthusiast can pick up this material if so inclined.
28. If, as Peter Sloterdijk claims, the use of chlorine gas in 1915 marked a shift in the targets of war away from individual subjects and toward the conditions of life, then the virus might be considered in terms of an opposite trajectory, a self-replicating force that exploits the conditions of life itself; Sloterdijk, *Terror from the Air*.

The "Collateral Murder" video was leaked to Wikileaks in 2010. It shows several sequences in which unarmed Iraqi civilians and journalists are shot with 30mm rounds from a U.S. Apache helicopter.

29. S. Weber, *Targets of Opportunity*, 4.
30. S. Weber, *Targets of Opportunity*, 5.
31. Processes that utilize this additive mode of construction include selective laser melting (SLM) or direct metal laser sintering (DMLS), selective laser sintering (SLS), and fused deposition modeling (FDM).
32. Gregory, "From a View to a Kill," 196.
33. Gregory, "From a View to a Kill," 196.
34. Latour, "Spheres and Networks," 141.
35. Hand, *Ubiquitous Photography*.
36. Cohen, "What Does the Photoblog Want?," 894.
37. Cohen, "What Does the Photoblog Want?,"896.
38. Harmon, "Stop Them before They Shoot Again."
39. In this, the piece maintains a close affinity to what fellow drone artist Trevor Paglen refers to as "entangled photography" or "relational photography." Echoing Nicolas Bourriaud's conception of "relational aesthetics," Paglen describes a "photography beyond photographs," a mode of practice that foregrounds the politics of image production over the content or finality of the image itself. Expanding this notion to network relations suggests that the parameters of "production" be expanded beyond the act of image capture so as to incorporate its circulation and redefinition via processes of exchange and remediation. Exemplary of Bourriaud's original concept is Félix González-Torres's "candy pieces," in which the audience literally constructs the work by taking or not taking pieces from a pile of candy, or Gillian Wearings's *Sign* series in which subjects were asked to caption their own self-portraits. See Curcio, "Seeing Is Believing."
40. Quoted from an interview in *Under the Shadow of the Drone*, a film directed by Brian McClave for the 2013 Brighton Festival.
41. Latour, "Morality and Technology," 258.
42. Harger, "Unmanned Aerial Ecologies."
43. A. Williams and Srnicek, "#ACCELERATE MANIFESTO for an Accelerationist Politics."
44. Shaviro, *Post-Cinematic Affect*, 48.
45. Shaviro, *Post-Cinematic Affect*, 48.
46. Dean, *Democracy and Other Neoliberal Fantasies*.
47. Williams and Srnicek, "#ACCELERATE MANIFESTO for an Accelerationist Politics."
48. Dean, "Communicative Capitalism," 54.
49. Mackay and Avenessian, *#Accelerate: The Accelerationist Reader*, 23.
50. Castells, *Networks of Outrage and Hope*, 7–9.
51. Der Derian, "The Desert of the Real," 931–48.
52. Gregory, "The Everywhere War," 239.
53. Harger, "Unmanned Aerial Ecologies."
54. Debord and Wolman, "A User's Guide to Détournement."

55. In this, the performance visualizes what John Arquilla and David Ronfeldt refer to as the "blurring" and "blending" of networks, dynamics that envelope not only individual nodes but the network itself. Arquilla and Ronfeldt, *Networks and Netwars*, 13.
56. Brassier, "Accelerationism."
57. Galloway and Thacker, *The Exploit*, 22; Lovink, *Networks without a Cause*, 164–69.
58. Galloway and Thacker, *The Exploit.*
59. Lovink, *Networks without a Cause*, 164–69.

9 THE CONTAINMENT ZONE

MADIHA TAHIR

WHAT HAD ONCE BEEN the frontier in British India had been "swallowed up in the interior," explained George Nathaniel Curzon, the former British Viceroy of India (1898–1905) during a lecture on frontiers in 1907.[1] Speaking of the British Indian Frontier, Curzon explained that "the title has passed, with the geographical fact which it represents, to the new North-West Frontier Province."[2] In present-day Pakistan, that province has now been renamed Khyber Pakhtunkhwa (KP), but the designation of "frontier" still lingers on its outer edges across a narrow territory along the Pakistan-Afghanistan border, formally known as the Federally Administered Tribal Areas (FATA). Since 2004, this territory has been the site of the most sustained American bombing by armed drones.

Hardly self-evident ontological facts, the frontier and its other, the sovereign nation-state, are co-constructed. If borders are cartographic lines dividing sovereign states, frontiers are zones with depth, ambiguously marked spaces that ebb and flow with the political tides.[3] Borders imply the consonance of nation, state, and territory as a permanent artifact; frontiers are subject to flexible, experimental governance, even extinguishment, as Curzon suggests. At the turn of the twentieth century, this "imaginative geography"[4] resulted in a policy of imperial frontier policing that exposed the targeted populations to particular forms of confinement, bombardment, and physical force as it aimed, alternately, to deter and to persuade subjects in order to maintain control.[5] Beginning in 1915, the aircraft became part of the apparatus of what would be called "air control" or "air policing" in the British Indian Frontier, with independent air raids deployed in 1917.[6] The first sustained bombing campaign in Waziristan and the North-West Frontier began in 1919 in a bid to quell rebellion, and it was part of a broader development of the use of aircraft to police not only the North-West Frontier but also Somaliland, Iraq, Afghanistan, Palestine, Yemen, Egypt, and elsewhere.[7]

To rationalize the bombing of villages and towns as an effective, even humane, method of control, air policing drew upon racialized cultural justifications.[8] Today, the official discourse on drone bombardment is usually shorn of explicitly racist tropes. Yet the idea that certain territories are somehow peculiar, inscrutable, and essentially lawless continues to circulate in the popular milieu, allowing President Barack Obama to claim special sanction for the actions of American troops because, as he puts it, "a sole reliance on law enforcement in territories that have no functioning police or security services—and indeed have no functioning law"—does not offer a "moral safe harbor."[9] Thus, it may not be so much that war is transforming into policing (aided by the drone) as it is that U.S. empire now returns to frontiers with a logic of violence that has historically been deemed appropriate for such territory. Indeed, the master code of the "war on terror" is not law but culture, embodied in the oft-repeated refrain that "they hate our way of life."

This is evident in Pakistan where drones bomb entirely within FATA, a territory that is administered through colonial-era regulations grounded in essentialist notions of preserving "native" custom. In other words, drone bombing is intrinsically tied to techniques of governance *on the ground.* These techniques format, enable, and shape drone bombardment by organizing and arranging the spatial order. While much academic work has usefully interrogated the construction of targets, the development of the notion of collateral damage, the visual regimes of drone bombardment, the algorithmic rationality of strikes, and other related issues, it has had less to say about how governance on the ground contributes to the apparatus of drone bombardment. Yet, without a particular arrangement on the ground, the drone apparatus cannot function as it does.

In what follows, I map the spatialization of FATA by the Pakistani security state.[10] To produce the Tribal Areas as available for overwhelming force requires considerable effort on the ground. I begin by sketching the spatial and administrative organization of FATA, then turn to some of the forms of violence to which it gives rise. I conclude by proposing a reconceptualization of the spatial order of the Tribal Areas.

The Spatial Order

In the years leading up to independence, British rule oscillated across a range of border policies in the North-West Frontier as it attempted to establish a buffer zone between British India and Afghanistan to its west while quelling rebellions in that territory and extending indirect rule.[11] The latter proceeded through colonial governance that claimed to leave cultural practices intact even as it hollowed out local customs and institutions and operationalized them as tactics of rule. In the frontier, this included the development of a system of monetary allowances, bribes, and collective fines on tribes; the identification of local leaders or *maliks* who could be tied to imperial rule through payments; the transformation of a collective local practice of the *jirga* into an administrative institution; and, finally, the establishment of militias and native security forces drawn from the tribes themselves.[12] Political officers prided themselves on their cultural knowledge and connections with the tribes.[13] Yet, when this knowledge failed them, the consequences could be harsh for the Tribal Areas. When the Afghan king, Amanullah Khan, invaded in 1919, the native militia system constructed by the British fell apart with many of the recruits joining the Afghan regulars.[14] The British army moved into Waziristan, and successive rebellions were suppressed with increasing use of air bombing campaigns.[15] Although imperial officers generally explained the uprisings as the religious fanaticism of the tribes, the agitations were often driven by more worldly concerns. In 1922 the editors of the newspaper *Al-Mujahid* decried how the land had been "cut to pieces" by roads, military posts, and camps, suggesting that a mobilizing concern centered on the threat of enclosure.[16] By 1939 Major General Charles Gwynn, a British officer who penned the manual *Imperial Policing*, could write of the North-West Frontier:

> Since the policy of maintaining a permanent garrison in the area, and of constructing roads through it, has been adopted, operations, whatever their scale, have acquired essentially a policing character. For although the administrative frontier has not been extended to include Waziristan, we exercise a more direct measure of control than formerly with machinery for maintaining order in normal times, the Army and Air Force giving assistance only on special occasions. Broadly speaking, political control is exercised through the tribal headmen, paid, in addition to other allowances, to maintain irregular forces of their

> own for which arms are supplied by us. These "Khassadars" are responsible for the safety of the roads and for keeping the turbulent elements of the tribes in order. But the political Resident has also under his own authority a force of levies commanded by British officers—the Tochi and South Waziristan Scouts recruited from border tribes—who to all intents and purposes are a military police.[17]

The system that Gwynn describes was largely maintained after independence. Even though Pakistan withdrew its forces in 1947, it reacted to uprisings in the area much as the British had. When the formidable anticolonial rebel Mirza Ali Khan, better known as the Faqir of Ipi, who had led several campaigns against the British, attacked outposts in Datta Khel, North Waziristan, and raised a demand for an independent state for ethnic Pashtuns, the Pakistan Air Force bombed the *lashkar*.[18]

The FATA is today organized into seven units known as "agencies," two of which—North Waziristan and South Waziristan—have been the site of the heaviest drone bombardment. Additionally, there are six "frontier regions," areas that provide a buffer between the Tribal Areas and what are called the "settled areas" of Pakistan, namely the country's four provinces. This slim band of territory running along the Pakistan-Afghanistan border is a space for experimental governance, instrumentalized for the security state's various aims, sometimes in concert with the United States. During the Cold War, it became a staging ground for raising the *mujahideen* for interventions into Kashmir and Afghanistan, the latter a critical site for the American effort against the Soviet Union. The Pakistan military's "strategic depth" policy in Afghanistan continues to necessitate the use of FATA as a securitized zone through and on which overwhelming violence can be enacted. All of this has meant that the Tribal Areas are administered through strategic forms of regulated enclosures enabled by draconian legislation, a configuration of security forces, and, when necessary, temporal and spatial closure—a system that, paradoxically, reproduces itself by claiming to preserve the autonomy of the tribes. According to the government: "The tribes regulate their own affairs in accordance with customary rules and unwritten codes, characterized by collective responsibility for the actions of individual tribemen [*sic*] and territorial responsibility for the area under their control. The government functions through local-level tribal intermediaries i.e. Maliks (representatives of the tribes) and Lungi-holders (representatives of sub-tribes or clans), who are influential members of their respective clan or tribe."[19] Governance, in other words, proceeds under the sign of "culture." It is a system enabled by the incorporation of FATA into Pakistan through the colonial-era Frontier Crimes Regulations (FCR). Under the FCR, a federally appointed political agent governs each agency, wielding extraordinary executive, administrative, and judicial power with no substantive accountability. The FCR allow for collective punishment of entire families or even tribes on mere suspicion, as well as arbitrary detention, economic blockades, destruction of property, and even imprisonment of children.[20] Adult franchise was extended to the Tribal Areas in 1996, and political parties have only been allowed to function since the last general elections in 2013. Even though FATA is (now) represented in Pakistan's Senate and National Assembly, its representatives are in the strange position of being part of a parliament whose laws and directives do not apply to their region.

Governmental reason, underwritten by essentialist notions of custom, also organizes the spatial order. The FATA is not only divided from the settled districts; it is also internally fragmented, broken up by topographies of law that are usually characterized as "protected" and "unprotected" areas, although, in practice, the borders of these zones are ambiguous.[21] In protected areas, with the locus of authority moving outward from public works, roads, offices, and government installations, the FCR vests the political agent with judicial powers in criminal and civil cases. Expanding out from unprotected areas, the levers of influence shift from direct administration by the Pakistan Army (PA) to exerting economic or political pressure on local maliks and other locals for effect.[22] It is a system that arranges space through the logic of cultural autonomy—the government says it only minimally interferes—but one whose final consequence in times of conflict is not the preservation of custom beyond the reach of governance but containment. In fact, several levels of security forces, from the sporadic lashkars raised to fight insurgents or settle disputes to more formal organizations, structure space and circulation in FATA.

In addition to the lashkars, the *khassadars* mentioned by Gwynn continue to function at the most local level. An untrained force, sometimes called the "tribal police," they were first raised by the British to assist maliks in maintaining roads and thwarting those that proved too troublesome to their authority.[23] The khassadars are now tasked with providing safe passage through their territory and serve under the PA. They are drawn from the tribes on a quota system that determines how many khassadars may be selected from each tribe depending on the tribe's size and influence.[24] These appointments are the right of the malik who pays them.[25] The malik, in turn, receives money from the government based on the amount of territory his tribe controls. As such, the khassadari system is oriented toward the malik and maintaining tribalized arrangements through which they are appointed. Khassadars are low paid, and the situation has disintegrated with bribes being exchanged for appointments and little oversight.[26]

Levies are also drawn from among tribes, and, unlike khassadars, who must have their own weapons, levies are provided arms by the government. They also serve under the political agent who appoints and pays them. Their duties overlap with those of the khassadars, and they are also underpaid and undertrained.[27]

A paramilitary force, the Frontier Constabulary draws its officers from the police while its ranks come from the Tribal Areas as well as Khyber Pakhtunkhwa, one of the provinces neighboring FATA.[28] Historically entrusted with preventing tribal raids into settled areas, it regulates movement between the Tribal Areas and the settled districts through a network of posts and checkpoints. The Constabulary also lists among its duties the protection of government installations, development projects, and senior personnel, providing security for multinational corporations and for trade on the Karakorum Highway. As conflicts have flared in various parts of the country, the Constabulary has added new policing zones and recruits from them: it now boasts seventeen areas of jurisdiction across Pakistan. In the country's capital, for instance, its "pivotal function," according to its website, is to "provide security to foreigners, diplomats, embassies, consulates, ambassadors and other installations as well to provide security to VVIPs in ICT (Islamabad Capital Territory)."[29]

If the Constabulary polices a border internal to Pakistan, each of the agencies is also subject to a paramilitary force that polices the Afghanistan-Pakistan border. Led by officers from the Pakistan Army, the Frontier Corps (FC) polices the Durand line while also serving as the supreme force responsible for law and order in FATA.[30] Although under the command of the Ministry of Interior, the FC is led by the Inspector General, a post that is generally filled by a major general; most of the recruits are drawn from FATA and ethnically Pashtun regions. During the 1970s and 1980s, the FC assisted in training the mujahideen. Since 9/11, it has increasingly been deployed in operations, and the United States has committed money and American trainers to equip and train this force, because—as part of the return to culture as an instrument in counterinsurgencies—the local and cultural knowledge of

Pashtun recruits is viewed as an asset.[31] The Pakistan military, however, also regards the FC contemptuously, with one military analyst writing that the officers see the militiamen "dressed in *shalwar* and *qameez* (traditional loose shirt and baggy pants worn by civilians) and *chaplis* (local sandals) and . . . dismiss them as a rabble."[32]

Taken together, these security forces all have their historical roots in colonial policing whose operative rationality was the maintenance of a buffer zone between the British Raj and Afghanistan. They also illustrate the intimacy of securitization. In addition to the Frontier Constabulary, whose numbers are not readily available, there were roughly 80,000 Frontier Corps troops, largely drawn from FATA and KP, with reportedly 55,000 of them in its Khyber Pakhtunkhwa division by 2008.[33] Additionally, there are currently 18,420 khassadars and 18,106 levies in FATA who also come from the Tribal Areas. In other words, an astonishing percentage of FATA's residents—a population of 3.18 million according to the last census conducted in 1998[34]—draw salaries or benefits from the security regime of the Pakistani state. Many in FATA consider the military as an outside force—its officers rotating through the Tribal Areas often have to rely on local Pashto translators, which locates them as outsiders—but these security forces are held in comparatively better regard. The FC, for example, has historically been better received in FATA than in Balochistan, Pakistan's largest province by landmass, where the FC's largely Pashtun troops also operate to suppress an ongoing ethnonationalist Baloch rebellion. The collaboration of the federal government and maliks in a (albeit unequal) governmental apparatus in which their authority and control is co-constitutive has resulted in a studied inability to structure other economic opportunities for FATA residents that are independent of state–malik authority. Consequently, securitization remains a viable labor market.

On the Road

Rather than sheer "lawlessness," then, FATA is immersed in a security economy in which the splintering of law across multiple, overlapping lines of jurisdiction also creates opportunities for illicit bribes, payoffs, and violence. Truckers who transport goods for NATO from Karachi through FATA and into Afghanistan mapped this economy for me during an interview at a truck stop in Khyber Agency en route to the Torkham border crossing:

> My name is Mohammad Umar. I loaded it for Bagram, three days before Ramzan. The charge for it was 1 lakh rupees. I've only 6,000 rupees left. From Peshawar to Kabul, the whole world demands money [bribes] from us. Every check post in Pakistan takes money from us. Then, the Afghan at the border takes money. Then in Jalalabad, he takes money. Then in Kabul, he takes money. And, of course, the truck has costs. Come with me right now. Come in the truck. You'll see how they treat us:
>
> "Get out of the truck asshole! Give us money!" He'll say, "Give me 500 rupees!"
>
> I'll say, "I don't have it. Just take 200."
>
> "Asshole! Give me 500!"
>
> Then what would you say? See for yourself. And, you'll say, "Just give him the money."
>
> They break your windshield with their Kalashnikov. They hit the vehicle. They damage it. That'll cost 5,000 rupees. So, 500 rupees is better than that, isn't it? What else can we do? We're obligated. They take money from everyone.[35]

A second trucker, Rahil Afridi, joined the conversation, relating how he had been beaten earlier that day for failing to pay a bribe. "You can't force them to back off. He has more power. He wears a uniform. He's a government man. You can't say anything."[36]

Both Umar and Afridi reveal how the securitized circulation of people and goods exposes them to risk, humiliation, harm, and abuse, that is, to precarity. Through the bureaucratic and spatial order of the administrative apparatus, the security forces, and the fragmentation of territory along protected and unprotected zones—the former of which, crucially, extend in and around roads—authorities regulate, curtail, block, shape, filter, and interrupt movement. Roads have been integral to this logic of control. Indeed, in neighboring Afghanistan, the United States has put significant effort into constructing roads. In his book *The Accidental Guerrilla* (2009), David Kilcullen says about roads:

> Once the road is through and paved, it is much harder to place IEDs [improvised explosive devices] under the tarmac surface or on the concrete verge, and IEDs are easier to detect if emplaced. The road provides an alternative works project to prevent people joining the

Taliban, the improved ease of movement makes business easier and transportation faster and cheaper, and thus spurs economic growth, and the graded black-top road allows friendly troops to move much more easily and quickly than before, along the valley floor, helping secure population centers and drive the enemy up into the hills where they are separated from the population—allowing us to target them more easily and with less risk of collateral damage, and allowing political, intelligence, aid, governance, education and development work to proceed with less risk.[37]

Although Kilcullen admits that the road is not a panacea, the range of projects in which it is inserted is illuminating. For Kilcullen, it is a technology of commerce and of securitization (quickly moving troops to "secure" population centers), that is, of movement and its arrest. It is a strangely contradictory geographic imagination that assumes a tidy, welcome cohabitation between the imperial army and the local population (as if military traffic were just like any other) and enables the total conflation between the literal road and the metaphorical and teleological "road" to success. Yet a visualization based on WikiLeaks data from 2004 to 2009 shows that the highest frequency of incidents occurred around the Kabul–Kandahar highway reconstructed by the United States.[38] Built to demonstrate the American commitment to Afghanistan's reconstruction, the highway also connects the two largest U.S. bases at Kandahar and Bagram and several smaller ones in between.[39]

In the Tribal Areas, too, the United States Agency for International Development (USAID) has funded roads in concert with the Pakistani government. During the inauguration of a sixty-five-mile stretch of road in South Waziristan in June 2012, USAID's acting director, Karen Freeman, once again echoed the dual use of the road. "We believe our joint efforts will bring commerce, jobs, trade, and long-term security to this important region in Pakistan."[40] However, the U.S. agency under whose auspices roads have been built in critical locations in FATA is the Bureau of International Narcotics and Law Enforcement (INL), and it has a narrower agenda: the securitization of the Afghanistan-Pakistan border through surveillance technologies, the construction of outposts and roads "to expand the presence of security forces" into hitherto inaccessible areas, and, finally, providing equipment to some of the forces.[41] With this bureaucratic and spatial organization, authorities can regulate movement and even enact closure through moveable barriers—checkpoints, blockades, roadblocks—that can be quickly erected to enforce curfews or interrupt movement. It is an apparatus that organizes spatial experience into one of anxiety, risk, and precarity.

During interviews I conducted in 2011 and 2012, one interviewee related to me how he had almost been killed for failing to note that a military convoy was passing: "You have to stop one hundred yards from a[n army] convoy. But, when we were crossing one turn, I didn't see them. They pointed guns at me." A second said: "This child gave the passing army [convoy] some sherbet. That day was hot. A blast happened just a short while after. The child was still nearby. They killed him. They killed the child who gave them sherbet." A third described: "There were Tablighis[42] nearby as an army convoy was passing. There was a road blast, and there were children nearby tending to the sheep. They opened fire and killed the children and took their bodies. This happened in FR Bakka Khel." A fourth recounted: "Sometimes people don't know. Two brothers were coming back from Bannu. . . . The army motioned at them. They [the brothers] didn't know what the army wanted. They went toward them and were shot. They [the soldiers] didn't give them [the brothers] time."

The juridical veracity of these anecdotes is less critical than the fact that they are utterly common and myriad, circulating as rumor, cautionary tale, or depiction of the casual ruthlessness of the security forces, particularly the military. These narratives form a low-level hum that rarely rises to the level of event. The bodies of FATA residents are thus marked, alternately, through displays of physical force and through "suspended violence," the latter of which produces anxiety, even fear, through the insinuation of physical force rather than its actual application.[43] It is not, therefore, sheer absence of law but a situation in which residents of the Tribal Areas must remain alert to the multiple, fluid jurisdictions that, as Lindsay Bremner puts it, "regulate the body in motion."[44] The flexible and mobile arrangements of time and space require one to be able to discern when to slow down, to stop, or to get off the road.

Securitized zones near check posts or blockades enable suspended violence in the name of deterring spectacular, physical violence by insurgent groups. Check posts refer, here, to more fortified permanent structures while checkpoints tend to be semi-permanent or temporary structures. The barrel of a gun peering out from a sandbagged checkpoint or from a heavily fortified check post, the sudden establishment of a curfew, and the passing of a military convoy all suggest the threat of physical force.[45] Nor are these merely side effects of securitized circulation. As Gwynn explained in *Imperial Policing*, the "moral effect" depended on the visual insinuation of threat by foregrounding lethal weapons:

> The sight of cold steel has a calming effect, and the steady advance of a line of bayonets has often sufficed to disperse a mob without resort to firing.[46]

> It is sometimes advocated that troops called out in aid of the civil power should be specially armed with non-lethal weapons, such as batons. . . . But the arguments against such a course are generally very strong. The moral effect of the appearance of troops depends largely on the fact that they carry lethal weapons. It is a warning to spectators that it is time to get away and it awakens the more moderate element to the seriousness of the situation.[47]

While the "moral effect" of suspended violence is clear when faced with the muzzle of a gun, it does not rise to the level of nameable event for editors in Islamabad, New York, and London. The rules of publicity demand the unexpected—that which "does not happen here." The very repetition and permanence of the architectures of suspended violence, paradoxically, enable the near total erasure of daily violence as that which always happens here. Even when security forces do deploy physical force, it too can be erased, as the inevitable consequence of the "lawlessness" of FATA.

Containment Zones and Filter Points

Indeed, lawlessness conceptualizes the spatial order of FATA as one in which islands of heavily fortified barracks and check posts are anchors in a sea of chaotic disorder.[48] For pro-war proponents, lawlessness provides a neat justification for deploying force by the state in order to establish "law and order." Yet, in FATA, it is unclear what reasserting the law means. As explained above, the legal regime in the Tribal Areas is the FCR, which exposes people to collective punishment, arbitrary detention, and corporal punishment. That *is* the law. The federal government's attempts to reform the FCR in 2011 met strong resistance from the Pakistani military. Only after the military was given sweeping powers of arrest and detention in "conflict zones" under the Actions in Aid of Civil Power (AACPR) law passed that year was the government able to install some changes in the FCR.[49] The AACPR rendered these reforms, such as minimal safeguards against arbitrary detention, meaningless. Mansur Khan Mehsud, who hails from South Waziristan and is the research director of the Islamabad-based FATA Research Center, summed up the situation tartly: "We are free to kill each other if we like as long as we don't do anything to the government."[50]

Free to kill each other as long as we don't do anything to the government encapsulates the culturalist governmental logic that organizes space into protected and unprotected areas, an imagination that maps the territory as government-held zones beyond which lies inscrutable terrain that oscillates between tribal autonomy and its double, lawlessness. The task of governance, then, is to distinguish between the exercise of proper circulation (culture/autonomy) and improper circulation (militancy/lawlessness). Indeed, functionaries of the Pakistani security regime explain their incursions and operations as temporary procedures to halt the slide from custom into lawlessness. The military commander who led the latest operation in Waziristan, Major General Zafarullah Khan Khattak, observed: "Whether it is rethink of the FCR [the Frontier Crimes Regulation that rules the Federally Administered Tribal Areas], or economic solutions, or good governance, we must understand what rules these people. The local code of Cholwashti [locals protecting their own land honourably] has to be brought back. What's always worked must work again. And for those who don't follow the local custom . . . We must kill them. We must fight them to the death."[51] The game of recognition, as Khattak reveals, always moves beyond drawing distinctions to establishing the very terms of what is properly culture and what is repugnant.[52] It is in this context that the security state spatializes the politics of recognition in FATA by engineering space into *containment zones* and *filter points*.

Containment zones are areas of temporal and spatial closure through curfews, shoot-on-sight policies, and checkpoints. They are also internally differentiated. So, while it remains possible for resident and nonresident Pakistani citizens to circulate through parts of Khyber Agency, other areas are under curfew (Bara, for example). North Waziristan, meanwhile, has remained entirely under continuous closure—nonresidents of Waziristan are not allowed in—and those who live there are subject to curfews. These zones are often difficult for ground forces that face attacks from insurgents; the government's political agents cannot traverse them with ease. That, however, does not mean that the area is beyond the state's reach. The cultural logic through which FATA's spatial order is organized as "autonomous" can be mobilized quickly to foreground the force inherent in the system and materialize it as containment zones. With curfews and checkpoints, a particular zone can be demarcated as troubled space and contained not only laterally across the surface but also vertically.[53] Containment zones are generally subject to the heaviest aerial bombardment, whether by the Pakistan Air Force or American drones.[54] Residents may also face mass expulsion on short notice. At times, a warning and a deadline is given after which security forces will strafe the neighborhood either by air or from mounted guns at a nearby towering check post. Containment zones are often established following an attack on security forces that, in turn, erect a curfew and display force through various means, including helicopter gunships that may patrol the airspace or fire.[55]

Bara, a *tehsil* or subdistrict in Khyber Agency, illustrates one version of the containment zone. After it became a stronghold for Mangal Bagh and his organization Lashkar-e-Islam (LeI), security forces enacted curfews and regulated movement at checkpoints. Within the containment zone, however, Bagh even took up policing duties through his own militia. It was not until the LeI had begun to threaten the takeover of the Khyber Pass, the main road that carries NATO supplies, that security forces began to articulate Bagh as a threat. The group's kidnapping in June 2008 of sixteen Christians in Peshawar, the capital city of KP province, further stoked fears that the frontier would spill over into settled areas.[56] These twin threats led to Operation Sirat-e-Mustaqeem (Righteous Path). The short twelve-day operation was mainly aimed at forcing insurgents away from Peshawar and the pass. Security forces have maintained the containment zone. In 2013, when Bara had already been subjected to a curfew over forty months long, security forces killed eighteen people in their homes near Dogra Check Post in Khyber Agency.[57] The killings followed an attack on a nearby check post that had killed seven soldiers a day earlier.[58] In an unusual move, the families protested, taking the bodies of the dead to the Governor's House in Peshawar. The protest was baton-charged and forcibly broken up. The Frontier Corps, meanwhile, released a statement blaming LeI militants wearing FC uniforms.[59] Because the territory vacillates between autonomy and lawlessness in the securitized imagination, it is always suspicious: it is never clear whether the "tribesman" will turn out to be an insurgent or the militiaman will turn out to be a militant literally wearing camouflage; hence, enclosure applies to the entire multitude.

The containment zone harbors an intensification of suspended violence and physical force. If biopolitics takes the population as its object over which the sovereign's power operates to "make live and let die," its escalation in the containment zone takes on a qualitatively different tenor.[60] Here, the regulation of bodies is not aimed at disciplining citizens but containing the multitude of categories—tribesmen, insurgents, women, and children—and, at the extreme, "inscribing them, when the time comes, within the order of the maximal economy now represented by the 'massacre.' "[61] Between May 2008 and late 2011, the Pakistan Air Force had already dropped 10,600 bombs in the region.[62] As of this writing, Zarb-e-Azb and now Khyber-1, the ongoing operations in FATA that have resulted in the expulsion and displacement of nearly one million people and an untold number of deaths, are only the latest examples of the consequences of the logic of containment.

This architecture is critical to the operation of American drones. With the exception of two attacks, which happened in territory abutting the Tribal Areas, armed drones also function within containment zones. In fact, the military mediates between the organization of terrestrial containment zones and their vertical extension into flight boxes, formally known as "Restricted Operating Zones," demarcated for the use of American drones. A 2008 diplomatic cable released by WikiLeaks reveals that Admiral Mike Mullen, U.S. Chairman of the Joint Chiefs of Staff, requested approval for a third zone over FATA from General Ashfaq Kayani.[63] By 2010 the United States was also pressuring the Pakistani military to allow armed drones to operate over Quetta, the capital of Balochistan.[64] Pakistani officials refused these requests even though the army is itself facing an ethnonationalist insurgency there.

Containment zones necessitate *filter points*, sites that regulate movement in and out of the area. At check posts or checkpoints, security forces may conduct "checking" of vehicles, people, and their identity documents. Although explained as instrumental to arresting the movement of insurgents, these filter points also serve as mechanisms that reinforce the unequal powers relationship between the people crossing the filter point and the security forces manning it. These focuses use a range of techniques, from petty annoyances to humiliation to prolonged wait times.[65] Here's how one person described to me the process of passing through these sites in 2015:

> There are various check posts primarily being controlled by the Pakistan Army in Waziristan. One has to show his/her identity documents including the National Identity Card before crossing the check post. Security personnel register names of all the passengers going to Waziristan. At

> Bakka Khel, which is an entry point into North Waziristan from district Bannu, the driver of a vehicle carrying passengers has to collect their ID cards and show them to a concerned Pakistan Army official at the check post. The driver is also required to provide a total number of passengers to the security official. When the vehicle reaches Khajuri Check Post, the other security official deployed there will check by counting the number of passengers if the number is correct. If someone is missing, then the driver has to explain where he dropped him/her. There are numerous cases where drivers have been badly beaten up by the security personnel for carrying an extra person.
>
> Sometimes, it takes hours at check posts to get security clearance due to the long queue of vehicles. It becomes very problematic when someone is carrying a patient.
>
> There are specific times when one can go to or leave Waziristan: at 6:00 a.m. in the morning till 6:00 p.m. in the evening. No one can travel at night.
>
> During curfews, no one is allowed to move on the main roads. If someone violates that, they would be shot and killed on the spot.
>
> There are even cases where the local tribesmen were tortured by being physically beaten up by security personnel for failing to communicate properly in Urdu. Thousands of local tribesmen cannot speak Urdu. And, at check posts, the government has deployed army personnel who cannot understand or speak Pashto.[66]

As this account demonstrates, the filter point is a system that reproduces the precise power relations between the security state and the people of FATA. In physically beating and torturing people who do not speak Urdu, the military engages in what has been a foundational disciplinary project for constructing the Pakistani nation. Language politics, or, rather, language as politics, have been a crucial site for congealing a modern Pakistani national identity.[67] The blows to the body link speech, violence, and subjectivity along three interrelated axes. They physically imprint the person being beaten as lacking the qualities proper to a Pakistani citizen. They mark the beaten subject as a "tribesman," that is, one who does not speak the language—literal and figurative—of the Pakistani citizen; he retains his mother tongue and in so doing is marked by "culture." Finally, the physical force applied to the body of the tribesman sacralizes that other body, the one not beaten, that of the proper Pakistani citizen. Indeed, customary laws like the FCR, wherever constructed by colonial authorities, have historically been characterized by corporal punishment.[68] One belongs to a forcibly mute geography of violence, the other to a communicative world of rights. Control is a matter of aural politics here as much as geographic control, or, rather, the geographic imagination of the security state is tied to a particular politics of aurality: the state draws a distinction between that which constitutes speech and that which is noise.

The description also illustrates the monopoly over time by the security apparatus. Filter points mediate and transform the relationship between space and time. People wait for hours. Journeys that are short as a measurement of linear units of distance become far longer as a measurement of a unit of time. Embodied distance is radically out of joint from representational distance on standard satellite images, maps, and other cartographic representations. Filter points thus elongate embodied distance, stretching it out until the Tribal Areas that circulate are "remote," "isolated," "distant," "faraway," and so on, as if these were natural features of the landscape rather than a mediated relationship into which an immense amount of labor, violence, and money has been poured. The time-space compression of modern drone warfare[69] necessitates this simultaneous distantiation. By obstructing, blocking, curfewing, and regulating through filter points, the security state re-presents containment zones as the remote, inscrutable (because inaccessible) frontier. Yet public opinion in support of state violence is also fortified by the suggested *nearness* of conflict zones. When the Tehreek-e-Taliban (TTP) held the district of Swat in 2009, for instance, domestic and international media repeatedly highlighted that the area was "only sixty miles" from the capital. The war on terror exploits the same double movement across a grander geographic scale. The threat that the frontiers might spill over at any moment is what calls out for their containment and even extinguishment, but it is a threat that can only be staged in the near total erasure of the structuring techniques that greatly produce the "chaos" of the frontier.

Postscript

How the colonial logic of frontier policing refracts, transforms, and organizes itself in a postindependence era is essential to understanding how imperial power appropriates and operates in the present. The turn toward reading empire as deterritorialized has generated interesting insight but has also, sometimes, overshadowed how localized techniques of governance attach to the imperial assemblage and how they structure the drone *dispositif*.

By itself, the juridical institutionalization of FATA as exceptional is not a sufficient explanation for the operation of drones in that region. The juridical status also requires labor on the ground, that is, tactics and strategies that arrange space as a containment zone. In that regard, FATA bears resemblance to several other sites, including aspects of the Occupied Palestinian Territories as well as the historical situation of reserves in apartheid South Africa—which were also rationalized as "self-governing" zones for tribalized natives. But, as Mahmood Mamdani has shown, when colonial reason applied a "politically enforced ethnic pluralism," it also cultivated political subjectivities as "tribal," "native," or "citizen."[70] In other words, power subjectivizes and, in so doing, formulates the terrain on which political struggles are fought—even in the postindependence era.[71]

Reading the spatial order of FATA as a "space of exception" obscures this productive axis of power in the Tribal Areas. Giorgio Agamben's eminently influential thesis mapping the metaphysics of the sovereign's power at its horizon cloaks necessary questions about how the legacies of indirect rule are now tied to a politics of cultural recognition that is fertile grounds for forms of agency, consent, and resistance in FATA.

Notes

There are more people than I am able to name who assisted me with this chapter by providing interviews, answering questions, and reading drafts. I am deeply indebted to my interlocutors who work, live, and endure in Pakistan's conflict zones. Without their cooperation and facilitation, my research would not be possible. I would especially like to thank Peter Lagerqvist, Darryl Li, and Saadia Toor for engaging with my work, reading successive versions, and offering thoughtful comments. Usama Khilji and Ihsanullah Tipu Mehsud provided generous assistance of many varieties and allowed me to pester them with questions, for which I am very grateful. The views expressed here, as well as any mistakes, are entirely my own.

1. Curzon, "Frontiers," 30.
2. Curzon, "Frontiers," 30.
3. Weizman, *Hollow Land*, 5.
4. Gregory, *The Colonial Present*, 19–28.
5. Khalili, *Time in the Shadows*, 32.

6. Omissi, *Air Power and Colonial Control.*
7. Omissi, *Air Power and Colonial Control.*
8. Lindqvist, *A History of Bombing*; Bady, "Tarzan's White Flights"; Satia, "The Defense of Inhumanity"; Satia, "Drones: A History."
9. Obama, "Remarks by the President at the National Defense University."
10. The state is not a singular entity anywhere. In the Pakistani context, it is significantly marked by the security apparatus. Here, I speak about the "security state" in order to foreground that situation.
11. Beattie, *Imperial Frontier*; Marsh, "Ramparts of Empire."
12. Marsden and Hopkins, *Fragments of the Afghan Frontier*; Haroon, *Frontier of Faith*. The concept of the tribe has a rich, troubled, and varied history. Sana Haroon and Robert Nichols have shown how colonial officers in the North-West Frontier compiled ethnographic manuals codifying genealogical trees and constructing the ahistorical tribal framework. However, following Haroon, the tribe is now both a category of governance and an idiom through which claims are articulated. See Haroon, *Frontier of Faith*, 25–26; Nichols, *Settling the Frontier*.
13. On the development of expertise by colonial officers, see Robert Nichols's discussion of Captain Robert Warburton, who served as political agent in Khyber. Nichols, "The Frontier Tribal Areas."
14. Tripodi, *Edge of Empire*, 133.
15. Haroon, *Frontier of Faith*; Tripodi, *Edge of Empire*.
16. Haroon, *Frontier of Faith*, 122. The editors warned that Yaghistan (loosely translated as "land of rebels") was in danger of being contained: "Mind that if the enemy succeeds even a little in Waziristan no other place in the frontier will be able to make any opposition to his aggressions because roads have long ago been constructed in the directions of Chakdarra, Chitral and the Khyber railway, Thal, Kurram and other grand roads have been fortified and defended so that the whole of *Yaghistan* is in the power of the enemy" (quoted in Haroon, *Frontiers of Faith*, 122). Importantly, Haroon notes that the *mullahs* made reasonable calculations about sustaining their power, including changing their stance on roads and other infrastructure depending on whether benefits would accrue to them.
17. Gwynn, *Imperial Policing*, 394.
18. Warren, *Waziristan*, 263.
19. FATA Government of Pakistan, "Administrative System," accessed February 1, 2015, https://fata.gov.pk/Global.php?iId=29&fId=2&pId=25&mId=13.
20. Amnesty International, *"As If Hell Fell on Me."*
21. FATA Government of Pakistan, "Administrative System"; Ali and Rehman, *Indigenous Peoples and Ethnic Minorities of Pakistan*.
22. Ali and Rehman, *Indigenous Peoples and Ethnic Minorities of Pakistan*.
23. Ahmad, "The Laws and Justice System."
24. Shinwari, *Understanding FATA*.
25. Gul, *The Most Dangerous Place*, 47–48.
26. International Crisis Group, *Pakistan*, 17.

27. See Gul, *The Most Dangerous Place*, 47–48; and S. Shah, "The FC and Levies."
28. Gul, *The Most Dangerous Place*, 48.
29. Frontier Constabulary, "Frontier Constabulary District Islamabad," accessed February 1, 2015, http://www.fc.gov.pk/internal.php?page=distgadoon.
30. Abbas, "Transforming Pakistan's Frontier Corps"; Imtiaz Gul, *Lawless Frontier*, 48.
31. On training the forces, see E. Schmitt, "U.S. Plan Widens Role"; and E. Schmitt and Perlez, "Distrust Slows U.S. Training of Pakistanis."
32. Quoted in Asfura-Heim, *Risky Business*, 47.
33. Ashraf, "The Pakistan Frontier Corps."
34. Currently, no reliable figures exist of FATA's population, but even doubling the census number would still produce a higher ratio of security forces to the population than the neighboring settled province of Khyber Pakhtunkhwa.
35. Tahir, "On the Road."
36. Tahir, "On the Road."
37. Kilcullen, *The Accidental Guerrilla*, 91.
38. Dewar et al., "Visualization of Activity in Afghanistan." See also Foust, "On the Roads Again in Afghanistan."
39. Gall, "Insurgency's Scars." The attacks ultimately necessitated sending in the Afghan National Army to protect the road without much help from the American forces, illuminating the manner in which domestic forces can be deployed as frontline proxies. In fact, the coordination with the United States was so poor that, in one incident, a passing American convoy opened fire on the Afghan troops guarding the road, wounding a soldier in the legs.
40. U.S. Embassy, "U.S. and FATA Secretariat Continue"; Yousaf, "Kayani Initiates USAID Project."
41. U.S. Department of State, "Border Security Program"; see also U.S. Department of State, "Afghanistan and Pakistan Programs"; and United States Government Accountability Office, "Securing, Stabilizing and Developing." By 2010 the Border Security Program had completed 209 miles (336 km) of what it calls "border security roads" in FATA, and another 45 miles (73 km) were under construction. It had also completed a total of 219 outposts in FATA and its neighboring provinces, Khyber Pakhtunkhwa and Balochistan. By 2013, the last set of figures available, completed road construction had jumped to nearly 621 miles (1,000 km). The 2013 data is unclear on whether the number of outposts also grew. The United States appears to count this assistance as no-military aid, according to Gene L. Dodaro, acting comptroller general of the Government Accountability Office, in *Combating Terrorism*. Much of the construction work is contracted to the Frontier Works Organization (FWO), an agency that is part of the Pakistani military's business nexus. See Siddiqa, *Military Inc.*, 153–54; T. Ali, "The Colour Khaki"; and Green, "US Plans Route to Stability."
42. "Tablighi" refers to adherents of the Tablighi Jamaat, a Deobandi missionary movement that received some attention when it turned out that a young American who joined the Taliban in Pakistan had done so on the encouragement of a Tablighi

missionary. Tablighis are often marked by their mode of dress and appearance. On the Tablighis, see Metcalf, "'Traditionalist' Islamic Activism," 1.

43. Azoulay and Ophir, "The Monster's Tail."
44. Bremner, "Border/Skin," 131.
45. Azoulay and Ophir, "The Monster's Tail."
46. Gwynn, *Imperial Policing*, 30.
47. Gwynn, *Imperial Policing*, 32.
48. The trope of lawlessness to depict the region has a long history. See Fowler, *Chasing Tales*.
49. Amnesty International, "*The Hands of Cruelty*," 39.
50. Farooq, "Pakistan's FATA."
51. Khan, "The Ghosts and Gains of North Waziristan."
52. Povinelli, *The Cunning of Recognition*, 4.
53. Weizman, "Politics of Verticality."
54. This pattern is also identifiable in the Occupied Palestinian Territories, where Gaza, subject to severe closure, is more heavily bombed than the West Bank. See Li, "The Gaza Strip as Laboratory."
55. On the range of tactics deployed in containment zones, see, for instance, M. T., "Waziris Mourn Their Dead"; on shoot-on-sight policies, see *Express Tribune*, "Bomb Blast"; on mass expulsion, see Shaheen, "30 More Terrorists Killed."
56. Zaidi, "A Profile of Mangal Bagh."
57. According to Amnesty International's Mustafa Qadri, Bara had been under a forty-month curfew by the time of the Dogra incident. See Grayson, "Peshawar Tribesmen Protest Killings at Bara."
58. Afridi, "In Memoriam."
59. Sherazi, "Tribesmen Forced to End Protest"; Aurakzai, "Burying Us Alive in Bara."
60. Foucault, "March 17, 1976," 241.
61. Mbembe, "Necropolitics," 34.
62. "PAF Conducted 5,500 Bombing Runs."
63. U.S. Embassy Cable, "CJCS Mullen's Meeting"; see also C. Woods, "Pakistan 'Categorically Rejects' Claim." The airspace for American drones is in addition to the airspace corridor over Pakistan referred to as "the Boulevard" that NATO forces use. A 2007 U.S. cable notes that "approximately 150 Coalition aircraft traverse 'the boulevard' each day." U.S. Embassy Cable, "Pakistan."
64. G. Miller, "US Wants to Widen Area"; CNN Wire Staff, "Pakistan Denies U.S. Request."
65. On checkpoints as sites of control, see Kotef and Amir, "Between Imaginary Lines"; Tawil-Souri, "Qalandia Checkpoint as Space and Nonplace"; and Razack, "A Hole in the Wall."
66. Personal communication with source by author, February 2015.
67. On the relationship between language and politics in Pakistan, see Toor, *The State of Islam*; K. Ali, "Communists in a Muslim Land"; and Tanqeed Editors, "Language and Politics."

68. Mamdani, "Beyond Settler and Native as Political Identities," 651–54.
69. Gregory, "From a View to a Kill," 192.
70. Mamdani, *Citizen and Subject*, 7.
71. Mamdani, "Historicizing Power and Responses to Power"; D. Scott, "Colonial Governmentality," 197.

10

STONERS, STONES, AND DRONES

Transnational South Asian Visuality from Above and Below

ANJALI NATH

My father's body was scattered in pieces and he died immediately, but I was unconscious for three to four days. . . . I have two younger brothers who . . . are home most of the day and they are very conscious of the fact that drones are hovering over them. [The presence of drones] intimidates them.

—Waleed Shiraz, quoted in International Human Rights and Conflict Resolution Clinic (Stanford Law School) and Global Justice Clinic (NYC School of Law), *Living under Drones*

Here we can think about *low theory* as . . . a kind of theoretical model that flies below the radar, that is assembled from eccentric texts and examples and that refuses to confirm the hierarchies of knowing that maintain the *high* in high theory.

Judith (Jack) Halberstam, *The Queer Art of Failure*

Drones in the morning, drones in the night / I'm trying to find a pretty drone to take home tonight.

—Himanshu "Heems" Suri, "Soup Boys (Pretty Drones)"

WALEED SHIRAZ'S chilling testimony describes surviving a drone attack in northwest Pakistan and illuminates the human cost of drone warfare. Although varying kinds of drones, or unmanned aerial vehicles (UAVs), have been present throughout the history of modern American warfare, armed UAVs have emerged as a potent symbol of contemporary asymmetric war in Pakistan, Yemen, Somalia, and Afghanistan, promoted as surgically precise alternatives to other forms of combat. After coming to office in 2009, President

Barack Obama vastly expanded the U.S. military's drone program, which proliferated with "advances" in military and satellite technology.[1] Estimates suggest that during Obama's tenure as commander in chief, drone strikes killed as many as four thousand people in Pakistan alone and injured many others. Shiraz's description foregrounds how these aerial attacks have vastly changed the physical and psychological landscape—as well as the perceptual skyscape—for many people in northwest Pakistan, where these attacks have been concentrated. Such somber testimonies from drone survivors enable anti-drone activism and, importantly, make palpable the bodily violence that UAVs inflict upon the communities that dwell below. In the face of such new warfare, this chapter looks to an unusual set of affective registers that challenge the visual logics of drone warfare. Alongside the somber and the sober, I consider the possible strategic interventions of irreverence, satire, and inebriation within diasporic South Asian cultural production.

In an age of drones, diasporic artists at times paint this bizarre militarized landscape in hues of the lowbrow, exemplifying what Jack (Judith) Halberstam calls *low theory* as quoted at the outset. As a reminder of the political project of cultural studies and in opposition to the relative elitism of *high* theory (where critique emerges from and is limited to a select few), Halberstam's *low theory* conjures an elsewhere: incoherence, irreverence, willful absurdity within the realm of the popular. This refusal of the terms that place particular cultural forms above others has been of great concern within cultural studies, from Stuart Hall's interests in the potentially subversive uses and abuses of popular culture to Pierre Bourdieu's exploration of *taste* as a cultural iteration of capitalist class distinction.[2] Such critiques point to the ways that high art aesthetics themselves are sites of power, exerting the sense that things are as they should be: an articulation of beauty as orderliness.[3] Lowbrow and popular expressions can undermine these logics through mass access to cultural productions and consumption practices that can be unruly, queer, and against the grain.[4] Thus, Halberstam's interest in what flies below the radar, or rather, in our case, what lives under drones, is more than mere metaphor; the spatiality of the low and the below bring into focus a situated site of critique. To this end I ask, what can an absurdist cultural production, engaging both the incoherent and the absurd, tell us about the visual logics of drone warfare and the politics of diasporic refusal? Put differently, how might a low theory illuminate drone optics and how drones—as military, visual, and aerial technologies—have changed the politics of diasporic visuality itself?

In this chapter, I consider one specific diasporic articulation of (and against) drone visuality: South Asian American rapper Himanshu "Heems" Suri's music video for the comedic hip-hop song "Soup Boys (Pretty Drones)," released in 2012 on YouTube and other music-sharing venues. The tune builds from a sample of "Why This Kolaveri Di," the 2011 viral Internet hit from Tamil musicians Anirudh Ravichander and Dhanush. Heems's song describes a South Asian American landscape, rendering drones as both troubling aerial presences and gendered recipients of Heems's sexual attention. Each song plays with the line between satire and nonsense, putting forth cheeky alternatives to overly didactic political commentary. Each is subversive within a visual and sonic field. Heems's video—featuring the artist rapping lyrics against a green screen montage of aerial shots, clips of New York City, and videos of homemade drones—furthers perceptual interventions into the regime of drone visuality that the song lyrically challenges.

"Soup Boys (Pretty Drones)" should not be understood within any articulation of a political hip hop per se; the music video features an apparently inebriated Heems, rapping about marijuana use against a montage of apparently disjointed images. I argue, however, that this perceptual alteration and deliberate flippancy only underscores the way the music video and song lyrically, sonically, and visually describe an Obama-era cartography of the "Af/Pak" region that has been created for consistent assault. Within "Soup Boys (Pretty Drones)," the lyrical and visual references to marijuana use become loci of contestation. In keeping with a cultural studies framework, I situate these references as part of a broader culture in which marijuana is entangled within racialized forms of policing and criminalization as well as a subcultural articulation of a nonhegemonic perspective. As Paul Willis argues in his study on the subcultures of drug users in England, perceptual alterations produced through encounters with drugs often present as counterhegemonic articulations that create communities of users.[5] But, as Curtiz Marez illuminates, in the United States, the war on drugs was a media spectacle in which black and brown producers and consumers throughout the Americas emerged in representational regimes that mapped the political economy of drug wars.[6] Hip hop emerged coevally with the war on drugs, the racially punitive Rockefeller Drug Laws, and the prison-industrial complex. For instance, a variety of rappers have articulated sensorial responses to state-sanctioned abandonment (for instance, Nas's famous mid-1990s refrain: "life's a bitch and then you die, that's why we get high, cuz you never know when you're going to go"). Others have self-styled and self-named based on outlaw drug lords, both fictive and real (Noriega, Scarface, Capone, etc.). These productions intervene, to varying degrees, in normative discourses of policing, drug enforcement, and racial discourses of criminality.

Correspondingly, I am less interested Heems's potential intent to produce a music video critical of drone warfare and more interested in how the narcotically inspired unruliness points at a transnational visual logics of war that is both brought into focus and refused. The song thus simultaneously emerges from and remaps a visual terrain in which South Asian and Middle Eastern bodies are constructed and killed, and whose lives are framed by the optic perception of drones. The subtitle of this chapter gestures toward precisely these politics of visuality, *from above and below*. I invoke these spatial metaphors for dual reasons. On the one hand, I reference the tradition of history from below, the practice of writing and rewriting accounts of past events in a way that centers the experiences, labors, and struggles of everyday people. This practice of a politics of *below* questions the authority of state narratives and corresponds to the political imperative of the *low*, a playful gesture toward the ability of cultural production to story-tell the present. But considering a drone history from above versus a drone history from below also quite obviously invokes the spatiality of the technology itself. As many geographers and science studies scholars argue, drones emerge from and exist within a visual and vertical politics of war. Initially theorized by Eyal Weizman in relation to the occupied territories in Gaza, *verticality* conceptually articulates the layeredness of contemporary occupation.[7] Geopolitics do not exist in two dimensions, as represented on paper or a flat-screen map. Instead, the aerial perspectives that create contemporary mapping projects and planetary visions are implicated in the social geographies of war; struggles over land, space, and social life themselves work against architectures of seeing, surveillance, and containment.

As Nicholas Mirzoeff argues, visuality "is not composed simply of visual perceptions in the physical sense, but is formed by a set of relations combining information, imagination, and insight into a rendition of physical and psychic space."[8] Accordingly, the significance of drone strikes extends far beyond the site of missile impact and into the very visual discourses of sobriety that belie the documentary impulses of those who seek to challenge drone warfare.[9] Drones have changed relations between ground and air for both Pakistanis (and Afghans) living within the space (as Shiraz's story illustrates) and the American teams assisting in the UAV operations. For contemporary drones, and other forms of aerial surveillance, UAVs provide specific views of the ground that are aided by satellite technology. Correspondingly, those living under the direct surveillance of drones are rendered by the overlapping histories of imperial conquest in the region, surviving British colonialism and American intervention as well as preemptive acts of military aggression during the Cold War and the war on terror.[10] Thus, even as drone warfare's specific material, psychological, and physical effects are felt most acutely within Pakistan, Afghanistan, Somalia, and Yemen, drone optics have broader implications within a racialized regime of visuality and American empire. As Stephen Graham and Lucy Hewitt illuminate, urban spaces like New York, where "Soup Boys (Pretty Drones)" partially unfolds, reflect "a classic neo-Orientalist tradition, [in which] cities are widely projected by state, military and security elites as complex, exotic and intrinsically devious three-dimensional spaces," implicating a continuity in vertical methods of domestic surveillance and policing with war geographies.[11] In this regard, my title gestures toward the spatial possibilities of contesting drone verticality and the politics of contemporary war. In other words, if signature strikes and precision strikes work through the domination of air and the mobilization and optical space *above*, what kinds of oppositional gazes and countertactics can be mobilized from a diaspora below?

My investments in diasporic cultural production follow the scholarship of Stuart Hall, Gayatri Gopinath, and others, who demonstrate how diasporas emerge from shifting racial regimes and thus work against stable notions of identity; diasporic cultural productions that afford affective purchase are always contingent on specific iterations of power and difference.[12] "Soup Boys (Pretty Drones)" is less interesting as a text that articulates an authentic experience of violence or a subjugated knowledge; to suggest so would erase the structuring categories of difference that produce uneven vulnerabilities to war. One can hardly assume a seamlessness between a Pakistani from rural Waziristan and a diasporic South Asian from Brooklyn. The text itself sharply diverges from the kinds of sober discourses of truth-telling that rely on such notions of authenticity. I consider this text then within the shifting terrains of diasporic cultural production that both shape and are shaped by ethnic categories always in motion, contingent on transnational animations of capital, labor, and war. Within this conception of diaspora, there are no fundamental meanings to categories of identification like South Asian, *desi*, Pakistani, Afghan, or Indian. Rather, these forms of belonging are constructed through nationalist, imperial, and hegemonic encounters, resulting in cultural forms that express forms of power and embodiments of difference. For instance, the emergence of the category Arab Middle Eastern Muslim and South Asian (AMEMSA) as an ethno-racial classification in the aftermath of 9/11 signified the nexus of issues that these populations dealt with around surveillance, hate crimes, and deportations.[13] This category reflects not a shared set of authentic cultural traditions but rather solely a politics of naming in the face of racial targeting. Similarly, "Soup Boys (Pretty Drones)" exemplifies this production of diaspora; this video, I argue, forsakes a "diasporic perspective on drones" for a contingent, strung-together set of subjective experiences and shifting vignettes through which the viewer experiences diaspora as it emerges from a contemporary militarized visual regime.

Drone Verticality and Discourses of Sobriety

In his seminal work on documentary cinema, Bill Nichols argues that documentary cinema works within a *discourse of sobriety*. Documentary films, in other words, with their oft serious subject matter and structured form, present proper and sobering ways to understand actualities through indexical narration.[14] I turn to Nichols's work on the documentary or testimonial impulse as a counterpoint; "Soup Boys (Pretty Drones)" invokes perhaps quite the opposite of a sober, serious, and coherent critique. Yet the music video for "Soup Boys (Pretty Drones)" meets the calculated and absurdist logic of drones with a pointedly absurd and stoned rejoinder. Instead of a discourse of sobriety, we encounter a discourse of inebriation. The sobering discourse of drone warfare meets the intoxicated and insubordinate. A visual history of drones clarifies this tension between the vertical militarism on the one hand and the irreverence of the diasporic on the other.

Although drones have been used for surveillance for several decades, since the late 1990s, their uses have more recently been applied to targeted killings, which have become all the more commonplace during the Obama administration. The scope and implementation of this form of aerial surveillance presents a significant shift. A 2012 article in the *New Yorker* put this stark material change rather succinctly: "In 2001, the military had just a few U.A.V.s. Now it has more than ten thousand."[15] There are drones that patrol the U.S.-Mexico border that—as of the writing of this chapter—are unarmed, though there are murmurs this may change.[16] In a few instances, domestic policing agencies have used drones, and after the FAA Modernization and Reform Act of 2012, this may become all the more ubiquitous.[17] There is also a do-it-yourself (DIY) drone hobby community in the United States, where amateur engineers build homemade UAVs, much like one would a model airplane. Although drone technology's potential uses are quite far-reaching, its primary use and development has been through and to serve the military-industrial complex. AeroVironment, one of the premier technology firms, for instance, is a major supplier of drones to the U.S. government.[18] The investment in UAV technology has changed both the visual field of domestic and international warfare and the practices of engagement on the battlefield itself.

The critique of the sober and rational can also extend to the discourses around the technological perception of drones themselves. Drone visuality is not simply mechanized, robotic, and rational. As Caren Kaplan argues, the notion that drones are *unmanned* deceptively obscures the labor of drone pilots. Instead, Kaplan suggests that "drone sight is always already embodied and affective because it is produced and analyzed, albeit in varying degrees, by human beings in specific sites."[19] Drone technology enables specific optical modes of perception for the persons guiding it, constructing ways of seeing and perceiving particular topographies that emerge from—and yet are irreducible to—other scopic regimes. In this regard, drone sight is less an extension of a politically neutral and scientific gaze; rather, it is a visuality that is produced in collaboration with a set of militarized and racial visualities born from conquest and expansion. Thus, drone visualities emerge from and enable racialized ways of seeing that are specifically intimate, not distantly dispassionate despite the spatial and technological segregations between "here" and "there." Drone operators located safely on military sites in Virginia, New Mexico, Nevada, and elsewhere engage the battlefield from remote distances, and their sensory perception is mediated by screens, satellites, and communications technologies that link them to on-the-ground forces. Critics of drone warfare have often argued that operating a drone provides a video game–like experience that distantiates the drone pilot from the ground. This distantiation, critics maintain, is what causes and sustains the collateral damage/civilian causalities of drone warfare.[20] However, paradoxically, as Derek Gregory has argued, distantiation does not conceptually account for the visual practices of drone piloting: "Contrary to critics who claim that these operations reduce war to a video game in which the killing space appears remote and distant, I suggest that these new visibilities produce a special kind of *intimacy* that consistently privileges the view of the hunter-killer, and whose implications are far more deadly."[21] This is not about "removing" soldiers from the battlefield but rather, as Gregory argues, creating new intimacies facilitated by UAV technology. Drone pilots often see the detailed aftermath far more accurately than airplane bombers would and are in close, immersive communication with on-the-ground troops in Afghanistan.[22]

Thus, these new technologies do more than extend the distant, phantasmic hand of U.S. empire. Instead, this particular optic regime facilitates what Matt Delmont calls the "drone encounter," the circuit of drone optic technology that creates the contact surface for visual mediation between American and Pakistani bodies.[23] The enemy body is produced through his or her appearance as an indistinct shape that, because of its unrecognizability, is killable.[24] Such a view would elide the specificity of the racialized gaze through which the drone is navigated as well as the relationships Gregory notes are forged through the encounter. These new aerial intimacies engendered by this technoracial visual system fall within what Keith Feldman calls "racialization from above," which works in step with the geography of imperialism and the afterlife of colonialism.[25] Gregory's reading of the documentation of a February 2010 drone attack in Afghanistan troubles the notion of the precise, rational, and surgical drone gaze, as military reviewers later argued the drone footage plainly showed civilians being killed. Gregory concludes that "high-resolution imagery is not a uniquely technical capacity but part of a techno-cultural system that renders 'our' space familiar even in 'their' space which remains obdurately Other."[26]

Thus, Gregory's assessment is correct that the killing of civilians is not simply a technological error but rather a *technocultural* practice, animated by the criminalization of Orientalized bodies: innately a technoracial visual system of interpellation. In this sense, the notion that greater precision gives surgical accuracy to drone strikes fails to recognize the racialized technocultural function of the drone optic and further conflates precision, categorization, and knowability with a more humane, less damaging form of killing. Thus, precision is itself about the production of racial knowledge. In the following section, I argue that "Soup Boys (Pretty Drones)" works against this precise, surgical gaze and in favor of a more complex diasporic gaze that refuses such knowability and visual coherence.

Diasporic Looks and the Inebriated Gaze

I move from the sobering technocultural rationalizations for drone warfare into diasporic cultural productions that rhetorically challenge these perceptual skyscapes. "Soup Boys (Pretty Drones)" emerges from within these shifting racial logics, as Heems addresses both the sensorial and cultural discourses that produce everyday people in the Middle East and South Asia as potential targets. As an emcee, Heems first gained popularity through the group Das Racist, formed by Suri and his college friend Victor Vasquez (aka Kool AD), who met while attending Wesleyan College. They were known for their subversive and satirical rhymes and performances of an inebriated, but nerdy, swagger and hipster panache. For instance, in their song "Fake Patois," both Heems and Kool AD bust rhymes in Jamaican patois, on the one hand parodying various emcees' appropriations of the Caribbean creole language yet on the other hand acknowledging Jamaican music's influence on hip hop. In other songs, they jest about their own ethnic backgrounds (Kool AD is Cuban): "which one's Dominican, wait who's the Indian?" Das Racist gained a reputation for their clever references to a bygone era of 1990s hip-hop classics, combining a throwback flow and slacker lyrics with references to specific black nationalist and Afrocentric 1990s hip-hop groups. Their rhymes bear both the reverence of close study and the intimacy of satire.

Heems's solo song "Soup Boys (Pretty Drones)" is stylistically consistent with this playful irreverence. The video was released in January 2013 through Pitchfork.tv's YouTube channel. The decline of music television and the rise of the Internet facilitated the production and circulation of low-budget music videos like "Soup Boys (Pretty Drones)," a video with a minimally sophisticated production value comprising mostly digital montage and chroma key acting.[27] Further, the circulatory practices YouTube enables is of particular importance within both this media moment and the broader context of visual culture. As Marwan Kraidy argues in the context of Arab music videos, these forms are "best understood as instruments of visibility in a symbolic economy that suffers from attention scarcity."[28] In other words, as a digital release, the video for "Soup Boys (Pretty Drones)" reflects a practice of authoring and consumption only possible within this digitally networked and politically vexed world.

"Soup Boys (Pretty Drones)" begins with a clip of White House correspondent Jessica Yellin interviewing President Obama in September 2012 about the use of drones.[29] The segment shifts to a talking head close-up of

President Obama, skirting the issue. He redirects, saying, "My first job, my most sacred duty as president and commander in chief, is to keep the American people safe." The clip ends as these words leave Obama's mouth and the first chords of the song drop while a chroma key effect allows Heems to enter from screen left, over Obama's face. Green screen projection constitutes the remainder of the video, in which Heems dances and raps over a montage (that one might even call Vertovian in some regards) of various images of South Asians in New York, followed by aerial shots (including New York City, what appears to be Afghanistan or Pakistan, and cloud-filled skies), and ending with images of homemade drones, satellite shots, and drone protests.[30] Notably, many of the images used within the montage—particularly those of diasporic communities—bear the aesthetic mark of home video: shaky, low-resolution, uncertain. The entire production itself possesses qualities of willful simplicity and minimal budget. As the music video finally draws to a close, we hear Obama's voice again, though disembodied from the original visuals and instead laid over a shot of the sky and a drone animation. The president's quote continues from where he left off: "What that means is we brought a whole bunch of tools to bear on those who would attack Americans. Drones are one tool, and our criteria for using them is very [unclear word]." Beginning with "and," the vocals for the second half of this sentence are slowed down to the point of incomprehension until the video draws to a close. Obama's voice bookends the entire video, positing Heems's surrealist and nonnarrative drone love song as an intervention into the president's statement justifying the use of UAVs.

The first few chords of "Soup Boys (Pretty Drones)" are borrowed nearly unaltered from "Why This Kolaveri Di," drawing the listener, particularly the South Asian and South Asian diasporic listener, into a transnational aural landscape shaped by communicative technologies that facilitate global consumption of media products. In other words, together, YouTube and hip-hop sample culture are implicated in and create the contemporary conditions for what Brent Hayes Edwards calls the *practice* of diaspora.[31] Indeed, Heems's title "Soup Boys (Pretty Drones)" is itself drawn from lyrics of Ravichander and Dhanush's song, which begins with the hailing of the listener: "Yo, boys. I am sing song. Soup Song. Flop Song." (In Tamil, "soup boy" refers to a heartbroken man.)[32] Several commentators have theorized both the success and the potential linguistic subversiveness of "Why This Kolaveri Di." The song simultaneously pokes fun at Indians who speak nonstandard English as well as Indian anglophiles by reversing the cultural cache of the English language. Despite its comical tone, the song had a high production value; Ravichander based the song on a folk rhythm using a mix of South Asian and Western instruments.[33] This satirical song (which one journalist called "a nonsensical Indian song about love and loss") provides the sonic referent and foundation for Heems's intervention into an American military optic; its comic tone coheres only in the context of a digitally mediated South Asian transnational cultural landscape.[34]

Moreover, that "Soup Boys (Pretty Drones)" emerges from a Tamil production underscores a disaffiliation with "diaspora" as a concept based on a presumed authentic relationship to categorized and static notions of culture, region, or ethnicity. As a South Indian production, "Why This Kolaveri Di" bears seemingly little relation to an "Af/Pak" geography or its attendant cultural imaginary. The song is thus particularly resistant to the sectarian—or communalist—identity politics that have troubled South Asian and diasporic cultural politics. Heems opens "Soup Boys (Pretty Drones)" by lyrically and visually inscribing the listener/spectator into the world of diasporic South Asians in Queens:

Indians jersey and an Om on my necklace
Outside Van Buren I'm parked in a Lexus
Waiting for the man, I'm waiting for a gram
I'm waiting for the man to put a gram up in my hand
And I'm looking fresh, you'll never find a flyer steeze
I'm in Richmond Hill smoking with the Guyanese
Hindus getting higher than a mother fucking fire, kid
Punjabis wild, yo, Himanshu is a Shayar man
They're throwing stones at the Mosque
I'm in tune with goons that's stoned at the Mosque
I'm throwing stones in the zone with my vox
You eating stones I'm seeing drones up top.

The opening phrases invoke a variety of South Asian experiences: Richmond Hill, for instance, is the contemporary home of large Indo-Guyanese, Indo-Trinidadian, and Punjabi communities. The accompanying chroma key montage shows outdoor shots of a vibrant diasporic New York City: ethnic businesses as storefronts in Queens, Gujarati folk dance in the street, handheld traveling shots of the well-known South Indian Ganesh temple in Flushing, and so on. These visual cues establish a diasporic point of view, a pastiche of different cultural and religious affiliations that situate the viewer squarely in a South Asian America. While in some ways this imagery for "Soup Boys (Pretty Drones)" may appear muddled (lyrical references to Hinduism and Islam, visual references to the Indian and Pakistani flag later in the song), it is precisely through this confusion—and the visual architecture of collision montage—that a visual politics is articulated. In other words, within the song's story-world, the point is not to pronounce an authentic aggrieved subject of the drone strike (an important but altogether different visual project) or to conjure the horror or experiential dimensions of drone bombings. Instead, diaspora becomes a site of irreverent critique rather than a location for reified identity or seamless continuity between an imagined *here* and *there*. I return to the multiple and shifting uses of the noun *stone* and the verb phrase *to be stoned* to elucidate this point later.

The lyrics excerpted above underscore the critical importance of imprecision and absurdity; these various references to South Asian communities are coeval with references to marijuana use and acquisition. Heems raps and dances in front of the green screen throughout the video as his loose movements, puffy eyes, and bewildered look suggest his own inebriation. The chorus underscores this stoned perception:

That drone cool, but I hate that drone
Chocolate chip cookie dough in a sugar cone
Drones in the morning, drones in the night
I'm trying to find a pretty drone to take home tonight

As he raps the chorus, Heems looks upward, pointing above the frame, toward the aerial. Yet he quickly flips the script, turning to the lyrically absurd ("chocolate chip cookie dough in a sugar cone") with gesturally comical and loose movements. The chorus's disjointed references, though arguably incoherent at first listen, point toward another form of intimacy and knowing. What could undermine the authority of the precision target more than an imprecision of perception resulting from drug use? Put differently, what cultural work is done by meeting the authoritative gaze of the drone with puffy stoner eyes?

And, indeed, the video itself places these two kinds of perception in conversation with each other; as Heems rhymes, "Hindus getting higher than a mother fucking fire, kid," the viewer sees an image of a rising helicopter, followed by aerial views of New York City and the sky (see figures 10.1 and 10.2). The chroma key montage suggests marijuana intoxication and the view from flight provides different kinds of sensory perceptive "highs";

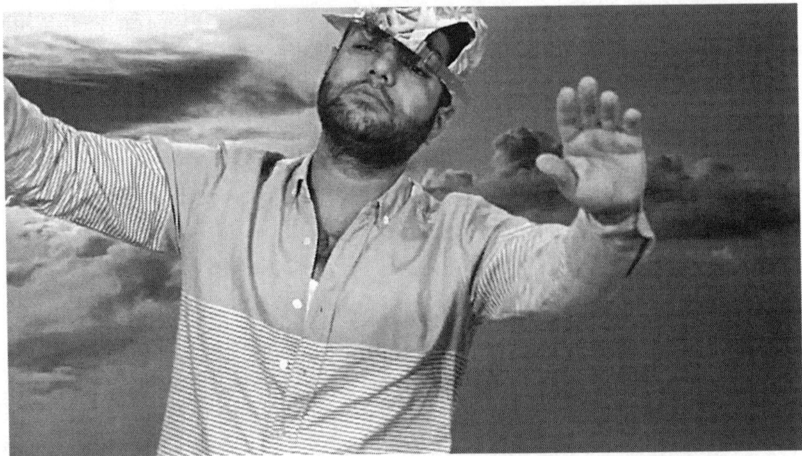

Figure 10.1. Heems, against green screen, high in the sky. ("Soup Boys [Pretty Drones]" official video screenshot)

Figure 10.2. Heems, against green screen, framed by aerial shot of New York City. ("Soup Boys [Pretty Drones]" official video screenshot)

as Heems raps this chorus, behind him are images of drones in flight. Situated below, he points to UAVs imagined above him. As perhaps an associatively postmodern lyric (or a reference to the munchies), "chocolate chip cookie dough in a sugar cone" welcomes the listener and spectator into the realm of the absurd: the bizarre proliferation of drones in everyday life befitting an outlandish inebriated conversation. Thus, the stoner gaze is returned by a fundamentally necropolitical visual technology, while simultaneously the Orwellian leanings of the drone program seem to conjure stoner paranoia. The inebriated gaze is visceral, embodied, subjective; being perceptively *high* only emerges from drugs, not from a deceptively "rational" and "precise" aerial skyscape view. Thus, in contrast with the new, murderous intimacies that Gregory posits as facilitated through the kill chain, Heems, lyrically inhabiting a space of a gazed-upon subject, counters this intimacy by intoxicatedly professing desire for the distant drone surveilling him.

Another lyric later in the song reiterates the slippage between the different meanings of "stoned," as noted in earlier mentioned rhymes linking mosque-stoning with pot-smoking: "I'm stoned, I'm stoned, I'm stoned at my parents' house / White Boys throwing stones at my parents' house, they dot-busting, hate crime, race war." In both instances, he counterposes the experience of being the target of racial violence with the escapism and altered perception of weed. Here, stone throwing is but one example of a logic of white supremacy that is not dissimilar in state-sanctioned and technomilitaristic forms of drone warfare. Such wordplay underscores both the underpinnings of power as well as the innate potentiality for subversion, as the multiple uses articulate not similarity but rather juxtaposition through sameness. Importantly, this juxtaposition illustrates the way an inebriated gaze confronts a racialized visual regime that targets specific bodies. To get stoned or to be stoned: both refer to rebel outcast figures and problematics taken up by a variety of hip-hop artists, such as what it means to be abandoned by the state and simultaneously resist its logic.

We are asked in this instantiation to look back at the state with an intimate and stoned view. We witness the disjointed montage through the gaze (or, an inebriated *kino-eye*, perhaps) of our narrator. Through montage, Heems's "Soup Boys (Pretty Drones)" articulates a radically different kind of diasporic perception. Moving from images of the South Asian diasporic in New York—undeniably subject to surveillance and profiling post 9/11—to images of aerial perspectives and Pakistani street life, the listener/viewer is drawn visually, sonically, and lyrically into a South Asian transnational landscape.[35] The viewer is not simply meant to understand the violence of drones as weapons but rather the violence of drone optics. This specific diasporic articulation of difference and disaffiliation disavows the very racial discourses of "precision" that authorize death. A surgical vocabulary of identity in which, as Gregory argues, "objects become rifles, praying a Taliban signifier, civilians 'military-aged males,' and children 'adolescents,'" is countered by the imprecision of inebriation, the unruliness of diasporic desire and perception.[36] In other words, racialized rationality meets diasporic imprecision, as signature strikes from above encounter inebriated rhymes below.

Yet even as Heems flips the script, he does so within a lyrically troubling gendered frame; his subversion of the drones' dominance works specifically—and only—through the heteronormative. Although he never directly uses the pronoun "she" for the drone (nor identifies himself as straight), the language reflects varying characterizations of cisgendered women. He ends the song rhyming, "That drone modest, but that drone flaunt / All of them drones do what them drones want." In his stoned state, Heems narratively feminizes the drone in order to render it as both irrational and an unruly femme fatale. He ends the song with the following lyrics: "Drones want to fire then drones want to kill / Drones want your dome and your bone and your grill." This last line highlights this problematic as he likens the new racial and violent intimacies generated by the drone's visual apparatus to potential sexual encounters with a troublesome woman; he merges the visceral physicality of those two encounters (the bone, the dome, and the grill). Although there is no direct feminine visual referent in the video, his body language changes at moments to suggest this sexualization of the drone. Even as this perceptive high speaks to the vertical architectures of drone warfare that engender new forms of intimacy, it does so within a heteronormative frame: comically subverting the drone's gaze by rendering it a *her* and rendering *her* a familiar and dismissible gendered subject. In this sense, we can think of the video as a diasporic production that is willfully absurd in the face of the punitive rationalizations of drone warfare but also relies on well-worn gendered tropes to assert a kind of mode of resistance.

Conclusion

In her work on overhead imagery, Lisa Parks calls for a "techno-reflexive way of writing history and conducting analysis" and suggests that "for every satellite view we need to conceptualize or imagine a reverse shot that would lead us to the orbital location, history, ownership of the satellite that gathered the image data."[37] In some ways, we can consider "Soup Boys (Pretty Drones)" as a reflexive visual and sonic production, turning a satirical gaze back at the imprecise violence of the drone. Although Heems's video does not speak directly to the material conditions of aerial image production, it gestures toward the bizarre visual landscapes and perceptual logics that both enable and are created by drones. Heems's video points toward a South Asian diasporic visuality not endlessly enmeshed in a politics of representation but rather one that emerges from the practices of looking, hailing, and seeing that produce forms of racialization. Unlike other instantiations of hip hop within the South Asian diaspora where, as Nitasha Sharma puts it, "desi artists express alternative desiness . . . [and] convey a diasporic sensibility to their Black peers and to multiracial audiences who may be more familiar with hip hop music centered on United States themes,"[38] Heems's work does not articulate a sense of ethnic identity vis-à-vis black cultural production, nor does it speak to a singular and knowable South Asian diaspora. Instead, the video, in its willful incoherence, escapes a narrative cogency and, in doing so, invokes powerful questions about drones, intimacy, and visual culture.

In a moment where drone visualities—and other forms of surveillance technology—can hail and create the subject as a racialized body, it is critical to betray the notion of visual optics as rational and precise. Waleed Shiraz's tragic testimony at the beginning of this chapter underscores the gravely deleterious effects of drone visuality on the lives of everyday Pakistanis. Furthermore, drone technologies are poised to become more thoroughly integrated into the U.S. borderlands and domestic life in new ways. As Nick Paumgarten dystopically notes, changing regulations may "eventually open the national airspace to unmanned aerial vehicles, or U.A.V.s, for commercial, scientific, and law-enforcement and public-safety use."[39] Drone use and development has thus far not been limited to the drone's instrumentality within the theater of foreign war; academic researchers and aeronautical engineering firms are at work on a variety of different applications for drone and other surveillance technologies that continue to change the landscape of the United States and law enforcement. The low-resolution chroma key montage of diasporic New York only underscores this apprehension about the futures of aerial surveillance that loom larger over U.S.-based communities of color. Yet the grainy piece itself exists on and circulates within the digital file-sharing platform of YouTube, which itself creates and engenders (imagined) communities through and across national boundaries.

Indeed, there is a particular cunning to resisting the Orwellian currents of surveillance culture through defying its logic within the lowbrow, or even through *mocking* empire, as Arundhati Roy once famously proclaimed.[40] As Robin Kelley argues, resistance is not always about didactic performance—musical or otherwise; sometimes resistance can be as simple as refusing to operate within the logic that is given, to use something differently, to subvert its authoritative gaze.[41] As a communicative intervention, "Soup Boys (Pretty Drones)" is thus subversive specifically because of its incoherence and refusal of the drone's punitively racial gaze. And yet the refusals of these forms of new intimacies specifically work through a mild form of sexism, gendered tropes that lend themselves to use within comedic and absurdist cultural productions. But, importantly, the song resists an "anti-drone" categorization, as Heems seems divested from articulating a contrarian or oppositional political stance. Instead, the piece draws the viewer into a diasporic South Asian transnational sensibility, asking us as viewers to collectively cast a stoned glance toward the sky.

Notes

I would like to thank Falu Bakrania and John Cheney-Lippold for their generous and generative comments on this piece.

1. Hough, "Aerial Torpedoes, Buzz Bombs, and Predators."
2. S. Hall, "Notes on Deconstructing the Popular," 40; Bourdieu, *Distinction*, 1–7.
3. Mirzoeff, "Introduction," xxxi.
4. Doty, *Flaming Classics*; S. Hall, "Notes on Deconstructing the Popular"; R. Williams, "Culture."
5. Willis, "The Cultural Meaning of Drug Use."
6. Marez, *Drug Wars*.
7. Weizman, "Introduction to the Politics of Verticality."
8. Mirzoeff, *The Right to Look*, 3.
9. B. Nichols, *Representing Reality*.
10. Mamdani, *Good Muslim, Bad Muslim*.
11. Graham and Hewitt, "Getting Off the Ground," 85.
12. S. Hall, *Critical Dialogues in Cultural Studies*, 7; Gopinath, *Impossible Desires*, 10–14.
13. "AMEMSA Fact Sheet."
14. B. Nichols, *Representing Reality*, 3–4, 9.
15. Paumgarten, "Here's Looking at You."
16. Democracy Now, "U.S. Border Patrol."
17. NPR, "Drones Moving from War Zones"; Bennett and Rubin, "Drones Are Taking to the Skies."

18. Paumgarten, "Here's Looking at You."
19. Kaplan, "Drone Sight."
20. Gregory, "From a View to a Kill."
21. Gregory, "From a View to a Kill," 193, emphasis added.
22. Gregory, "From a View to a Kill," 199–203.
23. Matt Delmont, "Drone Encounters: Noor Behram, Omer Fast, and Visual Critiques of Drone Warfare," *American Quarterly*, 65, no. 1 (March 2013): 193–202.
24. Delmont, "Drone Encounters," 201.
25. K. Feldman, "Empire's Verticality," 330.
26. Gregory, "From a View to a Kill," 201.
27. Edmond, "Here We Go Again," 305.
28. Kraidy, "Contention and Circulation," 271.
29. CNN, "Obama Reflects on Drone Warfare."
30. Vertov, "The Essence of Kino-Eye"; Fischer, "'Enthusiasm.'" Although Heems's video in many ways resists Vertov's primary interest in montage for its political functionality, in another sense the architecture of collision montage, the visual references to city symphony (combined with a new aeriality), and the referentiality to technologies of the image captures (camera/drones) resonate with Vertov's work. In this sense, though "Soup Boys (Pretty Drones)" consciously defies the politically didactic, this architecture engenders questions about the visual regimes of contemporary warfare that may arguably be considered Vertovian.
31. B. Edwards, *The Practice of Diaspora.*
32. Virmani, "Kolavari Di."
33. Singh, "Kolaveri di in Tamil and Punjabi."
34. Virmani, "Kolavari Di."
35. New York City Profiling Collaborative, "In Our Own Words."
36. Gregory, "From a View to a Kill," 203.
37. Parks, "Zeroing In," 89.
38. Sharma, *Hip Hop Desis*, 11.
39. Paumgarten, "Here's Looking at You."
40. Roy, "Confronting Empire."
41. Kelley, *Race Rebels,* 8–10.

PART III
BIOPOLITICS, AUTOMATION, AND ROBOTICS

11

TAKING PEOPLE OUT

Drones, Media/Weapons, and the Coming Humanectomy

JEREMY PACKER AND JOSHUA REEVES

The future may or may not bear out my present convictions, but I can not refrain from saying that it is difficult for me to see at present how, with such a principle brought to great perfection, as it undoubtedly will be in the course of time, guns can maintain themselves as weapons. We shall be able, by availing ourselves of this advance, to send a projectile at much greater distance, it will not be limited in any way by weight or amount of explosive charge, we shall be able to submerge it at command, to arrest it in its flight, and call it back, and send it out again and explode it at will, and, more than this, it will never make a miss, since all chance in this regard, if hitting the object of attack were at all required, is eliminated. But the chief feature of such a weapon is still to be told; namely, *it may be made to respond only to a certain note or tune, it may be endowed with selective power.* Directly such an arm is produced, it becomes almost impossible to meet it with a corresponding development. It is this feature, perhaps more than in its power of destruction, that its tendency to arrest the development of arms and to stop warfare will reside.

—Nikola Tesla, "Plans to Dispense with Artillery of the Present Type" (emphasis added)

NIKOLA TESLA, REMEMBERED for his farsighted vision into the realms of electrical production and dissemination, was anything but a Luddite. Yet in 1898 he saw that advances in the scientific application of technical media to ballistics—specifically the use of media to produce knowledge about the trajectory and guidance of weaponry—would ultimately lead to weapons that could determine for themselves which target to select. Autonomous artillery would thus be birthed through its capacity to take *note* of and *attune* itself to its surroundings. Artillery's ability to selectively capture and process information—to become media—should, according to Tesla, make obvious the need to avoid such a technological path. In point of fact, by the

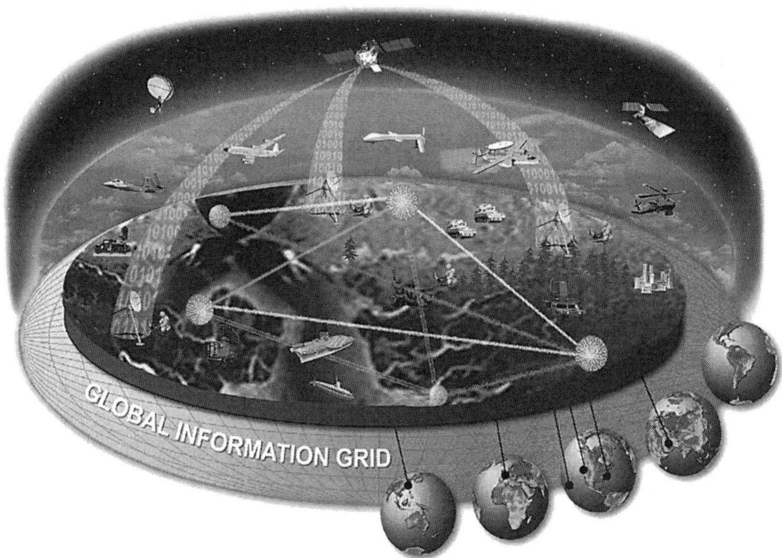

Figure 11.1. U.S. military's global information grid. (National Security Agency, "Global Information Grid")

1890s new forms of technical media, notably photography, were already being used scientifically to fine-tune the capacities of artillery and create "smarter" weapons.[1] Against such weaponry, no capable human response would be possible. Abolishing warfare altogether was the only logical response to such inevitability.

Rather than taking note of Tesla's warning to "dispense with Artillery of this type," the U.S. military is making plans to dispense instead with humans. Particularly since the Cold War, when the Americans were faced with Soviet numerical superiority, the U.S. military has resigned itself to maintaining *technological* superiority.[2] In particular, that superiority was oriented around what, during the Cold War, was called "electronic warfare."[3] Thus, while the Soviet strategy was oriented around recruiting and developing the human soldier, the American strategy was devoted to sacrificing the human in favor of technological innovation, especially innovation in communication and information technologies. According to this logic, it is hardly surprising that current U.S. defense policy now shows itself so willing to dispense with the human altogether.

In the present chapter, we describe this development of "humanectomy" through the stereoscopic lenses of media and communications theory. Our media-centric analysis draws upon three key operative understandings. First, following Friedrich Kittler, media are understood in terms of the selection, storage, processing, and transmitting of information.[4] Drones are thus increasingly prominent "earth-observing" media.[5] The production of military knowledge is foremost a media problem, and the world's militaries have been at the developmental front of media technologies for thousands of years.[6] More broadly, warfare is conducted according to communicative capacities. Even the size of singular permanent military formations, not to be composed of more than three thousand prior to the French Revolution, was dictated by the limits imposed by the soldier's perceptive capacity to see visual signaling technologies—flags.[7] In this and in related ways, command and *capacities* in war depend on the media created to collect data on self and enemy, use that information to develop strategy, transmit that strategy through the chain of command, and guide tactics in real time via perceptual engagements. Since its expansive reconfiguration during World War II, one valence of military strategy is represented by "the art or science of employing the economic, military, psychological, and technological forces of a nation to afford maximum support of national policies."[8] Military strategy at such a scale is produced via a form of electronic warfare or "Infowar" in which the world is informationalized in such a fashion that all realms of human, technological, and ecological activity might legitimately necessitate electronic/digital surveillance.[9] Accordingly, the U.S. military has been engaged in creating the global information grid (GIG), which entails a "globally interconnected, end-to-end set of information capabilities for collecting, processing, storing, disseminating, and managing information on demand to warfighters, policy makers, and support personnel" (see figure 11.1).[10]

Second, following Claude Shannon and Warren Weaver's classic theory, communications systems achieve optimal results through the creation of extensive feedback loops that work to reduce noise to enable greater amounts of information to be accurately transferred. Swarmed drones are being created with multipath cybernetic feedback loops.[11] Thus, the frontier of advancement in drone technologies is not so much ballistic superiority but rather *software* superiority. Insofar as military strategic goals must answer to the capacities of media and the conventions of communications theory, the U.S. military is experimenting with taking humans out of as many links in the chain of command as possible. Autonomatonization results. As with so many other systems-based approaches, humans can be counted on to insert noise into the system. They may introduce noise as an attack or hack,

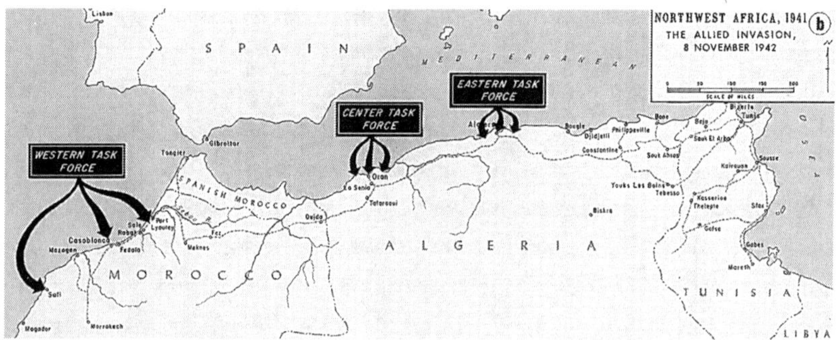

Figure 11.2. Allied Invasion of French North Africa, including Oran, 1942. [Wikimedia.org]

or they may do so because humans are inherently undependable when it comes to mediation—they have highly unreliable data collection, storage, and processing capacities. At any one of these points, even under benign circumstances, counting on humans to successfully operate as transformers or relays is doomed to inefficiencies and failure. Conversely, drones and other infoweapons instantiate emergent forms of military strategy that are largely responding to the conditions of Shannon and Weaver's classic consideration of communications as a mathematical problem whose solutions demand noise reduction.[12] Humans, as the noisiest of communicators, can be a lethal liability in the Infowar.

The third and related point also comes from Kittler, who has noted that, because war is noisy, "command in war must be digital."[13] This suggests that the answer to these problems of military command and communication is the application of digital certainty. As Gerfried Stocker points out, "There is no sphere of civilian life in which the saying 'war is the father of all things' has such unchallenged validity as in the field of digital information technology."[14] While the standard historical treatment of such sentiment relies on a narrative stemming from two World War II objectives, cryptography and ballistics prediction, it has been suggested that such a "digital telos" presents itself at least as early as the U.S. Civil War, when attempts to "digitize" semaphore telegraphy for the purposes of semiotic certainty and greater autonomous mobility were developed by the United States Army Signal Corps.[15] Regardless of its provenance, a digital telos still reigns in U.S. strategic thinking, and autonomy has been always been one of its perceived benefits.

These three considerations have continually set the stage for military strategic thinking. However, they do not guarantee that one military logic will prevail. Rather, military media capacities have been mustered to support two competing visions. Military centralization is founded on a hierarchical organization in which expert-trained generals depend on media to serve their needs—to give them perfect information and produce seamless chains of command.[16] The competing logic relies on autonomous tactical agents or regiments—for example, the "detachment" that can "think for itself" and act accordingly. At the forefront of such military-media machines is the drone. Drones have placed in bold relief a struggle between an old logic of "command and control" and an emergent vision of detachment or autonomy. Such internal military conflict had its electronics-induced birth during the Crimean War, when, in 1854, "commanders in the field were for the first time interfered with (they felt) by constant questions and suggestions (and sometimes orders) from distant military headquarters in London and Paris."[17]

What follows is an analysis of key historical moments in which military doctrine and objectives have been reoriented by media breakdowns and breakthroughs. That is, there has been a recurrent and recursive relationship between media and military strategy. To illustrate this tortured relationship, we begin by examining how hierarchical logics of military command have been fueled by evolving capacities for media to relay battlefield data and open up communications between soldiers and their commanding officers. To a great degree, military command has been vexed by Carl von Clausewitz's sentiment that the "great uncertainty of all data in War is a peculiar difficulty, because all action must, to a certain extent, be planned in a mere twilight, which in addition not unfrequently—like the effect of a fog or moonshine—gives to things exaggerated dimensions and an unnatural appearance."[18] The last 150 years have seen attempts to create media systems capable of piercing the fog of war to produce transcendent military intelligence that, by extension, should lead to unassailable strategy. Yet next-generation drone media are obliterating this commonsense impulse toward a hierarchical military command structure. Because innovations in digital media have unveiled the fallible, bumbling human as the true "fog of war," drones are now being designed with explicitly nonhuman forms of intelligence, cooperation, and communication. The demands of precise military command and organization, therefore, present us with a situation in which the human *must* be excised. The only way to solve the logical contradictions of seminal military doctrines like centralized control/decentralized execution, as well as the medial weaknesses of the soldiering human subject, is to perform a preventive humanectomy.

Centralized Control, Decentralized Execution

Visions of the heroic and autonomous World War I fighter pilot—which were widely and wildly documented in news and fictional accounts—were anachronistic before they truly took flight. One of the first technological breakthroughs the Americans brought to the Western Front in 1917 was airborne radio, "which transformed the airplane from a weapon of individual opportunity to a weapon capable of centrally commanded operation. The airborne radiotelephone made possible the application of the military principle of concentration of mass to aerial combat."[19] Long before Hitler's Panzer divisions were coordinated by very high frequency (VHF) radio, of which Kittler makes much ado,[20] American media transformed the airplane from a lone wolf into a pack. As Paul Clark notes, George Owen Squier, the same figure who invented the photo-chronograph for measuring the velocity of ballistics, pushed for the first successful application of radio use in airplanes when he was the Chief Signal Officer of the Signal Corps. Squier called for "combatant units to multiply their military strength" through the application of "weapons and agencies provided by scientists and engineers."[21] The pack is not merely a set measured according to addition. It is a "force multiplier."

It would be several decades, however, before U.S. Army doctrine caught up to the reality of these new technical capacities. In November 1942, as the German Sixth Army was beginning to freeze in Stalingrad, the Allies launched an invasion of French North Africa. In the early stages of Operation Torch (see figure 11.2), American forces stormed the Algerian beaches near Casablanca, Oran, and Algiers, striving to impose air superiority over this strategic sliver of Axis control. Calculating that French troops would not resist the American invasion, the Allies launched an amphibious assault with thirty-nine C-47 aircraft and 18,500 troops. As the Americans stormed the beaches at Oran, they used loudspeakers to woo French forces: "Ne tirez pas!" (Don't shoot!). When the French replied with machine gun fire, the Allies had to suddenly shift their invasion strategy from Option Peace to Option War.

The airborne C-47s, however, never got the message. Although the nearby anti-aircraft ship, the HMS *Alynbank*, tried to transmit this last-minute change of plans, the *Alynbank*'s operators reportedly used the wrong radio frequency. The result was a strategic disaster for the unseasoned American forces. Despite the fact that the French troops were ill equipped and outmanned, only fourteen of the Americans' thirty-nine C-47s landed unscathed. Although the Allies eventually took control of Oran and the rest of Algeria's strategic coastline, air forces would only play an auxiliary role.[22]

The Americans, however, learned from this notorious blunder in command and control. Just a few months after the invasion of Oran, the United States issued *War Department Field Manual FM 100-20: Command and Employment of Air Power*, which established its new doctrine of aerial warfare. This field manual, released on July 21, 1943, argued for a monumental shift in the U.S. military's relationship of forces. While theretofore airpower had been organized as supplementary and subordinate to ground forces, the new field manual's first lines emphasized: "Land power and air power are co-equal and interdependent forces; neither is an auxiliary of the other."[23] After asserting the necessary independence of airpower, the manual continues: "The inherent flexibility of air power is its greatest asset. This flexibility makes it possible to employ the whole weight of the available air power against selected areas in turn; such concentrated use of the air striking force is a battle winning factor of the first importance. Control of available air power must be centralized and command must be exercised through the air force commander if this inherent flexibility and ability to deliver a decisive blow are to be fully exploited."[24] In light of the communication failures at Oran, this plea for "centrality" established the need for an air force under the independent control of a specialized air command.[25] Yet, in an interesting tension with this emphasis on centrality, the manual also made the case for a "flexible" air force: "In order to obtain flexibility, the operations of the constituent units of a large air force must be closely coordinated. Flexibility enables air power to be switched quickly from one objective to another in the theater of operations."[26] While the authors sought an independent, centralized command, they also recognized that the unique nature of aerial warfare demanded a resilient flexibility from its units and pilots. This flexibility—as well as its apparent tension with "centralized" control—became a core mission of the U.S. Air Force when it was founded in 1947. In fact, "centralized control, decentralized execution" remained the essential doctrine of the air force for decades, and only now in the face of digital warfare has it been seriously called into question.

On the cusp of this monumental shift, air force official doctrine in 1997 emphasized, "Centralized control and decentralized execution of air forces are critical to force effectiveness. Air forces must be controlled by an airman who maintains a broad perspective in prioritizing the limited assets across the range of operations."[27] In 2011 doctrine expressed similar concerns: "Because of airpower's unique potential to directly affect the strategic and operational levels of war, it should be controlled by a single Airman who maintains the broad, strategic perspective necessary to balance and prioritize the use of a powerful, highly desired yet limited force."[28] This continued emphasis on a single "airman," of course, places the central responsibility on a seasoned, specially trained fighter who has honed his or her knowledge in a wide range of battlefield experiences. This wise leader then programs certain orders and strategies into the heads of pilots, who carry out their missions under the supervision of their leaders. While this basic hierarchical command-and-control strategy ensures the autonomy of air forces, it limits the reactive "flexibility" increasingly desired by air command.

Beginning in the 1990s, U.S. Air Force doctrine—under the weight of centuries of hierarchical military theory—sought to maximize this flexibility by developing a special brand of networked warfare.[29] Yet, because commands were still being filtered through a centralized node (or "controller"), advanced networking technologies simply reinscribed the military's traditional structures of centralized command and control. For example, the *Department of Defense Dictionary of Military and Associated Terms* defines "centralized control" the following way: "In joint air operations, placing within one commander the responsibility and authority for planning, directing, and coordinating a military operation or group/category of operations."[30] Decentralized execution, likewise, is defined as "the delegation of execution authority to subordinate commanders." In emphasizing the centrality of "one commander" who delegates tasks to subordinates, this doctrine essentially sacrifices the adaptability and operational autonomy sought—though left unfulfilled—by current forms of decentralized warfare.

For a new generation of military strategists, this centralization is proving to be one of the military's key obstacles. For example, Milan N. Vego, a strategist who teaches at the Naval War College, argues that the "most serious current problem in the Armed Forces is the trend toward over-centralized decisionmaking on the operational and strategic levels."[31] Yet, as Vego points out, attempts to decentralize command through networking have always fallen short of their promise: "Networking supposedly promises decentralization, affording greater initiative to subordinates. Evidence suggests the opposite: theater commanders increasingly use information technology to make decisions that would normally be the province of tactical commanders."[32] As Vego argues, "Advances in communications allow senior leaders to observe events in near real time from thousands of miles away. This promotes a false impression that remote headquarters can perceive the situation better than tactical commanders on the scene."[33] Technological advances that "clear the fog" for senior commanders, therefore, allow them to micromanage the battlefield from afar. For Vego, overcentralized command and control "encourages an unwillingness or inability on the part of subordinates to act independently and take responsibility for their actions."[34] This, of course, defeats the underlying purpose of networked decentralization. Advanced media of surveillance and communication, therefore, have actually worked against efforts to decentralize the work of war because they implicate senior commanders more deeply into the scene of battle, thereby remediating traditional structures of hierarchical command.

Vulnerable Media, Vulnerable Command

In a similar fashion, media that were designed to minimize battlefield noise have led to increased communications vulnerability. Reflecting on the radio communications systems of World War I, Kittler once remarked: "Technical media don't arise out of human needs, as their current interpretation in terms of bodily prostheses has it, they follow each other in a rhythm of escalating strategic answers."[35] Because telegraph cables were so vulnerable to enemy interception, Italian engineer Guglielmo Marconi developed a media solution based on wireless systems of radio communications. "But alas," as Kittler points out, "the new wireless medium of radio introduced even greater risks of interception than telegraphic cables."[36] Although radio was celebrated as a solution to the inherent limitations of cable telegraphy, opening up new possibilities for transatlantic communication, the new technology simply introduced new vulnerabilities that would have to be solved by new media.

This trend has been borne out in the bumpy development of postcentralized military command and control. As we have already seen, while new communications and surveillance technologies allowed for greater operational flexibility among pilot networks, they also exacerbated the problem of centralized command. To comprehensively tackle the prospect of decentralization, therefore, the U.S. military has begun to radically reconceptualize the ways in which battlefield data can be captured, stored, and processed. Technologies like autonomous vehicles, electromagnetic rail guns, and multi-phenomenology sensors are giving rise to what Robert Work and Shawn Brimley, scholars at the Center for a New American Security, call a "military technical revolution"[37]—that is, a disruptive technological convergence that promises to upturn the ways in which warfare is waged. One of the key teloi of this revolution is the development of technological solutions to the centralization problem. And as Kittler could have foreseen, these decentralizing technologies are creating new problems that are gradually leading to a singular technical solution—the elimination of the human from the chain of command and control.

Unmanned aerial vehicles, of course, are on the frontier of these efforts. Simply taking humans out of aircraft radically increases their flexibility on the battlefield. While a pilot can only stay in the air for twelve to fourteen hours, unmanned craft, with aerial refueling, can stay in the air for forty to fifty hours at a time.[38] The weight savings are also remarkable, allowing for a stealthier craft with higher endurance. And perhaps most of all, drones can partake in high-altitude and high-speed missions that are impossible for human pilots to safely endure.[39] Establishing air dominance in the age of drone warfare, therefore, requires activities in which humans simply cannot participate.

Faced with this shifting technological landscape, in 2010 then Secretary of Defense Robert Gates ordered the army and the air force to develop new multi-aircraft piloting technologies. In response, the army—which deploys its drone pilots to overseas bases—has developed a system by which pilots can oversee two vehicles at once. In 2015, therefore, the army began to field multi-aircraft control for their cutting-edge drone, the MQ-1C Gray Eagle.[40] This advance in unmanned warfare has been made possible only because the drones have a remarkable degree of autonomy, having the capacity to take off and land on their own, for example.[41] Yet this step forward in the autonomous operation of aerial vehicles creates a deluge of additional vulnerabilities. The Gray Eagle's present data transmission systems, for example, are highly sensitive to enemy hacking. Just as telegraph cables and then wireless radio transmissions enhanced the potential for message interception, drones' complex systems of satellite-based communications are highly vulnerable to penetration and sabotage. In fact, in order for drones to operate in the air, unmanned systems require constant, assured communications to remote pilots.[42] This communication link, therefore, is an Achilles's heel of unmanned craft: as Work and Brimley point out in *Preparing for War in the Robotic Age*, "an actor who dominates in cyber conflict can infiltrate command-and-control networks, generate misinformation and confusion, and potentially even shut down or usurp control over physical platforms. This will be especially true for unmanned systems."[43] To better secure these channels, the Department of Defense (DoD) is experimenting with high-bandwidth, protected communications like high-frequency satellites and laser and free-space optical communications.

Ultimately, however, new transmission media are not radical enough to solve this problem in all its complexity. In summer 2014 the Defense Advanced Research Projects Agency (DARPA), the principal research and development wing of the DoD, awarded a contract to Northrop Grumman for a post–satellite navigation system. Designed to allow navigation in "GPS-challenged" environments, DARPA's Chip-Scale Combinatorial Atomic Navigator (C-SCAN) program will be integrated with a microelectromechanical system (MEMS) and atomic inertial guidance technologies to form a single inertial measurement unit. In the words of Northrop Grumman vice president Charles Volk, "This microsystem has the potential to significantly reduce the size, weight, power requirement, and cost of precision navigation systems. . . . Additionally, the system will reduce dependence on GPS and other external signals, ensuring uncompromised navigation and guidance for warfighters."[44] Note the emphasis on reducing crafts' reliance on external navigation systems: by eliminating the vulnerabilities of external communications—even fully automated communications between crafts' navigational systems and their guiding satellites—craft autonomy can be significantly increased.

A number of recent innovations have energized this shift away from satellite communications (SATCOM), as researchers have demonstrated how simple it is to hack military satellite systems. According to a security consultant who produced a controversial white paper on the vulnerability of current-generation military SATCOM, "Multiple high risk vulnerabilities were uncovered in all SATCOM device firmware. . . . These vulnerabilities have the potential to allow a malicious actor to intercept, manipulate, or block communications, and in some cases, to remotely take control of the physical device."[45] Military SATCOM devices like the Cobham Aviator 700D, which have long served as secure communications and navigations systems for diverse military functions, are quickly becoming as hackable as telegraph lines were in the early twentieth century. The C-SCAN and kindred technological programs, therefore, are striving to develop navigation systems that are fully internal and thus process all locational data onboard.

Data security, however, is not the only communications challenge facing unmanned craft. According to the Department of Defense's 2013 "Unmanned Systems Integrated Roadmap," manpower and bandwidth are two of the costliest elements of their unmanned systems programs.[46] These costs, of course, are complementary: because unmanned systems cannot adequately process all the data they capture, they are required to use significant bandwidth to transmit these data back to humans on the ground.[47] In fact, the principal personnel burden for unmanned vehicles is the processing of all the surveillance data they generate.[48] Emphasizing that "one of the largest cost drivers in the budget of DoD is manpower," the Department of Defense "Roadmap" argues that "of utmost importance for DoD is increased system, sensor, and analytical automation that can not only capture significant information and events, but can also develop, record, playback, project, and parse out those data and then actually deliver 'actionable' intelligence instead of just raw information."[49] Remotely "piloting" drone aircraft requires remarkably little bandwidth; the vast majority of unmanned systems' bandwidth needs are devoted to transmitting their surveillance data to humans on the ground. Therefore, according to DoD, automated onboard data processing "can help minimize critical bandwidth necessary to transmit ISR data to the warfighter and may also be suitable for reducing the intelligence officer workload and decreasing the time in the kill chain."[50] According to DARPA estimates, automated image-processing technologies could reduce the personnel burden for wide-area drone sensors—which provide surveillance coverage for an entire city—from two thousand personnel to about seventy-five.[51] These onboard processing systems would scan the drones' surveillance data for anomalies and would only pass along to humans those items of potential interest. In the words of a Department of Defense report, "automated target recognition enables target discrimination, i.e., reporting contacts of interest instead of sending entire images for human interpretation."[52] Onboard computers, therefore, would autonomously determine which data should be shared with humans and which should be simply filtered out.

The Gathering Swarm

In other words, select war machines are now entrusted with the capacity to decide which battlefield data their controllers access. While at this time only humans are entrusted with "kill" decisions based on these data, this official DoD policy is being contradicted by autonomous media/weapons like Raytheon's new Close-In Weapon System, the Phalanx.[53] To compensate for the data vulnerability and financial cost of keeping humans in the command chain, these new military technologies are surrendering to automated computing systems the capacity to determine who is friend and who is enemy. Thus, in tracing the history of how new surveillance and communications technologies have been used to massage the tensions between centralized command, decentralized execution, and data security, we have been telling a story that has been built more or less logically on the computerized automation of enemy epistemology (and hence, eventually, the automation of kill decisions). This long drive toward decentralization, therefore, has serious epistemological and political implications.

In one of the cutting-edge developments of this military technical revolution, the figure of the "network" has receded into the figure of the *swarm*. While swarm warfare has important precedents in military history—such as in Alexander the Great's Central Asian campaigns, the Mongol invasions of Asia and Eastern Europe, Native American attacks on the western frontier, and postcolonial guerilla resistance in Asia and Africa[54]—logics of robotic autonomy have revolutionized the potential of the swarm. Many military strategists, faced with the failure of networks to solve the problem of overcentralization, have begun to realize that traditional models of intelligence and command—based, that is, on human cognition and human communication—are inadequate to the challenges of twenty-first-century warfare. While for now the Department of Defense is trying to keep humans in the kill chain of unmanned operations, a human-dominated control and command structure simply cannot fulfill the objectives of decentralized twenty-first-century warfare. The next step in the military technical revolution, therefore, relies on the development of nonhuman models of knowledge and communication. Observing this transition to animal intelligences, military strategist Paul Scharre has remarked that forces will shift "from fighting as a *network* to fighting as a *swarm*, with large numbers of highly autonomous uninhabited systems coordinating their actions on the battlefield. This will enable greater mass, coordination, intelligence, and speed than would be possible with networks of human-inhabited or even remotely controlled uninhabited systems."[55] While humans could retain a degree of supervisory contact with the swarm, "the leading edge of the battlefront across all domains would be unmanned, networked, intelligent, and autonomous."[56]

To many who work in military research and development, it is becoming increasingly clear that the only solution to the fog of war is the abandonment of human models of communication and command. The human—with its limited vision, its juvenile data-processing capacities, and its highly vulnerable communications processes—is the ultimate source of the fog of war. The human, however, was never intelligible as the source of this fog until it was possible to replace the human with digital media. Thus, with the development of extremely sophisticated systems for processing battlefield data, the human has suddenly emerged as an epistemological hindrance. This development helps us think more fully through the implications of Kittler's statement that "command in war must be digital precisely because war is noisy."[57] Of course, Kittler is not simply pinpointing the necessity of digitality in human-based communications and command. Noise elimination has its ultimate fulfillment in the elimination of humans' innate weaknesses in data selection, storage, and processing. For command to be truly digital, fully automated machine-to-machine command, control, and coordination must be developed.

With its extraordinary capacities for intercraft cooperation, the swarm is the ideal technological system for dispersing the fog of war. Upending the metaphorical connotations of "fog," swarms operate through a "combat *cloud*" that is driven by collective interoperability.[58] Traditional military networks, of course, had to safeguard their principal nodes of intelligence against enemy attack. But with swarms, this epistemological center of gravity is a thing of the past. In a radical departure from human-centered control and command, which requires communication between psychically isolated cooperating subjects, the swarm cloud possesses a continuously refined, emergent collective intelligence that is far beyond the grasp of humans' physiological capacity. These swarms continuously reorient their collective intelligence—they are even "self-healing" in the event of companion loss, which they compensate for by readjusting the epistemological topology of the swarm.[59] These decisions for topological restructuring can be accomplished by the use of "voting" mechanisms, which could allow swarms to achieve a decentralized epistemology that is inconceivable among networked human combatants.[60]

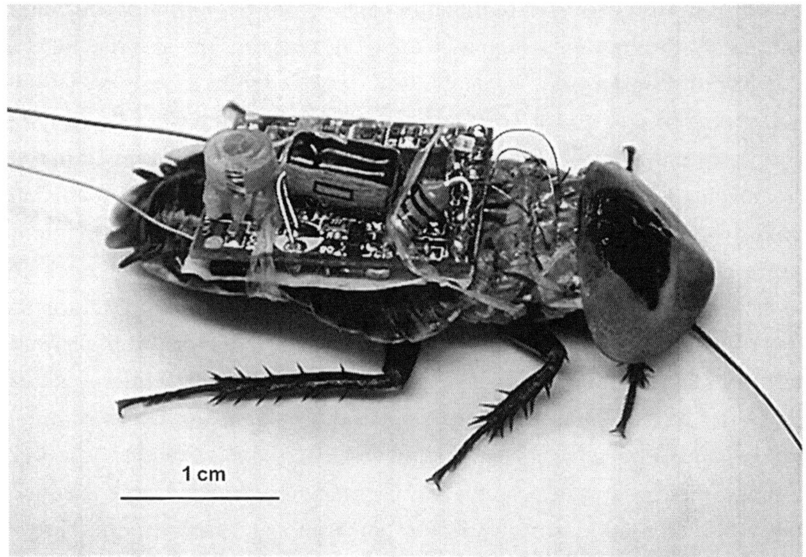

Figure 11.3. Specimen from DARPA's Hybrid Insect Micro-Electro-Mechanical System (HI-MEMS).

This emergent intelligence is made possible by what military strategists call "implicit communication," which is modeled on the cooperative epistemologies of flock and school animals like birds, ants, and fish.[61] New digital manufacturing technologies, such as 3-D printing, are providing the impetus for DoD affiliates to develop these sophisticated swarms that take the physical form of dragonflies, "robobees," houseflies, and other insects (see figure 11.3).[62] As 3-D printing has given rise to the mass production of these swarming minidrones,[63] and as computing and navigational systems continue to shrink and become more mobile, this development could allow DoD to deploy thousands or even billions of tiny, cheaply produced, cooperative drones that could be released into the field of combat in order to carry out reconnaissance and locate enemy combatants.[64]

Unlike schools of fish and flocks of birds, however, stigmergent robotic swarms are not necessarily composed of homogeneous parts. Of course, schools and flocks operate as collectives of whole organic units—each schooling fish has its own eyes, a lateral line sensory system, fins, teeth, bowels, and so forth. Yet military strategists have begun to imagine the emergence of a "swarmanoid," which is a heterogeneous assemblage of bots that each perform unique epistemological and kinetic functions. According to specifications developed by researchers at the University of Brussels, the swarmanoid could comprise three different components: "foot-bots," which specialize in moving through uneven and challenging terrains; "hand-bots," which climb vertical surfaces and manipulate objects; and flying "eye-bots," which collectively gather and process information that is then shared with the foot-bots and hand-bots.[65] Many swarms of the future will consist not of homogeneous swarming components but rather heterogeneous bots that collectively delegate tasks based on individual units' strengths in various kinetic or epistemological tasks.

Drawing on some of these emergent capacities, in the 2013 edition of its "Unmanned Systems Integrated Roadmap," the Department of Defense laid out its plans for unmanned systems during the next generation. In this document, the DoD foresees "smart teams of unmanned systems operating autonomously" and in concert.[66] Constructing a collective enemy epistemology, these swarms assess and classify their surroundings while carrying out nontraditional means of warfare, synchronizing electronic and kinetic attacks.[67] These swarms, in fact, are already being deployed on the battlefield in the form of advanced cruise missile systems, some of which are equipped with the capacity to autonomously determine and engage enemy targets. Outfitted with sophisticated onboard sensors, these swarms can perform battle damage assessments before they strike, thus enabling them to collectively refine their knowledge of the enemy and coordinate their attacks accordingly.[68] This process of enemy determination/incapacitation has reached an impressive degree of autonomy in naval warfare, where the craft in Lockheed Martin's Low-Cost Autonomous Attack System (LOCAAS) line collectively "vote" on which tactics and weapons to use against a determined target.[69] The cutting edge of these autonomous naval warfare technologies is currently the Control Architecture for Robotic Agent Command and Sensing system (CARACaS).[70]

The DoD's "Roadmap" also envisions a near future in which the air force will develop weaponized unmanned aerial systems that are designed to carry out autonomous swarm attacks. Calling these craft "loitering weapons," DoD envisions aerial swarms outfitted with imaging sensors that serve as "intelligent munitions."[71] Using data-processing systems like the LOCAAS, these swarming media/weapons are designed to "autonomously search and destroy critical mobile targets while aiming over a wide combat area."[72] While these swarming munitions are currently "man in the loop"—that is, in use while soldiers on the ground make decisions about lethal engagements—DoD suggests developing a data-processing "mothership" that could guide these

"Surveilling Miniature Attack Cruise Missiles." This artificially intelligent mothership, which will support four individual missiles, will aid the swarm in movement coordination, enemy determination, and attack protocols.[73] The DoD, therefore, foresees that the center of gravity for autonomous missions will be continuously deferred onto different machinic assemblages, as intelligent munitions are programmed to follow kill commands devised by machines, based on coordinates formulated by machines, and ultimately targeted at the enemies determined by machines.

Conclusion

As we have tried to make clear, the U.S. military has developed dueling compulsions and capacities that fluctuate according to the rise of new media technologies. On the one hand is the drive for fully centralized command and control, and on the other is the desire to have fully capable "on the ground" soldiers able to execute strategy based on their assessment of any given situation. One concern regarding autonomy is the rogue soldier or rogue platoon. Any *detachment* has the real potential to go rogue. The further and longer detached from central command and *oversight*, the more likely it becomes for the rogue to develop. Command in war necessitates clear lines of communication but also clear means of surveillance—you need to see both your enemy and yourself. Losing contact with your soldiers, no longer being able to track their whereabouts, can have negative consequences not just in terms of failed missions but for the development of counterinitiatives. This, of course, is an essential problem with drones: if they carry out their media logic to its full extent, they would remove human oversight to "close the loop."

These competing capacities, breakdowns, and reversals are organized through continuous innovations in communications technologies. Self-destructing orders move the chain of command into the realm of conjecture. Secret orders can be hidden from the externally known enemy as well as the potentially internal enemy. However, the existence of "secrets" means rogue orders can be invented and hidden behind the veil of secrecy that has long cast "deciphered" messages into question. An autonomous drone will be much like the detachment of old. Once sent on its mission, how it carries it out and how it interprets "the mission" remain open to a systemic feedback loop that is ideally hidden from human perception, let alone human decipherment. As with any sign that depends on intelligence to be given meaning, drone detachments must at some point give life to goals, to missions.

This bringing into being can only be accomplished through robotic autonomy. The drone must be able to freely choose how best to carry out the mission. Human communicative fallibility (with its narrow bandwidth, faulty memory, slow and irrational processing, weak signaling) must be systematically and surgically removed from military communications—extensively and intensively—for the drone to truly be free to carry out its mission. Any trace of the human is an insidious infection, a threat to the security and intelligence—to the very life—of the autonomous system. While a postoperative surgeon may check "the margins" in a search for remaining malignant tissue, humans may not be able to properly sense the ripple effects of their own presence in the system, however diminished. In that sense, humans cannot be counted on to remove all that is "human" from the drone. Only the drone can do that. The U.S. military's prognosis, alas, is clear: only a humanectomy can truly save us.

Notes

1. Paul Virilio (*War and Cinema*), Friedrich Kittler (*Gramophone, Film, Typewriter*), and Manuel DeLanda (*War in the Age of Intelligent Machines*) have all in their own way described the overlapping development of modern media technologies with those of guided artillery systems. What Tesla would likely have been well aware of was the expansive use in the 1890s of the scientific study of ballistics and artillery enabled by new forms of data collection—that is, of new media devices used to collect information about ballistics in increasingly specific and detailed fashion. Albert Cushing Crehore and George Owen Squier conducted groundbreaking research using photography and electromagnetism to measure the speed of ballistics. Their 1897 book, *The Polarizing Photo-Chronograph*, collected research previously published in the *Journal of the United States Artillery* that the U.S. military developed in 1892 for the scientific advancement of weaponry. Kittler (*Gramophone, Film, Typewriter*) noted that related research was also taking place in Europe.
2. Barton, *The Politics of Peace*, 165.
3. D. Gordon, *Electronic Warfare*.
4. Kittler, *Gramophone, Film, Typewriter*, 369.
5. See Packer and Reeves, "Romancing the Drone," which appeared in a special issue of the *Canadian Journal of Communication* devoted to "earth-observing media."
6. Kittler, *Gramophone, Film, Typewriter*; Sterling, *Military Communications*; Van Creveld, *Command in War*.
7. Van Creveld, *Command in War*, 24.
8. D. Gordon, *Electronic Warfare*, 10.

9. D. Gordon, *Electronic Warfare*; Stocker and Schopf, *INFOWAR: Information. Macht. Krieg*. Climate security is now considered one of the key considerations for U.S. military strategy. CNA Military Advisory Board, "National Security and the Accelerating Risks."
10. National Security Agency, "Global Information Grid."
11. Shannon and Weaver, *The Mathematical Theory of Communication*.
12. See Asaro, "Determinism, Machine Agency, and Responsibility," 271–74.
13. Kittler, "Media Wars," 119.
14. Stocker, "InfoWar."
15. Maddalena and Packer, "The Digital Body."
16. See Wall and Monahan, "Surveillance and Violence from Afar," 246–50.
17. Sterling, *Military Communications*, xxvii.
18. Von Clausewitz, *On War*, 106.
19. Clark, "Early Impacts of Communications," 1408.
20. While Kittler mentions the necessity of wireless communication for planes and submarines in World War I, it is the tank that receives the greatest attention. Kittler describes tanks as having suffered most from poor communication in World War I and having achieved the greatest force multiplier effect in World War II. See Kittler, *Gramophone, Film, Typewriter*, 95–105.
21. Clark, "Early Impacts of Communications," 1408.
22. Romero, "The Origins of Centralized Control," 8–10.
23. United States War Department, *War Department Field Manual*, 4.
24. United States War Department, *War Department Field Manual*, 4.
25. For more on the development of the early American discourse of airpower, see Kaplan, *Aerial Aftermaths*.
26. United States War Department, *War Department Field Manual*, 7.
27. See Romero, "The Origins of Centralized Control," 100.
28. United States Air Force, "Air Force Basic Doctrine," 38.
29. See Arquilla and Ronfeldt, *The Advent of Netwar*.
30. *Department of Defense Dictionary*, 33.
31. Vego, "Operational Command and Control," 101.
32. Vego, "Operational Command and Control," 102.
33. Vego, "Operational Command and Control," 101.
34. Vego, "Operational Command and Control," 101.
35. Kittler, "Media Wars," 121.
36. Kittler, "Media Wars," 121.
37. Work and Brimley, *Preparing for War*, 7.
38. Scharre, "Robotics on the Battlefield: The Coming Swarm"; cf. Crandall, "Ecologies of the Wayward Drone," 269.
39. Scharre, *Robotics on the Battlefield*, pt. I, *Range, Persistence, and Daring*, 10–11, 24.
40. Scharre, *Robotics on the Battlefield*, pt. I, 17.
41. Scharre, "Robotics on the Battlefield," video.
42. Scharre, *Robotics on the Battlefield*, pt. I, 31.

43. Work and Brimley, *Preparing for War*, 23.
44. Northrop Grumman Corporation, "Northrop Grumman Awarded Contract."
45. Santamarta, "A Wake-up Call for SATCOM Security," 1.
46. Department of Defense, "Unmanned Systems Integrated Roadmap FY2013–2038," 25, 49.
47. See Parks, "Zeroing In."
48. Scharre, *Robotics on the Battlefield*, pt. I, 17.
49. Department of Defense, "Unmanned Systems Integrated Roadmap," 29.
50. Department of Defense, "Unmanned Systems Integrated Roadmap," 85.
51. Scharre, *Robotics on the Battlefield*, pt. I, 17.
52. Department of Defense, "Unmanned Systems Integrated Roadmap," 89.
53. Stimson Center, "Recommendations and Report of the Task Force," 71. Although the DoD officially prohibits autonomous UAVs from launching weapons without human command, the 2014 task force on drone policy admitted that "current directives raise the possibility of permitting the use of such autonomous weapons in the future, with the approval of high-ranking military and civilian officials" (Stimson Center, "Recommendations and Report of the Task Force," 26). Indeed, DoD directive 3000.09, the notorious 2012 Autonomy in Weapon Systems policy document, establishes a legal loophole by which DoD officials can use their discretion to bypass all restrictions on lethal autonomous weapons (Department of Defense, "Directive Number 3000.09," 3). Further, as competing drone systems are developed in Russia, China, and elsewhere, it is hard to imagine that the U.S. military will fail to enhance their drone programs to the highest levels of sophistication.
54. See Arquilla and Ronfeldt, *Swarming and the Future of Conflict*; and S. Edwards, *Swarming and the Future of Warfare*.
55. Scharre, *Robotics on the Battlefield*, pt. I, 8.
56. Work and Brimley, *Preparing for War*, 29.
57. Kittler, "Media Wars," 119.
58. Stimson Center, "Recommendations and Report of the Task Force," 26.
59. Rubinstein and Shen, "A Scalable and Distributed Model"; Scharre, *Robotics on the Battlefield*, pt. I, 32.
60. Scharre, *Robotics on the Battlefield*, pt. II, *The Coming Swarm*, 26; see also *Defense Update*, "Low Cost Autonomous Attack System."
61. See Sharkey and Sharkey, "The Application of Swarm Intelligence"; Sarker and Dahl, "Bio-Inspired Communication."
62. Piore, "Rise of the Insect Drones."
63. Golson, "A Military-Grade Drone."
64. Scharre, *Robotics on the Battlefield*, pt. II, 20; see also Perry, "A Self-Organizing Thousand-Robot Swarm."
65. Dorigo et al., "Swarmanoid."
66. Department of Defense, "Unmanned Systems Integrated Roadmap," 72.
67. Center for a New American Security, "Robotics on the Battlefield."
68. Scharre, *Robotics on the Battlefield*, pts. I and II; Scharre, "Robotics on the Battlefield," video.

69. *Defense Update*, "Low Cost Autonomous Attack System."
70. See Smalley, "The Future Is Now."
71. Department of Defense, "Unmanned Systems Integrated Roadmap," 78.
72. Department of Defense, "Unmanned Systems Integrated Roadmap," 78.
73. Department of Defense, "Unmanned Systems Integrated Roadmap," 78.

12 THE LABOR OF SURVEILLANCE AND BUREAUCRATIZED KILLING

New Subjectivities of Military Drone Operators

PETER ASARO

THERE WAS A MASSIVE increase in the number of drone aircraft used by the United States military over the first decade of the twenty-first century.[1] Along with this, there was an expansion of the capabilities of drone technologies and an increase in the sophistication and types of missions and tasks for which drones are used. From 2001 to 2012 the number of unmanned aerial vehicles (UAVs) in the U.S. military grew from seventy to seven thousand. They were also armed for the first time with weapons, creating the new aircraft role of "hunter-killer," combining remote surveillance and lethal capabilities. This new role has largely been described as an economical and effective military tool for U.S. operations in the Iraq and Afghanistan wars and the Libyan civil war and as a politically expedient tool for the targeted killing of suspected terrorists in Pakistan, Yemen, and Somalia.[2] The New America Foundation estimates that as many as 2,600 people have been killed by drone strikes in Pakistan alone from their first use there in 2004 until 2012.[3] Following a more rigorous methodology, the Bureau of Investigative Journalism estimates the total number of people killed by the 344 drone strikes during that period in Pakistan as between 2,562 and 3,325, with as many as 881 of these being confirmed civilian deaths.[4] Casualties from drone strikes in Iraq and Afghanistan have not been tracked or analyzed by journalists, nor does the military release their own estimates, but the total is likely to be significantly higher given the greater number of missions flown in those war zones.

The U.S. military has strongly embraced the use of drones for a complicated set of reasons, alignments of interests, perceived military advantages, and internal policy and budgeting priorities. They are keenly interested in optimizing the effective use of drone technologies, which includes comprehensive reviews of missions, accidents, training programs, support infrastructure, operator performance and health, and other factors, including public perceptions of the use of drones.[5] Because the operators of these drones are an essential element of the complex socio-technical system that constitutes military drone operations, drone operators have been singled out as the subjects of a variety of research studies, especially studies of their psycho-physical performances and visual-motor skills. This particular focus has been due in part to perceived differences in the nature of "remote piloting" from "being in the plane" and the technological challenges of designing interfaces for such remote operations. Little, however, is known or discussed outside the military about the experiences of drone operators.

In this chapter, I will be investigating the people who operate these drones, as workers involved in the labor of surveillance and killing. In viewing drones as mobile platforms for surveillance, we can look to the operators of these systems, and the organization and management of their work, as constituting a particular form of the labor of surveillance. And insofar as these drones are armed with lethal weapons, we can also consider the relationships between this labor of surveillance and a unique form of the labor of killing. Of course, there are many jobs in contemporary society that involve surveillance (in prisons, hospitals, offices, factories, shopping centers, and numerous other places). Yet the kind of surveillance offered by remote-controlled flying robotic cameras is new and rapidly growing.[6] There are also many jobs that involve killing (in slaughterhouses, medical research labs, the military, and others).[7] What makes drone operators particularly interesting as subjects is not only that their work combines surveillance and killing but also that it sits at an intersection of multiple networks of power and technology, visibility and invisibility. Their work is a focal point of discourses about the ethics of killing, the effectiveness of military strategies for achieving political goals, the cultural and political significance of lethal robotics, and public concerns over the further automation of surveillance and killing.

While the work of killing performed by drone operators bears a certain resemblance to other forms of killing labor and shares with it certain cultural meanings, social stigmas, and psychological burdens, it is in many ways unique. Its uniqueness becomes most obvious when it is compared to other military jobs that also involve killing. Some of these involve killing at a great distance, such as the work of snipers, artillery gunners, aerial bombardiers, or ballistic missile operators. Among these, only snipers share the long and persistent voyeurism of drone operators, as they peer through their rifle scopes at potential targets. Yet snipers differ in being a mile or less from their targets, terrestrially bound, and in danger of being found out, tracked down, and killed. The sniper also feels the weather, smells the smells, and interacts with the local people in a way that a drone operator does not. The work of drone operators resembles in some ways the work of drawing up lists of aerial bombing targets. Since its invention in World War I, this work has been done in command posts by teams of workers who make their decisions based on maps and photos, intelligence reports of varying accuracy, consultations with lawyers and superior officers, collaborative decision processes, and often under intense time pressures. Yet these bombing planners do not ride along in the plane, nor are they called on to make judgments about events in real time and to change their targeting decisions based on live high-resolution video streams of potential targets.

In this chapter, I will use the phrase *bureaucratized killing* to refer to the particular form of labor that killing takes in the work of drone operators, which is constituted by the kind of bureaucratic labor organization developed within the military to do things like generate lists of bombing targets, in combination with the more "hands-on" work of deciding when and where to pull the trigger that more closely resembles the killing work of the sniper. Because this form of killing involves self-conscious processes and efforts at rationalization—at both the individual and organizational levels to make the processes more efficient, more accurate, and more manageable—it is most appropriate to approach this subject as a form of killing that has an elaborate and intentional bureaucratized structure as well as a psychological dimension.[8] Consequent with the historical emergence of this rational bureaucratization has been an intense computerization and technocratic management of the human labor involved in this complex system of remote surveillance and killing. And thus, there are certain parallels to be drawn between the regimes of scientific expertise applied to understanding and managing workers and the technologies they use in factories and offices and the kinds of scientific knowledge produced to understand the work of drone operators and the design of the technologies they use.

At this point, I should also clarify what I mean by the term *subjectivity* and why the subjectivity of drone operators is an interesting topic for study. Within sociological literature, there has been a rich discussion of the ways social "subjects" are constructed by the social structures in which they find themselves.[9] More recent theories have identified the formation of subjectivities in the day-to-day activities and habits of individuals, and still others have shown how "subjects" have been constructed through systems of knowledge by experts, systems of data collection, and modes of discourse.[10] In terms of the subjectivities of workers and labor, there is a long historical evolution of systems of expertise that have been deployed to construct and manage the subjectivity of workers and to respond to the emergent resistance to industrial and postindustrial modes of labor.[11] From Taylorism to mental hygiene, to the quality of working life, to business process reengineering, to the worker-as-entrepreneur, these attempts to actively construct and shape the subjectivities of individual workers in particular ways have had real consequences on large-scale social formations of labor, the subjective experience of workers, and the ways in which we conceive of and discuss their labor. This chapter will extend this notion of "subjectivity" to drone operators in order to better understand how systematic knowledge has been deployed to constitute their subjectivity, as well as how it falls short yet still grasps for greater control over the labor of bureaucratized killing.

From the Taylorist vision of observing and decomposing the movements of workers to ethnographies of the workplace, much of the science of labor organization and management seeks to make the practices, skills, and knowledge of workers more visible. Running against, or at least across, this trend are cultural imperatives to render invisible certain distasteful forms of work. From the "dirty" work around sanitation or sex work, to dealing with the materiality of human illness and mortality, to the low prestige and wages assigned to various forms of undesirable work, there are both explicit and implicit means within every society to render some forms of work "visible" and others "invisible."[12] This is tied up with cultural ideals and values and is often a source of political tension among groups of people who are systematically excluded from desirable forms of work, or whose work is systematically hidden, unrecognized, undervalued, or underpaid. Killing work in particular has been traditionally set apart from other forms of work in many societies.[13] Indeed, the formation of a separate social class of "warriors" to grapple with the ambivalent nature of socially sanctioned killing can be seen as a cultural expression and enforcement of the difference between killing work and other forms of work. From the execution chamber to the slaughterhouse to the battlefield, there are complicated politics surrounding the visibility and concealment of socially sanctioned forms of killing. Even while the work of drone operators has become increasingly important to the military, and to national and international politics, the actual work of drone operators has remained largely hidden from public view and increasingly protected from the prying eyes of journalists and social scientists. And even within the military, drone warriors are subject to powerful social pressures not to reveal or discuss their work or its psychological or emotional stresses.

Perhaps unsurprisingly for a technology that is often referred to as "unmanned," there has been relatively little public discussion about the people who operate these drone aircraft or the character of their work. What little public discussion there has been tends to be highly politically charged—not only because it deals with military service personnel but because it is also perceived as expressing implicit judgments on the U.S. policies that are being pursued using these technologies. While it may be both practically and theoretically impossible to completely understand what it is like to operate these drones in military missions with lethal consequences, it is worthwhile to examine the social semiotics—the signs, social relations, and systems of knowledge that constitute them—that have emerged in various attempts to describe this work. That is, as drone technologies have taken on increasing military and political significance, a range of discourses have emerged that attempt, in various ways, to describe the operators of these drones. These discourses range from the subjective and "what-it-is-like" to be a drone operator to the objective and techniques for the scientific understanding of the labor performed by drone operators and the means of improving or optimizing it. From a semiotic perspective, each of these discourses is trying, in its own way, to represent drone operators and their labor and, through these representations, to influence how the technology is developed and how it will be used to achieve military and political goals. This chapter provides a fresh perspective on the technological and political debates through a more careful analysis of the ways in which these discourses are framing and constructing the subjectivities of drone operators.

To say that the discussion of drone technologies and their appropriate uses is politically charged would be an understatement. There is, in fact, a powerful and highly developed rhetoric within military and foreign policy circles concerning the use of remote-piloted aircraft and unmanned aerial vehicles. This predominantly positive rhetoric touts the capabilities of the systems, primarily in the areas of intelligence, surveillance, and reconnaissance (ISR), as well as their emerging role as weapons in close air support of ground forces, support of manned air missions, and their use by special forces in targeted killings.[14] This rhetoric often focuses on the ability of military robotics, among which drones are the most prominent, to perform work that is "dull, dirty and dangerous" in ways that protect the operators and thus reduce the risk of conducting such operations. This is coupled with a positive economic cost-benefit analysis according to which these missions can be conducted at a greatly reduced cost when compared to manned aircraft and other technological alternatives, such as satellite imagery or special forces operations. More importantly, drone technologies are praised for their ability to protect their operators from the traditional threats of combat aviation by allowing them to conduct their work at a very great physical distance. I call these purported advantages collectively the "heroic myth" of drones, as it is a rhetorical framing that grants the technology itself agency in reducing costs and risks while increasing military capabilities. According to this myth, the technology serves to enhance the virtues of the pilots and operators and their ability to wage war ethically.[15]

There is also a critical rhetoric that expresses various concerns about drone technologies, especially their use in delivering lethal weapons. One such criticism focuses on the distance between operators and the combat zones where their actions take place, arguing that this creates emotional distance, ethical detachment, and psychological dissociation from the consequences of those actions. Another criticism concerns the video game–like nature of the interfaces these operators use and implies that they will increasingly treat real-world missions like video games, blurring the distinctions between reality and fantasy, again raising the specters of distance, detachment, and dissociation, or, even worse, a "trigger-happy" excitement like that experienced in fast-paced video games. Closely related to this is the notion that by making the use of lethal force so easy, like the so-called push-button war, it will increase killing overall and civilian casualties and accidents as well.[16] There is also a criticism that by failing to take any risk in face-to-face combat, or even being in an aircraft high above a combat zone, this form of military practice exhibits fear and cowardice or lacks the honor or justice of combat in which the soldiers from each side can both kill and be killed. Collectively, I call these purported dangers the "antiheroic myth" of drones, as it frames the technology as turning brave and virtuous warriors into unethical killers or even cowards.

Both mythologies, the heroic and the antiheroic, fail to capture the complexity of the reality presented by the use of drone technologies. In large part, this is because they both consider only the agency of the technology and fail to consider how human subjectivity and agency is transformed in using the technology in ways that are more than mere reactions to the technology. Yet they both capture relevant concerns about the use of lethal military force and the development, acquisition, and use of these technologies. By examining the kinds of subjectivities these technologies are creating, this chapter illuminates the transformations in how drone operators understand themselves, as members of the warrior class in modern society and as laborers in a bureaucratized system of killing.

This chapter is largely concerned with the labor and psychological demands placed on those who are doing the surveillance, analyzing the images, piloting the drones, and making decisions to use lethal force. There are numerous implications of these technologies for those who are observed as well, both obvious and subtle—from the constant fear of an imminent strike from the buzzing aircraft that circle overhead to the finger-pointing, rumors of tracking devices, and killing of suspected informants in the aftermath of a strike.[17] And while these implications are important to my larger research project, they will not be the focus of this chapter. I will, however, consider the implications of the new subject positions of drone operators to the larger discourse about using weaponized drones and their role in risk management.

The obvious challenge to studying the subjectivity of drone operators is that of access. Not only is their work systematically hidden from public view but much of it is also protected by official security policies that prohibit drone operators from discussing the details of their work with anyone who does not have the proper security clearances. Informally, they are also strongly discouraged from discussing their work with journalists and academics, even in its general structure or outline. The only scientific researchers allowed access to these operators are employed by either the military or the private contractors developing and evaluating the technologies. The few instances in which journalists or academics have been allowed to interview drone operators or visit their workplaces have been limited to training centers or noncritical operations, and the names and identities of operators have been withheld or obscured. While this is claimed to be for the protection of the drone operators, it is curious that these sorts of restrictions do not apply to soldiers or pilots serving in Iraq and Afghanistan, many of whom are interviewed in the press and who presumably have much more exposure to threats and harm. Regardless of the motives behind this policy, it presents a serious methodological challenge to gaining access to the work of drone operators. As such, I will elaborate this subjectivity through a variety of diverse and partial sources, each with its own limitations. More specifically, I will merge my analysis of a series of military medical reports with a journalistic account of a military inquiry into a friendly-fire drone strike and a critical analysis of a short art film that combines an interview with an actual drone operator with scripted scenes of an actor portraying a drone operator.

Stress and the Cognitive Demands on Drone Operators

There are various dimensions in which we might consider the "subjectivity" or "subject position" of drone operators as well as various discursive attempts to frame and articulate the subjectivity of drone operators. These subjectivities are interesting insofar as they become relevant to social and political debates about the military effectiveness of drones as well as the political, social, and moral implications of this form of warfare. One key area of interest and debate has focused on the psychological stress experienced by drone operators. With the increasing use of military drone aircraft, there have been numerous anecdotal reports of the increasing stress levels of their operators.[18] This additional stress has been attributed primarily to two factors: the psychological complexity of moving back and forth, on a daily basis, between remote combat operations in a foreign land and domestic and family life in the suburbs; and the intimate nature of the video surveillance that these operators conduct. That is, they could be surveying a potential target, such as a house or car, or tracking an individual for more than eight hours a day, using high-resolution cameras that allow operators to see and recognize the personal details and daily activities of their potential targets. They are also required to continue to survey the target after attacking it, in order to confirm the deaths of the targets and any civilians nearby. This intimacy, it has been suggested, puts greater emotional stress on drone operators than on individuals in other types of combat roles.[19]

Recently, there have been several medical and occupational psychology studies commissioned by the Pentagon and NATO to investigate how and why the people who inhabit the new subject positions of drone operators are experiencing higher levels of stress than other combat duty assignments.[20] Collectively, these scientific studies confirm some aspects of the anecdotal reports and disconfirm others. For the most part, they do find much higher levels of stress among drone operators than other civilian and military jobs. However, this stress was reported as primarily due to the massive increases in the use of these drones, placing greater labor demands on the relatively small number of pilots and analysts who must meet these demands. In this sense, the stress is perceived to be the predictable result of overwork rather than the peculiarities of the subject position. Yet there are other significant and interesting details within these studies that warrant more careful scrutiny and analysis and that point to the particular nature of the subject positions created by remote-controlled killing as being both unique and stressful. This chapter will thus seek to contextualize these studies into a larger framework for understanding the changing nature of the professional and psychological subjectivity of combatants placed in the roles of remote-control killing using drones.

The increased use of drones and its incumbent psychological impact on operators and implications for military strategy and foreign policy together raise a complex series of questions about the ethics and values of warriors, the value and nature of military interventions in contemporary international relations, the use of lethal force by states, and the labor of killing as performed by combatants. In many ways, the ascendancy of the drone as the weapon of choice in the early twenty-first century is the result of its perceived ability to reduce the costs and the risks, both political and economic, of collecting intelligence and using lethal force against remote and sparse enemies. As such, it has come to be seen as the politically ideal military weapon for the "global war on terror." Much like precision-guided munitions (PGMs) a decade earlier, which greatly lowered the cost-per-target of bombing, drones greatly reduce the costs of aerial surveillance, close air support, and other high-demand military missions. And also like PGMs, they raise a moral question of the practical implications of reducing the costs of using lethal force—by reducing collateral damage and its political costs as well as the economic cost of any given strike mission. The worry is that they enable increased use of lethal force in the form of more missions and longer targeting lists, ultimately leading to a greater overall lethal impact on both combatants and civilians, and may also influence the choice of strategies, or continued use of strategies, such as targeted killings. Drones lower the political costs of losing U.S. personnel in two powerful ways. Primarily this lies in their ability to lower the number of casualties, or the risk of such casualties, among pilots and sensor operators, thus reducing the political damage that such U.S. casualties might cause. They also reduce the severity of any international crises stemming from the loss of the aircraft or capture of U.S. forces. This was demonstrated clearly with Iran's capturing of a stealth U.S. drone flying over its territory,[21] which might have been a much more severe crisis for the United States had a pilot also been captured (as Francis Gary Powers was when his U-2 spy plane crashed in the Soviet Union in 1960).

While drones are often referred to as "unmanned vehicles," this term obscures the reality of the human labor involved in operating these remotely piloted aircraft. The reality is that, like traditional manned aircraft, drones require extensive maintenance and a significant number of technical specialists to keep them in the air and flight-ready as well as to arm them with munitions or remove unused munitions after a mission. Often these ground crews are also responsible for launching and landing the aircraft from airfields close to the area of operation, passing control back and forth to the remote pilots in Nevada and other locations, mostly in the continental United States. The military demands round-the-clock combat air patrols (CAPs), and there is always a demand for more. Often a single CAP will involve more than one crew change of drone operators (i.e., multiple labor shifts), as the Predator drone can fly for up to eighteen hours. As soon as the drone lands, it is serviced, refueled, and rearmed by ground crews and then launched again. A single Predator drone requires eighty service personnel to keep it operational.

What the military considers the "operators" is a relatively small group of individuals who typically work in a ground control station (GCS) at a great distance from the drone's area of flight operation and often at a great distance from the drone's launch and recovery air base. These operator crews vary depending on the particular type of drone and sometimes even the mission. This chapter is concerned primarily with the "large and lethal" drones (the MQ-1 Predator and the MQ-9 Reaper). For these drones, the operator crews consist of three people, with separate roles but often overlapping tasks and responsibilities. The "pilot" is an officer who is in command of the crew and in control of the aircraft, though much of the aircraft's actual maneuvering is done by automated systems. The "sensor operator" is not an officer but an enlisted service member who is primarily in charge of the various cameras, radars, and sensors onboard the aircraft and also responsible for targeting the weapons and guiding missiles in-flight. The final member of the crew is the "mission intelligence coordinator," whose main duty is to communicate with intelligence analysts and various databases, to manage the communications of the other crew members, and to verify information and assist in understanding and interpreting the intelligence being gathered by the drone.[22]

The tighter coupling of surveillance and the decisions to use lethal force, as is found in weaponized drones, place new and unique cognitive demands on drone operators. While in traditional air operations, which largely separated the gathering of intelligence from the use of lethal force, operators were able to focus on specialized tasks and avoid the distractions and demands of related tasks. A target was a target, and a pilot's job was to correctly identify it and destroy it. Selecting the target was someone else's job. A drone pilot, in consultation with the sensor operator and the mission intelligence coordinator, must now consider whether a potential target is in fact a valid target. The drone operators are much more aware of the complexities of making that judgment and the uncertainties inherent in it, and they ultimately share in the responsibility for any mistakes made. An operator will usually need to get permission to use lethal force from a superior officer, but depending on the "rules of engagement," there may be circumstances in which they are authorized to make that determination themselves. Similarly, sensor operators are much more aware of the consequences of their intelligence estimations and judgments as well as the operational pressures of the mission, which in traditional air operations would have been much more remote. And while the role of the mission intelligence coordinator has not changed much in its description, the reality of its practice has gone from preflight briefings and occasional interactions during a combat mission to a real-time interaction with the pilot and the sensor operator in a fast-paced multimedia and social media environment of intelligence gathering and killing.

As a result of this transformation, the traditional compartmentalization and separation of intelligence analysis and interpretation, as well as target designation and killing, has been broken down and reconfigured. This places greater psychological demands on all three roles because it becomes more difficult to shift responsibility to others or to ignore the consequences of one's own decisions and actions. Surprisingly, perhaps, the military studies found that this was not the largest source of stress among drone operators. Indeed, combat as a source of stress was not found to be significantly different for drone operators than for other combat-related military jobs, thus dispelling one of the speculated causes of anecdotal reports of high stress among drone operators. Yet this is perhaps only a result of the assumptions made by these studies and the bias in self-reporting, within which operators find it easier and more acceptable to discuss the stresses of their careers than to discuss the stresses of combat and killing. To better understand the new forms of labor experienced by drone operators, I turn now to an analysis of each role in turn.

Pilots

The demands of remote operating these drones have transformed each of the three crew roles relative to comparable roles in traditional manned aircraft. In a traditional crew, the aircraft itself would typically contain only a pilot, whose primary duty would be the constant hands-on control of the aircraft, along with operating and interpreting multiple radar and electronic warning systems and visual identification tasks with the unassisted eye. They are also responsible for maintaining communication with a flight operations center and commanding officers who give authorization for the use of lethal force in strike missions, the sensor operator, and the mission intelligence coordinator. While the pilots in traditional missions were in control of the aircraft and the release of the weapons, they rarely saw their target for any length of time prior to releasing their weapons because they traveled at high speeds and for relatively short periods of time. In most manned combat missions, the target is simply a set of geographic coordinates that were obtained from another source, such as soldiers on the ground, an aircraft or satellite up above, or the outcome of the analysis of multiple intelligence sources. Traditional pilots also rarely remained close to a target to observe the consequences of their attack, a task called "battle damage assessment" that was often given to unarmed surveillance aircraft or soldiers on the ground. This is very different from what ground-based drone pilots experience.

An air force study on drone-operator burnout and stress lists eleven duties for drone pilots, covering a broad range of piloting, surveillance, targeting, and battle damage assessment tasks.[23] The study also notes that these tasks must be conducted in a very complex environment of mediating technologies:

> An additional challenge related to piloting the aircraft is the demand to attend to and interpret visual and auditory data from several sources to sustain situational and spatial awareness. Specifically, pilots are required to multitask and sustain vigilance to multiple forms of input from the aircraft, other aircrew, and military personnel (*e.g.*, ground forces). These multiple tasks include translating two-dimensional imagery into mental representations while performing numerical calculations for maneuvering the aircraft. It is important to note that despite the automated nature of the MQ-1 Predator and MQ-9 Reaper during certain phases of flight, the pilot must manually maneuver the aircraft for deployment of weapons, battle damage assessment, strategic positioning for surveillance and reconnaissance, avoiding bad weather, and controlling the aircraft during equipment or system failures. For effective and efficient operations, the pilot also works closely with the [sensor operator], mission intelligence coordinator, and other military personnel on the ground and in the air for identification and discrimination of targets and deployment of weapons. . . . The pilot must draw from an inherent set of cognitive aptitudes and personality traits to successfully master a wide knowledge and skill set.[24]

While many of these tasks are similar to those of traditional pilots, much of the new complexity lies in working "closely with the sensor operator, mission intelligence coordinator, and other military personnel." This kind of interpersonal communication and coordination involves a variety of tasks that require the pilot to become a very sophisticated information processor. The pilot must interpret a variety of pieces of information from various sources, which are in turn mediated by various technologies and interfaces, and must both issue and receive commands as well as conduct analyses and make complex decisions in consultation with a variety of other people. In short, the pilot must multitask to an extraordinary degree. This complexity will be explored in greater detail below in discussing the role of the mission intelligence coordinator, whose job is to coordinate the communications with personnel outside the drone crew.

In addition to the information and communications complexity of pilots, they also have significant visual-motor skill demands. These were examined in some detail in a 2006 study that assessed the medical review requirements on drone pilots.[25] On the basis of the complexity of the tasks they are required to do, the study recommended that there should be a specialized set of medical standards for evaluating potential drone pilots. From a medical perspective, drone pilots fall somewhere between traditional pilots and traditional ground operations staff. This is not so surprising considering that "sudden incapacitation" of a drone pilot may not have the severe consequences that it might for a traditional pilot due to the many automatic flight controls, though it may still be more severe than the incapacitation of someone not in direct control of a massive piece of flying military hardware. But a closer reading of this medical study reveals that the "new demands" placed on pilots are primarily the number of distractions they are subject to in the form of information and communications media. In particular, the study recommends a test that combines the traditional visual-motor skill task with a difficult cognitive task requiring shifts in attention and memory recall (simulating the complex and dynamic information environment of the drone cockpit). That is, while the overall visual-motor skills of drone pilots are less demanding than those of traditional pilots, there are significantly more cognitive information-processing demands placed on drone pilots, and the study recommends testing these skills in potential drone pilots.

It is also important to note that the stress studies found that one of the most significant sources of stress for pilots stemmed from their frustration and difficulty with the computer interfaces and the design of the GCS, or drone cockpit.[26] The poor design of user interfaces was also cited as a key factor contributing to "human errors" by an earlier comprehensive study of all the reported "mishaps" involving drones up to 2005.[27] Mishaps are any accidents resulting in property damage in excess of $20,000 or human casualties. It is worth noting that this study found that approximately 80 percent of the mishaps attributed to human error were actually the result of poorly designed interfaces, insufficient training in the GCS systems, or both. There is a long tradition of ascribing the responsibility from the failures of poorly designed interfaces to the humans rather than the interfaces.[28] We should similarly recognize that when human errors are attributed to stress, a significant amount of that stress is in fact coming from the design of technology.

Sensor Operators

Sensor operators are essentially sophisticated camera operators, though instead of a tripod, dolly, or crane, their cameras are mounted in articulated pods in the nose and belly of a drone. These cameras provide very high-resolution video streams from the visible spectrum as well as thermal infrared imagery and sophisticated radio frequency imaging such as synthetic aperture radar. While the first generation of Predator drones carried a single cluster of instruments that could point in a single direction, newer models carry the Gorgon Stare system that can follow twelve independent ground locations, each with its own video feed (from one of the sensors), and the ARGUS-IS (Autonomous Real-time Ground Ubiquitous Surveillance Imaging System) for wide-area persistent surveillance, giving them the capability of following thirty independently controlled video streams from a single drone.[29] In addition to controlling the sensors collecting these video streams, sensor operators are also involved in monitoring the content of those streams, interpreting them, and offering opinions to the pilot and mission intelligence officer as to their meaning.

According to the burnout and stress study, while the sensor operator need not fly the drone, he or she still requires a set of sophisticated visual-motor and cognitive skills in order to accomplish the eleven duties.[30] These are primarily the cognitively demanding tasks of visual analysis and its contextualization within mission objectives and dynamic events:

> As can be surmised from [the list of sensor operator duties], this enlisted aircrew position requires a person to visually discriminate and synthesize various images and complex data on several electronic screens while maintaining heightened vigilance to numerous sources of visual and auditory information necessary for sustaining situational and spatial awareness. . . . The sensor operator must also effectively communicate with aircrew to report the identification and discrimination of targets and to assist in the deployment of weapons . . . [and] sustain visual targeting during and following the employment of weapons to ensure accuracy and damage assessment. This task includes visually observing the destruction of fixed and moving objects (such as buildings and cars), as well as the wounding and death of human combatants. Moreover, the sensor operator must be attentive to several procedural checklists and processes with advanced computer systems while simultaneously translating two-dimensional information from video screens into four-dimensional mental imagery and spatial analyses . . . in a confined environment with specific rules of engagement, tactics, and techniques.[31]

It is clear from this description that the job of the sensor operator is far more demanding and complicated than that of a traditional image analyst whose main responsibility is mostly limited to just one of these duties: "detecting, analyzing and discriminating between valid and invalid targets using SAR [SYNTHETIC APERTURE RADAR], electro-optical, low-light, and infrared full-motion video imagery, and other active or passive tracking systems." The study also elaborates on the career trajectory of these sensor operators. Many of them began as imagery analysts who were primarily trained in interpreting images. Needless to say, they find the new responsibilities involved in the direct control of the sensors, as well as the targeting decision processes and weapons guidance, much more demanding than their more traditional role in simply analyzing visual imagery, a task that they continue to perform as drone sensor operators.

Mission Intelligence Coordinators

While the researchers in the medical studies of burnout among drone operators conducted interviews with a significant number of mission intelligence coordinators, they do not describe the role or stresses of this crew member as explicitly as they do for pilots and sensor operators. It is thus more difficult to analyze just how their subjectivities have been shaped by the weaponization of drones and the bureaucratization of remote killing. However, it seems reasonable that they would experience most of the same forms of stress as other members of the drone crew, along with some forms specific to their specialized role. While their tasks often intersect and overlap with those of the pilot and sensor operator, the mission intelligence coordinator is the human interface between computer databases of intelligence information containing archived data and analyses as well as the person responsible for coordinating with human intelligence analysts at remote locations in real time through audio communications and text messaging.

Perhaps the best way to develop an understanding of what mission intelligence coordinators do and their subject position is to examine a journalistic account of a friendly fire incident reported in the *Los Angeles Times* in 2011.[32] Because this incident resulted in the accidental deaths of Marine Staff Sgt. Jeremy Smith and Navy Hospitalman Benjamin D. Rast, it was subject to significantly more scrutiny than most drone missions, including an official inquiry conducted by the Pentagon:

> The 381-page report, which has not been released, concludes that the Marine officers on the scene and the Air Force crew controlling the drone from half a world away were unaware that analysts watching the firefight unfold via live video at a third location had doubts about the targets' identity. The incident closely resembles another deadly mistake involving a Predator in early 2009. In that attack, at least 15 Afghan civilians were killed after a Predator crew mistook them for a group of Taliban preparing to attack a U.S. special forces unit. In that case, analysts located at Air Force Special Operations Command in Florida who were watching live battlefield video from the aircraft's high-altitude cameras also had doubts about the target. Their warnings that children were present were disregarded by the drone operator and by an Army captain, who authorized the airstrike.[33]

Within the team of drone operators, it is the role and responsibility of the mission intelligence coordinator to manage the complex streams of communications between the drone pilot, the sensor operator, superior officers, troops on the ground, and the host of analysts at other locations. In this friendly fire case, these communications broke down with tragic consequences:

> Smith, Rast and another Marine had separated from the others and had taken cover behind a hedgerow, where they were firing on insurgents in a cluster of nearby buildings. Infrared cameras on the Predator overhead had picked up heat signatures of the three men and detected muzzle flashes as they fired their weapons at insurgents. Air Force analysts who were watching the live video in Terre Haute, Indiana, noted that the gunfire appeared aimed away from the other Marines, who were behind the three. The analysts reported that gunshots were "oriented to the west, away from friendly forces," the Pentagon report says. But the Predator pilot in Nevada and the Marine commanders on the ground "were never made aware" of the analysts' assessment. The analysts, who communicated with the Predator pilot via a written chat system, were never certain who Smith and Rast were. At one point, the analysts described the pair as "friendlies," but withdrew that characterization a few seconds later. They later wrote, "Unable to discern who personnel were."[34]

Unfortunately, in this case, the communications were taking place directly between the pilot and the remote analysts, via a text-based chat application. In other words, the mission intelligence coordinator was failing to coordinate their communications. Contributing to this failure was the fact that the mission intelligence coordinator was a trainee, not yet fully skilled in performing the responsibilities of that role:

> Even a written assessment that the gunfire was aimed in the wrong direction was not passed along to the pilot by the Mission Intelligence Coordinator, a crew member responsible for relaying information to the pilot, the report says. The coordinator was a trainee supervised by a trainer. The report blames the attack on a fatal mix of poor communications, faulty assumptions and "a lack of overall common situational awareness." It recommends that a Marine lieutenant and two sergeants in Smith's platoon be "formally counseled" and suggests detailed reviews of battlefield procedures, but it said no one involved in the attack was "culpably negligent or derelict in their duties." "The chain of events . . . was initiated by the on-scene ground force commander's lack of overall situational awareness and inability to accurately communicate his friendly force disposition in relation to the enemy," the report said. The report, which was originally classified secret and written by a Marine colonel, criticizes the analysts for failing to make sure the pilot understood that the gunfire was aimed away from the Marines. The analysts "should have been more assertive," it says, and "should have persisted with their assessment until the crew either accepted or refuted the assessment."[35]

What becomes apparent in this breakdown of the system of people and technologies that constitute drone operations is the constructed nature of "situational awareness." This concept is often assumed to be something that simply exists, until it is missing or mistaken. Rather, situational awareness—the overall awareness of what is happening in a given situation—is the result of deliberate efforts, labor, and communications of a complex team. Moreover, the fact that the members of this team all have access to high-resolution imagery of the same situation does not mean that they all "see" the same thing. The visual content and interpretation of the visual scene are the products of analysis and negotiation among the team as well as the context given by the situational awareness—which is itself constructed. And while the team may often come to different interpretations of the same situation, in most cases of failure such as this one, they mistakenly believed that they had come to the same conclusions, or failed to communicate their alternate interpretations.

Through the absence of an effective mission intelligence coordinator in this case, we can begin to piece together the unique subject position that the coordinators are meant to occupy. As the only crew members not directly involved in controlling the drone or its surveillance sensors, their job is to operate the complex network of databases and communications with remotely located intelligence analysts who are viewing the same video streams as the drone crew. However, because they are physically located within the ground control station, they are in a superior position to assess the "situational awareness" of the drone crew as well as to second-guess and correct their interpretations and judgments. This is not the case for those remotely located analysts:

> The analysts in Indiana told investigators that they did not believe they should intervene to block an airstrike if U.S. troops were possibly in danger, even if they had doubts about the targets. When U.S. troops were under fire, the analysts told investigators, "they were to adopt a non-interference role, unless they observed an imminent violation" of the laws of war or women and children were present, the report said. The email chat system also contributed to the breakdown in communications, investigators said. After the Afghan civilians were mistakenly targeted in early 2009, the Air Force began installing equipment so drone video analysts could talk directly with drone pilots. The new equipment was not in place at the Indiana base in April, however.[36]

So we can see again that the technologies that deliver information and mediate communications are clearly also a source of "stress" for mission intelligence coordinators. Indeed, we can see more clearly how the "frustrations" with a technology can lead directly to system failures that result in friendly and civilian deaths.

While the responsibilities of coordinating communications and information are not new, the kind of subjectivity engendered by new communications technologies certainly is. As mentioned in the discussion of pilots, a major source of stress for drone operators is the poor design of their interfaces. Here we see a Pentagon report explicitly blaming the design of the e-mail chat system for contributing to the breakdown in communication that led to these mistaken deaths. Moreover, it is precisely the physical presence of the crew members, which is acknowledged to be so important to situational awareness, that has been radically transformed here. That is, by removing the drone operators from the combat theater, they are now completely dependent on the information provided by their mediating technologies in order to reach their decisions. So too are the analysts in Indiana, and this introduces yet another layer of remote mediation. In the context of such dependence, the interpretation and meaning of the images, the actions of soldiers, civilians, and suspected insurgents, and indeed the very identification of a figure in the image as one of those categories, is an active process that is shaped, influenced, and constituted by these mediated practices. What we find is a pilot in Nevada having a live chat with an imagery analyst in Indiana in order to select a target in Afghanistan on which they will fire a deadly laser-guided missile. Within such a mediation, shared understanding can be difficult to achieve, and misunderstandings and misinterpretations are likely to occur. The real work of the mission intelligence coordinator can thus be seen as coordinating these communications, keeping miscommunications in check, and correcting misunderstandings in real time.

Now that we have a clearer sense of the kinds of labor that drone operators perform, we now turn to a consideration of how their new subjectivities are related to their experience of stress and burnout.

Stress, Burnout, and PTSD

It is important to note that the two later military research reports on drone operator stress focus on what they call "burnout."[37] The subclinical diagnosis of burnout has emerged as a psychological condition that lies between the normal "stress" of day-to-day military work and the clinical diagnosis of posttraumatic stress disorder (PTSD), which entails possible medical interventions, loss of duty assignment, discharge from the military, and the lifelong impacts of a mental health disorder, including strained social relations, medical treatments and expenses, and limited employment opportunities in civilian life. As a medico-bureaucratic compromise, burnout can be severe enough to warrant managerial interventions, such as a temporary relief of duties (some time off to rest), without the grave professional and medical interventions that follow from PTSD (permanent loss of duty assignment or discharge from the military). That is, burnout is considered a normal reaction to high levels of stress rather than a clinical or pathological reaction to such stress. It is perceived as being alleviated through a contextual change (removing the stress) rather than as a psychological condition that requires treatment of the patient (reforming their mental life). The escalation of stress from an occupational issue to a medical issue also carries many implications, including dismissal from duty:

> According to USAF [U.S. Air Force] aeromedical policy, performing and operating in a high-demand, high-operational, and high-precision aviation-related position requires an optimal level of physical and psychological functioning. Although operators may be perceived to be generally healthy, if they suffer from a physical or psychological condition that has the potential to lead to degradation in the performance of their duties, then they are disqualified from such aviation-related operations. A general reason for holding operators to such high aeromedical standards is due to the perceived risk that subtle decrements in health can have on elevating the risk for an aviation mishap in which the threat to human life, national security, foreign relations, military operations, and loss of a multimillion dollar aircraft is often high. Although occupational burnout is not a categorical psychiatric diagnosis, it stands to reason that such a condition leads to performance degradation and, if untreated, may lead to significant emotional difficulties (e.g., anxiety and depression).[38]

By framing burnout as an occupational category instead of a medical category, it allows superior officers and support staff to try to manage the severe stress of drone operators without losing their skilled labor, which is in such high demand.

It is here where we begin to see the Taylorist aims of these studies most clearly. The studies, which are only indirectly concerned about the stress and psychological health of drone operators, are primarily concerned with attaining the "optimal level of physical and psychological functioning" of the drone operators as a means of maximizing their labor productivity and minimizing the risk of costly mishaps. In this sense, the health of the drone operators is not an end but a means to an end. There is also a clear distinction being made between psychological stress that interferes with job performance (burnout) and psychological stress that interferes with daily life or mental health (PTSD).

In one study, the researchers found that much of the reported stress was due to operators' long work hours and the stresses of late-night shift work:

"The most commonly cited stressors accentuating occupational stress for remote piloted aircraft operators included long hours (50+ hours a week), shift work, human-machine interface difficulties (ergonomic design of equipment and GCS), inefficiencies in computer-based input and command procedures, and difficulty juggling the demands of personal and domestic life with military operations."[39] Right after long hours, which might reasonably apply to any demanding form of labor, we find difficulties with the technology itself as the leading source of stress. This includes the human–machine interface and its effects on cognition, its ergonomic design and effects on the body, and frustration with the inefficiency of the rules and procedures governing the bureaucratized labor they perform, both those imposed by machines and those imposed by command procedures, protocols, and regulations. Earlier studies of medical review standards mentioned above noted that one of the most difficult aspects of drone operators' jobs was the coordination of precise hand-eye tasks along with complex verbal tasks. This may cause one to wonder which side of the human–machine interface is failing or to blame one side (the human or the machine) as inadequate, as in the report on the friendly fire incident above, which blames the analysts for not speaking up while merely noting that their communications technologies were making that difficult.

After these issues, the reports focus on the stresses that have long been the focus of post-Taylorist scientific labor management, such as the quality of working life movement's focus on ideals of job satisfaction, home life, and career prospects.[40] In its latest incarnations, productivity is sought by treating each individual in an organization as an "entrepreneur" who is constantly striving to increase her own productivity and advance the goals of the organization along with her own career. In this sense, these pilots have adopted the subjectivity of an entrepreneur within the military hierarchy. While military personnel have always sought promotions and better duty assignments, it is rather startling that these medical studies found one of the largest sources of occupational stress among drone operators coming not from combat, or even from the technical challenges of flying an aircraft and conducting operations halfway around the world, but from concerns over the future of their careers. This was closely followed by the stresses of managing a family life alongside a military career. A possible reason for this focus is that the uncertainties of the "pilot as career entrepreneur" can be rectified through organizational change, while the relief of other stresses requires far more complex technological interventions and social changes.

The career stress issue is an important one for understanding the subjectivity of drone operators in the broader context of military service. The first generation of drone pilots was chosen from pilots already flying manned aircraft. Second-generation drone pilots were initially trained in manned aircraft but never given a manned flight duty. With the heavy demand for drone pilots, the U.S. military is now training more of them than they are training pilots for all types of manned aircraft combined. They are also seeking to reduce the cost of that training by eliminating all manned aircraft flight training for future drone pilots—the U.S. Army has long trained drone pilots without any manned aircraft experience while the U.S. Air Force was more reluctant to do so. Thus, current trainees work primarily on simulators and eventually real remote-operated aircraft but no longer fly a manned plane in the course of their training.

Within the military hierarchy, and especially within the U.S. Air Force, being a pilot carries a special, prestigious status and identity. It is expensive to train pilots, and it is physically and mentally demanding to fly. Pilots are accordingly seen as a distinct and privileged class within the military. Indeed, only they are allowed to wear "flight wings" insignia on their uniform to designate them to all as pilots. They are only allowed to wear these wings for as long as they are certified to fly. Within the U.S. Air Force, only officers can be pilots, whereas the other branches permit enlisted service members to fly some types of aircraft. Initially, the U.S. Air Force did not grant pilot status, and wings insignia, to drone pilots, at least not for their drone training and duties alone. Because some drone pilots had wings before becoming drone operators, those that did not felt left out and perceived themselves as having a significantly lower status. In this way, the lack of wings and full pilot status for drone pilots led directly to one form of the "career stress" that Joseph Ouma, Wayne Chappelle, and Amber Salinas discuss. That is, for those who were manned aircraft pilots, moving to drones was seen as less prestigious than flying manned aircraft, and thus such an assignment meant a lowering of both current status and future career prospects. It also made it more difficult for them to acquire the flight time needed to keep their wings and, with no clear career route to return to flying manned aircraft, it could mean the eventual loss of their status as pilots. For those who came in without pilot's wings, there was little or no hope of ever getting them or the prestige and status associated with wearing them.

In 2009 the U.S. Air Force recognized this problem and addressed it with two major changes. First, it moved to recognize the hidden labor of drone operators by changing the official term for drones, which at the time was "unmanned aerial vehicles," because "unmanned" seemed to imply that the systems were autonomous or did not have a crew or pilot. Rather, they had a "remote" crew, and so the official term within the U.S. Air Force is now "remotely piloted aircraft" (RPA). It is interesting to note that the other service branches, in which pilot status is significant but not nearly as much so, have retained the term UAV. The U.S. Air Force also moved to designate drone pilots with the status of full-fledged pilots by giving them wing insignia for their uniforms, though they issued them special wings that distinguish drone pilots from the pilots of manned aircraft. Whether these moves ultimately served to alleviate the career stress of drone pilots is uncertain, but it was certainly a powerful symbolic gesture toward trying to instill prestige status to their work.

The career stress of sensor operators was similar to that of drone pilots. Many of them were initially trained as imagery analysts. Because the job of drone sensor operator involves rather unique and demanding skills, it is much more stressful than most imagery analysis jobs but lacks a clear career path toward advancement and promotion afterward. That is, while most image analysts could move up into more specialized fields of analysis, or to more sophisticated image platforms like satellite imagery, drone sensor operators are not likely candidates for such assignments. And due to the high demand for people to do the drone work, and their enlisted status, they are unlikely to ever be promoted out of that duty assignment.

The family and geographic location demands cited by the studies as additional sources of stress among drone operators are interesting because these are direct consequences of the remote operation of drones and also support the popular perceptions that remote warfare is stressful because of the shift between war zone and home life. If drone operators were "in theater" or in the aircraft, they would be based in Iraq, Kuwait, or Afghanistan and flying their missions from there. One of the perceived advantages of drones is that they do not require this, which is a huge cost savings. But this appears to come at a psychological price. While those who serve overseas often report being homesick and missing their families, and families report the stress of being without the service member, there are also psychological advantages to physical presence in the war zone. First, one is much more aware of what it is like to live in that place and its culture and society, as both a soldier and a civilian, which is difficult to understand from merely watching video streams. Moreover, there is a shared sense of hardship and comradery among soldiers serving together. This allows them to connect to one another emotionally and relate to a common shared experience, which offers a form of psychic relief that does not require the intervention of medical professionals.

Drone operators, however, must return to their family lives each day. This can mean killing insurgents remotely at night and taking the kids to school the next morning. On the one hand, this means that all of the usual stresses of home life are added to the stresses of work and combat. On the other hand, it means constantly moving back and forth between ordinary civilian life and military combat on a daily basis. For those who do experience combat stress, there is little chance that they would find comfort and shared understanding among the civilian population, and there are many powerful cultural forces within the military that would prevent them from discussing it with military colleagues.[41]

While it might be surprising that the demands of family and career should turn out to be more stressful than combat, we should take a moment to consider the biases inherent in the methodology of these studies. One must keep in mind that within military cultures, there is an imperative to show strength and hide weakness, especially emotional weakness. There is also a taboo against acknowledging the stress of combat. A clinical diagnosis of PTSD, or even anxiety or depression, can result in the end of one's military duty assignment or career, a discharge, and the stigma can even follow one to the civilian world, with a lifelong medical condition and bills and limited civilian employability. As such, it is difficult for drone operators to describe or admit to experiencing combat-related stress. Even under the conditions of these studies, which provided anonymity to the operators, they are not likely to discuss such experiences with a medical professional. In some cases, they may have even been in denial of the existence of these kinds of stresses in order to protect their military careers. The researchers admit as much in one study:

> Combat-related stressors were not rated as within the top sources of stress among participants. Such a finding is helpful for line commanders and medical personnel in understanding occupational stress. However, Chappelle *et al.* (2011) proposed that such a finding should also be interpreted cautiously when considering individual operators. It is likely that there are Predator/Reaper operators who perceive the deployment of weapons and exposure to live video feed of combat (*i.e.*, destruction/death of enemy combatants and ground forces) as

highly stressful even though it is not reported as the main source of occupational stress.[42]

The medical studies also claim that drone operators suffer from PTSD at similar rates as other combatants. This would mean that drone operators experience PTSD at a rate of about 4–17 percent, which is the estimated rate for units deployed to combat zones in the Iraq War.[43] Given that they interviewed over four hundred drone operators, it is statistically highly unlikely that none of the subjects were actually experiencing or would soon be diagnosed with PTSD. It seems more likely that they were simply failing to report it to the researchers. It is likely that all forms of combat stress were significantly avoided or underreported in the course of these studies, as they are more generally. To get a better understanding of the subjectivity of combat stress as experienced by drone operators, we must turn to other sources.

5,000 Feet Is the Best

The artist and filmmaker Omer Fast's submission to the 2011 Venice Biennale was a thirty-minute film titled *5,000 Feet Is the Best*.[44] The film consists of a series of scripted scenes involving an actor intercut with a documentary audio interview with a real drone operator that together offer insights and reflections on the new subjectivities of drone operators. For the purposes of this chapter, I will accept the documentary portion of the film as being an actual and accurate report of at least one individual operator's description of his own experiences. While the medical studies we have reviewed conducted such interviews, they did not reveal the content of those interviews but merely summarized them. The film thus offers a more detailed insight, if only into the experiences of a single operator.

Based on his description of his work, the documentary interview in the film is with a sensor operator who describes what he has seen during his five years of operating a Predator drone from an air base in Nevada. In the course of the interview, he acknowledges that he currently suffers from PTSD and left his assignment and the military as a result of it. While his psychological condition may only be shared with a percentage of drone operators, his subjective experience of his work is certainly shared with most if not all drone operators, or at least with Predator sensor operators operating in Iraq and Afghanistan.

One aspect of that subjectivity is that of the voyeurism of surveillance from high above. The drone operator tells us: "Five thousand feet is the best. We love it when we are sitting at five thousand feet. You get more description, plus at five thousand feet I mean, I can tell you what type of shoes you are wearing, from a mile away. I can tell you what type of clothes the person is wearing, if they have a beard, their hair color and everything else. So, there are very clear cameras on board. We have the IR infrared, which we can switch to automatically. That will pick up any heat signatures or cold signatures." He goes on to describe the strange world revealed by infrared thermal imaging, from the white blossoms where people sat down and then left to the glowing beacons of lit cigarettes to the disturbed soil around roadside bombs. In another vignette, the drone operator describes the stress of remote killing:

> Usually I wouldn't get home until about ten o'clock in the morning, jump in the shower, get some breakfast, play some video games for a few hours, then try to sleep. A lot of guys over there, believe it or not, play video games in their free time. I guess that's their way of unwinding. Mine were a lot of role-playing games, flight simulators. I guess Predator is similar to playing a video game, but playing the same video game four years straight every single day on the same level. One time I just watched the same house for a month straight—for at least eleven hours, every day, for a month. But then you have your moments where there is a real emergency going on. And that is just where stress comes into play. How do I hit that truck? And in what way do I hit that truck? How far away should I put the missile to get the truck? So that way I don't have any damage to the surrounding buildings or to the people or hurt anybody else's life that is around there. And sometimes I make mistakes.

In this account, we see some of the elements of the stresses of domestic life and also the cognitive and interpretative challenges that make the job stressful, according to the medical studies. It also addresses a popular idea that drone operators are "PlayStation warriors" and treat their work like a video game. While there are some similarities in terms of the interfaces and activities, drone operations are usually much more boring and tedious, with brief moments of incredible pressure and stress. And even for these operators, video games can be a form of relaxation, a way of decompressing from their work. Together this should make it clear that there is not a real danger that drone operators are confusing reality for a game or treating the work lightly.

It is also clear that they take the responsibility of using lethal force seriously and fear making mistakes. They do in fact make mistakes, and the killing of innocents is often cited as a source of PTSD. The drone operator in the film goes on to describe some of the combat stress he experienced, which is missing from the military medical studies:

> I mean, there are horror sides to working Predator. You see a lot of death. You know you see it all—as I said, I can tell you what kind of shoes you are wearing from a mile away; it is pretty clear about everything else that is happening. I mean, there came a point after five years of doing this that I just had to think about all this loss of life that was a direct result of me. I mean, there was a lot of personal stuff I had to go through, and a lot of chaplains I had to talk to just because of that. And the one factor that we talked about that helped me was that if it wasn't me who was doing it, then some new kid would be doing it, but worse. I was twenty-six at the time. A lot of people look at me like, how can you have PTSD if you weren't active in a war zone? Well, technically speaking every single day I was active in a war zone. I mean, I may not have been personally harmed but I was directly affecting people's lives over there every single day. There is stress that comes with that, with having to fire, with seeing some of the death, with seeing what is going on, having anxiety, looking back at a certain situation or incident over and over and over, you know, bad dreams, loss of sleep. You know, it's not like a video game; I can't switch it off. It's always there. There was a lot of stress with that. They call it virtual stress.

The operator goes on to describe the first time he killed someone as a drone operator. He says that it did not impact him immediately the first time he targeted a Hellfire missile at some insurgents who had planted a roadside bomb, but soon after that the bad dreams started. We can see in this passage a hint of how combat stress is also being managed in the boundaries between medical and psychological interventions and other forms of intervention. While the experiences described by the drone operator clearly constitute combat stress, and he is eventually diagnosed with PTSD, for many years his stress is managed in a variety of ways other than medical intervention or psychological treatment. For instance, rather than discuss his stress with a psychologist, which might lead to a diagnosis and stigma along with therapy, he gets most of his emotional and psychological counseling through a chaplain. While the military clergy are trained in dealing with combat stress, the methods and options are much more limited than what medical treatment can offer. While the chaplain provides the drone operator with a degree of counseling, he is able to do so without threatening the operator's job or military status. In the long run, however, this counseling is not sufficient to prevent the PTSD that later afflicts the operator.

Conclusion

The work of remote surveillance and killing that drone operators perform is difficult, stressful, and exhausting. Even the U.S. Air Force has recognized that this work deserves more respect than it often receives. Yet the military's strategy in studying this labor is primarily targeted at optimizing its efficiency. Toward this end, the U.S. military has incorporated elements of the quality of working life movement and its concerns about quality of life issues that affect job stress and performance, such as home life and satisfaction with geographic location, along with a conception of self-directed entrepreneurialism within military careers as a motivational strategy within a professional, postconscription military. The military is thus conscientious of developing career paths for striving drone operators to avoid these jobs becoming stigmatized as a "dead end" and to thereby reduce the career stress of the operators who perform them. Yet the remoteness of the work and the contextual shifts between combat zone and domestic life continue to present problems.

There are many complicated ethical issues raised by the management of combat stress. While there is a strong interest in managing the stress experienced by combatants, as well as PTSD, the technological means for doing this may impose a greater moral distance between those making combat decisions and further alienation from the lives of those directly affected by those decisions. Further analysis may be able to determine the extent to which many of the stresses of combat, and the bureaucratization of killing enacted through the use of drones, are in fact being redirected, projected, or simply denied by most drone operators. Until then, it is clear that drone technologies and the integration of surveillance with remote killing have created new and complex forms of human–machine subjectivity.

The mythologies surrounding the use of lethal drones, both the heroic and antiheroic, seem to fall short of the complexities of the new subjectivities of drone operators. The heroic myth, that the technology enables more precise use of lethal force and thus engenders a more ethical form of warfare, is only partly true. What is true is that the technology is capable of more deliberate and precise use of force than some military technologies. But what is also true is that the technology presents far more potential targets and shapes the interpretations and determinations of targets in unpredictable ways. It also puts far greater cognitive, moral, and emotional burdens on drone operators, who must engage with increasingly complicated information and communications systems in order to make these determinations. These burdens result in degrees of stress, burnout, and PTSD greater than in other military and combat operations. In other words, the work of surveillance and killing, once compartmentalized, isolated, and hidden, is now becoming formalized, collaborative, and visible within the ground control stations of lethal drones. Within this process of the bureaucratization of surveillance and killing, we find the mediating technologies as both enablers of these new bureaucratic forms of labor and themselves sources of stress and breakdown. This is in part because of poor design and misguided assumptions about how these systems will be used and the psychological needs of their users. But it is also because these technologies have exposed the hidden labor by failing to support it.

Some, but not all, aspects of the antiheroic myth are also proven by these studies of drone operators. Drone operators do not treat their jobs in the cavalier manner of a video game, but they do recognize the strong resemblance between the two. Many drone operators are often also video game players in their free time and readily acknowledge certain similarities in the technological interfaces of each. Yet the drone operators are very much aware of the reality of their actions and the consequences they have on the lives, and deaths, of the people they watch via video streams from half a world away, as they bear witness to the violence of their own lethal decisions. What they are less aware of, which is revealed by a careful analysis of the various accounts of their work surveyed in this chapter, is that their work involves the active construction of interpretations. The bodies and actions in the video streams are not simply "given" as soldiers, civilians, and possible insurgents—they are actively constructed as such. And in the process of this construction, the technology plays both an enabling and a mediating role. I use the term *mediating* here to indicate that it is a role of translation, not of truth or falsity directly but of transformation and filtering. On the one hand, there is the thermal imaging that provides a view into a mysterious and hidden world of relative temperatures. And thus these drone technologies offer a vision that contains more than the human alone could ever see. On the other hand, we can see that the lived world of human experience, material practices, social interactions, and cultural meanings that they are observing are difficult to properly interpret and fully understand from a lofty perch, and that even the highest resolution camera cannot resolve the uncertainties and misinterpretations. There is a limit to the fidelity that mediation itself can provide, insofar as it cannot provide genuine social participation and direct engagement. This applies both to surveillance and visuality, which is necessarily incomplete, but also to the limited forms of action and engagement that mediating technologies permit. While soldiers on the ground can use their hands to administer medical aid or push a stalled car as easily as they can hold a weapon, the drone operator can only observe and choose to kill or not to kill. Within this limited range of action, meaningful social interaction is fundamentally reduced to sorting the world into friends, enemies, and potential enemies—as no other categories can be meaningfully pursued.

Notes

A version of this chapter appeared as "The Labor of Surveillance and Bureaucratized Killing: New Subjectivities of Military Drone Operators," *Social Semiotics* 232 (2013): 196–224.

1. Sifton, "A Brief History of Drones"; Singer, *Wired for War*.
2. Department of Defense, "Unmanned Systems Integrated Roadmap"; Mayer, "The Predator War"; Sifton, "A Brief History of Drones."
3. New America Foundation, "Year of the Drone."
4. Bureau of Investigative Journalism, "Covert War on Terror."
5. Department of Defense, "Unmanned Systems Integrated Roadmap, FY2011–2036."
6. For concerns about domestic uses, see Stanley and Crump, "Protecting Privacy from Aerial Surveillance."
7. Pachirat, *Every Twelve Seconds*.
8. M. Weber, *Economy and Society*.
9. M. Weber, *Economy and Society*.
10. For the former, see Bourdieu, *Distinction*; and Bourdieu, *Outline of a Theory of Practice*. For the latter, see Thompson, *The Making of the English Working Class*; Foucault, *Discipline and Punish*; Rose, *Governing the Soul*; Rose, *Inventing Our Selves*; C. Taylor, *Sources of the Self*; T. Miller, *The Well-Tempered Self*; and Scott, *Seeing Like a State*.
11. P. Miller and Rose, "Production, Identity and Democracy"; Asaro, "Transforming Society by Transforming Technology."
12. Star and Strauss, "Layers of Silence, Arenas of Voice."

13. Pachirat, *Every Twelve Seconds.*
14. They are also being used extensively by the Central Intelligence Agency for targeted killings, but since these operations are almost completely opaque to public scrutiny and academic study, and outside the view of even the military studies on which my research draws, I will say little about these admittedly significant operations; Department of Defense, "Unmanned Systems Integrated Roadmap, FY2011–2036"; Singer, *Wired for War.*
15. See, for example, Strawser, "Moral Predators."
16. Plotnick, "Predicting Push-Button Warfare."
17. Wilson, "In Gaza, Lives Shaped by Drones."
18. Singer, *Wired for War.*
19. Singer, *Wired for War.*
20. Tvaryanas, "The Development of Empirically-Based Medical Standards"; Chappelle, McDonald, and King, "Psychological Attributes Critical to the Performance"; Ouma, Chappelle, and Salinas, "Facets of Occupational Burnout"; Chappelle, Salinas, and McDonald, "Psychological Health Screening."
21. Peterson and Faramarzi, "Iran Hijacked US Drone."
22. Chappelle, McDonald, and King, "Psychological Attributes Critical to the Performance."
23. Ouma, Chappelle, and Salinas, "Facets of Occupational Burnout."
24. Ouma, Chappelle, and Salinas, "Facets of Occupational Burnout."
25. "In particular, ground-based controller duty standards lacked sufficient rigor to address many of [the] concerns associated with current UAS operations while flying duty standards were unnecessarily restrictive. Therefore, it is recommended a separate set of medical standards be created for career UAS pilots flying large or weaponized UASs"; Tvaryanas, "The Development of Empirically-Based Medical Standards."
26. Ouma, Chappelle, and Salinas, "Facets of Occupational Burnout."
27. W. Thompson, Tvaryanas, and Constable, "U.S. Military Unmanned Aerial Vehicle Mishaps."
28. Hutchins, "How a Cockpit Remembers Its Speeds"; D. Woods and Shattuck, "Distant Supervision–Local Action."
29. Deptula, *Air Force Unmanned Aerial System.*
30. Ouma and Salinas, "Facets of Occupational Burnout."
31. Ouma and Salinas, "Facets of Occupational Burnout."
32. Zucchino and Cloud, "U.S. Deaths in Drone Strike"; Cloud, "Anatomy of an Afghan War Tragedy."
33. Zucchino and Cloud, "U.S. Deaths in Drone Strike."
34. Zucchino and Cloud, "U.S. Deaths in Drone Strike."
35. Zucchino and Cloud, "U.S. Deaths in Drone Strike."
36. Zucchino and Cloud, "U.S. Deaths in Drone Strike."
37. Chappelle, McDonald, and King, "Psychological Attributes Critical to the Performance"; Ouma, Chappelle, and Salinas, "Facets of Occupational Burnout."
38. Ouma, Chappelle, and Salinas, "Facets of Occupational Burnout."
39. Ouma, Chappelle, and Salinas, "Facets of Occupational Burnout."

40. P. Miller and Rose, "Production, Identity and Democracy."
41. Kime, "Study."
42. Ouma, Chappelle, and Salinas, "Facets of Occupational Burnout."
43. Richardson, Frueh, and Acierno, "Prevalence Estimates of Combat-Related PTSD."
44. It can be viewed in a linear form on the Internet; see http://www.gbagency.fr/en/42/Omer-Fast/#!/Works/tab-55.

13 LETTER FROM A SENSOR OPERATOR

BRANDON BRYANT

Dear Reader,

I'm writing this to you as a letter because that will get my point across a lot better. This was more difficult to write than I expected. Hopefully that is what makes it a better read.

You generally asked what it is like to be a drone crew member, specifically my role as a sensor operator (SO), and for a discussion of examples or situations that could help make that experience palpable to others. My work as an SO would be how one imagines television cops doing a stakeout. It's dark, mostly boring, quiet, while suffocating the soul, body, and mind. There is not one day that I ever enjoyed the work experience. I was proud that I was good—I would say the best, simply because of my motivations for doing the job—but I never enjoyed it.

During my time as a sensor operator, I was trained at the 11th Reconnaissance Squadron on Creech Air Force Base (AFB), April 12, 2006–November 18, 2006; imbedded with the 15th Recon Squadron on Nellis AFB, November 18, 2006—28, May 2007; deployed to the 46th Expeditionary Reconnaissance Squadron (ERS) on Balad Air Base (AB), Iraq, May 28, 2007–October 20, 2007; imbedded with the 3rd Special Operations Squadron on Nellis AFB, November 5, 2007– February 13, 2009; and then again with the 3rd Special Operations Squadron on Cannon AFB, February 13, 2009–April 17, 2011, when I was honorably discharged with eighty-three days of allowed terminal leave.

The container that I worked from is called a ground control station, or GCS. It is similar in size to a Formula 1 race-car trailer with processing computers on one long wall and the operator stations at the far end. There are fourteen monitors, two shared in the center detailing the pilot low side and mission coordinator low side screens. The central monitors on each station show the video camera feeds as controlled by the sensor operator or the nose camera for the pilot in weather situations. Above that is the GPS coordinate of the plane and maps of the local area. Going clockwise (counterclockwise for pilots) from there we have the mission coordinator's high side, the JSOC (Joint Special Operations Command) Information Automated Network (JIANT) server screen, the controls, and the head-down display (HDD) featuring technical flight data.

As a sensor operator, it was my task to control the multispectral targeting system (MTS) to provide the best picture possible for our intelligence analysts while being cognitively aware of all the activity going on, back up the pilot as a copilot—who is unqualified to fly the aircraft but has in-depth knowledge on how to fly—and be able to guide munitions to target locations. If none of that was going on, I just sat there and read: novels, occasionally my old Kindle, or a graphic novel. One person even made games on Excel spreadsheets for us to play during lulls in mission time. Leadership, of course, hated anything to do with sanity.

Our training was pretty inconsequential. For me it was weird and confusing. I started on April 12, 2006, with a montage video of strikes that had happened over the past year while some sort of pseudo–"I'm a badass" music played in the background. I had initiation and, because I was one of the last to get my orders to the place, they put me on casual status until the next class, where they had me show up to work every day to clean the squadron and read the horrible uneconomic monstrosity that was my "user manual." I had to do a *ton* of simulations simply to figure out the completely irrational menu keys. When I eventually started class again, they realized we were too big and had to split up the class, which delayed me by giving me another three months of just studying and doing simulations. I was good at my job not because I enjoyed it. . . . I sabotaged myself twice because I got cold feet when thinking whether I could actually do the job. The military used intimidation tactics to keep me doing my job, namely, humiliation and ridicule, which I will address later in a more general manner.

Training didn't really provide the ability to practice the basic skill set needed but provided the routine and methods to use. We would be told during training that being a sensor operator was an art form and not a science.

Through all of that, I excelled and struggled with convincing myself that it was all justified and my intuition was wrong.

Looking back, if I were to talk about what skills or qualities were necessary for a good operator to have . . . I'd say situational awareness, patience, and hand-eye coordination. The rest will fall into place.

While I was doing the work itself, I was mostly bored with life but fascinated by the activity I saw. Day in and day out I would be doing the same thing but seeing a wide variety of activities—a dualism that has probably never existed in our culture on this scale of life and death. It is almost enough to drive people mad.

My personal life was filled with mostly depression and loneliness. I had so many questions about what was happening, and all my leadership would do is tell me to shut up, stop questioning. I couldn't talk about this with any of my peers; the responses would be either I'm "too emotional" or that "God will work everything out." It was incredibly heartbreaking to be left alone in the dark for so long. While I was doing missions, sometimes I felt like I was the eyes of the mission: picking up what we see, acting on instinct, hunting down people, watching them live their lives like a Predator in the sky (sorry for the pun). . . . It was exhilarating when we were actually doing something, when we were studying our very human targets. But the exhilaration doesn't hide the discomfort, and when you're finally alone with your thoughts before bedtime you feel a bit of your soul crumble to dust.

Wash. Rinse. Repeat.

While I did have issues with how my life started in the military, I had sworn an oath. My great-grandfather once told me that "the only thing a man has of any worth in this world is his word, and if you cannot fulfill your word then you have no worth." I had to continue, regardless of what my instincts and conscience were telling me. In February 2012 I realized and found out that I was violating my oath by hunting down Anwar al-Awlaki, an American citizen who was also an imam for Islam. We had been flying unarmed over Yemen at this time. The government had let us in to do so, and we were going to capture "the traitor." I came in that day in February to see the flight operations supervisor looking very disturbed and very pale.

I asked him what was up, and he told me that he had just gotten off the phone with some very *very* higher-ups who told him that we will now be flying armed over Yemen, and if we have the ability to take out al-Awlaki, President Obama himself would call the crew to give the order. I asked him why he was upset when everyone seemed to want him to pay. He explained to me that it was a direct violation to assassinate American citizens and that they deserve a fair and free trial in front of a jury of their peers. He was unsure of what that meant overall for the community. It hit me then that I had no idea other than the basics of what our Constitution stood for. I had foolishly sworn an oath on something that I had no understanding of. I will admit that for a second after that conversation, I had felt this thrill of being the sensor that took this guy out. It would legitimize my place in the community, finally. Then I felt a weird sort of vertigo, a stretching of my reality, and I remembered why I wanted to get out of the community in the first place: too much sickness, and my soul was too sick to stay in that filth. When I left, I wanted to never hear anything about drones ever again—cut away completely. Something had other plans for me, if you believe in that sort of thing.

One interesting point about the work is that quite a few people compare it to video games and actually make fun of operators for it. When I had first come out about my experiences and talking about what I had discovered about myself, people would send me messages about how they also played video games and it made them feel bad. That was the mildest of them. While the skill set is very similar—the ability to be aware of multiple things at once while focusing on a single task—the comparison with games completely misses. It is nothing like a first person shooter but more like if a real-time strategy game had a baby with the Sims. And for me, the disconnect wasn't from our targets but with myself.

Another interesting comparison is with the American sniper. Being a drone operator is what happens when you take somebody who should be highly trained like a sniper, mass produce him, and make it a lot easier to get essentially the same results. You take away the pride and honor, give the operators a false sense of superiority and importance, then claim that they are essential to the war efforts—a recipe for disaster if I ever saw one.

Now what we see is vastly different from a sniper. We usually view everything in infrared (IR), as that gives us the best clarity, though sometimes we would switch to what we call the day TV camera (DTV). The quality is pretty low, but we can manage to see things like color of the clothing, markings on vehicles, buildings, etcetera. Eventually we got a software update that allowed us to blend both IR and DTV, which also gave us access to the low light (LL) camera. With that, we were able to see things like if lights were on in a building or if a car was driving around without its lights. We could blend the IR and LL cameras as well. Camera changes could be done at the click of a button on the control stick or manually via the head-up display (HUD) interface on the video screen.

There are a few incidents that stick out to me. The first one was when I saw an American convoy hit an improvised explosive device (IED) on my first mission. I had felt like a total failure. The burning wreckage, the screaming over the radio for backup, the frantic infrared activity on the screen while I was on the opposite side of the world allowing everyone to observe the first tragedy of war: the men and women you fight with will die.

The second event was the first time that I killed anyone. I was lonely, tired. I started having trouble sleeping after that first mission. I didn't want to be a failure. I was angry that the people I had been tasked to protect were killed by an unknown enemy. I wanted vengeance. I was a fool. When the flight operations supervisor told me I was going to shoot, I put up a half-hearted objection. My pain was at war with my conscience. I wasn't sure I could do it, but I was going to anyway.

Getting into the GCS was surreal. I can remember every moment like my very being was recording the event. It's probably one of the few memories I have that I'm not sure I ever wanted to keep. The sun was pale, the wind blowing like it was straight out of hell with enough sand to get into uncomfortable places. It was hot for a January late afternoon. The inside of the GCS was cold, arctic even, and the only lights inside were from the multitude of computer monitors on the other side of the trailer.

There were five men on top of a hill underneath a single tree shooting down the north face at a convoy of American troops. We were waiting for clearance when they decided that two F-16s would be the ones to drop bombs on this target. The Hellfire missile didn't have a large enough splash radius to get the desired weapons effect. The fighters had seen three individuals walking toward the firefight on a north by northwest road about ten kilometers away, and they wanted us to put eyes on the coordinates.

We found them, two of them arguing with each other and the third seemingly terrified while looking up at the sky. He heard the bombs drop. He lagged behind slightly. We were given the confirmation that they had weapons and then given the 9-line with the cleared "Hot." I was told to place the crosshairs at the feet of the two individuals in the front—better to get two than miss.

The missile left the rail with 16 seconds of flight time. At 1.2 seconds after firing, the missile hit the speed of sound and, due to the loss of kinetic energy, the sonic boom hit the target roughly 4 to 8 seconds before impact. The man in the back heard the boom and ran forward. The missile impacted right when he reached the front two. I had killed with the push of a button—four clicks, to be precise. Life became cheap, worthless. When the smoke cleared, the man who had run to the other two was rolling on the ground, clutching his leg in desperation, and I watched his life's blood spurt out in the rhythm of his heart. It was January in the mountains of Afghanistan. The blood cooled. He stopped moving, eventually losing enough body heat to become indistinguishable from the ground on which he died.

"No one is coming to pick up the body parts," our customer said over chat. "Prepare for new target."

I don't know how much longer the day was. I was in shock. People congratulated each other in the debriefing. Two people who were not involved at all gave one another a high-five. One pilot made the remark that I had "popped my cherry." The only thing I could think of was that I'd wounded my soul, violated a core belief for . . . now that I think back on it, I'm not sure. I can no longer justify it to myself. But somehow I did, and it was slowly killing me like a poison administered every day carefully enough to not be noticed by the victim. And I was damned. I learned the second lesson: nothing can protect your own soul from doing harm to another. Only the living suffer in war, mostly those who fight it.

The third instance that is solid in my memory was when I had taken a shot at a building. By my estimates, the child had probably heard the sonic boom and ran inside for cover. My supervisor told me that collateral damage happens. The official mission statement by the screener and pilot said that it was a dog. It was then I learned the most difficult lesson of all in war: the innocent die, same as the guilty, or as bad as die.

Those instances happened all within the first three months of active missions. I had a total of five shots, four that killed thirteen people, ten of whom I am unsure of their active role in our "war." It would be nearly four years after the start of my deployment to Iraq that I would get out. I had plenty of time to beat myself up over everything and plenty of excuses to continue to do so.

When I left, I didn't care about what anyone had thought. The program was a diseased thing. Everyone knew that I was at the end of my rope in dealing with all the bullshit. I was going to leave and never look back. Good riddance. Or so I had thought.

April 17, 2011, was my last day in the 3rd Special Operations Squadron. As I was saying good-bye to the people I had once called my brothers and sisters in arms, one of the lieutenants gave me a certificate that associated me with the deaths of over 1,626 individuals. All I could think about was the quote from Robert Oppenheimer after witnessing the drop of the atomic bomb:

> We knew the world would not be the same. A few people laughed, a few people cried, most people were silent. I remembered the line from the Hindu scripture, the Bhagavad-Gita; Vishnu is trying to persuade the Prince that he should do his duty and, to impress him, takes on his multi-armed form and says, "Now I am become Death, the destroyer of worlds." I suppose we all thought that, one way or another.[1]

I had once thought that I could leave with my thirteen dead: the thirteen who kept me from sleeping, who assaulted my psyche in my modes of consciousness. They became legion. I thought back to all the missions I had witnessed. I couldn't believe the numbers. I felt like my soul had fled and I knew my judgment would be damnation. But I was still there. I could still make things right.

I had ended up in the U.S. Air Force Survival Evasion Resistance and Escape program. With my terrible experience in the drone program, I had to leave my service with good skills and the feeling that I had actually served my country honorably. I had to wash off the filth that had anything to do with "drones." A year and a half later found me in Texas going through indoctrination after over four years of intense preparation. I had dreamed of this job since I joined. It was the one I had originally signed up to be. I fought to be there.

Within a few short weeks, my dreams (and my body) were shattered in a training accident. I had wanted the position so badly that I convinced everyone to let me continue training—broken face, injured spine, and more. It was the single most physically painful experience in my entire life. It paled in comparison to the emotional and psychic pain I had been feeling. I told myself that I would complete it no matter what or die trying. I had nothing else.

I only lasted six more days before I collapsed on the death truck march. My team had been beautifully supportive of me the whole time. They wanted me to succeed because they saw how badly I wanted it. And I had hoped to keep encouraging them to push forth and conquer. I remember arguing with one of the cadre members, then all of a sudden feeling extremely lightheaded. I was only out for a few seconds of eternity. It was my punishment by the universal karma machine (I no longer cared for any deities). I couldn't escape it. I woke up with the same cadre member standing over me with a concerned look on his face and slapping me in mine. I kept my eyes tightly shut because I couldn't believe my fate, didn't want to believe it was possible.

In the hospital, my dead stood in judgment of me in my nightmares. I was mocked and condemned for my actions by the legion crowd. My punishment was to live with what I had done, to die a broken man bereft of hopes and dreams. In my last true moment of clarity before the pain and drugs swept me away into the terror of the voice, I pled for a chance to make things right.

In the middle of October, *Der Spiegel*'s Nicola Abé contacted me for an interview to get some answers about the drone program. I told her I was willing to tell her whatever it is she wanted to know. Her duty is to inform the people of the truth that our government was keeping from them. It was supposed to be my last act of defiance before I had killed myself. The Veterans Administration had refused to see me after my reserves squadron kicked me to the streets and refused me medical treatment and medical discharge. They had put me in the inactive ready reserves (IRR) and told me it was my fault. I believed them. The only answer I could come up with was the Samurai ritual of Seppuku.

Leading up to the release of the *Der Spiegel* article,[2] I had convinced myself that more people would lend their voice to my outcry, that the people I left knew what was at stake and they would fix everything. Oh, how wrong I was. They attacked me for whichever reasons they wanted to justify to themselves. I confronted every single one of them, and all the random trolls, because I knew in my heart that what I had done was finally the right thing. If it hadn't been for them fighting with me like they had, I would have given in to my despairing path. A whole different history would have played out.

The rest you can find online as well as everyone's opinion of the matter. Here is what I have learned from this whole experience. I learned what worth really means. I learned that I can endure.

One of the board members who gave me the 2015 Whistleblower of the Year Award told me she had believed that a murderer did not deserve the prize. I told her I agreed. My original speech that I had written in my notebook had me declining the award. I did believe and still believe that I am unworthy of it. Many people that I knew and had told about the nomination had tried to convince me to accept it, saying it was a validation of what I had been saying all along. While I could understand that reasoning, it didn't sit well in my heavy heart. My little brother had told me that I was his hero, and while I didn't believe I was worthy of that title, for him I had to act like it. I couldn't let anyone go through what I experienced.

Our world and our species depend on us being actively involved in the decision-making processes that ensure our survival. Too often we are compelled into positions where we feel we have no power, but the reality is that we will always have the ability to decide our fates. In the end, we all die, and I can believe that we will face the repercussions of our actions. It is all about what we do in life, not what we believe in. No authority is given that can forgive a man of his actions. His loss and gain of honor is on his own merit. It cannot be displayed with deceit. Honesty and integrity will win out in the end, and a man of genuine change will show strength and champion reason. This breaks all boundaries of spirituality and politics. It is the hardest truth to understand.

The last thing my grandfather told me before he died was that he would never trust a man who never made a mistake. Go make some mistakes and fix them. Also remember to learn the lessons from other peoples' errors. Be wise and conquer.

Notes

This letter was written in response to a series of questions posed to Brandon Bryant by Lisa Parks in person and via e-mail.

1. J. Robert Oppenheimer, "Now I am become death . . ." This is an excerpt of an interview of Oppenheimer about the Trinity explosion (July 16, 1945), first broadcast as part of the television documentary *The Decision to Drop the Bomb* (1965), produced by Fred Freed, *NBC White Paper*.
2. Nicola Abé, "Dreams in Infrared."

14 MATERIALITIES OF THE ROBOTIC

JORDAN CRANDALL

Killer Robot

Of the many sentient forms that have emerged from the genre of science fiction, the humanoid monster reigns supreme—that hideous progeny of the gothic that returns, yet again, to congeal anxieties over technological change. This intelligent, enlivened machine will parallel human bodies, mechanics of action, and thought processes in a model of aberrant personification that provides the structural basis of the thrill, the enjoyment of being menaced by the very creature that one has brought to life. In turning against its creators, the synthetic entity will transform a narrative of technological triumph into one of betrayal. The delusions and dangers of our hubris will be exposed. Its narcissistic foundation, however, will remain entrenched.

In the encounter with the hostile robot, certain securities are provided. However the boundaries between human and machine may be troubled, the ground footing that guarantees the distinction will not. One can rely on the security of a terrestrial grip that will enable defiance or departure, fortification or traction. There is reassurance in knowing that you can get away from the thing.

The situation is infinitely different, however, if you are strapped inside the robot during its murderous spree. Extricating one's body from captivity within a vehicle is a prospect that is considerably more fraught, physically and conceptually, than simply running away. The body is dislodged from the security of its ground footing and the means of self-determined movement that enables. The capabilities afforded by its physical properties are wrested out of its command, the path from cognitive intention to corporeal expression severed. The body is subsumed into an action composite whose terms it cannot control—a composite of human and robot with which, from an exterior view, it is now coincident, in form, function, and intent.

Perhaps this is why the autonomous machine that transports people is never called a robot. The line between taking the vehicle and being taken by it is already thin enough. The nightmare scenario of the free-thinking vehicle is that the line disappears.

For those who seek authentic adventure, this is reason enough to get *in*—to enter the integrated materiality that a *vehicular* robot enacts and invest in the nature of agency there. Why settle for the surface effects of the storyline formulas when one can delve into their generative mechanisms, the code hierarchies that secure ease of use?

Alas, there is little dramatic potential. Gone is the delicious agony of having to fret about the latest robotic menace. Could the pleasurable fear of being menaced by the autonomous killer machines soon to be unleashed upon humanity be sustained if one were to think of them as transport vehicles in which the body must sit rather than Terminators from which one could flee? Lacking distinction from the machine and dislodged from the stability of a solid footing in relation to it, there is no structural basis for the thrill of the chase, no model of personification that secures the operations of the narrative. The exhilarating fear elicited in the heroic struggle between friend and foe is diffused when the differentiating gap that provides the basis of the conflict gives way to debilitating overlap.

The acceptance of such debilitation is progress, provided it does not simply involve rest. Immobilization along one axis of endeavor opens new avenues of mobility along others. The cinematic machine requires the immobilization of a viewer in order to sensitize the body to the rhythmic patterns to which it now must correspond: in conjunction with the transport machine that provides its informing background, to train the viewer-operator to be susceptible to the codes of the forms that will now menace it, the monsters that will chase it in order that it can move again willingly, with all the newfound sensory capacity that this will summon. Cinema, like transport, was fueled by the need for hasty departure as much as destinational allure, repulsions as much as attractions. To crave is a powerful propelling force but there is nothing quite like being an object craved to fire up the vital motor forces and functions, amplify the affect, escalate the rhythms—provided one's life is on the line.

Rhythms and tones move through the body, like music, as the body moves through them. Bodies inhabit the conditions that media apparatuses help implement, conditions that take hold in routines both on- and offscreen, the activity regimens incited by gears, motors, and patterns of light impressed into awareness through repetitive viewing and into corporeality through repeated enacting. In these regimens, which traffic between performance and depiction, and which combine procedures, techniques, and supports in generative movements, sensory capacities are retooled, functions are automated, and postures are formed. These automating and endo-shaping operations constitute the robotic. It *is* the apparatus of movement automation, not the automated form moved.

To get *in* the robotic vehicle, then, is not to enter into an enclosure. There is no entering it as one would a cabin, for its nature is operational, not spatial. In this, the autonomous vehicle holds a unique potential: that of facilitating a model of operation that does not rely on the structuring principle of interiority.

By way of the pilotless, we access the cabinless. We keep the operator but evacuate the enclosure. The robotic menace takes the form not of a transcendent object that stands in relation to the human but an intervention into the structure of its operations in the world. As a vehicle, it emphasizes principles that are based in transit, not territory—movement in practice, not form in production.

In this, the robotic is not by nature *hostile.* It is immanent to the materiality of form, not set in opposition to it. It disrupts the path from cognitive intention to corporeal expression not by severing it but by intervening in its constitutive procedures and technics, weaving action composites of reorganized capabilities and supports. It is only hostile when one regards these attributes as the sole province of a human corporeality, consolidated in terms of properties that it alone is seen to control—the agency it possesses now under siege, the body is swept from its ground footing and the command of its attributes pried away, including the authority that stems from their possession.

In contrast, consider the inviting nature of the robotic, its eros. We have much to gain by opening the field between deliberation and action rather than defending against perceived incursions, for this field is already well incurred upon in ways that elude our comprehension. If there is a battle, it is not here. A basic insight from neuroscience is that decisions are largely made before being consciously aware of having made them. Even the simplest operational tasks of driving a car involve immense realms of sensory, processing, and effecting activity at scales well below and above that of the individual and its conscious threshold—a much broader range and frequency of macro- and microdeliberations than can be contained corporeally and accommodated cognitively. Into the intricacies of these minute action composites, one needs to probe with care.

Within these intricacies of sensing, processing, and actuation, a level of complicity is to be acknowledged. When one hops in the driver's seat, the expectation is not to exploit the vehicle but to partake of the means that it provides. Entry into the robotic requires commitment to the facilitation of a joint course of action. In place of oppositional positions, we engage cooperative maneuvers: the realities of negotiating coordinated passage on surfaces, segueing in and out of paths, facilitating scalar correspondences, managing threshold transitions.

This erotics is not based in narcissistic reinforcement, not that of identified forms and personages, however deviant or monstrous, that attract and challenge humans by reflecting their centrality. It is not based on a fundamental separation between internal and external, the body and its extensions in the world—interchangeable attachments that, controllable via the architectures of the user interface, augment human faculties but do not disrupt its place. There is no essential corporeity that remains extricable from the robotic, no essential mind that remains separate from the body-as-vehicle, no complex of functions that can simply be embodied in a facile equivalence to the human frame.

How ironic that we apprehend the unmanned by getting *in*. Not by entering its cabin, which is not possible, but its infrastructure, which is. Possibilities of integrally moving into the vehicles to which we already have access in everyday life abound. Their attributes, principles, intelligibilities, and forms can be accessed through adroit operation, elucidated in informed driving. It is a materiality of and in the venture: plug in and test, retool and rerun, modify and try again. It is the route, insofar as it activates the routine. The vehicle's reality is in its inhabitation of the activity course rather than its representation of it, its means of operation more than its meaning. The paradigm is not that of the argument.

The narratives grind to a halt. Paths of movement are opened along other axes, provided one becomes sensitized to their conditions. The vehicular robotic holds the potential of decoupling action from its anthropocentric anchoring, broadening the capability for apprehending the activity that is actually occurring in the world through sources previously overlooked—sensitizing the human–machine conglomerate to the courses within which it already moves. The moves and postures have elucidating qualities and effects and open unforeseen modes of address. Intricacies of practice replace the drama of forms.

Unenclosure

I

At the close of the twentieth century, a progeny of aircraft was already on the ascendance, minus one salient characteristic of the phylum. The curious form of the windowless cockpit, which retained its bulbous shape but not its functions, announced the arrival of something long in development. The transfer of perceptual functions from humans to machines, ordinarily difficult to witness, suddenly became apparent by way of a bold material effect: the sealed volume of an uncanny form that retained the familiarity of the cockpit while negating its very essence.

In this sense, while the enclosed, globular form of the opaque cabin undoubtedly serves as an exemplar of the dislodging effects of the unmanned, its disturbing nature derives less from its function as representative than as renunciant. It maintains resemblance while rejecting the functionality associated. It institutes a repudiation of the sightline whose relevance in aviation history has always been clear, the visual path specific to a human no longer at the helm.

The cockpit from which persons have been jettisoned and exteriority walled off, along with its automated analogues on the ground—the surface vehicles not far behind in the dislodging process—certainly belong to a historical succession of forms. They are recent material iterations in a long history of the technological augmentation of human capacities. The history of the vehicle, whether terrestrial or aerial, is characterized by the advancing automation of cognitive functions, with the capacities of operators, historically assigned to humans, now being augmented or replaced by intelligent systems. The windowless bubble certainly announces the fact that machine cognition has advanced to the point that humans are no longer needed in the way they were before. But even more vividly, it makes apparent the radical nature of this new cognitive form, not by reflecting it but by performing it in an evacuating move.

The ontological break that has occurred with the wholesale sealing off of the cockpit from the exterior world and the displacement of its pilot is not simply indicative of a condition from which drivers on *this* side of the window are immune. A more pervasive displacement has been enacted. Viewers are jettisoned from their centers, subjects ejected from their bubbles of interiority, in ways that prompt a reconsideration of the modes of existence and knowledge long associated with these structuring conceits. In this, the dislodging occurs at a deeper core of the material, by way of a shift in the relational principles that underpin its constitution.

It is not simply that vehicles are being operated in the same way, with the difference that they are now controlled remotely or autonomously, however within or outside the enclosures of the flight deck. If there is any absence characteristic of this new cosmos of the unmanned, it is not simply that of the relocated human. It is, rather, the very condition of the interior, even as the appearance of the command enclosure remains. In an operational and ontological sense, it is not that there is no pilot inside, but that there is no inside.

II

The sleek transport capsule, like most objects of desire, becomes all the more alluring as it becomes opaque. The matter of accessing its concealed abundance becomes paramount, yet the demands of desire prohibit the easy access that will only dilute its hold. The glossy, alluring impenetrability of the windowless vehicle reaches its libidinous heights when it not only obscures the interior from visual possession but blocks entry to it, provided the possibility of entering remains.

Barred entry from the vehicle's soothing enclosure, as when a cab speeds by on an urban street ignoring one's frenzied attempts to hail it, the requirements of transport rise up into the field of awareness. Illusory surfaces give way to infrastructures and supply lines; routines cede to a bewildering array of options to be negotiated anew. Left outside the vehicle, one is "in" nothing but the constitutive ground of practices, immersed in the resources and procedures through which transport means must be harnessed. The horizontality of the base need is inflected by the verticality of improvement tension.

III

The interior-evacuating dynamics witnessed in vehicular forms are at work across the larger ecologies of resource procurement, assembly, distribution, and storage with which they configure in correspondence.

Just as the unmanned aerial vehicle (UAV) forfeited some of the defining characteristics of its progenitors, its support infrastructures have also encountered characteristic losses. Consider the warehouse. It never really had windows, but it did require floors, until the navigational actions of moving along one plane of action at a time within a vertical stack of platforms traversed by freight elevators gave way to omnidirectional movement within an open volumetric space, intelligent cabs now incorporating the lift and retrieval functions.

In the manner of the automated cockpit that supersedes its occupied ancestor, the automated guided vehicle (AGV) updates the elevator in a novel form that is an uncanny echo of old. It is easy to forget that the elevator too once had a human operator. The sudden emptying of its compartment during the industrial era surely incited some degree of trepidation in passengers, confronted as they were with the disappearance of a driver within a cabin that, while familiar enough to mount, required novel input actions. A transfer of functions from humans to machines was accomplished with a push of the button. Who could have imagined that passengers, newly welcomed into the command seat, would later become superfluous within a cab infrastructure that no longer required them to enter and, being occupied with other tasks, no longer need move them at all?

The AGV might just as well be positioned in the tradition of the forklift. No matter—its materiality is not simply that of its internal architecture but also that of the external arrangement with which it practices in conjunction, driven by the shared attributes that arise. Stacking and retrieval functions emerge among platform architectures that include computational hardware, sensors, data corridors, and rack systems. Forms are shaped within the parameters and procedures, between consolidation and reach.

Perhaps the AGV, laboring away along the volumetric racks of the warehouse, is the drone's unsung accomplice, saddled with attending to the logistical support systems that enable the resource availability on which the aerial vehicles depend. As the sublime UAV zooms across the boundless sky, shimmering with protective and invasive power, its squat counterpart lumbers along the tracks below, in ways too cumbersome and slow to captivate the imagination in the same way. Unlike the mastering overview that moves at the speed of light, it plods along the ground, complicating the dream of a frictionless machine.

We would do well to linger. Striking aerial images, analytics, and cartographies hide the majority of effort that such operations actually involve: the movement of enormous amounts of material across the ground and seas, between ports and centers, fabrication sites and storage facilities, distribution centers and operational zones. These fields of transfer and transmission and the configurations that form around them are part of a constitutive landscape that is far more generative than its more visible counterparts. It is not just a horizontal surface to be mapped but a volume with its own spatial and temporal dynamics, immersed in an infrastructure of practice that operates across scales and domains. While its quasi-urban zones and locales are distinct in their military and industrial protocols, they intersect, overlap, and share resources at key points.

To speak of a manufacturing landscape that is similarly devoid of the enclosures of factories, as these are conventionally regarded, is not to imply the evacuation of the shop floor but to foreground the reconstituted configurations that assume these roles. The material operators constitute a grammar to be worked with as a tool repertory—not for the purpose of description but for extracting principles from the mode of operation.

IV

Resources and components are shipped in and fabricated parts shipped out within larger ecologies of production, distribution, and storage. They draw on the instructing capabilities allowed by advances in software and networking, sensors and microprocessors, tracking and data management techniques. Systemic intelligence is integrated into hardware, applications, actuators, and build paths.

Unlike conventional methods that require parts to be machined all over again when mistakes are made, digital manufacturing methods enable testing and feedback throughout the production process. Structural problems can be detected early. Prototypes can be output rapidly and inexpensively, instructions modified and material composition changed based on performance. Each iterative output is subsequently discarded as the advancements are subsumed into the course and translated into subsequent models. Possibilities of direct intervention at the material level are increased. Build paths improve. Time windows shorten. Prototyping becomes adequate for end use. Planning is absorbed into production, testing into operation.

As the need for inventory is reduced, so can the factory be light on its feet. An aircraft or ship might carry a 3-D printer and download build files to produce components as needed—absolved of the need to carry replacement parts, yet required to stock powdered ingredients onboard like so

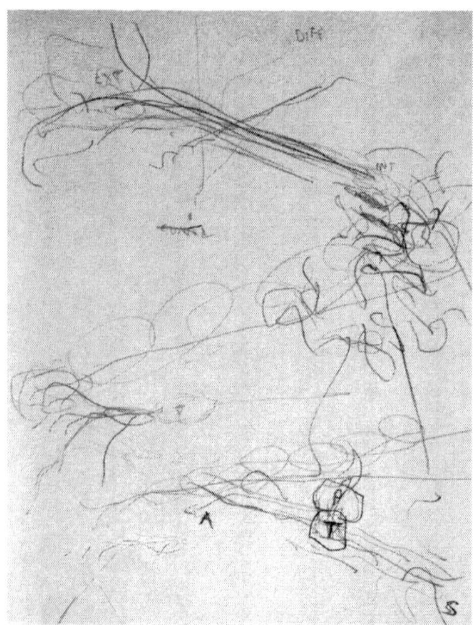

Figure 14.1. "Untitled Diagram, 2016." (Courtesy Jordan Crandall)

AUTOMAKER

R.P. is presenting plans for his company's new venture, a 3-D printer that can fabricate an automobile. From the schematics, I see that it will be about the same size as the car it fabricates. I wonder whether this constitutes progress. On the one hand, it reduces the factory, but on the other hand, it enlarges the printer.

It was not so long ago that computers required spaces that were nearly the size of factories. Is it any surprise that factories would shrink in tandem with the miniaturization of the sensing, processing, and storage platforms on which they now rely? In reducing the factory to the scale of a one-car garage, actions that once involved the molding and milling of objects within a space-time populated by laborers and tools, resources and industrial hardware, are condensed in an automating imperative.

Yet on the converse, we have not the shrinking factory but the expanding printer—swelled to the extent that it now subsumes the factory. The scenario is perhaps easier to visualize because it is more accommodating, considering the general desirability of roominess and the appeal of unfettered access to an apparatus whose inner workings are all but impenetrable, especially when requiring the extraction of jammed resources that it refuses to yield. Yet it may be more anxiety-inducing, given this "munching" tendency writ large, in the context of familiar body-devouring references of technological gigantism in horror films.

However ejected or ingested the innards, we are hard pressed to imagine this interiorless apparatus as anything nearly as uncanny as that of its cabinless consort up above.

many sacks of flour. Or perhaps it might instead harvest resources abundantly available in the local environment, in the manner of a solar-powered fabricator in the desert that draws from sand or a drone that sucks particulates from the atmosphere. Here, the build location achieves a remarkable degree of autonomy, not in the conventional sense of its harboring its own information-processing and actuation capability but in the sense of achieving its own supply chain. In this scenario, it is not a matter of whether the factory shrinks or expands in relation to the vehicle it fabricates. The vehicle devours the factory.

Driver fabricators orchestrate the proper intake, processing, and expenditure that will enable capabilities to adhere and traction to take place. Resource flows are proportionately converted, processed, and managed in correspondence with agglomerates joined in the routing, manufacture, and transport practices. Information architectures and analytics assist in orienting the modes of instruction that are harbored and conveyed within these flows—informing procedures that delimit ranges and rhythms of action. The miniaturization of technologies, the mobilization of resources, and the autonomization of supply corridors allow the stabilization of large-scale agglomerates: consider the emergence of massive sea-based factories and underground facilities on par with current data centers and the inevitable self-fabricating space outpost that will someday expand without territorial limitation. At the same time, one can imagine aircraft that are not only pilotless but that never need land.

V

Multiple units are linked in systems, enterprises joined through subcontracting and outsourcing, asymmetries overcome so that scalar differences can hold. Cooperative agreements allow sharing of equipment and labor resources, intelligence and forms of expertise—however, in materials science, software design, modeling, or stress testing. Techniques are integrated into routines that strive to amplify coherency and minimize unnecessary friction. Information drawn from cameras, microchips, accelerometers, location sensors, and proximity detectors, together with advanced processing capacity and analytics tools, enables resources, workers, goods, and vehicles to be tracked across ports, warehouses, manufacturing facilities, distribution centers, and test sites. Quantitative indicators harness movement to numerical values. Enterprise resource planning (ERP) databases and customized software applications manage global supply chains

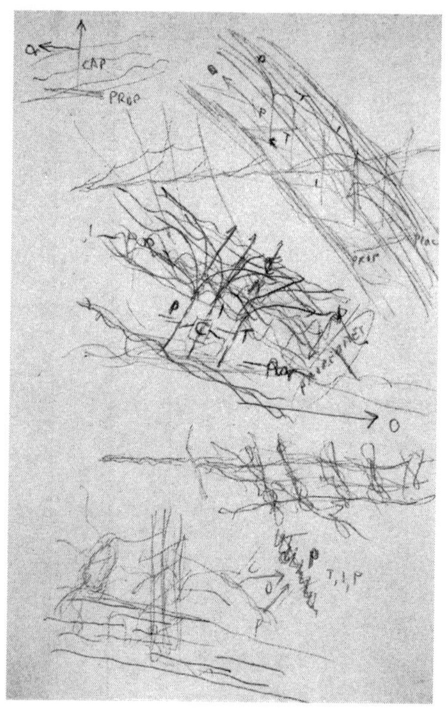

Figure 14.2. "Untitled Diagram, 2016." (Courtesy Jordan Crandall)

DRONES ON DEMAND

P.O. Lab is devising a novel infrastructure for vehicle-on-demand services. The cars do not arrive across roads but emerge within digital fabrication facilities. I wonder whether it is too much of a stretch. As if anticipating my skepticism, the director points out that, with the right resources, it is already possible to fabricate an automobile onsite in a matter of days. The body chassis can be 3-D printed in a single unit out of a reinforced thermoplastic composite, followed by installation of the critical structural and motoring components, which have necessarily been brought in from other sources.

I move with his line of reasoning, take his concept for a test ride. The paradigm is already in place in the case of encoded media, which, upon being summoned and received via transmission, is assembled locally within one's computer. A program writes to the console of the desktop or mobile device a sequence of images that upon reception is geared to transport the user. The infrastructure of this transmission along with much of its machine and assembly code is also that which causes vehicles to move through geographic space. Ever more bound up in transportation, it provides the means of monitoring, scheduling, and navigation at the internal and external, local and global levels.

Perhaps this plan is a logical outgrowth of ride-sharing services, which enable cars to be summoned on demand, their schedules carefully choreographed through location sensors and traffic-management algorithms. As automation increases, we might already imagine driverless vehicles perpetually circulating through the city and sky, tapping into the cognitive and energetic resources that the material infrastructure provides.

Will these relentlessly traveling vehicles even need to collect their drivers? Perhaps not, if the automobile begins to realize its full potential as UGV. In this case, it is not only the driver who is on the way out. The passenger, too, is in line for expunction. At this point, the automobile will have transubstantiated, having at long last fulfilled the level of self-determination anticipated by its prefix. A machine that was once primarily geared for transporting bodies will now attend to their needs in other ways or attend to other needs entirely.

No matter whether P.O.'s vision is practical. It helps elucidate what the vehicle already does: channel the system of transport. At one scale, it moves as a synchronous agglomeration across space in ways that are easily recognized as transport, while at other scales, it acts as a facilitator of movement that passes through it, however apparently fixed in place it remains. It is determined by instructing chords that run through as much as outlines that enclose. As it negotiates a course, it instantiates a build path. Among the consolidations and extensions is its contour en route.

Movements are instituted between points by way of transfers, but they also involve conversions among rates and protocols, formats and scales. Layers of translation occur in material constitutions and code architectures, and between points in space. The vehicle that moves from one place to another achieves identicality across space and time because it has conducted these translations with the stability and coherence required. It orchestrates a transferrable and situated integration by way of routes and routines of a sufficiently standardized nature. These intelligent infrastructures of movement and positioning, built on replicable procedures and data structures, help enact the frameworks of knowledge within which transport is understood.

---

and monitor organizational conditions, work efficiency, and financial performance in real time.

These integrated tools are often used willingly, however directly or indirectly, to manage performance across the circuits of daily life, in and out of vehicles in the workplace, at home, and on the road. The coded materialities of performance are endo-shaping and auto-regulating. As is the case more generally with large-scale social media, the software internalizes the patterns of practice as activity and analysis intertwine. Regulation happens by way of the synergetics of local improvisation. Systemic intelligence is variably channeled and stored by operators and harnessed in knowledge-making procedures.

The efficiency aim is to find the right dynamic between autonomy and integrated effort, local initiative and centralized control. It is more effective to engender the improvement pull that will facilitate entrance into the cycles of increase rather than enforce obedience via command center dictates.

VI

The component that would not have been achievable with conventional casting and machining methods might be indistinguishable from one that was. A part formerly produced in metal but now fabricated in a thermoplastic composite might appear the same but will actually be lighter and stronger than its metallic counterpart, its effecting capability now of a different nature than that conventionally associated with it. A blade for an engine might be made with multiple alloys such as titanium, aluminum, and nickel-chromium so as to optimize one end for strength and the other for heat resistance. A single part might combine functions of structural load-bearing with the power generation of blast resistance.

Assemblages formerly produced in several parts might instead be built additively in single units. An unrecognizable form might emerge from a bed of liquid resin or cobalt-chromium powder, reorganizing attributes within a novel support base. Functions bind material conglomerates into material uses that are often easy to overlook, diffusing their constitutive attributes beyond the boundaries of their forms. Use patterns are incorporated into retooled constitutions.

VII

As resources are managed and capabilities arranged in accordance with the situated properties in which they must lodge, trade corridors are active and exchange ratios ongoing. The reduction of a plane's weight might improve its ability to fly yet at the same time lower its energy absorption and worsen its impact performance. An increase of brittleness in crashes may be an advantageous tradeoff when the production of replacement parts, or entirely new vehicles, is no longer difficult, costly, or time intensive.

As vehicles become constellations of manufactured and composited parts of various levels of interchangeability, configurations of outputs in broader

MICROENHANCERS

Figure 14.3. "Untitled Diagram, 2016." (Courtesy Jordan Crandall)

For S.W., action is at the microlevel: auto-actuating material that is responsive to environmental change. He is leading an effort to embed control features in body panels, hulls, fairings, ailerons, stabilizers, and rudders. Combining the properties of newly synthesized composites with increased sensing, processing, and actuation capacity enables surface properties to auto-transform in response to external stimuli.

Optical fiber sensors are absorbed into the platform substrate to register stress loads in real time. Microactuators allow control of vibration by internally adjusting the force level of energy absorption elements and the friction level of aeroelastic forms. The responsiveness has a historical dimension: reconstructions in the microstructure can be performed through the retrievability of stored arrangements and values.

For S.W., the close integration of these capacities will offer real-time, onboard diagnostic abilities that minimize communication and data link requirements between vehicle and control center. They offer improvement in assessments that would otherwise be conducted from afar. The ultimate ambition: to enable recovery operations to be conducted midflight.

These formal constitutions depend on close integration and maintenance within larger-scale conglomerates—practice regimens on which their performative competency relies. Their form *is* the qualification and calibration of moves in these shaping practices—a condition to be "in" rather than a contour owned.

materializing circuits within which the base materiality resides, fashioned of parts and wholes with varying timelines and provisional stabilizations of tradeoff, there is the matter of what gets prioritized—the survival of the individual part, model, or plane or the production line itself.

The ease of digitally manufacturing replacements for damaged vehicles and easily repairing them en route might amplify the enduring resilience of prototypes by way of an increase in plasticity and disposability, amplifying their enduring priorities while accommodating their necessary vulnerability to the real and the risks associated with this exposure.

As vehicles are not entirely separate from the bodies that inhabit them, these risks include those that are particular to the human occupant. Yet the dislodging and relocation of the latter within integrated cognitive and corporeal systems makes the core of the susceptibility difficult to locate, the gambit difficult to gauge. The vehicle–operator composite is provisional and fluid, with the body of the driver extending to the car shell or fuselage and even beyond, retracting when necessary, as the composite that is traffic itself wells up and dilutes. The pilot driver hovers between the terrestrial vehicle rendered airborne and the airborne vehicle terrestrialized, along with the mutating lines of an interior compartment that once provided the locus of vulnerability.

Contraption

I

Against a horizon of the vehicular sublime populated by streamlined capsules whose excesses appear firmly contained behind windowless façades, there erupts a perplexing sight: the reemergence of the flying car, that diligent and whimsical standard of twentieth-century science fiction, and its contemporary analogue, the roadable plane. Their excesses are relatively unbound, their motivating impulses blatant. They instantiate the enduring impulse to transcend the limits of bodies and congested urban roadways, in continuously updated prototypes that, arising as they do amid crowded airways, seek to transcend the limits of the skies as well. Chugging along through the endless cycles of experimentation and enterprise, they harken back to the early days of aviation, when baffling contraptions strived for liftoff in endless test runs, their beleaguered human pilots strapped into or dangling out of them.

These confounding contrivances have no place in grand visions of the driverless sublime. They rarely make it to the commercial expositions and promotional spreads. They barely even get off the ground—at least for long. If you inquire of the driver where the thing is going you will likely receive a blank look. If it is going anywhere, it is back to the shop.

Also irrelevant is the question of what it is. Its ramshackle nature defies easy resolution. Even the most commonly appearing things have a contraption nature, their alluring surfaces belying their truth, so this is in any case not the best opener for the venturesome.

The contraption seems to endure precisely because it is poised on the brink of collapse. It seems to belong to the materializing circuits of attempting, endlessly cycling across the domains of production and prototyping, rehearsal and retooling, devoid of the investments of destination and description. In this it manifests a key feature of the vehicle: it is built to perform. Material and energetic resources must be integrated into generative, informing cycles, by way of the operational techniques best suited to the knowledge-making and powering requirements. The orientation is affirmative. One wants to make the thing work. If its performance is interrogated, it is for the purpose of improving it.

The drive is by nature a test drive. The aerial run is a flight test. You cannot believe the contrivance will work until you hop in and give it a try—mount it, adopt the appropriate function, and give it a test run. In production, the vehicle moves, but in practice, it moves within routines. Actions are relevant insofar as they constitute procedures. Elucidation happens in movements that repeat.

II

The contraption presses onward, between speculation of what could be and acquiescence to what is, however poised on the brink of collapse. Divorced from the ways and means through which it moves, it is not much. It requires drivers to lend orientation and motive force, drivers for whom achieving the end product is less important than enhancing the facility to engender it—the increase of the ability to conduct the actions that are appropriate and to engage with the contingencies that arise.

Adequacy must be demonstrated, not just once but repeatedly. Action requires support, its means of operation actively configured, not taken for granted. Unlike the viewer, reader, or user who is shielded from underlying

Figure 14.4. "Untitled Diagram, 2016." (Courtesy Jordan Crandall)

ROADOPLANE

T.L.O. is designing a roadable plane prototype built of lightweight metals reinforced with carbon fiber. He is at work on the chassis and retractable wings, which are being configured in compromises among size, weight, power consumption, and maneuverability. The ability to achieve liftoff will depend on the properties that best allow the deflection and contouring of flows, the optimum curves for harnessing the attributes of wind and speed, and the prime strength-to-weight ratios for maximizing the efficiency of the platform held aloft.

The trick, as ever, is to calibrate costs against expenditures. Speed is a priority, yet due to the roughness of terrain, it might need to be sacrificed in favor of the greater necessity of vibration reduction. Attributes of increased durability might need to be traded for attributes that offer temperature resistance. Strength-to-weight ratios are adjusted according to performance expectations. The reduction of weight might improve the ability to remain airborne yet at the same time lower energy absorption and worsen impact performance. The assurance of a smooth flight might not be worth the cost of a potentially catastrophic shattering.

Properties of mass, density, chemical composition, shape, and surface texture are adjusted based on tests. The right intake, conversion, and distribution of matter and energy will offer the properties that are most opportune. The right attachments, motoring devices, instructional inputs, and procedures will allow the platform to stabilize, gain momentum, and achieve elevation. It is a matter of the right ratio of exchange between the flow that will keep a resource moving and the contingencies that may threaten to obstruct it: between the standard move and the unique one that may offer advantage. Variability is to be stabilized to a degree sufficient for imitation and advance.

There is no instruction book. The task is to harness an instructability not based in the representational. Detecting and accommodating rather than overwriting with a default move. The conduits, regulators, and converters at work are not always evident. If one attempt does not work well, then another arrangement of inputs is in order, or a foregrounding of inputs that are already at work but unnoticed and in need of attention. The agency is in the action.

---

realities by spellbinding surfaces and their arrays of choices, the driver negotiates the vivid flows of the real at a level where the materiality of agency has to be sourced and sustained, rendered sufficient to do what it does.

The driver must be sufficiently equipped for performing in the manner and to the degree required; the designation does not apply simply by virtue of having gotten in the control seat. The wherewithal must be sourced and integrated into the practices through which performance qualification can be upheld. Information and fuel must be processed, programs deployed, platforms serviced and maintained, environmental conditions negotiated astutely, parameters intuited in terms of speed, rhythm, and range. Circumstances can turn on a moment's notice. The repercussions of disobeying regulations or neglecting to maintain the level of attention required are keenly evident. One is vulnerable to loss of resources, capabilities, and authority. The repercussions are not just those particular to arriving or achieving an end point but of not being able to do what needs to be done. Mastery is not assured through the reinforcement of position but through the adeptness of activity in time. Moves constituted in a structure of alternatives cede to maneuvers that are circumstantially astute.

Aligned with the infrastructures of transport and the techniques of assembly, the pilot fabricator is an aggregate of competency provisionally achieved. The vehicle is drawn in and around as the vehicle draws in and addresses this driver-assembler. Resources are integrated along with the sequences of operation particular to their use and the complex of skills that this operation entails. They are drawn into densities that are movable as uniform wholes, conglomerates that offer accordant maneuver within the flows of assembly. Lent traction, momentum, and elevation, matter is advanced into the regimens that will facilitate organization and direction in instituted form.

The piloted contraption is brazen in its needs, of both mechanical upkeep and social appropriation, its parts not sheathed beneath a continuous, undulating surface that defines them as its interior, and once so identified, discourages access to their workings. It is not shorn of embodiment but of the paradigm of the enclosure that would determine it as form.

Outfittings stick out and in. Pipes, conduits, antennae, attachments, feelers: extensions and incursions render the support as a topography, a structuring-registering baseline with no outside. It does not demarcate bodily forms so much as stabilize the resource integrations on the basis of which capabilities can transpire. The operative materiality is not an outlined but an outfitted one: the geared-up platform, not the delimiting frame. The stable consistency of the course replaces the consolidating function of the container.

III

One can imagine that the occupied forms of these contraptions will be even more perplexing than the unmanned aircraft that increasingly swarm the skies, due to their introduction of cockpits into vehicles that no longer require them. What will the driver pilot do as, peering out of the transparent optical portal of the control cabin, anchored in the sightline specific to its historical role at the helm, it confronts its disembodied understudy flying nearby?

A means of address might emerge along the flight path, provided the counterperspective of this disembodied stand-in is admitted. How does it register its object? Its sightline has no singular, discernible path particular to it, no locus. It is not just that the pilot has been evacuated or that the subject has been ejected but that interiority itself has been jettisoned from the structuring dynamic. If representation were to be operative (there is no need for it to be so), the form reflected would undoubtedly be baffling in its uncanniness, if not monstrous, retaining as it does the familiarity of the drone while negating its very essence. Its sudden emergence as a cognitive center will have been more alarming than its loss.

15

DRONE IMAGINARIES

The Technopolitics of Visuality in Postcolony and Empire

INDERPAL GREWAL

FOR EVERY SCHOLAR or writer who sees drones as manifestations of militarized state power,[1] there are those who see these technologies as useful for social justice projects, rescue operations, or environmental protection. While there are those who claim that even in war, drones can reduce violence and death through their greater precision and accuracy, others view technological advancement as a good in and of itself, or see drones as simply a commodity.[2] While much of the debate around drones in the United States concerns their use by the military, the power of privatized capital and corporations in this new century suggests that entities other than the state are developing and profiting from these technologies. Consequently, the consumption and production of these drones raises serious concerns. In the militarization of everyday life, the military and the consumer product are entangled not simply in the history of their origins or production but also in the technopolitics of visuality, that is, the ways that digital technologies become harnessed to struggles over power and inequality to address the violence of empire and postcolony.

In the contemporary phase of intensified economic and financial globalization and inequality, cultural critique has turned to drone technology to examine the operations of both empire and capital. Postcolonial, neocolonial, and national differences, allied to the material places, geographies, and deployments of war and global capital, have produced divergent drone aesthetics and imaginaries. In particular, a debate has emerged between those who advocate a more humanist response to militarized drones and those who locate resistance in narratives of the emergent subjects of this technology.[3]

The latter subjects may be posthuman or postnational, with the implication that liberal subjects and their institutions (legal, political, cultural) cannot respond adequately to the new sensoria and powers of neoliberal capital as it is allied with the practices and processes of empire and sovereignty that together subtend the drone. As much as some argue for visual witnessing of human rights abuses and assertions of national sovereignty to resist the military use of drones by the United States, there are others for whom these forms of liberal rights seem outmoded and ineffective against the dispersed and massive onslaught of violence by technosecuritized, neoliberal states, individuals, and corporations. In this debate, the drone has emerged as the latest avatar for a literary and cultural critique of technoscientific rationality, the security state as both empire and postcolony, and its imbrication with neoliberal economic processes.

As the chapters in this collection suggest, there is much to be learned from understanding how military drones produce both empire and its targets in national, regional, and global contexts. Transnational news organizations provide readers and viewers in the United States and in many other regions with narratives of drones dropping bombs in Pakistan, Yemen, and Afghanistan as part of the argument that this is a "smart" way to wage war, even though we learn that many civilians are being killed in the process. The drone as a "domestic" threat has emerged in the United States as well; one was found hovering over the White House and police have used these to monitor protests and crowds.[4] Yet the power of empire, so lethal for many outside the United States—and for minorities inside it—is also anxious and insecure precisely because the state is not the only sovereign entity that can use drones, since they are in the hands of individuals, corporations, NGOs, and states. Although many writers and scholars imagine the affective power of drones as a global, ubiquitous, and borderless technology, drones also produce insecurity for the empire since they contain the power of technologies and algorithms to create dispersed forms of sovereignty that challenge state and empire.[5] In such a context, the extreme privatization of aeromobility offered by the drone that is being sold globally as a part of consumer culture is both a promise and a threat to imperial power.[6] Imbricated within neoliberal economic processes and rationalities of private and corporate power that are both national and transnational, the power of such aeromobility threatens the sovereignty of the imperial state by breaking down the distinction between empire and postcolony, even as it adds to the securitization of everyday life that extends state power.

To examine the power and anxiety of empire and postcolonial states, I turn to two cultural texts: a short story set in a dystopic India of the future and a play about the contemporary politics of drone warfare within the United States. In bringing these together, I reveal the disparate and transnational effects of empire and capital. I do so to address the cultural imaginaries produced by two different national contexts as they grapple with the drone as both a weapon of war and a tool of a dystopian national-global economic future marked by technoscientific advances and extreme inequality. The short story "Drone" by Hari Kunzru presents a science fiction account of the drone as a metaphor for abjected labor as well as a technology for surveillance and the extraction of profits that enable oligarchic power. *Grounded*, a prize-winning, internationally staged play written by George Brant, focuses on an American female drone operator for whom the remote bombing of children produces anxiety, trauma, and posttraumatic stress disorder, or PTSD. Fears of robotic labor as drones, drone warfare, and surveillance capture both the particularity of American anxieties regarding the recent wars as well as the violence generated by India's contemporary economic policies. Although these texts differ in numerous ways, including in their genre and form, both emerge from U.S. contexts of war, globalization, and technoscientific changes. Both Brant and Kunzru try to capture the intensive political and aesthetic disruptions caused by the advent of drones, which they imagine as the extreme privatization, banalization, and commodification of the new technology of aeromobility. While they focus on different temporalities, one focusing on contemporary wars and the other on a dystopic future, both examine the visuality of the drone as violent and disruptive.

Hari Kunzru, the author of "Drone," is a well-known fiction writer and commentator on postcolonial politics, technology, race, and literature. The author of several highly regarded novels that focus on colonialism, race, identity, technology, and new digital worlds, he has been an editor at *Wired UK* magazine and currently contributes to the online leftist British magazine *Mute*, which takes as its object of analysis the structures and impacts of neoliberalism.[7] Kunzru lives in the United States, though he was born in Great Britain to a South Asian Muslim father and white English mother; he is often compared to Salman Rushdie and Zadie Smith. In interviews and writings, Kunzru speaks of his focus on the new worlds and subjectivities—cyborgian, algorithmic-controlled, and intensely and competitively individualist—being created by the emergence and circulation of new technologies through neoliberal capitalist globalization.[8] His novels and writings reveal the influence of science fiction, science and technology studies, and postcolonial and Marxist theory; Donna Haraway is clearly an influence, as are writers such as William Gibson and Michael Moorcock.

"Drone" captures some of Kunzru's politics of protest against the technologized subjects and regimes that are imbricated in globalized neoliberal capitalism. In novels such as *Transmission*, he focuses on the difference between the cosmopolitan elites who profit from the labor of new technologies and the noncosmopolitan but mobile subordinate classes, seeking to expose the contagion of capital by tracing the lives of those who subvert it.[9] In critiquing what he considers to be an outmoded politics that addresses liberal subjects and a liberal politics that cannot encompass both the migrants of the world and the viruses and contagions of technoscientific change as it is harnessed by capital and postcolony, Kunzru does not disavow history. Rather, he sees sedimented pasts being used and circulated by powerful men to create even greater inequalities across race, class, gender, sexuality, and religion.[10] Postcolonial difference remains important to understand which groups are abjected as labor and which use cultural power to become global oligarchs. The drone is, for Kunzru, an example of visuality being captured by power and violence, and there is no countervisuality that can escape this power.

George Brant's widely acclaimed and frequently staged plays concern social and political issues in the United States.[11] *Grounded* has become one of his most celebrated plays, creating a buzz not only because of its focus on the moral and ethical problems posed by drones and drone warfare but also due to his creation of a strong and powerful female figure as the main character of the play. In an interview, Brant has revealed that the character of the pilot (who is nameless and always referred to as "the Pilot") is based on a report he found about the first female pilot in the Air National Guard, Jackie Parker. In adopting Parker's "fierce independence" for his main character, Brant created a woman who signals her freedom and empowerment through her love of flying F-16 jets.[12] Brant recalls that Parker recounted that she had more in common with male pilots than with women, and his play references this female desire for the imagined fraternal camaraderie of the air force. Pilot is yet another figure in a long line of militant women who have appeared in popular media combining messages of female empowerment, equal rights, and national security. While many of these figures, such as the female protagonists of the television series *Homeland* or the film

Zero Dark Thirty, are shown to be powerful and effective, they are, like Pilot, also represented as anguished and traumatized subjects. Their obvious lack of femininity or proper heterosexuality—indeed, their queerness—is often shown to be tragic yet necessary for national security.[13] Pilot's trajectory highlights the liberal feminist equity discourse that draws in her audience, as does her traumatic relation to her job that is troubled by her maternal feelings.

Both "Drone" and *Grounded* direct their critiques not only at the violence of surveillance and war but also at economic policies—although each of these texts addresses the politics of U.S. empire and India as postcolony in quite different ways. *Grounded* focuses on the inequalities engendered by neoliberal economic arrangements that reduce the job of Pilot to that of a "drone operator." Moreover, the play suggests that even for the empire that deploys them, drones are dangerous; they not only enact surveillance of the enemy but also spy on their own citizens. The technology's visual power is double-edged since the drone monitors bring distant targets into close view even as that view has the ability to traumatize drone operators. In this play, the only innocent victims of drone attacks in distant regions of the Middle East and South Asia must be figured as children since only the very young can be unambiguously designated as innocent noncombatants. Even though accountability for these deaths is presumably dispersed across the drone's military and technology structure, Pilot comes to see herself as responsible. As the play unfolds, her maternal empathy for the children she has killed traumatizes her, and she ends up in military detention.[14]

Hari Kunzru's "Drone" also critiques the emergence of neoliberalism, but with an Indian specificity connected to the neocolonial and nationalist spread of global capitalism. The short story depicts a dystopian future where the immense wealth of a few is figured through one high-caste male oligarch who deploys Hindu nationalism as religion and tradition to capture labor and global capital through participation in the global economy and its designated economic zones that suggest Giorgio Agamben's camp.[15] While it may be tempting to contrast *Grounded* and "Drone" as completely divergent texts, they both critique global capitalism in the context of a neoliberal present. Their aesthetics reflect and engage the constant struggle, protests, and wars that have erupted in many nations and dispersed locations in recent years. At the same time, these texts articulate the violence of techno-scientific advancement in quite different ways. "Drone" eschews a liberal politics for a cyborgian and dystopian future in which neoliberal capitalism's emphasis on the entrepreneurial individual has dissolved ties of community and polity. There is not even liberal empire, since colonial power has been replaced by postcolonial, oligarchic power that uses caste and religion (particularly an authoritarian and homogenous version of Hinduism) as tools of control. The state is subject to such capital, as the market is unregulated and unbounded. A dystopic future is depicted as the result of territorially unbounded capital that creates profits from the "special economic zones" that are essentially labor camps. These zones, as spaces apart, are where the politics of visibility and visuality have been exhausted by the ubiquity of drones. Witnessing has been replaced by viewing and surveilling in a context absent of law and rights. Kunzru turns to a politics of a different sensorium, describing haptic effects that might better capture the violence of state and capital.

While "Drone" suggests liberal subjects are anachronistic to a new technosecurity capitalism, *Grounded* connects the subjects of empire and its targets to produce an American liberal subject. This new kind of subjectivity recognizes that both soldier and victim are traumatized by U.S. empire's lethal military and policing power. Yet this flattening of the violence of empire erases differentials and the arbitrage of global insecurity, resulting in a uniform and homogenized concept of neoliberalism and global war. Both texts, nonetheless, help us to critically understand the ways in which the drone as weapon and commodity has come to articulate emergent fears of a technoscience that has been captured by empire, postcolony, and neoliberal capital.

Grounded: PTSD in the Empire

As many neoliberal ideas have become policy in the United States, and as the imperial wars in the Middle East have drained U.S. resources, the resulting effects at "home" have become visible through inequalities based on gender, class, and race. Movements such as Occupy and Black Lives Matter have made these inequalities visible in public discourse. We have also witnessed a struggle in geopolitical arenas over the image of the United States as a superpower and as an exceptional nation, since the wars that have depleted the U.S. economy have produced inequalities similar to many other (even non-Western) nations across the globe. While the United States continues to assert global superiority in geopolitics, global financial markets, militarization at home, and wars abroad, there are still concerns about the waning of American power from the Cold War period.[16] It is not so much that the United States is no longer powerful militarily, since it has the lethal weaponry and the ability to kill or to allow the killing of many in distant regions, but its logic of insecurity and fear has come to pervade the culture of its empire, proposing it is less powerful than in the past. Not surprisingly, this insecurity is also now a project of transnational capital that both contributes to and benefits from precarity and surveillance.

Grounded captures the anxieties of this waning empire in a number of ways, from the bleak landscape of the Nevada location where the U.S. military's drone program is featured to the breakdown of Pilot, whose tedious exertions at the screen are seen as traumatizing. A staging of the play in 2015 in New York City starring Anne Hathaway and directed by Julie Taymor (who has had many successes on Broadway), though presented at the very small theater The Public, was a hit, with a sold-out house for most of the shows (echoing its success in many other theaters where it was previously staged). Audiences at The Public responded to the one-woman play with admiration for Hathaway's performance and for the effective staging and directing.

In the play, Hathaway's character, called simply "the Pilot," is a nameless woman who aspires to be a Top Gun–type air force pilot who revels in flying F-16s in what she calls the "blue." She has to become a drone operator once she becomes pregnant, is no longer allowed to pilot fighter planes, and needs a job. With her husband and child she moves to Nevada, where she is charged with monitoring and bombing so-called terrorists in Pakistan and Afghanistan. The constant attentiveness demanded for the job—and we are told she has to be working long hours at the screen every day—begins to cause her to unravel psychologically. The discrimination against a woman pilot demoted to remote drone operation is foregrounded as Pilot expresses her frustration and anger that she cannot remain flying in the sky—in the "blue." This loss renders her immobile and grounded. Because she has to carry out close surveillance for many hours each day of people in distant regions imagined as targets, she comes to believe someone is watching her everywhere and that there are cameras all around her. Even while shopping at the local mall with her child, she becomes concerned about surveillance: "But there's always a camera, right? / J.C. Penney or Afghanistan / Everything is witnessed."[17] She imagines those watching her to be like the nineteen-year-old (males, presumably) she works with or workers in India to whom surveillance has been outsourced; her disintegration is compounded by the thought of being watched by foreign brown men just as she has watched them through her monitor. As the play closes, she tells the audience that they are all being watched too, thus drawing her audience into both her psychic breakdown and the realization of the violence of this regime of war.

The play suggests that it is not family or husband that "ground" her; it is the U.S. military that is responsible for her situation. The tedium of commuting to and from work through a bleak desert, along with the long hours of looking at the screen, contrast intensely with the life of a pilot flying a fighter jet. As the character realizes that she has lost the excitement, pleasure, and sociality in being with other pilots, she loses her ambition and desire to work. Her achievement in becoming an air force pilot, the result of "sweat and brains and guts," signified by her flight suit, allowed her the thrill and empowerment of control of the "blue" sky:

> I'm in the blue for a reason
> I have missiles to launch
> I have Sidewinders
> I have Mavericks
>
> I rain them down on the minarets and concrete below me
> The structures that break up the sand
> I break them back down
> Return them to desert
>
> To particles
> Sand
>
> At least I think I do
> I'm long gone by the time the boom happens.[18]

The play suggests that it is not simply the thrill of flight that is exciting to Pilot but also her ability to rain down destruction from an F-16, especially in a Muslim country ("on the minarets"), without staying to see the destructive impact and deaths she causes on the ground.

While the play focuses on the trauma of viewing the results of "unmanned" missile attacks close up on the screen, the narrative moves too quickly over the violence of "manned" air attacks. While the monologue does mention the destruction caused by airpower, these violent acts of aerial bombing become imbued with Pilot's nostalgia for the joy and pleasure of flying. What further unhinges Pilot—"unmanning" her in a gendered sense because she no longer works among male pilots in the air force—is that she is presumably able to see the impact of the bombs more clearly than she might have from a fighter jet or a piloted bombing run. Once she sees that one of the missiles she releases has killed a child, she has a nervous breakdown. In this key moment, the play asks us to critique the use of drones as a weapon of war. At the same time, however, we come to realize the power of drone technology and its visual capabilities. Military technology's success, paradoxically, is that it can seemingly make us look more closely at the violence in which we share responsibility.

Many analysts of visual culture have critiqued the idea that only proximity will bring about empathy and identification with the victims and the targets of drone attacks.[19] Some scholars of visual culture also have argued for the particularity of "drone vision" as an emergent and important aspect of militarization of everyday life.[20] While the play suggests that remote vision, or what Caren Kaplan has called "remote sensing,"[21] does not simply distance us from the violence of war, it also signals that distance and proximity matter for visual politics. If drone vision creates proximity to the violence it causes, aerial war allows separation from the carnage: Pilot in her military aircraft can be "long gone by the time the boom happens."

Not only are distance or proximity foregrounded by drone warfare but also the greater capacities of the screen, cameras, and the hardware and software that traumatize those viewing the monitors. While suggesting that the military's technological and intelligence failure to distinguish between child and terrorist is responsible for Pilot's traumatic breakdown, it is also Pilot's ability to see the missile strike the child, a sight compounded by her maternal feelings, that is to blame. Yet such a logic of technologically proximate visibility—both triumphant and tragic—ignores the deaths of civilians and the foundational assumptions of contemporary wars in the Middle East and South Asia through which all Muslims have come to be seen as threatening.[22]

As much as the play suggests that it is the viewing of harm to the child that undoes the imperial subject, war's spectacle has other effects. As Thomas Blom Hansen and Finn Stepputat argue, empire has to stage spectacles of violence, and the effective spectacle of violence on itself makes its sovereignty even more powerful.[23] Pilot's breakdown marks the power of empire over its subjects. Empire's move between spectacular and hidden violence is visible through its traumatic effect on the white, female, and American body of the drone operator.

Elise Morrison suggests that the staging of the play positions its audience as surveilling the action while also learning to be empathetic to the effects of such surveillance and bombing.[24] In this reading, empathy and humanity are the universals of the play, shared by Pilot and extended to Pakistani, Yemeni, and Afghan children. However, this moral logic remains a limited critique because empathy can only be directed at particular subjects, such as children, rather than adults who may not elicit similar empathy or presumptions of innocence.[25]

The play's staging at The Public also suggested more than simply the production of empathy. The minimal stage, with only sand on the ground, the action occurring below and in the center of the circle of rows of seats, enable the action to focus on the breakdown of Pilot rather than the violence that Pilot has both seen and rained down on targets far away. The play's directions state that "the audience is The Pilot's confidante, to varying degrees of familiarity, until perhaps the final pages." Julie Taymor, the director at The Public, interpreted the audience as both confidante and witness for Pilot. Seated in a circle around her, the audience becomes protector and witness as they watch her disintegration. To the extent that some of the activism against the use of drones for bombing has come from charging the United States with human rights abuses and extrajudicial killings of its own citizens and of distant Others, the play's moral trajectory emphasizes the power of witnessing and visuality. Yet if the audience is both witness and court of justice, the spectators come to understand the violence of U.S. war through its effect on a figure who shares some responsibility for that violence. The play asks that only the distant child and Pilot be mourned.[26] In this way, the play enacts the limits of visibility that have become part of militarized vision in the United States, allowing us to see only certain kinds of violence on specific bodies, and to mourn only that which can be seen; in this case, the violence is perpetrated on the drone operator rather than on those being bombed in South Asia and the Middle East. This is the limited vision of the technopolitics of violence of drone warfare.

Thus, even as some of the violence of drone warfare is made visible, so much remains hidden. Drone missiles often kill within buildings, and their effects remain secret. It is only in sporadic cases that we hear about the effects of bombings. Because the regions where such drones operate are what Eyal Weizman calls "frontier" zones where researchers and reporters often cannot enter, it might be reasonable to believe that Pilot is the best witness to the deaths caused by drone war. Yet such witnessing limits empathy while it distributes blame. Weizman has argued that drone warfare, like many other forms of contemporary war, requires witnessing and accountability that have to come from a shift from testimony to "forensics."[27] This term designates both the use of technology to uncover the harm of military technologies and the "forum" that reveals evidence of violence via the use of digital technology. The art of the forum, according to Weizman, needs a triangulation of testimony between technology (satellite, digital architecture, and remapping) that uncovers the destruction, the human witness who has suffered the violence and who comes from the targeted regions, and the expert or translator who can bring these narratives together to reveal the complex causality of war. If one follows Weizman to analyze *Grounded,* neither Pilot as witness nor the audience as the court of justice who sees only the trauma of Pilot can adequately testify to either the visible or the hidden and extensive violence of military drones. The play does not reveal the pervasive and unseen violence of drone wars or the multiple ways that technoscience and the imperial state formulate its human and nonhuman targets and weapons. It cannot, crucially, reveal why some regions can be subject to drone attacks. As Jacob Burns argues, it is the long history of colonial law in South Asia through which such "frontier" and tribal zones are produced as places where sovereignty is left as a "politically productive zone of exception."[28] The history of colonial and nationalist powers that created these "frontier" zones suggests that designations of targets, subjectivity, and sovereignty are palimpsestic, while their designation is designed to defeat both distant and proximate seeing.

In addition, as so much of recent war involves "boots on the ground," from both U.S. military and private security companies who have killed civilians and others with impunity, the play is unable to move beyond a liberal critique of war to examine the imbrication between and co-construction of war machines, capitalism, and imperial histories. That the drone is imagined as a new technology that creates new fears for humans and humanity means that every iteration of its technological power and novelty can disguise the longue durée of technologized war and its lethal consequences as well as the multiple means—legal, geopolitical, economic—through which new technologies and their targets come into existence.

Pilot's nostalgia for manned, aerial war serves to make that earlier form of warfare more human, less distancing, and more intimate, evoking the nostalgia for lost community—gendered as a fraternity—that seems to accompany each new technology. The humanity of manned warfare is conveyed through

Pilot's memories of the fraternal camaraderie between military pilots flying planes in war and her desire to recapture the thrill of flying F-16s. In this way, the play erases the violence of a history of empire and aerial bombardment.[29] Its reliance on empathy as the powerful ethic to resist new wars remains limited by a refusal to address any difference between the history of empire and its historical targets, even as it cannot but exhibit the power of imperial war and violence. Human witnessing and human embodiment by Americans become the play's tools for resistance. The power and limit of this embodied witnessing emerges via the white body of Pilot, who is brought down by the empire for whom she has become an insignificant, easily replaceable operative. Here, even the impact of neoliberal politics remains confined to an American subject, rather than to its broader, global effects.

There is little doubt that *Grounded* was inspired by reports that drone operators were found to be suffering from PTSD.[30] Peter Asaro has examined drone operators as new subjectivities constructed through surveillance and remote agency combined with post-Fordist labor practices that distribute agency and responsibility across technology and its multiple producers and consumers. Reports and research have shown that the stress, long hours, and horrors of war seen "close-up," in tandem with the scorn with which drone operators are treated by others in the air force, have contributed to considerable turnover. The play also draws on news reports on gender equity issues in the military as the protagonist sees herself demeaned by being relegated, because of her pregnancy, from the position of jet pilot to what she calls the "Chairforce." The issue of gendered equality and discrimination is then factored into neoliberal working conditions and the realization of pervasive surveillance that leads to her traumatic breakdown. In addition, because she is a mother of a little girl, the killing of a child by a missile from the drone in a remote location is shown to be even more affecting. Finally, it is only Pilot's traumatized self who can warn the audience of the ubiquitous surveillance that surrounds us, thereby aligning, quite problematically, this surveillance of an American audience with those who live in the particular areas that are considered available for bombardment and who endure the constant hum and shadow of death by drones in the "frontier" zones of South Asia and the Middle East.

"Drone": Labor and Oligarchs in the Postcolony

If *Grounded* produces a critique of drone war and surveillance by revealing the harm these technologies cause to an American white woman in the military, Hari Kunzru's "Drone" takes us to a dystopic future set somewhere in South Asia in a "special economic zone," where drones carry out surveillance over labor camps that enrich wealthy oligarchs. If the global economy can be critiqued for the inequality that it produces, and the ways that neoliberal capitalism has empowered corporate and oligarchic sovereignties that have undermined the state, including U.S. empire, "Drone" pushes this critique further. It does so by suggesting that neoliberalism's future is the production of hypercompetitive individuals that include both oligarch and various classes of workers. Postcolonial nationalism has disappeared, replaced by oligarchic power. In this context, the oligarch can be both global and postcolonial, Hindu and Indian. This is a postliberal dystopia where witnessing seems redundant because there is no legal redress or remedy to exploitation. In the locale of Kunzru's story, colonial, national, and international law have designated some regions as zones without laws or government, giving them over to unregulated capital. Thus, drones operate outside community; anyone who can afford a drone can use it to look anywhere, but looking is not about witnessing. Drones are operated by so many heterogeneous entities that neither spectacle nor its counter is able to produce either justice or empathy. If the narrator shows us that the witnessing gaze is disinterested, what emerges is a different kind of political understanding: one that must be more broadly sensorial, both haptic and sonic. It is only by descriptions of the sensoria of the "special economic zone," which is the mining camp, that one can know the postcolony's banal necropolitics. But even that knowing is without a goal, without any futurity. Such a failure of sight, then, and the excess of the sensorium mark the divergent aesthetics of the postcolony's drone economy.

In Kunzru's text, Indian nationalism has disappeared to be replaced by a Hindu nationalism that is subservient to capital. Inequalities flourish, depending on primitive accumulation from histories of race, caste, and class. In the story, postcolonial elites are both cyborg and genetically enhanced to be as superior as possible, their bodies inscribed with Hindu caste and religious hierarchies and symbols. The oligarch controls all natural resources, ensuring that whatever is "natural" or "pure" is kept for the enjoyment and use of a select few. All others compete with each other at various levels of the economy. While all the bodies in this story are either genetically engineered or cyborgs, only the oligarch claims humanness, perfecting himself to be as handsome as the local ideal of masculinity might imagine. While Kunzru offers neoliberal empire as global and postcolonial, differences based on caste and religion are important because they are used to produce power and to exploit. Yet Kunzru does not offer a project of reclaiming humanity in the name of universals, nor is his story a project of cultural or civilizational difference. In "Drone," postcolonial elites rule by controlling capital and culture on national and global scales. There is no possibility of being external to this power, and no depiction of anything outside the dystopia of the economic zones.

The use of security forces to protect the expansion of capital has become an important aspect of contemporary Indian neoliberalism. It is well known by now that the Indian state has recently been buying drones for military use from Israel and is also developing its own drones, but little attention has been paid to this program in the Indian news media (much of which is also under corporate control). The digital economy has received much greater attention in the news, as its development and growth continue to be most important for politicians, businesspeople, and journalists. Neoliberal economic policies have become powerful due to the importance given to the private and corporate sectors as engines of development,[31] even though there is some continued emphasis on distribution of resources and welfare. This focus on economic growth means that corporations are seen as corrupt only if they collude with politicians or the state to amass wealth. With the rise of Hindu nationalism and the coming to power of Narendra Modi as prime minister with a history of pogroms against Muslims, there is continued disenfranchisement of religious minorities, Dalits, and the poor through neoliberal privatization on multiple scales. Modi's political party, the Bharatiya Janata Party, has continued the policy of the previous administration of appropriating the lands of indigenous peoples for mining corporations. Its goal is to control knowledge production through disenfranchising religious minorities. Tools of biometric identification are being sold as essential to development and poverty reduction, giving rise to fears among minorities, indigenous groups, and Dalits that new forms of upper-caste control are emerging. Given such conditions, it is not surprising that Kunzru's short story suggests that economic globalization has produced oligarchs who rely on right-wing Hindu nationalism to control economy and state, further disenfranchising labor.

By locating his short story in a postcolony and in a "camp" that is a "special economic zone" where rare minerals for the new economies are mined, Kunzru's story takes us to another space of exception than that in *Grounded*, but it is one that cannot be targeted by bombing because its condition of entropy enables exploitation. This entropy makes it possible for necropolitics to flourish. In Kunzru's story, the capitalist is called "the Seth" (a term that translates as "merchant," "banker," or "trader"), who is also a high-caste Hindu. Seth lives in an apartment building that towers over the slums below. Here "tower" is a reference to the house built by one of the richest men in contemporary India, the Mumbai-based billionaire Mukesh Ambani. Ambani's house, Antilia, is a twenty-seven-story building with helipads, floating gardens, and swimming pools built at the reported cost of a billion dollars, and it towers over other apartment buildings and the slums of Mumbai. Kunzru incorporates this building into his story with an additional fictional twist: the owner has also purchased the air rights around it so that nothing can intrude on his privacy. While Seth initially designed the tower as a Tuscan fantasy, he has turned it into a "Hindu" version in order to be seen as a true patriot and to use religion to control the state and the population.

As the story begins, there are crowds at the temple in the courtyard of the tower. Men claiming to be gurus (popularly known as "godmen" in India), priests of "every orthodox sect," rub shoulders with businessmen and bureaucrats. All those present are high-caste men, all genetically augmented with legally mandated religious and caste marks on their bodies; these marks are not just inscribed but have become genetically incorporated into the bodies themselves. Since every person with money can be modified to become attractive, these men are all "generically handsome." They all look up to the oligarch with slavish attention, aspiring to become oligarchs themselves. As this large group gathers to participate in a religious ceremony in the courtyard, the police chief monitors the crowds below him while the state bureaucrats "inhale the scent of burning sandalwood, their noses twitching with jealousy and awe" (17).[32] The sandalwood is not a virtual or genetically modified product but comes from the last groves of the trees existing in the world, which are owned by Seth, who "controls everything from raw materials to staggeringly abstract forms of intellectual property" (17). Seth is part of a system that seems to be so powerful that it appears immune to resistance. Thus, the narrator says of Seth: "So entangled is he in the global economy that it is impossible to imagine how he could be excised" (17).

The inequality of this economy is conveyed through the narrator's emphasis on jostling bodies, their proximity to power, and the smell of sandalwood that evokes pleasures and desires that are unattainable for many in this world. Seth and his cronies designate this exploitative and unequal context as "Ramrajya," the mythical kingdom of God defined in the epic Ramayana as the most ethical state.

Unlike everyone else, however, Seth is an ascetic, and he is kept in that state by vast sums of money. The narrator compares him to Mahatma Gandhi in this regard, linking anticolonial nationalism's cultural politics to their more recent capture by capital. Seth eats only the freshest food, the most natural, nonsynthetic products, and the last wild animals and fishes left on earth. He relies on what are called "Vedic" principles to structure his life and work. In this, the narrator references Indian prime minister Narendra Modi and the Hindu nationalists who are now claiming to run the government and to conduct science on neo-Vedic principles, constructing a theology of profit-making and exploitation. The narrator tells us that even Seth's seventh wife is "headhunted from an isolated rural community" and becomes a "vessel" after "compliance with stringent genetic and astrological tests" (18). In this story, the combination of oligarchic masculinity and control over women, decontextualized theology and science, and invented tradition is deliberately staged as the source of the oligarch's wealth and power. Seth's daughter from this wife is similarly eugenically designed since the "biological matter that makes up her body has flowed in from the purest sources" (18). She is designed to be beautiful and trained to be obedient, since Seth is "molding a family aesthetic, a brand that can be passed on," an aesthetic that is both visual and material (19). She lives with constant surveillance and monitoring, with care offered by the "warm nebulous presence" of an entity that is both servant and dog that "exists in her sensorium as a repertoire of gestures, a nuzzling, a pleading, the scrabble of tiny paws on her skin" (19).

Despite his power, however, Seth is worried that his daughter, whom he surveils obsessively by watching her every move, seems to be interested in something outside his house. His surveillance mechanisms show that she is spending time, via a drone, in the networks of one of his mining companies. What Seth's daughter looks at is the benighted landscape of a mine, one of the last ones in the world where rare minerals are to be found, and she is taking an interest in Jai, one of the miners. This is a "special economic zone," which is "in a state of continual, undeclared war, the war of each against each" (23). It is designated to be outside any government or rule of law, and it exemplifies the kind of location where Seth is able to extract profits. The zone is called a "camp," and it is a location where bodies, all "blue-black" (21) and thus racially differentiated from anyone outside the camp, are constantly mutating, created by jumbled-up "organic and inorganic" fragments that rise up and disappear (22). "Teeming, swarming," the camp is a "mess of sensory fragments," where poor miners "know what it means to be exhausted, to lie down at the top of the pit, gasping through their masks"; they know "the feel of mud cakes on skin," and the mud waits for their bodies when they die (22). Those in power wear hazmat suits and have ventilators to protect themselves from the mud.

In this camp, the miners labor endlessly while "drones and chakras" enforce their labor. Chakras, based on Hindu and Buddhist religious concepts, are rotating wheels that reference the energy swirling in bodies. Along with drones, chakras enact surveillance on the miners. The numerous chakras are everywhere, producing a constant hum, a sonic reverberation that never ceases. "After a storm," we learn, "the ground is crunchy underfoot with little electronic corpses" (23). The miners are all seen as a security risk and "must participate in network identification and trust protocols to demonstrate they are not a threat" (23). They take the "precious dust" they have mined to dealers who are women—"fat and glossy"—working for governments or "any of the dozen other factions that depend on mining revenue to continue their obscure insurgencies" (23). The division of labor here positions miners as far more subject to necropolitical power than the women dealers who work behind shields that protect them from the miners and the noxious air of the camp.

Within the camp, there are other zones that are even more highly entropic. One of these is the "red-light district known as the Cages" (27), where the miners can go for sexual gratification. Here, the "process" offers "every type and quality of peak, dip, spread and intensification" (27). The narrator tells us that "whores" are "grafted onto walls [that] display available orifices or scroll out stims that grab the crotch"; there is a confusion of "tacky skins and feelies" (27). When one of the miners, Jai, ventures into this zone, semen "spatters the optics of his sensorium," and he is "brushed by nipples, hair, lubricated hands" (27). Women disappeared even as sex workers; only female body parts and genitals remain. Necropolitics produces the abject male as labor and fragments women into sexual fragments or figures who profit from their place on the border of the economic zone. Only the haptic captures the abjection of labor; the miners, we are told by the narrator, "want the hard stuff" (27).

The only other female figure in "Drone" is Seth's daughter, who is seemingly outside the power of capital while being created by it. She watches Jai, a nineteen-year-old "human, a man," described as "beautiful" with "blue-black skin" and a "high strong voice" (25).[33] He is alone, "part of no tribe or community that he can remember," and finds "unremarkable" the horrors he has seen in his short life. Unlike the other miners, he is not covered with mud and dust, and wherever he moves, he is accompanied by "tiny drones and flyers" (25). Yet is it not clear who sends these machines, and the other miners wonder at the swarm of drones around Jai. The drones are described as "low grade personal devices" that "come from far away, carried on the wind" (25). These devices also see and feel, because they have "optics and sometimes haptics, but there may not be anyone watching or feeling." Every person, we learn, knows that they are being watched, if not by humans then by "some algorithm trained to sift through the feeds for porn or lulz or evidence of crime" (25). Drones are owned by numerous people and groups who send them to watch anyone they wish, so that "privacy is a quaint word, like chivalry, or superego" (26). People all over the world send these drones to look at things: "Go find something to look at. Not that, this. Not this, that. Floating about on solar-cell gossamer. Some are directed, others almost completely autonomous, trained to go in search of a particular kink of flavor. The famous put up security; otherwise they'd live in a swarm of angry voyeuristic bees" (25).

In this story, drones are manifestations of hyperindividualization and hypersurveillance; anyone can surveil anyone if they can purchase a drone. As well as surveilling, they offer commodities and services for purchase. But none of these drones surveil the mine in order to help the miners. No drone appears to protect Jai or any of the other miners from their miserable lives, and there is no other authority or power to turn to in this special economic zone. Jai dies after he buys a robotic arm; it is supposed to help him work better in the mine, but it infects him. Seriously ill, he has no money to take advantage of the numerous offers from the buzzing drones to protect him from the viruses that are replicating in his body. As he dies, offers come to him for his organs: "Offers run right through him, subprime bids for his organs, corporate indentures. Your fatal condition cured in return for ten years' labour: new life just a click away" (30). He cannot take the offers and is too weak to do anything but die at the door of his hut, as the drones watch: "Overhead the plume swarms and wheels, eyes trained down on him" (31).

While Seth's daughter has sent her drone to look at Jai, and perhaps she is the agent for the drone buzzing over Jai at the end, she does not come to his rescue. Although she makes Seth worried and anxious about her desires, she cannot reduce the entropy in the Cages. She is, however, a female cyborg who desires something else. What to make of her remains unclear; it seems that postliberal and postcolonial politics have unclear and heterosexual desires, although their rupture is promising. The narrator cannot tell us what she wants or why she looks at Jai. Her desires, in effect, defeat the narrator's ability to survey the scene.

In Kunzru's short story, the drone is both the embodiment of human labor available for expropriation and a technology produced by economic regimes that have come to reduce everyone to a competitive individualism. While the oligarch ruthlessly extracts and uses resources for himself, state bureaucrats, priests and godmen, dealers, and traders all compete against each other by becoming various types of cyborgs. Even workers work obsessively to improve their productivity. No collaborations are possible that may resist this structure; the power of sight does not produce community. The drones are commodities, deployed by numerous nameless and unknown people and machines; these drones fly and buzz around looking around for pleasure or for surveillance. Visuality has lost the ability to shock or elicit emotion. There are so many drones that privacy has become "a quaint word," an "evolutionary relic, a kink that is being ironed out by the forces of order" (26). There are no futures possible, as is the case with most dystopias, only extraction, exploitation, surveillance, and death allied to a hyperindividualized culture of both unbounded and deterritorialized capitalism that instrumentalizes Hindu nationalism for profit. In this text, drones are not there to kill as they are in *Grounded*, nor are they assigned to an agency separate from that of the cyborg whose commands they carry out. They are simply instruments of various desires and powers, many violent and many who just want to look, though their looking does not help reduce the violence. While nameless and countless consumers use drones to look at others without offering connection or community, the capitalists use them for control over the camp.

Conclusion

In these texts, as the latest avatars of technoscientific progress allied to neoliberal capital and militarized empire, drones evoke insecurity and exploitation. Whereas *Grounded* blames the state and the empire for this exploitation precisely because its violence has now "come home" to the empire, "Drone" sees the state and the empire at the service of capital that is in the hands of postcolonial oligarchs and cannot offer any visual counterpolitics. If, at the end of *Grounded*, Pilot exhorts the audience in the empire to remember that they are all being surveilled, in order to produce a politics of resistance to empire through visual witnessing and recognition of the insecurity produced within it, the postcolonial dystopia in "Drone" provides no such possibility. There is no emergent force of resistance by the cyborg,[34] and resistance is foreclosed because individuals, as securitized and militarized consumers, are no longer capable of being in community, nor can they defeat the powers of capital. Although there are ruptures to this power from unexpected entities, their direction and intent remain unclear.

By collapsing the meaning of drone as abjected labor and military and consumer technology, Kunzru's postcolonial critique, then, turns to production and labor in those economic zones to understand the effects of unregulated global capital as a totalizing power. If visuality produces no recourse from violence, and individual use of drones cannot be witness to violence, descriptions of the haptic also continue to reveal immiseration without any possibility of ending it. While visuality is clearly unable to turn to witnessing, the haptic dwells in the violence of abjection in the postcolony. While the haptic does more than the visual, its goals are not about rights or solidarity or interruptions to dystopia. Postcolonial politics then concerns more than that which can be seen, since it is the scale of the widespread and dispersed violence of empire, capital, and postcolony that cannot be captured by the visual. Even as researchers such as Eyal Weizman produce visual evidence as central to claims made at the United Nations, or at other national and international courts, or even in transnational news media or social media, the fate and uses of such evidence are limited to particular cases rather than the broader structural violence of contemporary capitalism and imperialism. We know that while the U.S. government has provided small sums as reparation for civilian deaths in Pakistan and Afghanistan, and that such sums can help in individual and limited cases, minimal reparation has not stopped the war, the bombing, or the destruction of ways of living.[35] Given the massive outpouring of images from all sorts of entities and all kinds of groups, as well as the control of media by transnational corporations, there are limits to what sort of images can be seen, stored or circulated, or used for reparation or redress. If international law designates spaces of expropriation as outside law, then the history of looking is of limited use. For critical media activists such as Kunzru, the new modes of exploitation and violence are to be understood by other sensorial means, such as touch. Yet even as Kunzru's critique gestures to the widespread violence and the unnamed numbers who suffer it, it is unable to grasp as the many ruptures, resistances, and movements that disrupt power and its effects. As much as visuality cannot grasp the extent of violence, Kunzru's postcolonial politics, confined to its dystopic sensorium, cannot capture how the violence is lived in complex, heterogenous ways that are not only necropolitical.

Postcolonial theorists have come to see the politics of representation as limited in its remit. While scholars debate the Anthropocene as demanding a new politics that is both planetary and regionally and locally accountable,[36] they turn to the many protests and migrations of the new century as evidence of the failure of nationalism's cultures to control the excesses of capital and the inability of either humanism or capitalist democracy to change the inequalities and hierarchies of the emergent order. Yet postcolonial politics still offers compelling approaches to understand these inequalities within historical and emergent cultures in the Global South, the logics of hierarchy and difference based on articulations and intersections of caste, race, gender, nation, and religion that enable accumulation by dispossession.

Notes

I dedicate this essay to my late colleague Mark Poster. Mark's research inaugurated a whole new field of historical cultural theory on digital media, and his work has long been a great inspiration for many, especially in paying attention to the complexities of technology and the history of the relation between technology and culture. He read Kunzru's work long before I did and gave me his copy of Kunzru's first novel. I am indebted to him for many kindnesses and comradeship. My thanks also go to Laura Wexler, my good friend and colleague, who found the *Granta* issue and, purchased it for me, the Theory and Media Studies Colloquium in the Yale Department of English, especially to Julia Chan for her comments on this chapter that came from her brilliant research on dystopic fiction, and to Peter Raccuglia and Anna Shechtman for inviting me to share this work. I also thank Caren Kaplan and Lisa Parks for their patience, encouragement, and excellent comments.

1. Benjamin, *Drone Warfare.*
2. Naylor, "Look, Up in the Sky!"
3. Evangelista and Shue, *The American Way of Bombing.*
4. Schmidt, "Secret Service Arrests Man"; Sengupta, "Rise of Drones in U.S."
5. Hansen and Stepputat, *Sovereign Bodies*; Brown, "American Nightmare."
6. Drone Tech Report, "News and Product Reviews of Personal Drones and UAVs," http://www.dronetechreport.com.
7. Kunzru, *Transmission*; Kunzru, *The Impressionist*; Kunzru, *Memory Palace*; Kunzru, *Gods without Men*; Kunzru, *My Revolutions: A Novel*; see also the website for *Mute*, www.metamute.org.
8. Haiven, "An Interview with Hari Kunzru."
9. Leonard, "'A Revolution in Code'?"
10. Haiven, "An Interview with Hari Kunzru."
11. A full list of George Brant's plays and their staging appears on his website, http://www.georgebrant.net/plays.html.
12. Simakis, "Writer George Brant."
13. For an extended discussion of these figures in popular culture, see my forthcoming book *Saving the Security State: Exceptional Citizens in Twenty-First Century America*, Duke University Press, 2017.
14. For more on the relationship between war and medicine, see Terry, "Significant Injury" and *Attachments to war.*
15. Agamben, *Homo Sacer.*
16. Nye, "The Future of American Power"; Wallerstein, *The Decline of American Power.*
17. Brant, *Grounded*, 47.
18. Brant, *Grounded*, 9–10.
19. Boltanski, *Distant Suffering*; Mirzoeff, *Watching Babylon.*
20. Stahl, "What the Drone Saw."
21. Kaplan, "Sensing Distance."
22. Rana, *Terrifying Muslims*; Razack, *Casting Out*; McAlister, *Epic Encounters.*
23. Hansen and Stepputat, introduction to *Sovereign Bodies.*
24. Morrison, "Ambushed by Empathy."
25. From scholarly studies of emotion and affect, we know that empathy is a historical project that has now become intricately configured into new, more "realistic" digital games in order to produce particular affects. As video game cultures are imbricated in military projects, and because games elicit feelings that are part of game design, who or what can elicit empathy is also a question of the power of militarized image-making. The production of affect from the visual is both critique and mastery of a technology that shared much with the culture of virtual games; Moore, "Invigorating Play."
26. Butler, *Precarious Life.*
27. Weizman, *Forensic Architecture.*
28. Burns, "Persistent Exception," 400.
29. Kaplan, Loyer, and Daniels, "Precision Targets."

30. Chappelle, Salinas, and McDonald, "Psychological Health Screening"; Bumiller, "Air Force Drone Operators"; R. Martin, "Report"; Trimble, "Study"; Kaag, "Drones, Ethics and the Armchair Soldier"; Gettinger, "Burdens of War."
31. Shah, *In the Shadows of the State.*
32. All parenthetical page numbers refer to Kunzru, "Drone."
33. *Jai* is a diasporic and popular name—easily pronounced globally. It translates into victory and is thus ironic because the dystopia does not allow any victory for workers like Jai.
34. Haraway, "A Cyborg Manifesto."
35. Bashir and Crews, introduction to *Under the Drones*, 7. The editors mention that, in 2010, the U.S. government paid about $2,900 each to those wounded and $4,800 each to families of those killed.
36. See, for instance, Chakrabarty, "The Climate of History."

BIBLIOGRAPHY

Abbas, Hassan. "Transforming Pakistan's Frontier Corps." *Terrorism Monitor* 5, no. 6 (2007). https:jamestown.org/program/transforming-pakistans-frontier-corps/.

Abé, Nicola. "Dreams in Infrared: The Woes of an American Drone Operator." *Spiegel Online*, December 14, 2012. http://www.spiegel.de/international/world/pain-continues-after-war-for-american-drone-pilot-a-872726.html.

Abramson, Albert. *Zworykin, Pioneer of Television*. Champaign: University of Illinois Press, 1995.

Ackerman, Spencer. "Airstrike in Yemen Kills 15 Wedding Guests Mistaken for al-Qaeda." *Guardian*, December 13, 2013.

———. "41 Men Targeted but 1,147 People Killed: US Drone Strikes—The Facts on the Ground." *Guardian*, November 24, 2014.

———. "Only Three of 116 Guantánamo Detainees Were Captured by US Forces." *Guardian*, August 25, 2015.

———. "US Cited Controversial Law in Decision to Kill American Citizen by Drone." *Guardian*, June 23, 2014.

"Africa: Djibouti." Internet World Stats, 2016. http://www.internetworldstats.com/africa.htm#dj.

Afridi, Said Nazir. "In Memoriam: The Bara 15." *Pak Tea House*, January 20, 2013. http://pakteahouse.net/2013/01/20/in-memorium-the-bara-15/.

afrol News. "Djibouti Opposition Boycotts Election." *afrol News*, March 11, 2011. http://afrol.com/articles/37560.

———. "Mass Protests Shake Djibouti." *afrol News*, February 26, 2011. http://afrol.com/articles/38194.

Agamben, Giorgio. *Homo Sacer: Sovereign Power and Bare Life*. Translated by Daniel Heller-Roazen. Stanford, CA: Stanford University Press, 1998.

———. *Remnants of Auschwitz: The Witness and the Archive*. Translated by Daniel Heller-Roazen. New York: Zone Books, 1999.

———. *State of Exception*. Translated by Kevin Attell. Chicago: University of Chicago Press, 2005.

Ahmad, Naveed. "The Laws and Justice System in FATA with Recommendations for Reformations." LLM diss., University of South Asia, 2008.

Ahmed, Manan [Sepoy]. "Waziristan, U.S." *Chapati Mystery* (blog), April 16, 2014. http://www.chapatimystery.com/archives/homistan/waziristan_us.html.

Akulov, Andrei. “Asia Pivot Declared, US Army Eyes Africa.” *Global Research*, November 21, 2013. http://www.globalresearch.ca/asia-pivot-declared-us-army-eyes-africa/5358964.

Ali, Kamran Asdar. “Communists in a Muslim Land: Cultural Debates in Pakistan’s Early Years.” *Modern Asian Studies* 45, no. 3 (2011): 501–34.

Ali, Shaheen Sardar, and Javaid Rehman. *Indigenous Peoples and Ethnic Minorities of Pakistan: Constitutional and Legal Perspectives*. Richmond, Surrey: Curzon, 2001.

Ali, Tariq. “The Colour Khaki.” *New Left Review* 19 (January–February 2003): 5–28.

Allbritton, Chris. “Pakistan Helps U.S. Drone Campaign.” *Reuters*, January 22, 2012.

Alston, Philip. “The CIA and Targeted Killings beyond Borders.” *Harvard National Security Journal* 2 (2011): 283–446.

———. “Report of the Special Rapporteur on Extrajudicial, Summary or Arbitrary Executions: Study on Targeted Killings.” Submitted to the UN Human Rights Council, May 28, 2010. http://www2.ohchr.org/english/bodies/hrcouncil/docs/14session/A.HRC.14.24.Add6.pdf.

Alwazir, Atiaf. “US War on Yemen: Invisible Casualties.” *Al-Akhbar,* August 20, 2012.

Amar, Paul. *The Security Archipelago: Human-Security States, Sexuality Politics, and the End of Neoliberalism*. Durham, NC: Duke University Press, 2013.

“AMEMSA Fact Sheet.” *Asian Americans/Pacific Islanders in Philanthropy*, November 2011. http://aapip.org/files/incubation/files/amemsa20fact20sheet.pdf.

American Civil Liberties Union. “Al-Aulaqi v. Panetta—Constitutional Challenge to Killing of Three U.S. Citizens.” June 4, 2014. https://www.aclu.org/cases/al-aulaqi-v-panetta-constitutional-challenge-killing-three-us-citizens.

Amnesty International. *“As If Hell Fell on Me”: The Human Rights Crisis in Northwest Pakistan*. London: Amnesty International, 2010.

———. *“The Hands of Cruelty”: Abuses by Armed Forces and Taliban in Pakistan’s Tribal Areas*. London: Amnesty International, 2012.

———. *“Will I Be Next?”: US Drone Strikes in Pakistan*. London: Amnesty International, 2013.

Amoore, Louise. *The Politics of Possibility: Risk and Security beyond Probability*. Durham, NC: Duke University Press, 2013.

———. “Security and the Incalculable.” *Security Dialogue* 45, no. 5 (2014): 423–39.

Amoore, Louise, and Marieke de Goede. “Transactions after 9/11: The Banal Face of the Preemptive Strike.” *Transactions of the Institute of British Geographers* 33, no. 2 (2008): 173–85.

Anderson, Kenneth. “Readings: The Canonical National Security Law Speeches of Obama Administration Senior Officials and General Counsels.” Lawfare Institute blog, June 11, 2012. https://www.lawfareblog.com/readings-canonical-national-security-law-speeches-obama-administration-senior-officials-and-general.

———. “Targeted Killing and Drone Warfare: How We Came to Debate Whether There Is a ‘Legal Geography of War.’ ” Stanford, CA: Board of Trustees of the Leland Stanford Junior University, 2011. http://media.hoover.org/sites/default/files/documents/FutureChallenges_Anderson.pdf.

Andrejevic, Mark. "Becoming Drones: Smartphone Probes and Distributed Sensing." In *Locative Media*, edited by Rowan Wilken and Gerald Goggin, 193–207. London: Routledge, 2015.

Appelbaum, Jacob, Matthias Gebauer, Susanne Koelbl, Laura Poitras, Gordon Repinski, Marcel Rosenbach, and Holger Starkmy. "Obama's Lists: A Dubious History of Targeted Killing in Afghanistan." *Spiegel Online*, December 28, 2014. http://www.spiegel.de/international/world/secret-docs-reveal-dubious-details-of-targeted-killings-in-afghanistan-a-1010358.html.

Aradau, Claudia. "The Signature of Security: Big Data, Anticipation, Surveillance." *Radical Philosophy* 191 (May/June 2015): 21–28.

Arquilla, John, and David Ronfeldt. *The Advent of Netwar*. Santa Monica, CA: RAND, 1996.

———. *Networks and Netwars: The Future of Terror, Crime, and Militancy*. Santa Monica, CA: RAND, 2001.

———. *Swarming and the Future of Conflict*. Santa Monica, CA: RAND, 2000.

Arteh, Abdourahim. "Protests Hit Djibouti as Opposition Leaders Held." *Reuters*, February 19, 2011. http://www.reuters.com/article/us-djibouti-protests-idUSTRE71I1BQ20110219.

Asad, Talal. *On Suicide Bombing*. New York: Columbia University Press, 2007.

Asaro, Peter. "Determinism, Machine Agency, and Responsibility." *Politica and Societa* 2 (2014): 265–92.

———. "Transforming Society by Transforming Technology: The Science and Politics of Participatory Design." *Accounting, Management and Information Technologies* 10, no. 4 (2000): 257–90.

Asfura-Heim, Patricio. *Risky Business: The Future of Civil Defense Forces and Counterterrorism in an Era of Persistent Conflict*. Arlington, VA: Center for Strategic Studies, 2014.

Ashraf, Tariq Mahmud. "The Pakistan Frontier Corps in the War on Terrorism." *Terrorism Monitor* 6, no. 15 (2008). https://jamestown.org/program/the-pakistan-frontier-corps-in-the-war-on-terrorism-part-one/.

Associated Press. "Al-Shabab Showed Gruesome Social Media Savvy during Attack." CBS News, September 24, 2013. http://www.cbsnews.com/news/al-shabab-showed-gruesome-social-media-savvy-during-attack/.

———. "John Kerry Says Drone Strikes Could End as Bilateral Talks Resume." *Guardian*, August 1, 2013.

———. "Surveillance Drone Crashes in Somali Capital." *Yahoo News*, February 3, 2012. http://news.yahoo.com/surveillance-drone-crashes-somali-capital-134652928.html.

———. "Unidentified Drone Crashes in Mogadishu." *Army Times*, February 3, 2012. http://www.armytimes.com/article/20120203/NEWS/202030310/Unidentified-drone-crashes-Mogadishu.

———. "US-Pakistan Relationship Increasingly Strained." *Dawn*, March 18, 2011. http://www.dawn.com/news/614081/us-pakistan-relationship-increasingly-strained.

Atherton, Kelsey D. "Australian Eagle Takes Down a Drone in a Split Second." *Popular Science*, August 12, 2015. http://www.popsci.com/watch-australian-eagle-attack-drone.

———. "Trained Police Eagles Attack Drones on Command." *Popular Science*, February 1, 2016. http://www.popsci.com/eagles-attack-drones-at-police-command.

Aurakzai, Rashid Khan. "Burying Us Alive in Bara." *Tanqeed*, February 2013. http://www.tanqeed.org/2013/02/burying-us-alive-in-bara-rashid-khan-aurakzai/#sthash.9yAWmARG.dpbs.

Axell, Albert, and Hideake Kase. *Kamikaze: Japan's Suicide Gods*. London: Longman, 2002.

Azoulay, Ariella, and Adi Ophir. "The Monster's Tail." In *Against the Wall: Israel's Barrier to Peace*, edited by Michael Sorkin, 2–27. New York: New Press, 2005.

Bachman, Jan, Colleen Bell, and Caroline Holmqvist, eds. *War, Police and Assemblages of Intervention*. New York: Routledge, 2014.

Bady, Aaron. "Tarzan's White Flights: Terrorism and Fantasy before and after the Airplane." *American Literature* 83, no. 2 (2011): 305–29.

Baker, Peter. "Obama Apologizes after Drone Kills American and Italian Held by Al Qaeda." *New York Times*, April 23, 2015.

Bamford, James. *The Shadow Factory*. New York: Doubleday, 2008.

Barnes, Julian, and Greg Miller. "Pakistan Gets a Say in Drone Attacks on Militants." *Los Angeles Times*, May 13, 2009.

Barry, Tom. "The Political Economy of Drones." *CounterPunch*, May 1, 2013. http://www.counterpunch.org/2013/05/01/the-political-economy-of-drones/.

Barton, John H. *The Politics of Peace: An Evaluation of Arms Control*. Stanford, CA: Stanford University Press, 1981.

Bashir, Shahzad, and Robert D. Crews. Introduction to *Under the Drones: Modern Lives in the Afghanistan-Pakistan Borderlands*, edited by Shahzad Bashir and Robert D. Crews, 1–16. Cambridge, MA: Harvard University Press, 2012.

Battles, Matthew. "The Feral Drones." *HiLoBrow*, December 6, 2011. http://hilobrow.com/2011/12/06/the-feral-drones/.

Bayoumy, Yara. "Insight: In Yemen, al-Qaeda Gains Sympathy amid US Drone Strikes." *Reuters*, December 13, 2013.

BBC. "Suspected US Drone Crashes in Somalia's Lower Shabelle." BBC, May 28, 2013.

Beattie, Hugh. *Imperial Frontier: Tribe and State in Waziristan*. London: Curzon Press, 2002.

Becker, Jo, and Scott Shane. "Secret 'Kill List' Proves a Test of Obama's Principles and Will." *New York Times*, May 28, 2012.

Bell, Colleen. "Hybrid Warfare and Its Metaphors." *Humanity* 3, no. 2 (2012): 225–47.

———. "War and the Allegory of Medical Intervention." *International Political Sociology* 6, no. 3 (2012): 325–28.

Bell, David. "In Defense of Drones: A Historical Argument." *New Republic*, January 26, 2012. https://newrepublic.com/article/100113/obama-military-foreign-policy-technology-drones.

Bengali, Shashank. "U.S. Military Investing Heavily in Africa." *Los Angeles Times*, October 20, 2013.

Benjamin, Medea. *Drone Warfare: Killing by Remote Control*. New York: OR Books, 2012.

Benn, Aluf. "Obama Is Learning from the IDF." *Haaretz*, November 4, 2009. http://www.haaretz.com/obama-is-learning-from-the-idf-1.4815.

Benn, Aluf, and Amos Harel. "Kitchen Cabinet Okays Expansion of Liquidation List." *Haaretz*, July 17, 2001. http://www.haaretz.com/print-edition/news/kitchen-cabinet-okays-expansion-of-liquidation-list-1.64082.

Ben-Naftali, Orna, and Keren R. Michaeli. "Justice-Ability: A Critique of the Alleged Non-Justiciability of Israel's Policy of Targeted Killings." *Journal of International Criminal Justice* 1, no. 2 (2003): 368–405.

———. "We Must Not Make a Scarecrow of the Law: A Legal Analysis of the Israeli Policy of Targeted Killing." *Cornell International Law Journal* 36, no. 2 (2003): 233–92.

Bennett, Brian, and Joel Rubin. "Drones Are Taking to the Skies in the U.S." *Los Angeles Times*, February 15, 2013.

Benson, Bruce, and Zafar Siddiqui. "*Pashtunwali*—Law for the Lawless, Defense for the Stateless." *International Review of Law and Economics* 37 (March 2014): 108–20.

Benton, Lauren. "Spatial Histories of Empire." *Itinerario* 30, no. 3 (2006): 19–34.

Benvenisti, Eyal. "The Legal Battle to Define the Law on Transnational Asymmetric Warfare." *Duke Journal of International Law* 20, no. 3 (2009–10): 339–59.

Bezabeh, Samson A. "Citizenship and the Logic of Sovereignty in Djibouti." *African Affairs* 110, no. 441 (2011): 1–20.

Biltgen, Patrick, and Stephen Ryan. *Activity-Based Intelligence: Principles and Applications*. Norwood, MA: Artech House, 2016.

Bisharat, George. "Legitimation in Lawyering under Israeli Occupation." *Law and Social Inquiry* 20 (1995): 349–405.

Bittel, Jason. "Want a Drone-Hunting License in Colorado? Get in Line." *Slate*, September 5, 2013. http://www.slate.com/blogs/future_tense/2013/09/06/deer_trail_co_sees_applications_for_nonexistent_drone_hunting_license.html.

Blake, Matt. "'This One Won't Spy on Muslims Again': Somali Militants Publish Pictures of US Drone They 'Shot Down.'" *Daily Mail*, May 31, 2013.

Blank, Laurie. "Defining the Battlefield in Contemporary Conflict and Counterterrorism: Understanding the Parameters of the Zone of Combat." *Georgia Journal of International and Comparative Law* 39, no. 1 (2010–11): 1–38.

Blau, Uri. "License to Kill." *Haaretz*, November 27, 2008. http://www.haaretz.com/license-to-kill-1.258378.

Bobich, Joshua. "'Who Authorized This?!': An Assessment of the Process for Approving U.S. Covert Action." *William Mitchell Law Review* 33, no. 3 (2007): 1111–42.

Boltanski, Luc. *Distant Suffering: Morality, Media and Politics*. Cambridge: Cambridge University Press, 1999.

Bolter, Jay, and Richard Grusin. *Remediation: Understanding New Media*. Cambridge, MA: MIT Press, 1999.

Bonnington, Christina, and Spencer Ackerman. "Apple Rejects App That Tracks US Drone Strikes." *Wired*, August 30, 2012. http://www.wired.com/dangerroom/2012/08/drone-app/.

Borger, Julian. "Israel Trains U.S. Assassination Squads in Iraq." *Guardian*, December 9, 2003.

Bourdieu, Pierre. *Distinction: A Social Critique of the Judgement of Taste*. Translated by Richard Nice. Cambridge, MA: Harvard University Press, 1984.

———. *Outline of a Theory of Practice*. Translated by Richard Nice. New York: Cambridge University Press, 1977.

Bowden, Mark. "The Killing Machines." *Atlantic*, September 14, 2013.

Brant, George. *Grounded*. London: Oberon Books, 2013.

Brass, Jennifer N. "Djibouti's Unusual Resource Curse." *Journal of Modern African Studies* 46, no. 4 (December 2008): 523–45.

Brassier, Ray. "Accelerationism." Lecture given at Goldsmiths, University of London, September 4, 2010. http://moskvax.wordpress.com/2010/09/30/accelerationism-ray-brassier/.

———. "Concepts and Objects." In *The Speculative Turn: Continental Materialism and Realism*, edited by Levi R. Bryant, Nick Srnicek, and Graham Harman, 47–66. Melbourne: re.press, 2011.

Breau, Susan, Marie Aronsson, and Rachel Joyce. "Discussion Paper 2: Drone Attacks, International Law, and the Recording of Civilian Casualties of Armed Conflict." Oxford Research Group, June 2011. http://www.oxfordresearchgroup.org.uk/sites/default/files/ORG%20Drone%20Attacks%20and%20International%20Law%20Report.pdf.

Bremner, Lindsay. "Border/Skin." In *Against the Wall: Israel's Barrier to Peace*, edited by Michael Sorkin, 122–35. New York: New Press, 2005.

Brown, Wendy. "American Nightmare: Neoliberalism, Neoconservatism, and De-Democratization." *Political Theory* 34, no. 6 (2006): 690–714.

Browne, Simone. "Digital Epidermalization: Race, Identity and Biometrics." *Critical Sociology* 36, no. 1 (2010): 131–50.

Brownstone, Sydney. "Your iPhone Can Now Alert You When a Drone Attacks." *Fast Company*, October 27, 2011. http://www.fastcoexist.com/3026320/your-iphone-can-now-alert-you-when-a-drone-attacks.

Buckley, Chris. "Chinese Navy Returns Seized Underwater Drones." *New York Times*, December 20, 2016. https://www.nytimes.com/2016/12/20/world/asia/china-returns-us-drone.html?_r=0.

Bumiller, Elisabeth. "Air Force Drone Operators Show High Levels of Stress." *New York Times*, December 18, 2011.

Bureau of Investigative Journalism. "The Bush Years: Pakistan Strikes 2004–2009." *Bureau of Investigative Journalism*, August 10, 2011. https://www.thebureauinvestigates.com/2011/08/10/the-bush-years-2004-2009/.

———. "Covert War on Terror—The Data." Reprinted in *Global Research News*, October 27, 2012. http://www.globalresearch.ca/covert-war-on-terror-the-data/5309831.

———. "Drone War." February 15, 2017. https://www.thebureauinvestigates.com/projects/drone-war.

Burns, Jacob. "Persistent Exception: Pakistani Law and the Drone War." In *Forensis: The Architecture of Public Truth*, edited by Forensic Architecture, 400–408. Berlin: Sternberg Press, 2014.

Butler, Judith. *Frames of War: When Is Life Grievable?* London: Verso, 2010.

———. *Precarious Life: The Powers of Mourning and Violence.* London: Verso, 2006.

Cacho, Lisa Marie. *Social Death: Racialized Rightlessness and the Criminalization of the Unprotected.* New York: New York University Press, 2012.

Cartwright, Lisa. *Screening the Body: Tracing Medicine's Visual Culture.* Minneapolis: University of Minnesota Press, 1995.

Castells, Manuel. *Networks of Outrage and Hope: Social Movements in the Internet Age.* London: Polity, 2012.

Cenciotti, David. "Pentagon Confirms Drone Crash in Somalia. But It Doesn't Say It Was an Austrian Made Psyops-Capable Camcopter." *Aviationist,* May 29, 2013. http://theaviationist.com/2013/05/29/schiebel-s-100/#.UcRf12ZwbIU.

Central Intelligence Agency (CIA). "Djibouti." *The World Factbook.* https://www.cia.gov/library/publications/the-world-factbook/geos/dj.html.

Chairman of the Joint Chiefs of Staff. "No-Strike and the Collateral Damage Estimation Methodology." Washington, DC, October 12, 2012. https://publicintelligence.net/cjcs-collateral-damage/.

Chakrabarty, Dipesh. "The Climate of History: Four Theses." *Critical Inquiry* 35, no. 2 (2009): 197–222.

Chamayou, Grégoire. "Patterns of Life: A Very Short History of Schematic Bodies by Grégoire Chamayou." *The Funambulist: Bodies, Designs and Politics* (blog), December 14, 2014. http://thefunambulist.net/2014/12/04/the-funambulist-papers-57-schematic-bodies-notes-on-a-patterns-genealogy-by-gregoire-chamayou/.

———. *Théorie du drone.* Paris: La fabrique, 2013.

———. *A Theory of the Drone.* Translated by Janet Lloyd. New York: New Press, 2015.

Chappelle, Wayne, Kent McDonald, and Raymond E. King. "Psychological Attributes Critical to the Performance of MQ-1 Predator and MQ-9 Reaper U.S. Air Force Sensor Operators." Air Force Research Labs Technical Report AFRL-SA-BR-TR-2010-0007. June 2010.

Chappelle, Wayne, Amber Salinas, and Kent McDonald. "Psychological Health Screening of Remotely Piloted Aircraft (RPA) Operators and Supporting Units." Paper presented at the Symposium on Mental Health and Well-Being across the Military Spectrum, Bergen, Norway, April 12, 2011.

Chesney, Robert. "Military-Intelligence Convergence and the Law of the Title 10/Title 50 Debate." *Journal of National Security Law and Policy* 5, no. 2 (2011): 539–629.

Chow, Rey. *The Age of the World Target: Self-Referentiality in War, Theory, and Comparative Work.* Durham, NC: Duke University Press, 2006.

CIA Office of Transnational Issues. "Best Practices in Counterinsurgency: Making High-Value Targeting Operations an Effective Counterinsurgency Tool." July 7, 2009. WikiLeaks, December 18, 2014. https://wikileaks.org/cia-hvt-counterinsurgency/WikiLeaks_Secret_CIA_review_of_HVT_Operations.pdf.

Clark, Paul W. "Early Impacts of Communications on Military Doctrine." *Proceedings of the IEEE* 64, no. 9 (September 1976): 1407–13.

Cline, Donna. "An Analysis of the Legal Status of CIA Officers Involved in Drone Strikes." *San Diego International Law Journal* 15, no. 1 (2013): 51–115.

Cloud, David S. “Anatomy of an Afghan War Tragedy.” *Los Angeles Times*, April 10, 2011.

CNA Military Advisory Board. “National Security and the Accelerating Risks of Climate Change.” May 2014. https://www.cna.org/cna_files/pdf/MAB_5-8-14.pdf.

CNN. “Obama Reflects on Drone Warfare.” *Security Clearance* (blog), September 5, 2012. http://security.blogs.cnn.com/2012/09/05/obama-reflects-on-drone-warfare/.

CNN Wire Staff. “Pakistan Denies U.S. Request to Expand Drone Access, Officials Say.” *CNN*, November 22, 2010. http://www.cnn.com/2010/WORLD/asiapcf/11/22/pakistan.us.drones/.

Cobain, Ian. “Obama’s Secret Kill List—The Disposition Matrix.” *Guardian*, July 14, 2013.

Cockburn, Andrew. *Kill-Chain: Drones and the Rise of the High-Tech Assassins*. New York: Henry Holt, 2015.

Cohen, Kris R. “What Does the Photoblog Want?” *Media, Culture and Society* 27, no. 6 (2005): 883–901.

Cohn, Marjorie, ed. *Drones and Targeted Killing: Legal, Moral, and Geopolitical Issues.* Northampton, MA: Olive Branch Press, 2015.

Cole, David. “The Drone Memo: Secrecy Made It Worse.” *New York Review of Books*, June 24, 2014.

———. “‘We Kill People Based on Metadata.’” *New York Review of Books*, May 10, 2014.

Coll, Steve. “The Unblinking Stare: The Drone War in Pakistan.” *New Yorker*, November 24, 2014.

Comaroff, John. “Colonialism, Culture, and the Law: A Foreword.” *Law and Social Inquiry* 26, no. 2 (2001): 305–14.

Committee to Protect Journalists. “Police arrest Djibouti journalist covering demonstration,” Aug. 12, 2014. Accessed February 12, 2017. https://cpj.org/2014/08/police-arrest-djibouti-journalist-covering-demonst.php.

Constitution Project. *The Report of the Constitution Project’s Task Force on Detainee Treatment*. Washington, DC: Constitution Project, 2013.

Cowen, Deborah. *The Deadly Life of Logistics: Mapping Violence in Global Trade*. Minneapolis: University of Minnesota Press, 2014.

Cowen, Deborah, and Emily Gilbert. *War, Citizenship, and Territory*. New York: Routledge, 2007.

Craig, Tim. “Pakistani Military Says Its Drone Killed Three Suspected Militants.” *Washington Post*, September 7, 2015.

Crandall, Jordan. “Ecologies of the Wayward Drone.” In *From Above: War, Violence, and Verticality*, edited by Peter Adey, Mark Whitehead, and Alison J. Williams, 263–87. London: Hurst, 2013.

———. “Unmanned.” http://jordancrandall.com/main/+UNMANNED/index.html.

———. “Unmanned.” In *Concerning War: A Critical Reader in Contemporary Art*, edited by Maria Hlavajova and Jill Winder, 60–74. Utrecht: BAK, 2010.

Crane, David. “Blucher Systems Ghost Soldier Camouflage and Spectraflage Vehicle Camo: Multispectral Combat Camouflage Fabric Technology That Provides Anti-

Thermal/IR (Infrared) Camo for 21st Century Special Warfare (Specwar)." *Defense Review*, April 19, 2011. http://www.defensereview.com/blucher-systems-ghost-and-spectralflage-multispectral-combat-camouflage-fabric-technology-anti-thermalir-infrared-soldier-camouflage-and-vehicle-camouflage-for-21st-century-warfare-operations/.

Crehore, Albert Cushing, and George Owen Squier. *The Polarizing Photo-Chronograph: Being an Account of Experiments at the U.S. Artillery School, Fort Monroe, Va., in Developing This Instrument*. New York: John Wiley and Sons, 1897.

Cullen, Tim M. "The MQ-9 Reaper Remotely Piloted Aircraft: Humans and Machines in Action." PhD diss., Massachusetts Institute of Technology, 2011.

Curcio, Seth. "Seeing Is Believing: An Interview with Trevor Paglen." *Daily Serving*, February 24, 2011. http://dailyserving.com/2011/02/interview-with-trevor-paglen.

Currier, Cora, Glenn Greenwald, and Andrew Fishman. "US Government Designated Prominent Al Jazeera Journalist as 'Member of al Qaeda.'" *Intercept*, May 8, 2015. https://theintercept.com/2015/05/08/u-s-government-designated-prominent-al-jazeera-journalist-al-qaeda-member-put-watch-list/.

Curzon, George Nathaniel. *Frontiers: The Romanes Lectures, 1907, Delivered in the Sheldonian Theatre, Oxford, November 2, 1907*. Oxford: Clarendon, 1907.

Daggett, Cara. "Drone Disorientations: How 'Unmanned' Weapons Queer the Experience of Killing in War." *International Feminist Journal of Politics* 17, no. 3 (2015): 361–79.

Dakwar, Jamil. "In the Name of Justice." *Adalah's Newsletter* 19 (October 2005).

Darcy, Shane, and John Reynolds. "'Otherwise Occupied': The Status of the Gaza Strip from the Perspective of International Law." *Journal of Conflict and Security Law* 15, no. 2 (2010): 211–43.

Daskal, Jennifer. "The Geography of the Battlefield: A Framework for Detention and Targeting Outside the 'Hot' Conflict Zone." *University of Pennsylvania Law Review* 161, no. 5 (2013): 1165–234.

Dawar, Rasool, and Asif Shahzad. "U.S. Drone Strike Said to Kill Pakistani Militant." WBUR News, May 29, 2013. http://www.huffingtonpost.com/2013/05/29/waliur rehman-dead-pakistan-no-2-killed-drone-strike_n_3351939.html.

Dean, Jodi. "Communicative Capitalism: Circulation and the Foreclosure of Politics." *Cultural Politics* 1, no. 1 (2005): 51–74.

———. *Democracy and Other Neoliberal Fantasies: Communicative Capitalism and Left Politics*. Durham, NC: Duke University Press, 2009.

Dearden, Lizzie. "The Man Who Says He's on America's Kill List and Can't Get Off It." *Independent*, April 17, 2016.

Debord, Guy, and Gil Wolman. "A User's Guide to Détournement." Translated by Ken Knabb. Bureau of Public Secrets, 1956. http://www.bopsecrets.org/SI/detourn.htm.

Defense Update. "Low Cost Autonomous Attack System." *Defense Update* 4 (2004). http://defense-update.com/products/l/locaas.htm.

de Goede, Marieke, Stephanie Simon, and Marijn Hoijtink. "Performing Preemption." *Security Dialogue* 45, no. 5 (2014): 411–22.

de Goede, Marieke, and Gavin Sullivan. "The Politics of Security Lists." *Environment and Planning D: Society and Space* 34, no. 1 (2016): 67–88.

De Landa, Manuel. *War in the Age of Intelligent Machines*. New York: Zone, 1991.

Deleuze, Gilles. *Difference and Repetition*. Translated by Paul Patton. New York: Columbia University Press, 1994.

Deleuze, Gilles, and Félix Guattari. *Anti-Oedipus: Capitalism and Schizophrenia*. London: Continuum, 2004.

Delmont, Matt. "Drone Encounters: Noor Behram, Omer Fast, and Visual Critiques of Drone Warfare." *American Quarterly* 65, no. 1 (2013): 193–202.

Democracy Now. "U.S. Border Patrol Considers Using Weaponized Drones." *Democracy Now*, July 3, 2013. http://www.democracynow.org/2013/7/3/headlines/us_border_patrol_considers_using_weaponized_drones.

Denbeaux, Mark, et al. *Report on Guantanamo Detainees: Profile of 517 Detainees through Analysis of Department of Defense Data*. Newark, NJ: Seton Hall University School of Law Publisher, 2006.

Department of Defense. "Directive Number 3000.09." November 21, 2012. http://www.dtic.mil/whs/directives/corres/pdf/300009p.pdf.

———. "The National Defense Strategy of the United States of America." March 2005. http://archive.defense.gov/news/Mar2005/d20050318nds1.pdf.

———. "Unmanned Systems Integrated Roadmap FY2011–2036." Reference number 11-S-3613, 2011.

———. "Unmanned Systems Integrated Roadmap FY2013–2038." Reference number 14-S-0553, 2013.

Department of Defense Dictionary of Military and Associated Terms. Washington, DC: Joint Chiefs of Staff, 2010. http://www.dtic.mil/doctrine/dod_dictionary/.

Department of Homeland Security. "Implementing the 9/11 Commission Recommendations," Progress Report. Washington, DC, 2011

Department of the Navy and CIA World Factbook. "An End to Drone Flights from Camp Lemonnier, Djibouti." *Washington Post*, September 24, 2013.

Deptula, Dave. *Air Force Unmanned Aerial System (UAS) Flight Plan 2009–2047*. Washington, DC: Headquarters, U.S. Air Force, 2009.

Der Derian, James. "The Desert of the Real and the Simulacrum of War." *International Affairs* 84, no. 5 (2008): 931–48.

———. *Virtuous War: Mapping the Military-Industrial-Media-Entertainment Network*. Boulder, CO: Westview, 2001.

Deveraux, Ryan. "Family of Grandmother Killed in US Drone Strike Arrive for Congress Visit." *Guardian*, October 27, 2013.

de Volo, Lorraine Bayard. "Unmanned? Gender Recalibrations and the Rise of Drone Warfare." *Politics and Gender* (September 7, 2015): 1–28.

Dewar, Mike, Drew Conway, John Myles White, and Harlan Harris. "Visualization of Activity in Afghanistan Using the Wikileaks Data." Vimeo, 2011. http://vimeo.com/14200191.

de Yoanna, Michael, and Mark Benjamin. "I Am under a Lot of Pressure to Not Diagnose PTSD." *Salon*, April 8, 2009. http://www.salon.com/2009/04/08/tape/.

DeYoung, Karen. "Al-Qaeda Seen as Shaken in Pakistan." *World Security Network*, June 1, 2009. http://www.worldsecuritynetwork.com/Terrorism-United-States-Pakistan/DeYoung-Karen-1/Al-Qaeda-Seen-as-Shaken-in-Pakistan.

———. "Secrecy Defines Obama's Drone War." *Washington Post*, December 19, 2011.

Dillon, Michael. *Deconstructing International Politics*. London: Routledge, 2013.

Dillon, Michael, and Julian Reid. *The Liberal Way of War: Killing to Make Life Live*. New York: Routledge, 2009.

"Djiboutians Rally to Oust President." *Al Jazeera English*, February 18, 2011.

Dodaro, Gene L. *Combating Terrorism: US Efforts to Address the Terrorist Threat in Pakistan's Federally Administered Tribal Areas Require a Comprehensive Plan and Continued Oversight*. Testimony, GAO-08-820T. Washington, DC: U.S. Government Accountability Office, 2008.

Donavan, Kevin P., and Aaron K. Martin. "The Rise of African SIM Registration: The Emerging Dynamics of Regulatory Change." *First Monday* 19, no. 2 (2014). http://firstmonday.org/ojs/index.php/fm/article/view/4351/3820.

Dorigo, Marco, et al. "Swarmanoid: A Novel Concept for the Study of Heterogeneous Robotic Swarms." *IEEE Robotics and Automation Magazine* 20, no. 4 (2013): 60–71.

Dörmann, Knut. "The Legal Situation of 'Unlawful/Unprivileged Combatants.'" *International Review of the Red Cross* 85, no. 849 (2003): 45–74.

Dorrien, Gary. *Imperial Designs: Neoconservatism and the New Pax Americana*. New York: Routledge, 2004.

Doty, Alexander. *Flaming Classics: Queering the Film Canon*. London: Routledge, 2000.

Drake, Bruce. "Obama and Drone Strikes: Support but Questions at Home, Opposition Abroad." Pew Research Center, May 24, 2013. http://www.pewresearch.org/fact-tank/2013/05/24/obama-and-drone-strikes-support-but-questions-at-home-opposition-abroad/.

Drew, Christopher. "Military Is Awash in Data from Drones." *New York Times*, January 11, 2010.

Drone Wars UK. "Drone Crash Database." Accessed February 19, 2017. http://dronewars.net/drone-crash-database/.

Druckery, Timothy. "Deadly Representations or Apocalypse Now." *Ten.8* 2, no. 2 (1991): 16–27.

Dunlap, Col. Charles J., Jr. "Does Lawfare Need an Apologia?" *Duke Law Scholarship Repository Working Papers* 43, no. 1 (2010): 121–43.

———. *Law and Military Interventions: Preserving Humanitarian Values in 21st Century Conflicts*. Farnham, UK: Ashgate, 2012.

———. "Lawfare Today: A Perspective." *Yale Journal of International Affairs* 3, no. 1 (2008): 146–54.

Dunn, Elizabeth Cullen, and Jason Cons. "Aleatory Sovereignty and the Rule of Sensitive Spaces." *Antipode* 46, no. 1 (2014): 92–109.

Edgerton, Gary. *Columbia History of Television*. New York: Columbia University Press, 2010.

Editorial Board. "A Thin Rationale for Killing." *New York Times*, June 23, 2014.

Edmond, Maura. "Here We Go Again: Music Videos after YouTube." *Television and New Media* 15, no. 4 (2014): 305–20.

Edwards, Brent Hayes. *The Practice of Diaspora: Literature, Translation, and the Rise of Black Internationalism*. Cambridge, MA: Harvard University Press, 2003.

Edwards, Sean J. A. "Swarming and the Future of Warfare." Diss., the Pardee Rand Graduate School, 2005.

Ehrenreich, Barbara. Foreword to *Drone Warfare: Killing by Remote Control*, by Medea Benjamin, vii–ix. New York: OR Books, 2012.

Elden, Stuart. "Governmentality, Calculation, Territory." *Environment and Planning D: Society and Space* 25, no. 3 (2007): 562–80.

———. "Land, Terrain, Territory." *Progress in Human Geography* 34, no. 6 (2010): 799–807.

Emmerson, Ben. "Report of the Special Rapporteur on the Promotion and Protection of Human Rights and Fundamental Freedoms while Countering Terrorism." Report A/HRC/25/59. March 11, 2014. https://documents-dds-ny.un.org/doc/UNDOC/GEN/G14/119/49/PDF/G1411949.pdf?OpenElement.

Engel, Richard. "Former Drone Operator Says He's Haunted by His Part in More Than 1,600 Deaths." June 6, 2013. http://investigations.nbcnews.com/-news/2013/06/18787450-former-drone-operator-says-hes-haunted-by-his-part-in-more-than-1600-deaths.

Entous, Adam. "Obama Kept Looser Rules for Drones in Pakistan." *Wall Street Journal*, April 26, 2015.

Entous, Adam, and Jessica Donati. "How the US Tracked and Killed the Leader of the Taliban." *Wall Street Journal*, May 25, 2016.

Entous, Adam, and Siobhan Gorman. "CIA Strikes Strain Ties with Pakistan Further." *Wall Street Journal*, August 29, 2011.

Entous, Adam, Siobhan Gorman, and Julian Barnes. "US Tightens Drone Rules." *Wall Street Journal*, November 4, 2011.

Entous, Adam, Siobhan Gorman, and Evan Perez. "US Unease over Drone Strikes." *Wall Street Journal*, September 26, 2012.

Entous, Adam, Damian Paletta, and Felicia Schwarz. "American, Italian Hostages Killed in CIA Drone Strike in January." *Wall Street Journal*, April 23, 2015.

Erakat, Noura. "No, Israel Does Not Have the Right to Self-Defense in International Humanitarian Law against Palestinian Occupied Territory." *Jadaliyya*, December 5, 2012. http://www.jadaliyya.com/pages/index/8799/no-israel-does-not-have-the-right-to-self-defense.

European Parliament. "Joint Motion for a Resolution on the Use of Armed Drones." February 25, 2014. http://www.europarl.europa.eu/sides/getDoc.do?pubRef=-//EP//TEXT+MOTION+P7-RC-2014-0201+0+DOC+XML+V0//EN.

Evangelista, Matthew, and Henry Shue, eds. *The American Way of Bombing: Changing Ethical and Legal Norms, from Flying Fortresses to Drones*. Ithaca, NY: Cornell University Press, 2014.

Express Tribune. "Bomb Blast: Explosion Kills Two Soldiers in Khyber." *Express Tribune*, June 19, 2013. http://tribune.com.pk/story/579455/bomb-blast-explosion-kills-two-soldiers-in-khyber/.

———. "PAF Conducted 5,500 Bombing Runs in FATA since 2008." *Express Tribune*, November 14, 2011. http://tribune.com.pk/story/291762/paf-conducted-5500-bombing-runs-in-fata-since-2008/.

———. "Thousands Flee North Waziristan Fearing Military Action." *Express Tribune*, January 26, 2014. http://tribune.com.pk/story/663657/thousands-flee-north-waziristan-fearing-military-action/.

———. "3,400 Militants Killed in Operation Zarb-e-Azb: ISPR." *Express Tribune*, December 12, 2015. http://tribune.com.pk/story/1008791/3400-militants-killed-in-operation-zarb-e-azb-ispr/.

Fahrney, Delmar. "The Genesis of the Cruise Missile." *Astronautics and Aeronautics* (January 1982): 34–39, 53.

———. "The History of Pilotless Aircraft and Guided Missiles." Unpublished manuscript, United States Navy, Washington, DC, 1957. Collected Records of D. S. Fahrney, Record Group (RG) 72, National Archives (NARA) II.

Faint, Charles, and Michael Harris. "F3EAD: Ops/Intel Fusion 'Feeds' the SOF Targeting Process." *Small Wars Journal*, January 31, 2012. http://smallwarsjournal.com/jrnl/art/f3ead-opsintel-fusion-"feeds"-the-sof-targeting-process.

Fair, C. Christine. "Ethical and Methodological Issues in Assessing Drones' Civilian Impacts in Pakistan." *Monkey Cage* (blog), October 6, 2014. http://www.washingtonpost.com/blogs/monkey-cage.

Fang, Lee. "Ahmed Mohamed's Clock Was 'Half a Bomb,' Says Anti-Muslim Group with Ties to Trump, Cruz." *Intercept*, September 18, 2015. https://theintercept.com/2015/09/18/prominent-anti-muslim-group-says-ahmed-mohameds-clock-resembles-ied-trigger-produced-iranians.

Fanon, Frantz. *Black Skin, White Masks*. New York: Grove Press, 1967.

Farocki, Harun. "Phantom Images." *Public* 29 (2004): 12–24.

Farooq, Umar. "Pakistan's FATA: Lawless No More?" *Al Jazeera English*, March 22, 2014.

Fast, Omer, dir. *5,000 Feet Is the Best*. Denmark: Commonwealth Projects, 2011. 30 min.

Feigenbaum, Anna. "From Cyborg Feminism to Drone Feminism: Remembering Women's Anti-Nuclear Activism." *Feminist Theory* 16, no. 3 (2015): 265–88.

Feinberg, Ashley. "Giant Portrait Shows Drone Operators That People Aren't 'Bug Splats.'" *Gizmodo*, April 6, 2014. http://gizmodo.com/giant-portrait-shows-drone-operators-that-people-arent-1559460573.

Feldman, Allen. "On the Actuarial Gaze: From 9/11 to Abu Ghraib." *Cultural Studies* 19, no. 2 (2005): 203–25.

Feldman, Keith. "Empire's Verticality: The Af/Pak Frontier, Visual Culture, and Racialization from Above." *Comparative American Studies* 9, no. 4 (2011): 325–41.

Feldman, Yotam, and Uri Blau. "Consent and Advise." *Haaretz*, February 5, 2009. http://www.haaretz.com/consent-and-advise-1.269127.

Femia, Will. "Richard Engel's Full Drone Pilot Interview." MSNBC, June 8, 2013. http://www.msnbc.com/rachel-maddow-show/richard-engels-full-drone-pilot-interview.

Fernandez, Manny, Richard Pérez-Peña, and Fernanda Santos. "Gunman in Texas Shooting Was F.B.I. Suspect in Jihad Inquiry." *New York Times*, May 4, 2015.

Fiore, Mark. "Drones Come to Technopolis." Animated cartoon, December 4, 2013. https://www.markfiore.com/mark-fiore-blog/cartoons/drones-come-to-techopolis.html.

Fischer, Lucy. "'Enthusiasm': From Kino-Eye to Radio-Eye." *Film Quarterly* 31, no. 2 (1977–78): 25–34.

Fisher, Mark. *Capitalist Realism: Is There No Alternative?* Washington, DC: Zero Books, 2009.

Flynn, Michael T., Rich Juergens, and Thomas Cantrell. "Employing ISR: SOF [Special Operations Forces] Best Practices." *Joint Forces Quarterly* 50, no. 3 (2008): 56–61.

Forensic Architecture, ed. *Forensis: The Architecture of Public Truth*. Berlin: Sternberg Press, 2014.

Foucault, Michel. *Discipline and Punish: The Birth of the Prison*. Translated by Alan Sheridan. New York: Vintage Books, 1975.

———. "March 17, 1976." In *"Society Must Be Defended": Lectures at the Collège de France, 1975–1976*, edited by Mauro Bertani and Alessandro Fontana, translated by David Macey, 239–64. New York: Penguin, 2003.

———. *Security, Territory, Population: Lectures at the Collège de France, 1977–1978*. Edited by Arnold I. Davidson. New York: Palgrave Macmillan, 2007.

Foust, Joshua. "The Islamabad Drone Dance." PBS, March 19, 2013. http://www.pbs.org/wnet/need-to-know/opinion/the-islamabad-drone-dance/16519.

———. "On the Roads Again in Afghanistan." PBS, August 31, 2010. http://www.pbs.org/wnet/need-to-know/opinion/on-the-roads-again-in-afghanistan/3223/.

Fowler, Corinne. *Chasing Tales: Travel Writing, Journalism and the History of British Ideas of Afghanistan*. New York: Rodopi, 2007.

Freud, Sigmund. "Inhibitions, Symptoms and Anxiety." In *The Standard Edition of the Complete Psychological Works of Sigmund Freud*, vol. 20, *1925–1926*, edited by James Strachey, 75–175. 24 vols. London: Hogarth Press, 1953.

Friedersdorf, Conor. "Every Person Is Afraid of the Drones: The Strikes' Effect on Life in Pakistan." *Atlantic*, September 25, 2012.

Fulghum, David A., and Robert Wall. "Israel Pursues High Tech Despite War Costs." *Aviation Weekly and Space Technology* (June 24, 2002): 78–80.

———. "Israel Refocuses on Urban Warfare." *Aviation Weekly and Space Technology* (May 13, 2001): 24–26.

Funnell, Anthony. "Predictive Policing: Putting Data on the Beat." *Future Tense*, August 23, 2015. http://www.abc.net.au/radionational/programs/futuretense/predictive-policing3a-putting-data-on-the-beat/6702640.

Gall, Carlotta. "Insurgency's Scars Line Afghanistan's Main Road." *New York Times*, August 13, 2008.

Galloway, Alexander R., and Eugene Thacker. *The Exploit: A Theory of Networks*. Minneapolis: University of Minnesota Press, 2007.

Gannon, Kathy, Kimberly Dozier, and Sebastian Abbot. "Timing of US Drone Strike Questioned." Associated Press, August 2, 2011.

Gardner, Frank. "US Military Steps Up Operations in the Horn of Africa." BBC, February 7, 2014. http://www.bbc.co.uk/news/world-africa-26078149.

Gardner, Lloyd C. *Killing Machine: The American Presidency in the Age of Drone Warfare*. New York: New Press, 2013.

Gates, Kelly. *Our Biometric Future: Facial Recognition Technology and the Culture of Surveillance*. New York: New York University Press, 2011.

Gates, Sara. "Predator Drone Toy on Amazon Sold Out after Users Write Sarcastic Parody Review." *Huffington Post*, February 17, 2013. http://www.huffingtonpost.com/2013/02/17/predator-drone-toy-amazon-sold-out_n_2707164.html.

Gellman, Barton, and Ashkan Soltani. "NSA Tracking Cellphone Locations Worldwide, Snowden Documents Reveal." *Washington Post*, December 4, 2013.

General Staff, Army Headquarters, India. *Operations in Waziristan 1919–1920*. Calcutta: Government Printing, 1921.

Gettinger, Dan. "Burdens of War: PTSD and Drone Crews." Center for the Study of the Drone, April 21, 2014. http://dronecenter.bard.edu/burdens-war-crews-drone-aircraft/.

"A Giant Art Installation Targets Predator Drone Operators." April 6, 2014. https://notabugsplat.com/2014/04/06/a-giant-art-installation-targets-predator-drone-operators/.

Gilani, Sabrina. "'Spacing' Minority Relations: Investigating the Tribal Areas of Pakistan Using a Spatio-Historical Method of Analysis." *Social and Legal Studies* (January 2015): 359–80.

Gilbert, Emily. "Money as a 'Weapons System' and the Entrepreneurial Way of War." *Critical Military Studies* 1, no. 3 (2015): 202–19.

Ginsburg, Tom. "An Economic Interpretation of the *Pashtunwali*." *University of Chicago Legal Forum* 2011, no. 1 (2011): 89–114.

Golson, Jordan. "A Military-Grade Drone That Can Be Printed Anywhere." *Wired*, September 16, 2014. http://www.wired.com/2014/09/military-grade-drone-can-printed-anywhere/.

Goodman, Amy. "Death by Metadata: Jeremy Scahill and Glenn Greenwald Reveal NSA Role in Assassinations Overseas." *Democracy Now!*, February 10, 2014. http://www.democracynow.org/2014/2/10/death_by_metadata_jeremy_scahill_glenn.

Goodman, Ryan. "Social Science Data on Public Reactions to Drone Strikes and Civilian Casualties." *Just Security* (blog), July 3, 2014.

———. "10 Years of Drone Strikes in Pakistan—But Do You Know Whether It's an 'Area of Active Hostilities'?" *Just Security* (blog), June 18, 2014. https://www.justsecurity.org/11828/drone-strikes-pakistan-fata-area-active-hostilities/.

Goodman, Ryan, and Derek Jinks. "Military Targeting Based on Cellphone Location." *Just Security* (blog), February 18, 2014. https://www.justsecurity.org/7200/military-targeting-based-cellphone-location/.

Gopinath, Gayatri. *Impossible Desires: Queer Diasporas and South Asian Public Cultures*. Durham, NC: Duke University Press, 2005.

Gordon, Don E. *Electronic Warfare: Element of Strategy and Multiplier of Combat Power*. New York: Pergamon, 1981.

Gordon, Neve. "Rationalising Extra-Judicial Executions: The Israeli Press and the Legitimisation of Abuse." *International Journal of Human Rights* 8, no. 3 (2004): 305–24.

Gosztola, Kevin. “Contemporary Colonialism: The Permanent US Drone War Base in Djibouti.” *Shadow Proof*, October 26, 2012.

Graham, Stephen. *Cities under Siege: The New Military Urbanism*. London: Verso, 2010.

———. *Vertical: The City from Satellites to Bunkers*. London: Verso, 2017.

Graham, Stephen, and Lucy Hewitt. “Getting Off the Ground: On the Politics of Urban Verticality.” *Progress in Human Geography* 37, no. 1 (2012): 72–92.

Grayson, Carol Ann. “Peshawar Tribesmen Protest Killings at Bara.” *Radical Sister Blog*, January 16, 2013. https://activist1.wordpress.com/2013/01/16/peshawar-tribesmen-protest-killings-at-bara-bodies-of-the-dead-carried-to-governor-house/.

Green, Matthew. “US Plans Route to Stability in Tribal Region.” *Financial Times*, February 10, 2011.

Greenberg, Karen J., and Joshua L. Dratel, eds. *The Enemy Combatant Papers: American Justice, the Courts, and the War on Terror.* Cambridge: Cambridge University Press, 2008.

Greenwald, Glenn. *No Place to Hide: Edward Snowden, the NSA, and the US Surveillance State*. New York: Random House, 2014.

———. “The Real Criminals in the Tarek Mehanna Case.” *Salon*, April 13, 2012. http://www.salon.com/2012/04/13/the_real_criminals_in_the_tarek_mehanna_case/.

———. “XKeyscore: NSA Tool Collects ‘Nearly Everything’ a User Does on the Internet.” *Guardian*, July 31, 2013.

Greenwald, Glenn, and Ewan MacAskill. “Boundless Informant: The NSA’s Secret Tool to Track Global Surveillance Data.” *Guardian*, June 11, 2013.

Gregory, Derek. “Angry Eyes: Air Strikes and the Geography of Militarised Vision.” *Geographical Imaginations* (blog), October 1, 2015. https://geographicalimaginations.com/2015/10/01/angry-eyes-1/.

———. *The Colonial Present: Afghanistan, Palestine, Iraq*. Malden, MA: Blackwell, 2004.

———. “Death Sentences.” *Geographical Imaginations* (blog), April 12, 2016. https://geographicalimaginations.com/2016/04/12/death-sentences.

———. “Drone Geographies.” *Radical Philosophy* 183 (January/February 2014): 7–19.

———. “The Everywhere War.” *Geographical Journal* 177, no. 3 (2011): 238–50.

———. “From a View to a Kill: Drones and Late Modern War.” *Theory, Culture and Society* 28, nos. 7–8 (2011): 188–215.

———. “The Individuation of Warfare?” *Geographical Imaginations* (blog), August 26, 2013. http://geographicalimaginations.com/2013/08/26/the-individuation-of-warfare/.

———. “Lines of Descent.” In *From Above: War, Violence and Verticality*, edited by Peter Adey, Mark Whitehead, and Alison Williams, 41–70. London: Hurst, 2013.

———. “Theory of the Drone 10: Killing at a Distance.” *Geographical Imaginations* (blog), September 15, 2013. http://geographicalimaginations.com/2013/09/15/theory-of-the-drone-10-killing-at-a-distance/.

———. “Untargeted Killing.” *Geographical Imaginations* (blog), December 29, 2012. https://geographicalimaginations.com/2012/12/29/untargeted-killing/.

Grewal, Inderpal. *Exceptional Citizens? Advanced Neoliberalism, Surveillance, and Security in the Contemporary United States*. Durham, NC: Duke University Press, 2017.

Grewal, Inderpal, and Caren Kaplan, eds. *Scattered Hegemonies: Postmodernity and Transnational Feminist Practices*. Minneapolis: University of Minnesota Press, 1994.

Groeger, Lena, and Cora Currier. "Stacking Up the Administration's Drone Claims." *ProPublica*, September 13, 2012.

Gross, Michael. "Fighting by Other Means in the Mideast: A Critical Analysis of Israel's Assassination Policy." *Political Studies* 51, no. 2 (2003): 350–68.

Guiora, Amos. "Targeted Killing as Active Self Defense." *Case Western Reserve Journal of International Law* 36, no. 2 (2004): 319–34.

Gul, Imtiaz. *The Most Dangerous Place: Pakistan's Lawless Frontier*. New York: Penguin, 2010.

Gusterson, Hugh. *Drone: Remote Control Warfare*. Cambridge, MA: MIT Press, 2016.

———. "Toward an Anthropology of Drones: Remaking Space, Time, and Valor in Combat." In *The American Way of Bombing: Changing Ethical and Legal Norms from Flying Fortresses to Drones*, edited by Matthew Evangelista and Henry Shue, 191–206. Ithaca, NY: Cornell University Press, 2014.

Gwynn, Charles. *Imperial Policing*. London: Macmillan, 1939.

Hacking, Ian. "Kinds of People: Moving Targets." *Proceedings of the British Academy* 151 (2007). doi: 10.5871/bacad/9780197264249.003.0010.

Haiven, Max. "An Interview with Hari Kunzru: Networks, Finance Capital and the Fate of the Novel." *Wasafiri* 28, no. 3 (September 1, 2014): 8–23.

Hajjar, Lisa. "Anatomy of the US Targeted Killing Policy." *Middle East Report* 264 (fall 2012): 10–17. http://www.merip.org/mer/mer264/anatomy-us-targeted-killing-policy.

———. "International Humanitarian Law and 'Wars on Terror': A Comparative Analysis of Israeli and American Doctrines and Policies." *Journal of Palestine Studies* 36, no. 1 (2006): 21–42.

———. "Is Gaza Still Occupied and Why Does It Matter?" *Jadaliyya*, July 14, 2014. http://www.jadaliyya.com/pages/index/8807/is-gaza-still-occupied-and-why-does-it-matter.

———. "Universal Jurisdiction as Praxis: An Option to Pursue Accountability for Superpower Torturers." In *When Governments Break the Law: The Rule of Law and the Prosecution of the Bush Administration*, edited by Austin Sarat and Nasser Hussein, 87–120. New York: New York University Press, 2010.

Halberstam, Judith. *The Queer Art of Failure*. Durham, NC: Duke University Press, 2011.

Hall, James. *American Kamikaze*. Titusville, FL: J. Bryant, 1984.

Hall, Matthew. "Did Former SDSU Grad Student Anwar al-Awlaki Inspire the Charlie Hebdo Attack?" *San Diego Union Tribune*, January 9, 2015. http://www.utsandiego.com/news/2015/jan/09/anwar-al-awlaki.

Hall, Stuart. *Critical Dialogues in Cultural Studies*. New York: Routledge, 1996.

———. "Notes on Deconstructing the Popular." In *People's History and Socialist Theory*, edited by Raphael Samuel, 227–40. London: Routledge, 1981.

Hallion, Richard P. "Precision Guided Munitions and the New Era of Warfare." Working Paper 53. Air Power Studies Centre, 1995. http://www.fas.org/man/dod-101/sys/smart/docs/paper53.htm.

Hambling, David. "Drones Tag and Track Quarry Using Nanoparticle Sprays." *New Scientist* 2931 (August 24, 2013). https://www.newscientist.com/article/mg21929315-100-drones-tag-and-track-quarry-using-nanoparticle-sprays/.

Hand, Martin. *Ubiquitous Photography.* London: Polity, 2012.

Handwerk, Brian. "5 Surprising Drone Uses (Besides Amazon Delivery)." *National Geographic*, December 2, 2013.

Hansen, Thomas Blom, and Finn Stepputat, eds. *Sovereign Bodies: Citizens, Migrants, and States in the Postcolonial World.* Princeton, NJ: Princeton University Press, 2005.

Haraway, Donna. "A Cyborg Manifesto: Science, Technology, and Socialist-Feminism in the Late Twentieth Century." In *Simians, Cyborgs, and Women*, 149–81. New York: Routledge, 1991.

———. *Simians, Cyborgs, and Women: The Reinvention of Nature.* New York: Routledge, 1991.

Harger, Honor. "Unmanned Aerial Ecologies: Protodrones, Airspace and Canaries in the Mine." *honor harger* (blog), April 21, 2013. http://honorharger.wordpress.com/2013/04/21/unmanned-aerial-ecologies-proto-drones-airspace-and-canaries-in-the-mine.

Harmon, Amy. "Stop Them Before They Shoot Again." *New York Times*, May 5, 2005.

Haroon, Sana. *Frontier of Faith: Islam in the Indo-Afghan Borderland.* New York: Columbia University Press, 2007.

Harvey, Adam. "Stealth Wear Summary." January 17, 2013. http://ahprojects.com/projects/stealth-wear/.

Harwood, Graham. "Endless War: On the Database Structure of Armed Conflicts." *Rhizome*, March 17, 2014. http://rhizome.org/editorial/2014/mar/17/endless-war-database-structure-armed-conflict/.

Hastings, Michael. "The Rise of the Killer Drones: How America Goes to War in Secret." *Rolling Stone*, April 16, 2012.

Hawthorne, Nathaniel. *Twice-Told Tales.* Boston: American Stationers' Company, 1837.

Hayden, Michael. "To Keep America Safe, Embrace Drone Warfare." *New York Times*, February 19, 2016.

Heller, Kevin Jon. "'One Hell of a Killing Machine': Signature Strikes and International Law." *Journal of International Criminal Justice* 11, no. 1 (2013): 89–119.

Hersh, Seymour. "The Killing of Osama bin Laden." *London Review of Books* 37, no. 10 (2015): 3–12.

———. "Manhunt: The Bush Administration's New Strategy in the War against Terror." *New Yorker*, December 23 and 30, 2002.

Hilali, A. Z. "The Costs and Benefits of the Afghan War for Pakistan." *Contemporary South Asia* 11, no. 3 (2002): 291–310.

Hodge, Nathan. "U.S. Sharing Predator Video with Afghanistan, Pakistan." *Wired*, November 17, 2008. https://www.wired.com/2008/11/in-a-presentati/.

Holder, Eric. "Attorney General Eric Holder Speaks at Northwestern University School of Law." March 5, 2012. https://www.justice.gov/opa/speech/attorney-general-eric-holder-speaks-northwestern-university-school-law.

Holmqvist, Caroline. "Undoing War: War Ontologies and the Materiality of Drone Warfare." *Millennium: Journal of International Studies* 41, no. 3 (2013): 535–52.

Horgan, John. "Unmanned Flight: The Drones Come Home." *National Geographic*, October 2015.

"Hormuud Telecom Services Disrupted by Militant Group." *TeleGeography*, February 4, 2014. https://www.telegeography.com/products/commsupdate/articles/2014/02/04/hormuud-telecom-services-disrupted-by-militant-group/.

Horton, Scott. "Lawfare Redux." *Harper's Magazine*, March 12, 2010. http://harpers.org/blog/2010/03/lawfare-redux/.

———. *Lords of Secrecy: The National Security Elite and America's Stealth Warfare*. New York: Nation Books, 2015.

Hough, Kenneth. "Aerial Torpedoes, Buzz Bombs, and Predators: The Long Cultural History of Drones." *Origins* 6, no. 11 (2013). http://origins.osu.edu/article/aerial-torpedoes-buzz-bombs-and-predators-long-cultural-history-drones.

House, Tamzy J. (Col.), James B. Near Jr. (Lt. Col.), William B. Shields (LTC, USA), Ronald J. Celentano (Maj.), Ann E. Mercer (Maj.), James E. Pugh (Maj.). *Weather as a Force Multiplier: Owning the Weather in 2025*. A Research Paper Presented to Air Force 2025. August 1996. http://csat.au.af.mil/2025/volume3/vol3ch15.pdf.

Human Rights Watch. "'Between a Drone and Al-Qaeda': The Civilian Cost of US Targeted Killing in Yemen." October 22, 2013. https://www.hrw.org/report/2013/10/22/between-drone-and-al-qaeda/civilian-cost-us-targeted-killings-yemen.

———. "Djibouti: Allow Peaceful Protests." April 4, 2011. http://www.hrw.org/news/2011/04/04/djibouti-allow-peaceful-protests.

———. "Pakistan: Withdraw Repressive Counterterrorism Law." July 3, 2014. https://www.hrw.org/news/2014/07/03/pakistan-withdraw-repressive-counterterrorism-law.

Hussain, Murtaza. "Who Tried to Silence Drone Victim Kareem Khan?" *Intercept*, February 25, 2014. https://theintercept.com/2014/02/25/tried-silence-drone-victim-kareem-khan/.

Hussain, Nasser. "The Sound of Terror: Phenomenology of a Drone Strike." *Boston Review*, October 16, 2013. https://bostonreview.net/world/hussain-drone-phenomenology.

Hussain, Zahid. "Battleground North Waziristan." *Dawn*, November 19, 2014. http://www.dawn.com/news/1145359.

Hutchins, Edwin. "How a Cockpit Remembers Its Speeds." *Cognitive Science* 19, no. 3 (1995): 265–88.

International Crisis Group. *Drones: Myths and Reality in Pakistan*. Asia Report 247. Brussels: International Crisis Group, 2013.

———. *Pakistan: Countering Militancy in FATA*. Brussels: International Crisis Group, 2009.

International Human Rights and Conflict Resolution Clinic (Stanford Law School) and Global Justice Clinic (NYU School of Law). *Living under Drones: Death, Injury, and Trauma to Civilians from US Drone Practices in Pakistan*. Stanford, CA: Stanford Law School; New York: New York University School of Law, 2012.

Iqtidar, Humeira, and Noor Akbar. "Caught between Drones and Army Raids, Pakistanis in 'Tribal Areas' Feel Betrayed." *Conversation*, November 17, 2014. https://

theconversation.com/caught-between-drones-and-army-raids-pakistanis-in-tribal-areas-feel-betrayed-34216.

"Israel Convicts Journalist for Disclosing Assassinations." *Alakhbar English*, July 5, 2012. http://english.al-akhbar.com/node/9299.

Israel Foreign Affairs. "Salah Shehadeh—Special Investigatory Commission." November 8, 2015. http://israelforeignaffairs.com/2015/11/salah-shehadeh-special-investigatory-commission-2/.

Israeli Ministry of Foreign Affairs. "Findings of the Inquiry into the Death of Salah Shehadeh." August 2, 2002. http://www.mfa.gov.il/mfa/pressroom/2002/pages/findings%20of%20the%20inquiry%20into%20the%20death%20of%20salah%20sh.aspx.

Issacharoff, Samuel, and Richard H. Pildes. "Drones and the Dilemma of Modern Warfare." *New York University Public Law and Legal Theory Working Papers* 404 (June 1, 2013).

———. "Targeted Warfare: Individuating Enemy Responsibility." *New York University Law Review* 88, no. 5 (2013): 1521–99.

Jabareen, Hassan. "On Legal Advocacy and Legitimation of Control." *Jadal* 13 (May 2012).

———. "Transnational Lawyering and Legal Resistance before National Courts: Palestinian Cases before the Israeli Supreme Court." *Yale Human Rights and Development Journal* 13, no. 1 (2010): 65–83.

Jabri, Vivienne. *War and the Transformation of Global Politics*. New York: Palgrave Macmillan, 2007.

Jaffer, Jameel. "The Drone Memo Cometh." *Just Security* (blog), June 21, 2014. https://www.justsecurity.org/11986/drone-memo-cometh/.

Jahangir, Asma. "Civil and Political Rights, Including the Questions of Disappearances and Summary Executions." Report of the Special Rapporteur. Commission on Human Rights, UN Doc. E/CN.4/2003/3. January 13, 2003. http://repository.un.org/handle/11176/242638.

Jansen, Bart. "Small Drone Crashes near the White House Despite Ban Against Flights in D.C." *USA Today*, October 9, 2015. http://www.usatoday.com/story/news/2015/10/09/drone-crash-white-house-ellipse-us-park-police-federal-aviation-administration/73641812/.

Jarmakani, Amira. *Imagining Arab Womanhood: The Cultural Mythology of Veils, Harems, and Belly Dancers in the U.S.* New York: Palgrave Macmillan, 2008.

Jasanoff, Sheila, ed. *States of Knowledge: The Co-Production of Science and the Social Order*. New York: Routledge, 2004.

Johns, Fleur. "Guantánamo Bay and the Annihilation of the Exception." *European Journal of International Law* 16, no. 4 (2005): 613–35.

Johnsen, Gregory. *The Last Refuge: Yemen, Al-Qaeda and America's War in Arabia*. New York: W. W. Norton, 2013.

Johnston, John. "Machinic Vision." *Critical Inquiry* 26, no. 1 (1999): 27–48.

Jones, Bryan Williams. "Creech AFB UAV Operations." *Jonesblog*, February 22, 2008. http://prometheus.med.utah.edu/~bwjones/2008/02/creech-afb-uav-operations/.

Jones, Craig. "Lawfare and the Juridification of Late Modern War." *Progress in Human Geography* 40, no. 2 (2016): 221–39.

Jordan, Taryn. "The Politics of Impossibility: CeCe McDonald and Trayvon Martin—The Bursting of Black Rage." Master's thesis, Georgia State University, 2014.

Junod, Tom. "The Lethal Presidency of Barack Obama." *Esquire*, July 9, 2012.

———. "The Murderous Core of Obama's Drone Memo." *Esquire,* June 24, 2014.

Kaag, John. "Drones, Ethics and the Armchair Soldier." *Opinionator* (blog), March 17, 2013. http://opinionator.blogs.nytimes.com/2013/03/17/drones-ethics-and-the-armchair-soldier/.

Kaag, John, and Sarah Kreps. *Drone Warfare.* Cambridge: Polity Press, 2014.

Kahn, Paul. "Imagining Warfare." *European Journal of International Law* 24, no. 1 (2013): 199–216.

Kang, Cecilia. "Google to Use Balloons to Provide Internet Access to Remote Areas." *Washington Post*, June 14, 2013.

Kaplan, Caren. *Aerial Aftermaths: Wartime from Above.* Durham, NC: Duke University Press, 2017.

———. "Air Power's Visual Legacy: Operation Orchard and Aerial Reconnaissance Imagery as *Ruses de Guerre*." *Critical Military Studies* 1, no. 1 (2015): 61–78.

———. "The Balloon Prospect: Aerostatic Observation and the Emergence of Militarized Aeromobility." In *From Above: War, Violence and Verticality*, edited by Peter Adey, Mark Whitehead, and Alison Williams, 19–40. London: Hurst, 2013.

———. "Dead Reckoning: Aerial Perception and the Social Construction of Targets." *Vectors* 2, no. 2 (2007). http://www.vectorsjournal.org/projects/index.php?project=11.

———. "Drone Sight." *Public Books*, February 14, 2013. http://publicbooks.org/artmedia/soldier-exposures-and-technical-publics.

———. "Mobility and War: The Cosmic View of US 'Air Power.' " *Environment and Planning A* 38, no. 2 (2006): 395–407.

———. Precision Targets. 2010. http://www.precisiontargets.com/

———. "Precision Targets: GPS and the Militarization of U.S. Consumer Identity." *American Quarterly* 58, no. 3 (2006): 693–714.

———. "Sensing Distance: The Time and Space of Contemporary War." *Social Text* (June 17, 2013). http://socialtextjournal.org/periscope_article/sensing-distance-the-time-and-space-of-contemporary-war/.

Kaplan, Caren, Erik Loyer, and Ezra Claytan Daniels. "Precision Targets: GPS and the Militarization of Everyday Life." *Canadian Journal of Communication* 38, no. 3 (2013): 397–420.

Keenan, Thomas, and Eyal Weizman. "Israel: The Third Strategic Threat." *Open Democracy*, June 8, 2010. https://www.opendemocracy.net/thomas-keenan-eyal-weizman/israel-third-strategic-threat.

Kellenberger, Jakob. "International Humanitarian Law at the Beginning of the 21st Century." International Committee of the Red Cross, May 9, 2002. https://www.icrc.org/eng/resources/documents/statement/5e2c8v.htm.

Kelley, Robin D. G. *Race Rebels: Politics, Culture, and the Black Working Class.* New York: Simon and Schuster, 1996.

Kember, Sarah, and Joanna Zylinska. *Life after New Media: Mediation as a Vital Process.* Cambridge, MA: MIT Press, 2012.

Khalili, Laleh. *Time in the Shadows: Confinement in Counterinsurgencies.* Stanford, CA: Stanford University Press, 2012.

Khan, Wajahat. "The Ghosts and Gains of North Waziristan." *The News*, November 18, 2014.

Kilcullen, David. *The Accidental Guerrilla.* Oxford: Oxford University Press, 2009.

Kime, Patricia. "Study: Troops Still Fear Reporting PTSD." *Air Force Times*, December 16, 2011.

Kitchen, Rob, and Martin Dodge. *Code/Space: Software and Everyday Life.* Cambridge, MA: MIT Press, 2011.

Kittler, Friedrich. *Gramophone, Film, Typewriter.* 1987. Reprint. Stanford, CA: Stanford University Press, 1999.

———. "Media Wars: Trenches, Lightning, Stars." In *Essays: Literature, Media, Information Systems*, 117–29. Amsterdam: Overseas Publishers, 1997.

Klaidman, Daniel. "Drones: How Obama Learned to Kill." *Daily Beast*, May 28, 2012. http://www.thedailybeast.com/videos/2012/06/07/drones-how-obama-learned-to-kill.html.

———. *Kill or Capture: The War on Terror and the Soul of the Obama Presidency.* New York: Houghton Mifflin Harcourt, 2012.

Knefel, John. "Three Troubling Lessons from the Latest US Drone Strikes." *Rolling Stone*, June 17, 2014.

Knuckey, Sarah. "Analysis of the Stimson Drone Task Force Report." *Just Security* (blog), June 27, 2014. https://www.justsecurity.org/12357/stimson-drone-task-force-report-knuckey/.

———. "Key Findings in New UN Special Rapporteur Report on Drones." *Just Security* (blog), March 4, 2014. https://www.justsecurity.org/7819/key-findings-special-rapporteur-report-drones/.

Koh, Harold. "The Obama Administration and International Law." Remarks at the Annual Meeting of the American Society of International Law, March 25, 2010. http://www.state.gov/s/l/releases/remarks/139119.htm.

Kotef, Hagar, and Merav Amir. "Between Imaginary Lines: Violence and Its Justifications at the Military Checkpoints in Occupied Palestine." *Theory, Culture and Society* 28, no. 1 (2011): 55–81.

Kraidy, Marwan. "Contention and Circulation in the Digital Middle East: Music Video as Catalyst." *Television New Media* 14, no. 4 (2013): 271–85.

Krasmann, Susanne. "Targeted Killing and Its Law: On a Mutually Constituted Relationship." *Leiden Journal of International Law* 25, no. 3 (2012): 665–82.

Kretzmer, David. *The Occupation of Justice: The Supreme Court of Israel and the Occupied Territories.* Albany: State University of New York Press, [illegible].

Kunzru, Hari. "Drone." *Granta* 130 (March 14, 2015): 15–31.

———. *Gods without Men.* New York: Vintage, 2013.

———. *The Impressionist.* [2002]. New York: Plume, 2003.

———. *Memory Palace.* Edited by Laurie Britton Newell and Ligaya Salazar. London: V and A, 2013.

———. *My Revolutions: A Novel.* [2007]. New York: Plume, 2008.

———. *Transmission.* [2004]. New York: Plume, 2005.

Kurgan, Laura. *Close Up at a Distance: Mapping, Technology, and Politics.* Cambridge, MA: MIT Press, 2013.

Kutz, Christopher. "How Norms Die: Torture and Assassination in American Security Policy." *Ethics and International Affairs* 28, no. 4 (2014): 425–49.

Kuyers, Josh. "CIA or DoD: Clarifying the Legal Framework Applicable to the Drone Authority Debate." National Security Law Brief, April 4, 2013. http://www.nationalsecuritylawbrief.com.

Land, Nick. *Fanged Noumena: Collected Writings, 1987–2007.* Falmouth, UK: Urbanomic, 2011.

Landay, Jonathan. "Do U.S. Drones Kill Pakistani Extremists or Recruit Them?" McClatchy Newspapers, April 7, 2009. http://www.mcclatchydc.com/news/nation-world/world/article24532831.html.

———. "Leaked U.S. Justification for Drone Killings Assailed as Rewriting Definition of 'Imminent Threat.'" McClatchy Newspapers, February 5, 2013. http://www.mcclatchydc.com/news/nation-world/world/article24744379.html.

———. "U.S. Secret: CIA Collaborated with Pakistan Spy Agency in Drone War." McClatchy Newspapers, April 9, 2013. http://www.mcclatchydc.com/news/nation-world/world/article24747829.html.

Latour, Bruno. "Morality and Technology: The End of the Means." *Theory, Culture and Society* 19, nos. 5–6 (2002): 247–60.

———. *Pandora's Hope: Essays on the Reality of Science Studies.* Translated by Catherine Porter. Cambridge, MA: Harvard University Press, 1999.

———. "Spheres and Networks: Two Ways to Reinterpret Globalization." A lecture delivered to Harvard Graduate School of Design, February 17, 2009. *Harvard Design Magazine* 30 (spring/summer 2009): 138–44. http://www.bruno-latour.fr/sites/default/files/115-SPACE-HARVARD-GB.pdf.

Leander, Anna. "Technological Agency in the Co-constitution of Legal Expertise and the US Drone Program." *Leiden Journal of International Law* 26, no. 4 (2013): 811–31.

Leghari, Faryal. "Dealing with FATA: Strategic Shortfalls and Considerations." *Perspectives on Terrorism* 2, no. 10 (2008). http://www.terrorismanalysts.com/pt/index.php/pot/article/view/54/html.

Leonard, Philip. "'A Revolution in Code'? Hari Kunzru's *Transmission* and the Cultural Politics of Hacking." *Textual Practice* 28, no. 2 (2014): 267–87.

Lewis, Michael. "Drones and the Boundaries of the Battlefield." *Texas International Law Journal* 47, no. 2 (2011–12): 293–314.

———. "The Misleading Human Rights Watch and Amnesty International Reports on U.S. Drones." *Opinio Juris*, November 8, 2013. http://opiniojuris.org/2013/11/08/misleading-human-rights-watch-amnesty-international-reports-u-s-drones.

Li, Darryl. "The Gaza Strip as Laboratory: Notes in the Wake of Disengagement." *Journal of Palestine Studies* 35, no. 2 (2006): 38–55.

Liang, Aislinn. "US Drone 'Shot Down by al-Shabaab in Somalia.'" *Telegraph*, May 29, 2013.

Lichty, Patrick. "Drone: Camera, Weapon, Toy: The Aestheticization of Dark Technology." *Furtherfield*, May 30, 2013. http://www.furtherfield.org/blog/patrick-lichty/drone-camera-weapontoy-aestheticization-dark-technology-0.

Lindqvist, Sven. *A History of Bombing*. New York: New Press, 2003.

Lovink, Geert. *Networks without a Cause: A Critique of Social Media*. Cambridge: Polity Press, 2012.

Lubell, Noam, and Nathan Derejko. "A Global Battlefield? Drones and the Geographical Scope of Armed Conflict." *Journal of International Criminal Justice* 11, no. 1 (2013): 65–88.

Lyon, David. "Everyday Surveillance: Personal Data and Social Classifications." *Information, Communication and Society* 5, no. 2 (2002): 242–57.

Mack, Pamela. *Viewing the Earth: The Social Construction of the Landsat Satellite System*. Cambridge, MA: MIT Press, 1990.

Mackay, Robin, and Armen Avanessian. *#Accelerate: The Accelerationist Reader*. Falmouth, UK: Urbanomic, 2014.

MacKenzie, Donald A. *Inventing Accuracy: A Historical Sociology of Nuclear Missile Guidance*. Cambridge, MA: MIT Press, 1993.

Maddalena, Kate, and Jeremy Packer. "The Digital Body: Telegraphy as Discourse Network." *Theory, Culture and Society* 32, no. 1 (2015): 93–117.

Mahler, Jonathan. "What Do We Really Know about Osama bin Laden's Death?" *New York Times Magazine*, October 15, 2015.

Mamdani, Mahmood. "Beyond Settler and Native as Political Identities: Overcoming the Political Legacy of Colonialism." *Society for Comparative Study of Society and History* 43, no. 4 (2001): 651–54.

———. *Citizen and Subject: Contemporary Africa and the Legacy of Late Colonialism*. Princeton, NJ: Princeton University Press, 1996.

———. *Good Muslim, Bad Muslim: America, the Cold War, and the Roots of Terrorism*. New York: Three Leaves Press, 2004.

———. "Historicizing Power and Responses to Power: Indirect Rule and Its Reform." *Social Research* 66, no. 3 (1999): 859–86.

Manjikian, Mary. "Becoming Unmanned: The Gendering of Lethal Autonomous Warfare Technology." *International Feminist Journal of Politics* 16, no. 1 (2014): 48–65.

Mann, Itamar. "The Dual Foundation of Universal Jurisdiction: Toward a Jurisprudence for the 'Court of Critique.'" *Transnational Legal Theory* 1, no. 4 (2010): 485–521.

Manovich, Lev. "The Mapping of Space: Perspective, Radar and 3-D Graphics." 1993. http://manovich.net/content/old/03-articles/01-article-1993/01-article-1993.pdf.

Maoz, Asher. "War and Peace: An Israeli Perspective." *Constitutional Forum* 24, no. 2 (2005): 35–76.

March, Andrew. "A Dangerous Mind?" *New York Times*, April 21, 2012.

Marez, Curtis. *Drug Wars: The Political Economy of Narcotics*. Minneapolis: University of Minnesota Press, 2004.

Marsden, Magnus, and Benjamin D. Hopkins. *Fragments of the Afghan Frontier*. London: Hurst, 2011.

Marsh, Brandon Douglas. "Ramparts of Empire: India's North-West Frontier and British Imperialism, 1919–1947." PhD diss., University of Texas, 2009.

Martin, Gary, and Viveca Novak. "Drones: Despite Problems, a Push to Expand Domestic Use." *OpenSecrets Blog*, November 27, 2012. https://www.opensecrets.org/news/2012/11/drones-despite-problems-a-push-to-e.html.

Martin, Jim. "Best Quadcopters 2015/16." *TechAdvisor*, October 14, 2015. http://www.pcadvisor.co.uk/test-centre/gadget/best-quadcopter-2015–2016-drone-buying-guide-3601312/.

Martin, Rachel. "Report: High Levels of 'Burnout' in U.S. Drone Pilots." *NPR*, December 19, 2011. http://www.npr.org/2011/12/19/143926857/report-high-levels-of-burnout-in-u-s-drone-pilots.

Masco, Joseph. *The Theater of Operation: National Security Affect from the Cold War to the War on Terror*. Durham, NC: Duke University Press, 2014.

Masood, Salman, and Pir Zubair Shah. "Drone Attack Kills Civilians in Pakistan." *New York Times*, March 17, 2011.

"Mass Arrests Stopped Further Djibouti Protests." *afrol News*, February 27, 2011. http://www.afrol.com/articles/37449.

Massumi, Brian. "Fear (The Spectrum Said)." *Positions* 13, no. 1 (2005): 31–48.

———. "The Future Birth of the Affective Fact: The Political Ontology of Threat." In *The Affect Theory Reader*, edited by Melissa Gregg and Gregory J. Seigworth, 52–70. Durham, NC: Duke University Press, 2010.

———. *Ontopower: War, Powers, and the State of Perception*. Durham, NC: Duke University Press, 2015.

———. "Potential Politics and the Primacy of Preemption." *Theory and Event* 10, no. 2 (2007): 1–34.

Mayer, Jane. "The Hidden Power: The Legal Mind behind the White House's War on Terror." *New Yorker*, July 26, 2006.

———. "The Predator War." *New Yorker*, October 26, 2009.

Mazzetti, Mark. "How a Single Spy Helped Turn Pakistan against the United States." *New York Times*, April 9, 2013.

———. "Rise of the Predators: A Secret Deal, Sealed in Blood." *New York Times*, April 6, 2013.

———. "A Secret Deal on Drones, Sealed in Blood." *New York Times*, April 7, 2013.

Mazzetti, Mark, and Matt Apuzzo. "Deep Support in Washington for CIA's Drone Program." *New York Times*, April 25, 2015.

Mazzetti, Mark, and Eric Schmitt. "First Evidence of a Blunder in Drone Strike: 2 Extra Bodies." *New York Times*, April 23, 2015.

Mazzetti, Mark, and Declan Walsh. "Pakistan Says U.S. Drone Killed Taliban Leader." *New York Times*, May 29, 2013.

Mbembe, Achille. "Necropolitics." Translated by Libby Meintjes. *Public Culture* 15, no. 1 (2003): 11–40.

McAlister, Melani. *Epic Encounters: Culture, Media, and U.S. Interests in the Middle East Since 1945*. Berkeley: University of California Press, 2001.

McGarry, Brendan. "Drones Most Accident-Prone U.S. Air Force Craft: BGOV Barometer." *Bloomberg Business*, June 17, 2012. http://www.bloomberg.com/news/articles/2012-06-18/drones-most-accident-prone-u-s-air-force-craft-bgov-barometer.

McKelvey, Tara. "Interview with Harold Koh, Obama's Defender of Drone Strikes." *Daily Beast*, April 8, 2012. http://www.thedailybeast.com/articles/2012/04/08/interview-with-harold-koh-obama-s-defender-of-drone-strikes.html.

McNabb, Miriam. "Chicago Now a No Drone Zone: Heavy Restrictions Passed." *DroneLife.com*, November 13, 2015. http://dronelife.com/2015/11/13/chicago-now-a-no-drone-zone-heavy-restrictions-passed/.

McVeigh, Karen. "Drone Strikes: Tears in Congress as Pakistani Family Tells of Mother's Death." *Guardian*, October 29, 2013.

Mead, Corey. *War Play: Video Games and the Future of Armed Conflict*. New York: Houghton Mifflin, 2013.

Mégret, Frédéric. "War and the Vanishing Battlefield." *Loyola University Chicago International Law Review* 9, no. 1 (2011–12): 131–56.

Mejias, Ulises. *Off the Network: Disrupting the Digital World*. Minneapolis: University of Minnesota Press, 2013.

Menkhaus, Ken. "Al-Shabaab and Social Media: A Double-Edged Sword." *Brown Journal of World Affairs*, spring/summer 2014. https://www.brown.edu/initiatives/journal-world-affairs/sites/brown.edu.initiatives.journal-world-affairs/files/private/articles/Menkhaus.pdf.

Menthe, Lance, Myron Hura, and Carl Rhodes. *The Effectiveness of Remotely Piloted Aircraft in a Permissive Hunter-Killer Scenario*. Santa Monica, CA: RAND, 2014.

Merleau-Ponty, Maurice. *Phenomenology of Perception*. Translated by Colin Smith. [1945]. Reprint. New York: Routledge, 2002.

Metcalf, Barbara D. "'Traditionalist' Islamic Activism: Deoband, Tablighis, and Talibs." ISIM Papers, 2002.

Michel, Arthur Holland. "The Age of Drone Vandalism Begins with an Epic NYC Tag." *Wired*, April 30, 2015. http://www.wired.com/2015/04/age-drone-vandalism-begins-epic-nyc-tag/.

Miethe, Terance D., et al. "Public Attitudes about Aerial Drone Activities: Results of a National Survey." UNLV Center for Crime and Justice Policy, July 2014. http://www.unlv.edu/sites/default/files/page_files/27/CCJP-PublicAttitudesAboutAerialDrones-2014.pdf.

Milgram, Stanley. *Obedience to Authority: An Experimental View*. New York: Harper and Row, 1974.

Miller, Greg. "CIA Flew Stealth Drones into Pakistan to Monitor bin Laden House." *Washington Post*, May 17, 2011.

———. "Lawmakers Seek to Stymie Plan to Shift Control of Drone Campaign from CIA to Pentagon." *Washington Post*, January 15, 2014.

———. "Plan for Hunting Terrorists Signals U.S. Intends to Keep Adding Names to Kill Lists." *Washington Post*, October 23, 2012.

———. "Under Obama, an Emerging Global Apparatus for Drone Killing." *Washington Post*, December 27, 2011.

———."US Wants to Widen Area in Pakistan Where It Can Operate Drones." *Washington Post*, November 20, 2010.

Miller, Greg, and Julie Tate. "CIA Shifts Focus to Killing Targets." *Washington Post*, September 1, 2011.

Miller, Greg, Julie Tate, and Barton Gellman. "Documents Reveal NSA's Extensive Involvement in Targeted Killing Program." *Washington Post*, October 16, 2013.

Miller, Greg, and Bob Woodward. "Secret Memos Reveal Explicit Nature of U.S., Pakistan Agreement on Drones." *Washington Post*, October 24, 2013.

Miller, Peter, and Nicholas Rose. "Production, Identity and Democracy." *Theory and Society* 24, no. 3 (1995): 427–67.

Miller, Toby. *The Well-Tempered Self: Citizenship, Culture and the Postmodern Subject*. Baltimore: Johns Hopkins University Press, 1993.

Mirzoeff, Nicholas. Introduction to *The Visual Culture Reader*, third edition, edited by Nicholas Mirzoeff, 3–13. London, Routledge, 2012.

———. *The Right to Look: A Counterhistory of Visuality*. Durham, NC: Duke University Press, 2014.

———. *Watching Babylon: The War in Iraq and Global Visual Culture*. New York: Routledge, 2005.

Moallem, Minoo. *Between Warrior Brother and Veiled Sister: Islamic Fundamentalism and the Politics of Patriarchy in Iran*. Berkeley: University of California Press, 2005.

———. "The Unintended Consequences of Equality within Difference." *Brown Journal of World Affairs* 22, no. 1 (2015): 335–49.

Mohamed, Hamza. "Al-Shabab Say They Are Back on Twitter." *Al Jazeera*, December 16, 2013.

Moore, Christopher. "Invigorating Play: The Role of Affect in Online Multiplayer FPS Games." In *Guns, Grenades and Grunts: First Person Shooter Games*, edited by Gerald A. Voorhees, Joshua Call, and Katie Whitlock, 341–64. London: Continuum Books, 2012.

Morrison, Elise. "Ambushed by Empathy: George Brant's *Grounded*." *TDR/The Drama Review* 58, no. 4 (2014): 163–69.

M. T. "Waziris Mourn Their Dead after Army Attacks." *Tanqeed*, November 2012. http://www.tanqeed.org/2012/11/waziris-mourn-their-dead-after-army-attacks/#sthash.ktmpwbgr.8wMRtTh1.dpbs.

Mulrine, Anna. "Warheads on Foreheads." *Air Force Magazine* 91, no. 10 (2008): 44–47.

Munro, Campbell. "The Entangled Sovereignties of Air Police Mapping the Boundary of the International and the Imperial." *Global Jurist* 15, no. 2 (2015): 117–38.

———. "Mapping the Vertical Battlespace: Towards a Legal Cartography of Aerial Sovereignty." *London Review of International Law* 2, no. 2 (2014): 233–61.

Murphy, Margi. "15 UK Companies Using Drones." *Techworld*, November 11, 2015. http://www.techworld.com/picture-gallery/personal-tech/6-best-uses-of-drones-in-business-3605145/#13.

Murray, Peter. "Drones Close in on Farms, the Next Step in Precision Agriculture." *Singularity Hub*, May 28, 2013. http://singularityhub.com/2013/05/28/drones-close-in-on-farms-the-next-step-in-precision-agriculture/.

Najmabadi, Afsaneh. *Women with Mustaches and Men without Beards: Gender and Sexual Anxieties of Iranian Modernity*. Berkeley: University of California Press, 2005.

Naseemullah, Adnan. "Shades of Sovereignty: Explaining Political Order and Disorder in Pakistan's Northwest." *Studies in Comparative International Development* 49, no. 4 (2014): 501–22.

National Commission on Terrorist Attacks upon the United States. The 9/11 Commission Report. New York: W. W. Norton, 2004.

National Naval Aviation Museum. "TDR-1 Edna III." http://www.navalaviationmuseum.org/attractions/aircraft-exhibits/item/?item=tdr.

National Security Agency. "Global Information Grid." November 14, 2008. Last modified April 23, 2012. http://www.acqnotes.com/Attachments/DoD%20GIG%20Architectural%20Vision,%20June%2007.pdf.

Naval History and Heritage Command. "U.S. Navy Personnel in World War II: Service and Casualty Statistics." April 28, 2015. https://www.history.navy.mil/research/library/online-reading-room/title-list-alphabetically/u/us-navy-personnel-in-world-war-ii-service-and-casualty-statistics.html.

Naylor, Brian. "Look, Up in The Sky! It's a Drone, Looking at You." *NPR*, December 5, 2011. http://www.npr.org/2011/12/05/143144146/drone-technology-finding-its-way-to-american-skies.

Negarestani, Reza. "A Vertiginous Enlightenment." In *Savage Objects*, edited by Godofredo Pereira, 101–18. Lisbon: INCM, 2012.

———. "Globe of Revolution." *Journal of Politics, Gender and Culture* 17 (2011): 25–54.

Neocleous, Mark. *War Power, Police Power*. Edinburgh: Edinburgh University Press, 2014.

New America Foundation. "Drone Wars Pakistan: Analysis." Accessed February 19, 2017. http://securitydata.newamerica.net/drones/pakistan-analysis.html.

Newcome, Lawrence. *Unmanned Aviation: A Brief History of Unmanned Aerial Vehicles*. Reston, VA: American Institute of Aeronautics and Astronautics, 2004.

New York City Bar Association Committee on International Law. "The Legality under International Law of Targeted Killing by Drones Launched by the United States." New York, June 16, 2014. http://www2.nycbar.org/pdf/report/uploads/20072625-TheLegalityofTargetedInternationalKillingsbyUS-LaunchedDrones.pdf.

New York City Profiling Collaborative. "In Our Own Words: Narratives of South Asian New Yorkers Affected by Racial and Religious Profiling." March 2012. http://saalt.org/wp-content/uploads/2012/09/In-Our-Own-Words-Narratives-of-South-Asian-New-Yorkers-Affected-by-Racial-and-Religious-Profiling.pdf.

Nichols, Bill. *Representing Reality: Issues and Concepts in Documentary Film*. Bloomington: Indiana University Press, 1991.

Nichols, Robert. "The Frontier Tribal Areas, 1840–1990." *Afghanistan Forum*, August 1995.

———. *Settling the Frontier: Land, Law and Society in the Peshawar Valley, 1500–1900*. Oxford: Oxford University Press, 2001.

Niva, Steve. "Disappearing Violence: JSOC and the Pentagon's New Cartography of Networked Warfare." *Security Dialogue* 44, no. 3 (June 2013): 185–202.

———. "Palestinian Suicide Bombings, Israeli Provocations and the Cycle of Violence." *Peace Review* 15, no. 1 (2003): 33–38.

Nordland, Rod. "Germany and Sweden Are Said to Help Make Afghan 'Kill Decisions.'" *New York Times*, September 4, 2015.

Northrop Grumman Corporation. "Northrop Grumman Awarded Contract to Develop Miniaturized Inertial Navigation System for DARPA." June 5, 2014. http://news.northropgrumman.com/news/releases/northrop-grumman-awarded-contract-to-develop-miniaturized-inertial-navigation-system-for-darpa.

Noys, Benjamin. "Drone Metaphysics." *Culture Machine* 16 (2015): 1–22.

———. *The Persistence of the Negative: A Critique of Contemporary Continental Theory*. Edinburgh: Edinburgh University Press, 2010.

NPR. "Drones Moving from War Zones to the Home Front." *NPR*, April 17, 2012. http://www.npr.org/2012/04/17/150817060/drones-move-from-war-zones-to-the-home-front.

Nye, Joseph S. "The Future of American Power." *Foreign Affairs*, November 1, 2010. https://www.foreignaffairs.com/articles/2010-11-01/future-american-power.

Obama, Barack. "Remarks by President Obama and Prime Minister Shinawatra in a Joint Press Conference." Bangkok, Thailand, November 18, 2012. https://www.whitehouse.gov/the-press-office/2012/11/18/remarks-president-obama-and-prime-minister-shinawatra-joint-press-confer.

———. "Remarks by President Obama at NATO Summit Press Conference." Newport, Wales, September 25, 2012. http://www.whitehouse.gov/the-press-office/2014/09/05/remarks-president-obama-nato-summit-press-conference.

———. "Remarks by the President at the National Defense University." Fort McNair, Washington, DC, May 23, 2013. http://www.whitehouse.gov/the-press-office/2013/05/23/remarks-president-national-defense-university.

Ohnuki-Tierney, Emiko. *Kamikaze, Cherry Blossoms, and Nationalisms: The Militarization of Aesthetics in Japanese History*. Chicago: University of Chicago Press, 2002.

———. *Kamikaze Diaries: Reflections of Japanese Student Soldiers*. Chicago: University of Chicago Press, 2006.

Olsen, Erik. "Drone Racing Dreams." *New York Times*, November 11, 2015.

Omar, Feisal, Abdi Sheikh, and George Obulutsa. "Drone Crashes in Southern Somalia, May Have Been Shot Down." *Reuters*, May 28, 2013. http://www.reuters.com/article/2013/05/28/us-somalia-conflict-idUSBRE94R0JP20130528.

Omissi, David E. *Air Power and Colonial Control: The Royal Air Force, 1919–1939*. Manchester: Manchester University Press, 1990.

Oppenheimer, J. Robert. "Now I am become death . . ." Excerpt of a July 16, 1945, interview about the Trinity explosion, first broadcast as part of the television documentary *The Decision to Drop the Bomb* (1965), produced by Fred Freed, *NBC White Paper*. Accessed February 12, 2017. http://www.atomicarchive.com/Movies/Movie8.shtml.

Osman, Ahmed. "Somalia Powerless to Stop Al-Shabaab Mobile Internet Shutdown." Inter Press Service, February 16, 2014. http://www.ipsnews.net/2014/02/somalia-powerless-stop-al-shabaab-mobile-internet-shutdown/.

Ouma, Joseph A., Wayne L. Chappelle, and Amber Salinas. "Facets of Occupational Burnout among U.S. Air Force Active Duty and National Guard/Reserve MQ-1 Predator and MQ-9 Reaper Operators." Air Force Research Labs Technical Report AFRL-SA-WP-TR-2011-0003. June 2011.

Pachirat, Timothy. *Every Twelve Seconds: Industrialized Slaughter and the Politics of Sight*. New Haven, CT: Yale University Press, 2011.

Packer, Jeremy. "Screens in the Sky: SAGE, Surveillance, and the Automation of Perceptual, Mnemonic, and Epistemological Labor." *Social Semiotics* 23, no. 2 (2013): 173–95.

Packer, Jeremy, and Joshua Reeves. "Romancing the Drone: Military Desire and Anthropophobia from SAGE to Swarm." *Canadian Journal of Communication* 38, no. 3 (2013): 309–31.

Page, Jeremy. "US Missile Strike Kills Six in Pakistan Village." *Times*, November 19, 2008.

Pagnamenta, Robin. "My Dead Mother Wasn't an Enemy of America, She Was Just an Old Lady." *Times*, November 20, 2012.

Palestinian Centre for Human Rights. "Assassination Reports." Accessed February 17, 2017. http://pchrgaza.org/en/?cat=60.

Parks, Lisa. *Coverage: Vertical Mediation and the War on Terror*. New York: Routledge, forthcoming.

———. *Cultures in Orbit: Satellites and the Televisual*. Durham, NC: Duke University Press, 2005.

———. "Digging into Google Earth: A Critical Analysis of 'Crisis in Darfur.'" *Geoforum* 40 (2009): 535–45.

———. "Drone Media: Grounded Dimensions of the US Drone War in Pakistan." In *Place, Scale and Mediated Communication: Exploring Context Collapse*, edited by Carolyn Marvin and Sun-ha Hong, 13–28. New York: Routledge, forthcoming 2017.

———. "Drones, Infrared Imagery, and Body Heat." *International Journal of Communication* 8 (2014): 2518–21. http://ijoc.org/index.php/ijoc/issue/archive.

———. "Drones, Vertical Mediation, and the Targeted Class." *Feminist Studies* 42, no. 1 (2016): 227–35.

———. "Vertical Mediation: Geospatial Imagery and the US Wars in Afghanistan and Iraq." In *Mediated Geographies and Geographies of Media*, edited by Susan Mains, Julie Cupples, and Chris Lukenbeal, 159–75. New York: Springer, 2015.

———. "Zeroing In: Overhead Imagery, Infrastructure Ruins, and Datalands in Afghanistan and Iraq." In *Communication Matters: Materialist Approaches to Media, Mobility and Networks*, edited by Jeremy Packer and Stephen B. Crofts Wiley, 78–92. New York: Routledge, 2013.

Parks, Lisa, and Jo Ellen Fair. "Africa on Camera: Television News Coverage and Aerial Imaging of Rwandan Refugees." *Africa Today* 48, no. 2 (2001): 35–57.

Pater, Ruben. *Drone Survival Guide*. http://www.dronesurvivalguide.org/.

Paumgarten, Nick. "Here's Looking at You: Should We Worry about the Rise of the Drone?" *New Yorker*, May 14, 2012.

Pelton, Robert Young. "Enter the Drones: An In-Depth Look at Drones, Somali Reactions, and How the War May Change." *Somalia Report*, July 6, 2011. http://www.somaliareport.com/index.php/post/1096.

Perry, Caroline. "A Self-Organizing Thousand-Robot Swarm." *Harvard School of Engineering and Applied Sciences*, August 14, 2014. http://www.seas.harvard.edu/news/2014/08/self-organizing-thousand-robot-swarm.

Peterson, Scott, and Payam Faramarzi. "Iran Hijacked US Drone, Says Iranian Engineer." *Christian Science Monitor*, December 15, 2011.

Piore, Adam. "Rise of the Insect Drones." *Popular Science*, January 29, 2014. http://www.popsci.com/article/technology/rise-insect-drones.

Plotnick, Rachel. "Predicting Push-Button Warfare: US Print Media and Conflict from a Distance, 1945–2010." *Media, Culture and Society* 34, no. 6 (2012): 655–72.

Porter, Gareth. "How McChrystal and Petraeus Built an Indiscriminate 'Killing Machine.'" *Truthout*, September 26, 2011. http://www.truth-out.org/news/item/3588:how-mcchrystal-and-petraeus-built-an-indiscriminate-killing-machine.

———. "Why Pakistani Military Demands a Veto on Drone Strikes." Inter Press Service, August 16, 2011. http://www.ipsnews.net/2011/08/why-pakistani-military-demands-a-veto-on-drone-strikes/.

Povinelli, Elizabeth A. *The Cunning of Recognition: Indigenous Alterities and the Making of Australian Multiculturalism*. Durham, NC: Duke University Press, 2002.

Power, Matthew. "Confessions of a Drone Warrior." *GQ*, October 22, 2013.

Priest, Dana. "NSA Growth Fueled by Need to Target Terrorists." *Washington Post*, July 21, 2013.

———. "U.S. Military Teams, Intelligence Deeply Involved in Aiding Yemen on Strikes." *Washington Post*, January 27, 2010.

Puar, Jasbir. *Terrorist Assemblages: Homonationalism in Queer Times*. Durham, NC: Duke University Press, 2007.

Pugliese, Joseph. "Prosthetics of Law and the Anomic Violence of Drones." *Griffith Law Review* 20, no. 4 (2011): 931–61.

———. *State Violence and the Execution of Law*. New York: Routledge, 2013.

Rana, Junaid. *Terrifying Muslims: Race and Labor in the South Asian Diaspora*. Durham, NC: Duke University Press, 2011.

Raytheon. "Raytheon AST Surveillance and Reconnaissance Solutions." YouTube, November 8, 2011. https://www.youtube.com/watch?v=UtpURMoT1Qg.

Razack, Sherene. *Casting Out: The Eviction of Muslims from Western Law and Politics*. Toronto: University of Toronto Press, 2008.

———. "A Hole in the Wall; a Rose at the Checkpoint: The Spatial Colonial Encounters in Occupied Palestine." *Journal of Critical Race Inquiry* 1, no. 1 (2010): 90–108.

Reisner, Col. Daniel. "Israel Ministry of Foreign Affairs Press Briefing." November 15, 2000. http://mfa.gov.il/MFA/PressRoom/2000/Pages/Press%20Briefing%20by%20Colonel%20Daniel%20Reisner-%20Head%20of.aspx.

Replogle, Jill. "The Drone Makers and Their Friends in Washington." *Fronteras*, July 5, 2015. http://www.fronterasdesk.org/content/drone-makers-and-their-friends-washington.

Reporters Sans Frontiers. "Djibouti Authorities Step up Harassment of Journalists," January 19, 2016. https://rsf.org/en/news/djibouti-authorities-step-harassment-journalists.

Reprieve. "You Never Die Twice: Multiple Kills in the US Drone Program." November 2014. http://www.reprieve.org/wp-content/uploads/2014_11_24_PUB-You-Never-Die-Twice-Multiple-Kills-in-the-US-Drone-Program-1.pdf.

Reprieve (London) and Foundation for Fundamental Rights (Islamabad). "The Situation in Afghanistan: The Use of Drone Strikes in Pakistan." Communication to the Office of the Prosecutor, International Criminal Court, February 19, 2014. http://www.reprieve.org.uk/wp-content/uploads/2015/04/2014_02_20_PUB-ICC-drones-complaint.pdf.

Resnick, Judith. "Detention, the War on Terror, and the Federal Courts." *Columbia Law Review* 110, no. 2 (2010): 579–686.

Rich, B. Ruby. "Sundance at Thirty." *Film Quarterly* 67, no. 2 (winter 2013): 85–91.

Richardson, Lisa K., Christopher Frueh, and Ronald Acierno. "Prevalence Estimates of Combat-Related PTSD: A Critical Review." *Australian and New Zealand Journal of Psychiatry* 44, no. 1 (2010): 4–19.

Risen, James, and David Johnson. "Threats and Responses: Bush Has Widened Authority of CIA to Kill Terrorists." *New York Times*, December 15, 2002.

Riza, M. Shane. *Killing without Heart: Limits on Robotic Warfare in an Age of Persistent Conflict*. Washington, DC: Potomac Books, 2013.

Rizer, Arthur, and Joseph Hartman. "How the War on Terror Has Militarized the Police." *Atlantic*, November 7, 2011.

Robinson, Jennifer. "'Bugsplat': The Ugly US Drone War in Pakistan." *Al Jazeera*, November 29, 2011.

Rodriguez, Alex. "Pakistan Denounces U.S. Drone Strike." *Los Angeles Times*, March 18, 2011.

Roe, Andrew. "Friends in High Places: Air Power on the North-West Frontier of India." *Air Power Review* 11, no. 2 (2008): 3–42.

———. *Waging War in Waziristan: The British Struggle in the Land of Bin Laden, 1849–1947*. Lawrence: University of Kansas Press, 2008.

Rogers, Ann, and John Hill. *Unmanned: Drone Warfare and Global Security*. London: Pluto Press, 2014.

Rohde, David, and Mohammed Khan. "Ex-fighter for Taliban Dies in Strike in Pakistan." *New York Times*, June 19, 2004.

Romero, Rene F. "The Origins of Centralized Control and Decentralized Execution." Master's thesis, US Army Command and General Staff College, 2003.

Ron, James. *License to Kill: Israeli Undercover Operations against "Wanted" and Masked Palestinians*. New York: Human Rights Watch, 1993.

Rose, Nicholas. *Governing the Soul: The Shaping of the Private Self.* London: Routledge, 1989.

———. *Inventing Our Selves: Psychology, Power, and Personhood.* New York: Cambridge University Press, 1996.

Rosenzweig, Ido, and Yuval Shany. "Update on Universal Jurisdiction: Spanish Supreme Court Affirms Decision to Close Inquiry into Targeted Killing of Salah Shehadeh." *Terrorism and Democracy*, no. 17 (April 5, 2010).

Ross, Alice. "CIA Drone Strikes outside Pakistan's Tribal Regions." *Bureau of Investigative Journalism*, November 21, 2013. https://www.thebureauinvestigates.com/2013/11/21/cia-drone-strikes-outside-pakistans-tribal-regions.

———. "High Court Rejects First UK Challenge to CIA's Drone Campaign." *Bureau of Investigative Journalism*, December 22, 2012. https://www.thebureauinvestigates.com/2012/12/22/court-of-appeal-rejects-first-uk-challenge-to-cias-drone-campaign/.

———. "Leaked Official Document Records 330 Drone Strikes in Pakistan." *Bureau of Investigative Journalism*, January 29, 2014. https://www.thebureauinvestigates.com/2014/01/29/leaked-official-document-records-330-drone-strikes-in-pakistan.

Rothenberg, Daniel. "What the Drone Debate Is Really About." *Slate*, May 6, 2013. http://www.slate.com/articles/technology/future_tense/2013/05/drones_in_the_united_states_what_the_debate_is_really_about.html.

Rothstein, Adam. *Drone.* London: Bloomsbury, 2015.

Roy, Arundhati. "Confronting Empire." *Outlook India*, January 30, 2003. http://www.outlookindia.com/article.aspx?218738.

Rubinstein, Michael, and Wei-Min Shen. "A Scalable and Distributed Model for Self-Organization and Self-Healing." In *Proceedings of the 7th International Joint Conference on Autonomous Agents and Multiagent Systems,* vol. 3, 1179–82. Richland, SC: International Foundation for Autonomous Agents and Multiagent Systems, 2008.

Rumsfeld, Donald. "Secretary Rumsfeld Press Conference at NATO Headquarters, Brussels, Belgium." U.S. Department of Defense News transcript, June 6, 2002. www.defense.gov/transcripts/transcript.aspx?transcriptid=3490.

Ryan, Klem. "What's Wrong with Drones? The Battlefield in International Humanitarian Law." In *The American Way of Bombing: Changing Ethical and Legal Norms from Flying Fortresses to Drones*, edited by Matthew Evangelista and Henry Shue, 207–23. Ithaca, NY: Cornell University Press, 2014.

Ryan, Maria. "'War in Countries We Are Not at War With': The 'War on Terror' on the Periphery from Bush to Obama." *International Politics* 48, no. 2 (2011): 364–89.

Sadat, Leila N., and Jing Geng. "On Legal Subterfuge and the So-Called 'Lawfare Debate.'" *Case Western Reserve Journal of International Law* 43, no. 1 (2010): 153–61.

Said, Wadie. *Crimes of Terror: The Legal and Political Implications of Federal Terrorism Prosecutions.* New York: Oxford University Press, 2015.

Salaita, Steven. *Israel's Dead Soul.* Philadelphia: Temple University Press, 2011.

Salama, Vivian. "Death from Above: How American Drone Strikes Are Devastating Yemen." *Rolling Stone*, April 14, 2014.

Santamarta, Rube. "A Wake-up Call for SATCOM Security." IOActive, 2014. www.ioactive.com/pdfs/IOActive_SATCOM_Security_WhitePaper.pdf.
Sarker, Muhammad Omar Faruque, and Torbjørn S. Dahl. "Bio-Inspired Communication for Self-Regulated Multi-Robot Systems." In *Multi-Robot Systems: Trends and Development*, edited by Toshiyuki Yasuda, 367–92. Rijeka, Croatia: Intech, 2011.
Satia, Priya. "Attack of the Drones." *Nation*, November 9, 2009.
———. "The Defense of Inhumanity: Air Control and the British Idea of Arabia." *American Historical Review* 3, no. 1 (2006): 16–51.
———. "Drones: A History from the British Middle East." *Humanity* 5, no. 1 (2014): 1–31.
Savage, Charlie. "Before Osama bin Laden Raid, Obama Administration's Secret Legal Deliberations." *New York Times*, October 28, 2015.
———. "Brian Egan's ASIL Speech." April 2, 2016. http://www.charliesavage.com/?p=954.
———. "Secret U.S. Memo Made Legal Case to Kill a Citizen." *New York Times*, October 8, 2011.
Scahill, Jeremy. *The Assassination Complex*. New York: Simon and Schuster, 2016.
———. *Dirty Wars: The World Is a Battlefield*. New York: Nation Books, 2013.
———. "The Secret US War in Pakistan." *Nation*, November 23, 2009.
Scahill, Jeremy, and Glenn Greenwald. "The NSA's Secret Role in the U.S. Assassination Program." *Intercept*, February 9, 2014. https://theintercept.com/2014/02/10/the-nsas-secret-role/.
Scharre, Paul. "Robotics on the Battlefield: The Coming Swarm." Center for a New American Security. Eighth Annual Conference, Washington, DC, June 11, 2014. https://www.youtube.com/watch?v=_WuxwBHI6zY.
———. *Robotics on the Battlefield*. Part I, *Range, Persistence and Daring*. Washington, DC: Center for a New American Security, 2014.
———. *Robotics on the Battlefield*. Part II, *The Coming Swarm*. Washington, DC: Center for a New American Security, 2014.
Scheer, Peter. "Connecting the Dots between Drone Killings and Newly Exposed Government Surveillance." *Huffington Post*, August 8, 2013. http://www.huffingtonpost.com/peter-scheer/drones-surveillance_b_3408487.html.
Schiebel Group. "Schiebel CAMCOPTER® S 100 UAS PSYOP Capability Demo Fort Bragg." YouTube, February 27, 2013. https://www.youtube.com/watch?v=plbmgVU4U8E.
Schmidt, Michael S. "Secret Service Arrests Man after Drone Flies Near White House." *New York Times*, May 14, 2015.
Schmitt, Carl. *The Concept of the Political*. Translated by George Schwab. Chicago: University of Chicago Press, 2007.
Schmitt, Eric. "U.S. Plan Widens Role in Training Pakistani Forces in Qaeda Battle." *New York Times*, March 2, 2008.
Schmitt, Eric, and Mark Mazzetti. "In a First, U.S. Provides Pakistan with Drone Data." *New York Times*, May 13, 2009.
Schmitt, Eric, and Jane Perlez. "Distrust Slows U.S. Training of Pakistanis." *New York Times*, July 11, 2010.

Schmitt, Eric, and Thom Shanker. *Counterstrike: The Untold Story of America's Secret Campaign against Al Qaeda*. New York: Times Books/Henry Holt, 2011.

Scott, David. "Colonial Governmentality." *Social Text* 43 (autumn 1995): 191–220.

Scott, James C. *Seeing Like a State: How Certain Schemes to Improve the Human Condition Have Failed*. New Haven, CT: Yale University Press, 1999.

Selk, Avi. "Ahmed Mohamed Swept Up, 'Hoax Bomb' Charges Swept Away as Irving Teen's Story Floods Social Media." *Dallas Morning News*, September 15, 2015.

Senate Select Committee on Intelligence. "Committee Study of the Central Intelligence Agency's Detention and Interrogation Program." December 3, 2014. http://fas.org/irp/congress/2014_rpt/ssci-rdi.pdf.

Sengupta, Somini. "Rise of Drones in U.S. Spurs Efforts to Limit Uses." *New York Times*, February 15, 2013.

Serle, Jack. "Naming the Dead Project Records the Names of over 700 Killed by Drones in Pakistan." *Bureau of Investigative Journalism*, July 31, 2014. https://www.thebureauinvestigates.com/2014/07/31/naming-the-dead-project-records-the-names-of-over-700-killed-by-drones-in-pakistan/.

Serle, Jack, and Abigail Fielding-Smith. "Monthly Updates on the Covert War: US Drone War: 2014 in Numbers." *Bureau of Investigative Journalism*, January 7, 2015. https://www.thebureauinvestigates.com/2015/01/07/us-drone-war-2014-in-numbers/.

Serwer, Adam. "Does Posting Jihadist Material Make Tarek Mehanna a Terrorist?" *Mother Jones*, December 16, 2011. http://www.motherjones.com/politics/2011/12/tarek-mehanna-terrorist.

Shachtman, Noah. "Drone 'Surge'; Predator Flights up 94% in 2008." *Wired*, February 5, 2009. https://www.wired.com/2009/02/drone-surge-pre/.

———. "U.S. Military Joins CIA's Drone War in Pakistan." *Wired*, December 10, 2009. https://www.wired.com/2009/12/us-military-joins-cias-drone-war-in-pakistan.

Shah, Alpa. *In the Shadows of the State: Indigenous Politics, Environmentalism, and Insurgency in Jharkhand, India*. Durham, NC: Duke University Press, 2010.

Shah, Naureen, Rashmi Chopra, et al. "The Civilian Impact of Drones: Unexamined Costs, Unanswered Questions." Center for Civilians in Conflict. Washington, DC, 2012. http://civiliansinconflict.org/uploads/files/publications/The_Civilian_Impact_of_Drones_w_cover.pdf.

Shah, Pir Zubair. "My Drone War." *Foreign Policy*, February 27, 2012.

Shah, Syed Fida Hassan. "The FC and Levies: Front-Line in Pakistan's War." *Qissa Khwani*, February 1, 2013. http://www.qissa-khwani.com/2013/02/the-fc-and-levies-front-line-in.html.

Shaheen, Sardar Sikander. "30 More Terrorists Killed in NWA, Khyber Agency Strikes." *Daily Times*, June 22, 2014. http://www.dailytimes.com.pk/national/22-Jun-2014/30-more-terrorists-killed-in-nwa-khyber-agency-strikes.

Shakhsari, Sima. "Killing Me Softly with Your Rights: Queer Death and the Politics of Rightful Killing." *Queer Necropolitics* (January 1, 2014): 93–110.

Shane, Scott. "The Lessons of Anwar al-Awlaki." *New York Times*, August 27, 2015.

———. *Objective Troy: A Terrorist, a President, and the Rise of the Drone*. New York: Tim Duggan Books, 2015.

Shannon, Claude, and Warren Weaver. *The Mathematical Theory of Communication.* Urbana: University of Illinois Press, 1949.

Sharkey, Amanda J. C., and Noel Sharkey. "The Application of Swarm Intelligence to Collective Robots." In *Advances in Applied Artificial Intelligence*, edited by John Fulcher, 157–85. Hershey, PA: Idea Group Publishing, 2006.

Sharma, Nitasha. *Hip Hop Desis: South Asian Americans, Blackness, and Global Race Consciousness.* Durham, NC: Duke University Press, 2010.

Shaviro, Steven. *Post-Cinematic Affect.* London: Zero Books, 2010.

Shaw, Ian G. R. "Intervention—'Ghosts in the Machine: Drone Warfare Will Haunt the Future.'" *Antipode*, March 10, 2014. http://antipodefoundation.org/2014/03/10/ghosts-in-the-machine/.

———. *Predator Empire: Drone Warfare and Full Spectrum Dominance.* Minneapolis: University of Minnesota Press, 2016.

Shaw, Ian G. R., and Majed Akhter. "The Dronification of State Violence." *Critical Asian Studies* 46, no. 2 (2014): 211–34.

———. "The Unbearable Humanness of Drone Warfare in FATA, Pakistan." *Antipode* 44, no. 4 (2012): 1490–1509.

Sheers, Owen. *I Saw a Man.* London: Faber, 2015.

Shehadeh, Raja. *Occupier's Law: Israel and the West Bank.* Washington, DC: Institute for Palestine Studies, 1985.

Shephard News. "Schiebel Demonstrates CAMCOPTER® S-100 Together with Boeing in Psychological Operations Role." *Shephard News*, December 16, 2009. https://www.shephardmedia.com/news/uv-online/schiebel-demonstrates-camcopter-s-100-to/.

Sherazi, Zahir Shah. "Tribesmen Forced to End Protest after Police Moved In." *Dawn*, January 16, 2013. http://www.dawn.com/news/779241/relatives-of-slain-bara-tribesmen-march-towards-governors-house.

Shinwari, Naveed Ahmad. *Understanding FATA: Attitudes Towards Governance, Religion and Society in Pakistan's Federally Administered Tribal Areas.* Vol. 5. Peshawar: Community Appraisal and Motivation Program, 2011.

Siddiqa, Ayesha. *Military Inc.: Inside Pakistan's Military Economy.* London: Pluto Press, 2007.

Siegel, Greg. *Forensic Media: Reconstructing Accidents in Accelerated Modernity.* Durham, NC: Duke University Press, 2014.

Sifton, John. "A Brief History of Drones." *Nation*, February 7, 2012.

Simakis, Andrea. "Writer George Brant and the Star of 'Grounded' at the Cleveland Play House Talk Sexy Fighter Pilots, Drones and Why We Love Dark, Complicated Characters (Preview)." *Plain Dealer*, May 8, 2014.

Singer, Peter W. *Wired for War: The Robotics Revolution and Conflict in the Twenty-First Century.* New York: Penguin, 2009.

Singh, Birinder Pal. "Kolaveri di in Tamil and Punjabi." *Hindu*, January 21, 2012. http://www.thehindu.com/opinion/open-page/kolaveri-di-in-tamil-and-punjabi/article2820858.ece.

Sloterdijk, Peter. *Terror from the Air.* Translated by Amy Patton and Steve Corcoran. Los Angeles: Semiotext(e), 2009.

Smalley, David. "The Future Is Now: Navy's Autonomous Swarmboats Can Overwhelm Adversaries." Office of Naval Research, 2014. http://www.onr.navy.mil/Media-Center/Press-Releases/2014/autonomous-swarm-boat-unmanned-caracas.aspx.

Spark, Nick T. "Command Break: The Battle over America's Secret WWII Cruise Missile." 2005. http://stagone.org/?page_id=20.

Speri, Alice. "Al-Shabaab Is Confiscating Camera-Equipped 'Spy' Phones," *Vice News*. March 20, 2014. https://news.vice.com/article/al-shabaab-is-confiscating-camera-equipped-spy-phones.

Stahl, Roger. "What the Drone Saw: The Cultural Optics of the Unmanned War." *Australian Journal of International Affairs* 67, no. 5 (September 20, 2013): 659–74.

Stanley, Jay, and Catherine Crump. "Protecting Privacy from Aerial Surveillance: Recommendations for Government Use of Drone Aircraft." ACLU Report, December 2011. https://www.aclu.org/files/assets/protectingprivacyfromaerialsurveillance.pdf.

Star, Susan Leigh, and Anselm Strauss. "Layers of Silence, Arenas of Voice: The Ecology of Visible and Invisible Work." *Computer Supported Cooperative Work* 8, no. 1 (1999): 9–30.

Stares, Paul B. *The Militarization of Space: U.S. Policy, 1945–1984*. Ithaca, NY: Cornell University Press, 1985.

Sterio, Milena. "The United States' Use of Drones in the War on Terror: The (Il)legality of Targeted Killings under International Law." *Case Western Reserve Journal of International Law* 45, no. 1 (2012): 197–214.

Sterling, Christopher H., ed. *Military Communications: From Ancient Times to the 21st Century*. Santa Barbara, CA: ABC-CLIO, 2008.

Steussy, Lauren. "Source of Mystery Drone Crash Revealed." NBC San Diego, December 6, 2012. http://www.nbcsandiego.com/news/local/-Source-of-Mystery-Drone-Crash-Revealed-182407811.html.

Stimson Center. "Recommendations and Report of the Task Force on US Drone Policy." June 26, 2014. http://www.stimson.org/content/recommendations-and-report-stimson-task-force-us-drone-policy-0.

Stocker, Gerfried. "InfoWar." *Information. Macht. Krieg-Theory [Part 02]. Ars Electronica*. 1998. http://90.146.8.18/en/archives/festival_archive/festival_catalogs/festival_artikel.asp?iProjectID=8442.

Stocker, Gerfried, and Christine Schopf. *INFOWAR: Information. Macht. Krieg*. Vienna: Springer, 1998.

Strawser, Bradley Jay. "Moral Predators: The Duty to Employ Uninhabited Aerial Vehicles." *Journal of Military Ethics* 9, no. 4 (2010): 342–68.

Suchman, Lucy. *Human-Machine Reconfigurations: Plans and Situated Actions*. Cambridge: Cambridge University Press, 2007.

Suchman, Lucy, and Jutta Weber. "Human-Machine Autonomies." In *Autonomous Weapons Systems: Law, Ethics, Policy*, edited by Nehal Bhuta et al., 75–102. Cambridge: Cambridge University Press, 2016.

Sultany, Nimer. "The Legacy of Justice Aharon Barak: A Critical Review." *Harvard International Law Journal Online* 48 (April 30, 2007): 83–92.

"The Surveillance Hummingbird: Watch It Spy and Fly." *Time*, 2015.

Tahir, Madiha. "On the Road." *Tanqeed*, August 2015. http://www.tanqeed.org/2013/08/on-the-road/.

———, dir. *Wounds of Waziristan*. Madiha Tahir and Paragon Films, 2013.

Tanaka, Yuki, and Marilyn B. Young, eds. *Bombing Civilians: A Twentieth-Century History*. New York: W. W. Norton, 2009.

Tanqeed Editors. "Language and Politics." *Tanqeed* 8 (January 2015). http://www.tanqeed.org/2015/01/issue-8-editorial-urdu/#sthash.eaWBecgj.dpbs.

Tawil-Souri, Helga. "Qalandia Checkpoint as Space and Nonplace." *Space and Culture* 14, no. 1 (2011): 4–26.

Taylor, Charles. *Sources of the Self: The Making of the Modern Identity.* Cambridge: Cambridge University Press, 1992.

Taylor, Robert. 2012. "Predator Drone Strikes: 50 Civilians Are Killed for Every 1 Terrorist, and the CIA Only Wants to Up Drone Warfare." *Policy Mic*, October 20, 2012. http://mic.com/articles/16949/predator-drone-strikes-50-civilians-are-killed-for-every-1-terrorist-and-the-cia-only-wants-to-up-drone-warfare.

Telegraph. "Al-Qaeda's 22 Tips for Dodging Drone Attacks." *Telegraph*, February 21, 2013.

Tenold, Vegas. "The Untold Casualties of the Drone War." *Rolling Stone*, February 18, 2016.

Terry, Jennifer. *Attachments to War: Biomedical Logics and Violence in Twenty-First-Century America*. Durham, NC: Duke University Press, 2017.

———. "Killer Entertainments." *Vectors* 13, no. 1 (fall 2007). http://www.vectorsjournal.org/index.php?page=7&projectId=86.

———. "Significant Injury: War, Medicine, and Empire in Claudia's Case." *WSQ: Women's Studies Quarterly* 37, no. 1 (2009): 200–225.

Tesla, Nikola. "Plans to Dispense with Artillery of the Present Type." *Sun*, November 21, 1898. http://www.tfcbooks.com/tesla/1898-11-21.htm.

Thomas, Will. "Nano Chemtrails." *Cosmic Convergence: 2012 and Beyond.* July 17, 2014. http://cosmicconvergence.org/?p=7679.

Thompson, Charis. *Making Parents: The Ontological Choreography of Reproductive Technologies*. Cambridge, MA: MIT Press, 2005.

Thompson, E. P. *The Making of the English Working Class*. New York: Vintage, 1966.

Thompson, Mark. "The Rules of Drone Warfare." *Time*, December 29, 2013.

Thompson, William T., Anthony P. Tvaryanas, and Stefan H. Constable. "U.S. Military Unmanned Aerial Vehicle Mishaps: Assessment of the Role of Human Factors Using Human Factors Analysis and Classification System (HFACS)." USAF 311th Human Systems Wing Technical Report HSW-PE-BR-TR-2005-0001. March 2005.

Toor, Saadia. *The State of Islam: Culture and Cold War Politics in Pakistan*. London: Pluto Press, 2011.

Trimble, Stephen. "Study: Flying Predators Bad for Pilot's Health, Family Life." *DEW Line*, April 2008. http://flightglobal.rbiblogs.co.uk/the-dewline/2008/04/study-flying-predators-bad-for/?replytocom=19989.

Tripodi, Christian. *Edge of Empire: The British Political Officer and Tribal Administration on the North-West Frontier, 1877–1947*. London: Ashgate, 2011.

Tsukayama, Hayley. "Google Buys Drone Maker Titan Aerospace." *Washington Post Blog*, April 14, 2014. http://www.washingtonpost.com/blogs/the-switch/wp/2014/04/14/google-buys-drone-maker-titan-aerospace-2/.

Turse, Nick. "Behind the Veil of Secrecy over US Military Operations in Africa." *Mother Jones*, April 14, 2014. http://www.motherjones.com/politics/2014/04/us-military-africa-secrecy-operations.

———. "The Increasing US Shadow Wars in Africa." *Mother Jones*, July 12, 2012. http://www.motherjones.com/politics/2012/07/us-shadow-wars-africa.

———. "The Startling Size of US Military Operations in Africa." *Mother Jones*, September 6, 2013. http://www.motherjones.com/politics/2013/09/us-military-bases-africa.

Turse, Nick, and Tom Englehardt. *Terminator Planet: The First History of Drone Warfare, 2001–2050*. Lexington, KY: Dispatch Books, 2012.

Tvaryanas, Anthony P. "The Development of Empirically Based Medical Standards for Large and Weaponized Unmanned Aircraft System Pilots." USAF 311th Human Systems Wing Technical Report HSW-PE-BR-TR-2006-0004. October 2006.

"20 Great UAV Applications Areas for Drones." *Air-Vid*, September 2, 2014. http://air-vid.com/wp/20-great-uav-applications-areas-drones/.

United Nations Security Council. "Report of the Secretary-General on the Protection of Civilians in Armed Conflict." Report S/2015/453. June 18, 2015. http://reliefweb.int/report/world/report-secretary-general-protection-civilians-armed-conflict-s2015453.

Uricchio, William. "Television's First Seventy-Five Years: The Interpretive Flexibility of a Medium in Transition." In *The Oxford Handbook of Film and Media Studies*, edited by Robert Kolker, 286–305. Oxford: Oxford University Press, 2008.

United States Air Force. "Air Force Basic Doctrine, Organization, and Command: Air Force Doctrine Document 1." LeMay Center for Doctrine Development, 2011. http://www.bits.de/NRANEU/others/END-Archive/AFDD1(11).pdf.

United States Air Force, Accident Investigation Board. "Executive Summary: Abbreviated Aircraft Accident Investigation MQ-1B, 07-3249, Republic of Djibouti 17 May 2011." May 2011. http://usaf.aib.law.af.mil/ExecSum2011/MQ-1B_Djibouti_ExecSum_17%20May%2011.pdf.

———. "Executive Summary: Aircraft Accident Investigation MQ-1B, T/N 04-3125 Camp Lemonnier, Djibouti 21 Feb 12." http://usaf.aib.law.af.mil/ExecSum2012/MQ-1_Djibouti_ExecSum_21%20Feb%2012.pdf.

———. "MQ-1B T/N 06-3173 432D Wing Creech Air Force Base, Nevada." July 28, 2011. http://usaf.aib.law.af.mil/ExecSum2011/MQ-1B_Djibouti_7%20May%2011.pdf.

———. "Summary of Facts and Statement of Opinion Aircraft Accident Investigation MQ-1B Predator, T/N 04–3126 Near Horn of Africa (HoA)." March 15, 2011. http://usaf.aib.law.af.mil/ExecSum2011/MQ-1B%2C%20Near%20Horn%20of%20Africa%2C%2015%20Mar%2011.pdf.

United States Government Accountability Office. "Securing, Stabilizing and Developing Pakistan's Border Area with Afghanistan." GAO-09-263SP. Washington, DC, February 2009.

United States War Department. *War Department Field Manual FM 100-20: Command and Employment of Air Power*. Washington, DC: Government Printing Office, 1943.

U.S. Department of State. "Afghanistan and Pakistan Programs." May 15, 2013. http://www.state.gov/j/inl/rls/fs/209449.htm.

———. "Border Security Program: Pakistan." May 3, 2010. http://www.state.gov/j/inl/rls/fs/141576.htm.

U.S. Embassy. "U.S. and FATA Secretariat Continue to Build Roads for the FATA People." Islamabad, June 18, 2012. http://islamabad.usembassy.gov/pr_061812.html.

U.S. Embassy Cable. "CJCS Mullen's Meeting with COAS General Kayani." 08ISLAMABAD1272. *WikiLeaks*, March 24, 2008. https://cablegatesearch.wikileaks.org/cable.php?id=08ISLAMABAD1272&q=operating%20restricted%20zone.

———. "Pakistan: Attempted Intercepts of Coalition Aircraft." 07ISLAMABAD5283. *WikiLeaks*, December 14, 2007. https://cablegatesearch.wikileaks.org/cable.php?id=07ISLAMABAD5283&q=boulevard%20pakistan.

U.S. Government. "U.S. Policy Standards and Procedures for the Use of Force in Counterterrorism Operations outside the United States and Areas of Active Hostilities." May 23, 2013. https://www.whitehouse.gov/the-press-office/2013/05/23/fact-sheet-us-policy-standards-and-procedures-use-force-counterterrorism.

Van Creveld, Martin. *Command in War*. Cambridge, MA: Harvard University Press, 1985.

Vandiver, John. "Workers Protesting Work Force Cuts at US Base in Africa." *Stars and Stripes*, July 10, 2013. http://www.stripes.com/news/africa/workers-protesting-work-force-cuts-at-us-base-in-africa-1.229711.

Vego, Milan N. "Operational Command and Control in the Information Age." *Joint Force Quarterly*, no. 35 (2004): 100–107.

Vertov, Dziga. "The Essence of Kino-Eye." In *Kino-Eye: The Writings of Dziga Vertov*, 49–50. Berkeley: University of California Press, 1984.

Virilio, Paul. *War and Cinema: The Logistics of Perception*. London: Verso, 1989.

Virmani, Priya. "Kolavari Di: How India's 'Tamglish Soup Song' Went Viral." *Guardian*, February 6, 2012.

von Clausewitz, Carl. *On War*. New York: Kegan, 1908.

Wall, Tyler, and Torin Monahan. "Surveillance and Violence from Afar: The Politics of Drones and Liminal Security-Scapes." *Theoretical Criminology* 15, no. 3 (2011): 239–54.

Wallerstein, Immanuel. *The Decline of American Power: The U.S. in a Chaotic World*. New York: New Press, 2003.

Walsh, Declan. "US Disavows 2 Drone Strikes over Pakistan." *New York Times*, March 4, 2013.

Warf, Barney. "Dethroning the View from Above: Toward a Critical Social Analysis of Satellite Occularcentrism." In *Down to Earth: Satellite Technologies, Industries, and Cultures*, edited by Lisa Parks and James Schwoch, 42–60. New Brunswick, NJ: Rutgers University Press, 2012.

Warren, Alan. *Waziristan, the Faqir of Ipi, and the Indian Army: The North West Frontier Revolt of 1936–37*. Oxford: Oxford University Press, 2000.

Washington Times. "Editorial: Drones at Home." May 29, 2013.

Weber, Greta. "This Is the Year's Best Drone Photography." *National Geographic*, July 8, 2015.

Weber, Jutta. "Keep Adding: On Kill Lists, Drone Warfare and the Politics of Databases." *Environment and Planning D: Society and Space* 34, no. 1 (2016): 107–25.

Weber, Max. *Economy and Society.* 1922. 4th ed. Berkeley: University of California Press, 1978.

Weber, Samuel. *Targets of Opportunity: On the Militarization of Thinking.* New York: Fordham University Press, 2005.

Weheliye, Alexander. *Habeas Viscus: Racializing Assemblages, Biopolitics, and Black Feminist Theories of the Human.* Durham, NC: Duke University Press, 2014.

Weisberger, Mindy. "Drone-Hunting Eagles Can Snatch Devices Out of the Sky." CBS News, February 8, 2016. http://www.cbsnews.com/news/drone-hunting-eagles-can-snatch-the-devices-out-of-the-sky/.

Weizman, Eyal. *Forensic Architecture: Notes from Fields and Forums.* Documenta 13. Ostfildern, Germany: Erschienen im Hatje Cantz Verlag, 2012.

———. *Hollow Land: Israel's Architecture of Occupation.* London: Verso, 2012.

———. "Introduction to the Politics of Verticality." *Open Democracy*, April 24, 2002. http://www.opendemocracy.net/ecology-politicsverticality/article_801.jsp.

———. "Lawfare in Gaza: Legislative Attack." *Open Security*, March 1, 2009. https://www.opendemocracy.net/article/legislative-attack.

———. *The Least of All Possible Evils: Humanitarian Violence from Arendt to Gaza.* London: Verso, 2012.

———. "Legislative Attack." *Theory, Culture and Society* 27, no. 6 (2010): 11–32.

———. *The Politics of Verticality.* London: Verso, 2007.

Wessler, Nathan Freed. "The Government's Pseudo-Secrecy Snow Job on Targeted Killing." *ACLU Blog*, June 26, 2012. https://www.aclu.org/blog/governments-pseudo-secrecy-snow-job-targeted-killing.

Weymouth, Lally. "Moscow's Invisible 'War of Terror' inside Pakistan." *Washington Post*, March 13, 1988.

Whitlock, Chris, and Greg Miller. "U.S. Moves Drone Fleet from Camp Lemonnier to Ease Djibouti's Safety Concerns." *Washington Post*, September 24, 2013.

Whitlock, Craig. "Defense Secretary Panetta Visits U.S. Base in Djibouti, Then Travels to Afghanistan." *Washington Post Blog*, December 13, 2011. http://www.washingtonpost.com/blogs/checkpoint-washington/post/panetta-visits-us-base-in-djibouti-that-exemplifies-shift-in-military-approach/2011/12/13/gIQAnKTSrO_blog.html.

Whittle, Richard. *Predator: The Secret Origins of the Drone Revolution.* New York: Henry Holt, 2014.

WikiLeaks. "Press Release: Secret US Embassy Cables." *WikiLeaks*, September 12, 2011. https://wikileaks.org/Press-Release-Secret-US-Embassy.html.

Wilke, Christiane. "The Optics of War: Bombing, Performances and Fantasies of Distinction in International Law." Paper presented at Philosophy and the Social Sciences, Czech Academy of Sciences, Prague, Czech Republic, May 2013.

Williams, Alex. "Escape Velocities." *E-Flux*, no. 46 (2003). http://www.e-flux.com/journal/escape-velocities/.

Williams, Alex, and Nick Srnicek. "#ACCELERATE MANIFESTO for an Accelerationist Politics." *Critical Legal Thinking: Law and the Political*, May 14, 2013. http://

criticallegalthinking.com/2013/05/14/accelerate-manifesto-for-an-accelerationist-politics/.

Williams, Brian Glyn. *Predators: The CIA's Drone War on al Qaeda.* Washington, DC: Potomac Books, 2013.

Williams, Raymond. "Culture." In *Keywords: A Vocabulary of Culture and Society*, 87–93. London: Croom Helm, 1976.

Willis, Paul. "The Cultural Meaning of Drug Use." In *Resistance through Rituals: Youth Subcultures in Post-War Britain*, edited by Stuart Hall and Tony Jefferson, 88–99. London: Routledge, 1993.

Wilson, Scott. "In Gaza, Lives Shaped by Drones." *Washington Post*, December 3, 2011.

Wirsing, Robert. "Pakistan and the War in Afghanistan." *Asian Affairs* 14, no. 2 (1987): 57–75.

Wood, David. "Drone Strikes: A Candid, Chilling Conversation with Top US Drone Pilot." *Huffington Post*, May 15, 2013. http://www.huffingtonpost.com/2013/05/15/drone-strikes_n_3280023.html.

Woods, Chris. "CIA's Pakistan Drone Strikes Carried Out by Regular US Air Force Personnel." *Guardian*, April 14, 2014.

———. "Don't Call It a Comeback." *Foreign Policy*, June 19, 2014.

———. "Leaked Pakistani Report Confirms High Civilian Death Toll in CIA Drone Strikes." *Bureau of Investigative Journalism*, July 22, 2013. https://www.thebureauinvestigates.com/2013/07/22/exclusive-leaked-pakistani-report-confirms-high-civilian-death-toll-in-cia-drone-strikes/.

———. "Pakistan 'Categorically Rejects' Claim That It Tacitly Allows Drone Strikes." *Bureau of Investigative Journalism*, September 28, 2012. http://www.thebureauinvestigates.com/2012/09/28/pakistan-categorically-rejects-claim-that-it-tacitly-allows-us-drone-strikes/.

———. *Sudden Justice: America's Secret Drone Wars.* New York: Oxford University Press, 2015.

Woods, David D., and Lawrence G. Shattuck. "Distant Supervision–Local Action Given the Potential for Surprise." *Cognition, Technology and Work* 2, no. 4 (2000): 86–96.

Woodward, Bob. *Obama's Wars.* New York: Simon and Schuster, 2010.

Work, Robert O., and Shawn Brimley. *Preparing for War in the Robotic Age.* Washington, DC: Center for a New American Security, 2014.

World Bank Group. "Mobile Cellular Subscriptions (per 100 people)—Somalia," 2016. http://data.worldbank.org/indicator/IT.CEL.SETS.P2?locations=SO.

Wright, Tom, and Rehmat Mehsud. "Pakistan Slams Drone Strike." *Wall Street Journal*, March 18, 2011.

Yashuvi, Na'ama. "Activity of the Undercover Units in the Occupied Territories." B'Tselem, Jerusalem, 1992. http://www.btselem.org/publications/summaries/199205_undercover_units.

Yousaf, Kamran. "Kayani Initiates USAID Project in S. Waziristan." *Express Tribune*, June 19, 2012. http://tribune.com.pk/story/395817/kayani-initiates-usaid-project-in-s-waziristan/.

Zaidi, Manzar. "A Profile of Mangal Bagh." *Long War Journal* (November 11, 2008): 1–13.

Zarrella, Tabatha. "Working Together, Sharing a Common Mission, Bond." Combined Joint Task Force, Horn of Africa, January 27, 2014. http://www.hoa.africom.mil/story/7844/working-together-sharing-a-common-mission-bond.

Zucchino, David, and David S. Cloud. "U.S. Deaths in Drone Strike Due to Miscommunication, Report Says." *Los Angeles Times*, October 14, 2011.

Zworykin, V. K. "A Flying Torpedo with an Electric Eye." April 25, 1934, Sirnoff Library Materials, RCA Collection, Hagley Library Manuscripts Collection, Wilmington, DE. Reprinted in *RCA Review* 7, no. 3 (September 1946): 293–302.

CONTRIBUTORS

PETER ASARO, a philosopher of science, technology, and media, is Associate Professor at the New School. His current research focuses on the social, cultural, political, legal, and ethical dimensions of military robotics and unmanned aerial vehicles from a perspective that combines media theory with science and technology studies. He has written widely cited papers on lethal robotics from the perspective of just war theory and human rights. Asaro's research also examines agency and autonomy, liability and punishment, and privacy and surveillance as they apply to consumer robots, industrial automation, smart buildings, and autonomous vehicles. His research has been published in international peer-reviewed journals and edited volumes, and he is currently writing a book that interrogates the intersections between military robotics, interface design practices, and social and ethical issues.

BRANDON BRYANT was a staff sergeant of the United States Air Force with service dates from July 5, 2005 to July 4, 2011, active duty, and July 5, 2011 to January 1, 2013, reserves. Honorably discharged, he has been an advocate for transparency in the U.S. military's use of armed drones in perpetuating global war. He was named the 2015 Whistleblower of the Year by the International Association of Lawyers Against Nuclear Arms and the Federation of German Scientists. He hopes to work toward peace with his fellow veterans in the world.

KATHERINE CHANDLER is Assistant Professor in the Edmund A. Walsh School of Foreign Service at Georgetown University in the Culture and Politics Program. She examines interconnections between social and political theory, science and technology studies, and new media. Her current research, "Unmanning: The Dissociative Politics of Drone Flight and Failure, 1936–1992," studies the prehistory of pilotless technologies to interrogate multiple entanglements between human, machine, and enemy coproduced by drones and their political consequences.

JORDAN CRANDALL is a media artist, theorist, and performer. He is Professor in the Visual Arts Department at the University of California–San Diego. In 2011 he received the Vilém Flusser Theory Award for outstanding theory and research-based digital arts practice, given by the Transmediale in Berlin, in collaboration with the Vilém Flusser Archive of the University of Arts, Berlin. His current project, UNMANNED, blends performance art, political theater, philosophical speculation, and intimate reverie. It explores new ontologies of distributed systems and the status of the human in a militarized landscape increasingly dependent on automated technology. The work was developed in an honorary residency at the Eyebeam center for art and technology in New York City and subsequently performed in 2012 at the V2_ Institute for the Unstable Media in Rotterdam and 2015 at Transmediale, Berlin. Crandall is a researcher at the California Institute for Telecommunications and Information Technology and codirector of the Gallery@CALIT2.

RICARDO DOMINGUEZ is a cofounder of the Electronic Disturbance Theater, a group that developed virtual sit-in technologies in 1998 in solidarity with the Zapatista communities in Chiapas, Mexico. His Electronic Disturbance Theater project with Brett Stabaum, Micha Cardenas Amy Sara Carroll, and Elle Mehrmand, the *Transborder Immigrant Tool* (a GPS cell-phone safety net tool for crossing the U.S.-Mexico border), was the winner of the "Transnational Communities Award," which was funded by Cultural Contact, Endowment for Culture Mexico–U.S. He is also a cofounder of *particle group*, with artists Diane Ludin, Nina Waisman, and Amy Sara Carroll. Dominguez is an Associate Professor at UCSD in the Visual Arts Department, a principal investigator at CALIT2 as well as the Performative Nanorobotics Lab at SME (UCSD), and he is also the lead researcher of the UCSD Center for Drone Policy and Ethics.

DEREK GREGORY is the Peter Wall Distinguished Professor at the University of British Columbia in Vancouver. Since publishing *The Colonial Present: Afghanistan, Palestine, Iraq* (2004), his research has focused on the genealogies and geographies of later modern war, exploring the ways in which military violence has and has not changed over the last hundred years. He is completing a new book based on his Tanner lectures, "Reach from the Sky: Aerial Violence and the Everywhere War," which places today's drone wars in the longer history of bombing, and is currently working on casualty evacuation from war zones, 1914–2014. He was awarded the Founder's Medal of the Royal Geographical Society in 2006 and is a Fellow of both the British Academy and the Royal Society of Canada. He blogs at http://www.geographicalimaginations.com.

INDERPAL GREWAL is Professor of Women's, Gender, and Sexuality Studies at Yale University. She is the author of *Home and Harem: Nation, Gender, Empire, and the Cultures of Travel* (Duke University Press, 1996); *Transnational America: Feminisms, Diasporas, Neoliberalisms* (Duke University Press, 2005); and *Exceptional Citizens? Advanced Neoliberalism, Surveillance, and Security in the Contemporary United States* (Duke University Press, 2017). With Caren Kaplan, she has written and edited *Gender in a Transnational World: Introduction to Women's Studies* (2001) and *Scattered Hegemonies: Postmodernity and Transnational Feminist Practices* (1994). With Victoria Bernal, she has edited *Theorizing NGOs: States, Feminisms, and Neoliberalism* (Duke University Press, 2014).

LISA HAJJAR is Associate Professor of Sociology at the University of California–Santa Barbara. She is the author of *Courting Conflict: The Israeli Military Court System in the West Bank and Gaza* (2005) and *Torture: A Sociology of Violence and Human Rights* (2012) as well as numerous other publications relating to war and conflict, human rights, and political violence. She serves on the editorial committees of *Middle East Report*, *Journal of Palestine Studies*, and *Societies without Borders* and is a founding coeditor of *Jadaliyya*.

CAREN KAPLAN is Professor of American Studies at the University of California–Davis. She is the author of *Aerial Aftermaths: Wartime from Above* (Duke University Press, 2018) and *Questions of Travel: Postmodern Discourses of Displacement* (Duke University Press, 1996) and the coauthor/editor of *Introduction to Women's Studies: Gender in a Transnational World* (2001), *Between Woman and Nation: Transnational Feminisms and the State* (Duke University Press, 1999), and *Scattered Hegemonies: Postmodernity and Transnational Feminist Practices* (1994) as well as two digital multimedia scholarly works, *Dead Reckoning* and *Precision Targets*.

ANDREA MILLER is a PhD student in Cultural Studies at the University of California–Davis. Her research addresses genealogies of policing, surveillance, and preemptive practices in U.S. colonialism and her work has appeared in *Media Fields Journal*. Miller holds a master's degree in Women's, Gender, and Sexuality Studies from Georgia State University and cofounded the Society for Radical Geography, Spatial Theory, and Everyday Life.

ANJALI NATH is Assistant Professor of American Studies at the University of California–Davis. Nath's research focuses on wartime visual cultures, with a particular emphasis on the study of American military imprisonment. Her writing has appeared in *Cultural Studies Critical Methodologies*, *American Quarterly*, *Visual Anthropology*, and other academic journals.

JEREMY PACKER is Associate Professor at the University of Toronto, where he is a faculty member in the Institute for Communication, Culture, Information and Technology (Mississauga) and the Information School (St. George). His primary research investigates the historical, political, and cultural dimensions of communication technologies as they relate to mobility, security, and military automation. He is the author or editor of the following books: *Communication Matters: Materialist Approaches to Media, Mobility, and Networks* (2012), *Secret Agents: Popular Icons beyond James Bond* (2009), *Mobility Without Mayhem: Cars, Safety and Citizenship* (Duke University Press, 2008), *Thinking with James Carey: Essays on Communications, Transportation, History* (2006), and *Foucault, Cultural Studies, and Governmentality* (2003).

LISA PARKS is Professor of Comparative Media Studies at MIT and was previously Professor of Film and Media Studies at the University of California–Santa Barbara. Parks is the author of *Cultures in Orbit: Satellites and the Televisual* (Duke University Press, 2005) and *Coverage: Vertical Mediation and the War on Terror* (forthcoming). She is coeditor of *Signal Traffic: Critical Studies of Media Infrastructures* (2015); *Down to Earth: Satellite Technologies, Industries, and Cultures* (2012); and *Planet TV* (2003).

JOSHUA REEVES is Assistant Professor of New Media Communications and Speech Communication at Oregon State University. He is the author of *Citizen Spies: The Long Rise of America's Surveillance Society* (2017) and served as coeditor (with Rachel Hall and Torin Monahan) of a recent special issue of *Surveillance and Society*. His work has appeared in such publications as *Communication and Critical/Cultural Studies*, *Critical Studies in Media Communication*, *Philosophy and Rhetoric*, and *Surveillance and Society*.

THOMAS STUBBLEFIELD is Assistant Professor of Art History at the University of Massachusetts–Dartmouth. He is the author of *9/11 and the Visual Culture of Disaster* (2014), which was awarded the Rollins Prize by the New England Popular Culture Association in 2015. His research interests include the visual culture of disaster, network theory, the interplay between digital and analog media, and the history and theory of photography. Recent publications include "The City from Afar: Urbanization and the Aerial View in Alvin Coburn's *The Octopus*" in the *Journal of Urban History* and "How to Disappear Completely (Into Surveillance Video): Peter Bergmann and the North Pond Hermit" in *Media Fields*.

MADIHA TAHIR is a doctoral candidate at Columbia University and the director of *Wounds of Waziristan*, a short documentary film about the aftermath of drone attacks in Pakistan's Tribal Areas. Tahir is also a freelance journalist. Her work has appeared in a host of media outlets, including *Al Jazeera*, *Vice*, *Foreign Affairs*, *Caravan*, *Guernica*, the *New Inquiry*, the *Columbia Journalism Review*, and the *Wall Street Journal* as well as on Democracy Now!, PRI and BBC's "The World," and elsewhere. She is the coeditor of a volume of essays, *Dispatches from Pakistan* (2014), with Vijay Prashad and Qalandar Bux Memon. In 2012 she cofounded *Tanqeed* (http://www.tanqeed.org), a magazine of politics and culture, with Mahvish Ahmad. Tahir holds a master's degree in Near Eastern Studies from New York University and a master's of science from the Columbia Journalism School.

INDEX

Page numbers followed by *f* indicate illustrations.